THE CLAY SANSKRIT LIBRARY
FOUNDED BY JOHN & JENNIFER CLAY

WWW.CLAYSANSKRITLIBRARY.COM
WWW.NYUPRESS.ORG

First Edition 2006.

The Clay Sanskrit Library is co-published by
New York University Press
and the JJC Foundation.

Further information about this volume
and the rest of the Clay Sanskrit Library
is available on the following Websites:
www.claysanskritlibrary.com
www.nyupress.org.

ISBN-13: 978-0-8147-1996-1 (cloth : alk. paper)
ISBN-10: 0-8147-1996-1 (cloth : alk. paper)

Artwork by Robert Beer.
Typeset in Adobe Garamond at 10.25 : 12.3+pt.
XML-development by Stuart Brown.
Editorial input from Dániel Balogh, Tomoyuki Kono,
Eszter Somogyi & Péter Szántó.
Printed in Great Britain by St Edmundsbury Press Ltd,
Bury St Edmunds, Suffolk, on acid-free paper.
Bound by Hunter & Foulis Ltd, Edinburgh, Scotland.

"THE LADY OF THE JEWEL NECKLACE" AND "THE LADY WHO SHOWS HER LOVE"

BY HARṢA

TRANSLATED BY

WENDY DONIGER

NEW YORK UNIVERSITY PRESS
JJC FOUNDATION
2006

Library of Congress Cataloging-in-Publication Data
Harṣavardhana, King of Thānesar and Kanauj, fl. 606-647.
[Ratnāvalī. English & Sanskrit]
The lady of the jewel necklace ; and,
The lady who shows her love / by Harṣa ;
translated by Wendy Doniger.
p. cm. – (The Clay Sanskrit library)
Plays.
In English and Sanskrit (romanized) on facing pages;
includes translations from Sanskrit.
Includes bibliographical references and index.
ISBN-13: 978-0-8147-1996-1 (cloth : alk. paper)
ISBN-10: 0-8147-1996-1 (cloth : alk. paper)
1. Sanskrit drama–Translations into English.
2. Harṣavardhana, King of Thānesar and Kanauj,
fl. 606-647–Translations into English.
I. Harṣavardhana, King of Thānesar and Kanauj,
fl. 606-647. Priyadarśikā. English & Sanskrit.
II. Title. III. Title: Lady of the jewel necklace ;
and, The lady who shows her love.
IV. Title: Lady who shows her love.
PK3794.H3R313 2006
891'.22–dc22
2006033976

CONTENTS

CSL CONVENTIONS

SANSKRIT ALPHABETICAL ORDER

Vowels:	*a ā i ī u ū ṛ ṝ ḷ ḹ e ai o au ṃ ḥ*
Gutturals:	*k kh g gh ṅ*
Palatals:	*c ch j jh ñ*
Retroflex:	*ṭ ṭh ḍ ḍh ṇ*
Dentals:	*t th d dh n*
Labials:	*p ph b bh m*
Semivowels:	*y r l v*
Spirants:	*ś ṣ s h*

GUIDE TO SANSKRIT PRONUNCIATION

a	b*u*t
ā, â	f*a*ther
i	s*i*t
ī, î	f*ee*
u	p*u*t
ū, û	b*oo*
ṛ	vocalic *r*, American p*ur*dy or English p*re*tty
ṝ	lengthened *ṛ*
ḷ	vocalic *l*, ab*le*
e, ê, ē	m*a*de, esp. in Welsh pronunciation
ai	b*i*te
o, ô, ō	r*o*pe, esp. Welsh pronunciation; Italian s*o*lo
au	s*ou*nd
ṃ	*anusvāra* nasalizes the preceding vowel
ḥ	*visarga*, a voiceless aspiration (resembling English *h*), or like Scottish lo*ch*, or an aspiration with a faint echoing of the preceding vowel so that *taiḥ* is pronounced *taih*[i]
k	lu*ck*
kh	blo*ckh*ead
g	*g*o
gh	bi*gh*ead
ṅ	a*n*ger
c	*ch*ill
ch	mat*chh*ead
j	*j*og
jh	aspirated *j*, he*dgeh*og
ñ	ca*ny*on
ṭ	retroflex *t*, *t*ry (with the tip of tongue turned up to touch the hard palate)
ṭh	same as the preceding but aspirated
ḍ	retroflex *d* (with the tip of tongue turned up to touch the hard palate)
ḍh	same as the preceding but aspirated
ṇ	retroflex *n* (with the tip of tongue turned up to touch the hard palate)

t	French *t*out	*y*	*y*es
th	ten*t h*ook	*r*	trilled, resembling the Italian pronunciation of *r*
d	*d*inner	*l*	*l*inger
dh	guil*dh*all	*v*	*w*ord
n	*n*ow	*ś*	*sh*ore
p	*p*ill	*ṣ*	retroflex *sh* (with the tip of the tongue turned up to touch the hard palate)
ph	u*ph*eaval	*s*	hi*ss*
b	*b*efore	*h*	*h*ood
bh	a*bh*orrent		
m	*m*ind		

CSL PUNCTUATION OF ENGLISH

The acute accent on Sanskrit words when they occur outside of the Sanskrit text itself, marks stress, e.g. Ramáyana. It is not part of traditional Sanskrit orthography, transliteration or transcription, but we supply it here to guide readers in the pronunciation of these unfamiliar words. Since no Sanskrit word is accented on the last syllable it is not necessary to accent disyllables, e.g. Rama.

The second CSL innovation designed to assist the reader in the pronunciation of lengthy unfamiliar words is to insert an unobtrusive middle dot between semantic word breaks in compound names (provided the word break does not fall on a vowel resulting from the fusion of two vowels), e.g. Maha·bhárata, but Ramáyana (not Rama·áyana). Our dot echoes the punctuating middle dot (·) found in the oldest surviving forms of written Indic, the Ashokan inscriptions of the third century BCE.

The deep layering of Sanskrit narrative has also dictated that we use quotation marks only to announce the beginning and end of every direct speech, and not at the beginning of every paragraph.

CSL PUNCTUATION OF SANSKRIT

The Sanskrit text is also punctuated, in accordance with the punctuation of the English translation. In mid-verse, the punctuation will not alter the *sandhi* or the scansion. Proper names are capitalized. Most Sanskrit metres have four "feet" *(pāda):* where possible we print the common *śloka* metre on two lines. In the Sanskrit text, we use French *Guillemets* (e.g. *«kva saṃcicīrṣuḥ?»*) instead of English quotation marks (e.g. "Where are you off to?") to avoid confusion with the apostrophes used for vowel elision in *sandhi*.

Sanskrit presents the learner with a challenge: *sandhi* ("euphonic combination"). *Sandhi* means that when two words are joined in connected speech or writing (which in Sanskrit reflects speech), the last letter (or even letters) of the first word often changes; compare the way we pronounce "the" in "the beginning" and "the end."

In Sanskrit the first letter of the second word may also change; and if both the last letter of the first word and the first letter of the second are vowels, they may fuse. This has a parallel in English: a nasal consonant is inserted between two vowels that would otherwise coalesce: "a pear" and "an apple." Sanskrit vowel fusion may produce ambiguity. The chart at the back of each book gives the full *sandhi* system.

Fortunately it is not necessary to know these changes in order to start reading Sanskrit. For that, what is important is to know the form of the second word without *sandhi* (pre-*sandhi*), so that it can be recognized or looked up in a dictionary. Therefore we are printing Sanskrit with a system of punctuation that will indicate, unambiguously, the original form of the second word, i.e., the form without *sandhi*. Such *sandhi* mostly concerns the fusion of two vowels.

In Sanskrit, vowels may be short or long and are written differently accordingly. We follow the general convention that a vowel with no mark above it is short. Other books mark a long vowel either with a bar called a macron (*ā*) or with a circumflex (*â*). Our system uses the macron, except that for initial vowels in *sandhi* we use a circumflex to indicate that originally the vowel was short, or the shorter of two possibilities (*e* rather than *ai*, *o* rather than *au*).

When we print initial *â*,	before *sandhi* that vowel was *a*
î or *ê*,	*i*
û or *ô*,	*u*
âi,	*e*
âu,	*o*
ā,	*ā* (i.e., the same)
ī,	*ī* (i.e., the same)

ū,	*ū* (i.e., the same)
ē,	*ī*
ō,	*ū*
āi,	*ai*
āu,	*au*
’, before *sandhi* there was a vowel *a*	

FURTHER HELP WITH VOWEL SANDHI

When a final short vowel (*a*, *i* or *u*) has merged into a following vowel, we print ’ at the end of the word, and when a final long vowel (*ā*, *ī* or *ū*) has merged into a following vowel we print ” at the end of the word. The vast majority of these cases will concern a final *a* or *ā*.

Examples:

What before *sandhi* was *atra asti* is represented as *atr’ âsti*

atra āste	*atr’ āste*
kanyā asti	*kany” âsti*
kanyā āste	*kany” āste*
atra iti	*atr’ êti*
kanyā iti	*kany” êti*
kanyā īpsitā	*kany” ēpsitā*

Finally, three other points concerning the initial letter of the second word:

(1) A word that before *sandhi* begins with *ṛ* (vowel), after *sandhi* begins with *r* followed by a consonant: *yatha” rtu* represents pre-*sandhi* *yathā ṛtu*.

(2) When before *sandhi* the previous word ends in *t* and the following word begins with *ś*, after *sandhi* the last letter of the previous word is *c* and the following word begins with *ch*: *syāc chāstravit* represents pre-*sandhi* *syāt śāstravit*.

(3) Where a word begins with *h* and the previous word ends with a double consonant, this is our simplified spelling to show the pre-*sandhi* form: *tad hasati* is commonly written as *tad dhasati*, but we write *tadd hasati* so that the original initial letter is obvious.

COMPOUNDS

We also punctuate the division of compounds (*samāsa*), simply by inserting a thin vertical line between words. There are words where the decision whether to regard them as compounds is arbitrary. Our principle has been to try to guide readers to the correct dictionary entries.

EXAMPLE

Where the Deva·nágari script reads:

कुम्भस्थली रक्षतु वो विकीर्णसिन्दूररेणुर्द्विरदाननस्य ।
प्रशान्तये विघ्नतमश्छटानां निष्ठ्यूतबालातपपल्लवेव ॥

Others would print:

kumbhasthalī rakṣatu vo vikīrṇasindūrareṇur dviradānanasya /
praśāntaye vighnatamaśchaṭānāṃ niṣṭhyūtabālātapapallaveva //

We print:

kumbha|sthalī rakṣatu vo vikīrṇa|sindūra|reṇur dvirad'|ānanasya
praśāntaye vighna|tamaś|chaṭānāṃ niṣṭhyūta|bāl'|ātapa|pallav" êva.

And in English:

"May Ganésha's domed forehead protect you! Streaked with vermilion dust, it seems to be emitting the spreading rays of the rising sun to pacify the teeming darkness of obstructions."

"Nava·sáhasanka and the Serpent Princess" I.3 by Padma·gupta

DRAMA

Classical Sanskrit literature is in fact itself bilingual, notably in drama. There women and characters of low rank speak one of several Prakrit dialects, an "unrefined" *(prākṛta)* vernacular as opposed to the "refined" *(saṃskṛta)* language. Editors commonly provide such speeches with a Sanskrit paraphrase, their "shadow" *(chāyā)*. We mark Prakrit speeches with ⌜opening and closing⌟ corner brackets, and supply the Sanskrit *chāyā* in endnotes. Some stage directions are original to the author but we follow the custom that sometimes editors supplement these; we print them in italics (and within brackets, in mid-text).

WORDPLAY

Classical Sanskrit literature can abound in puns *(śleṣa)*. Such paronomasia, or wordplay, is raised to a high art; rarely is it a *cliché*. Multiple meanings merge *(śliṣyanti)* into a single word or phrase. Most common are pairs of meanings, but as many as ten separate meanings are attested. To mark the parallel senses in the English, as well as the punning original in the Sanskrit, we use a *slanted* font (different from *italic*) and a triple colon *(⁝)* to separate the alternatives. E.g.

> yuktaṃ Kādambarīṃ śrutvā kavayo maunam āśritāḥ
> *Bāṇa/dhvanāv* an|adhyāyo bhavat' îti smṛtir yataḥ.

> It is right that poets should fall silent upon hearing the Kádambari, for the sacred law rules that recitation must be suspended when *the sound of an arrow ⁝ the poetry of Bana* is heard.
>
> Soméshvara·deva's "Moonlight of Glory" I.15

INTRODUCTION

Who was Harsha?

HARSHA (ALSO CALLED Harsha·várdhana, Shri Harsha, Harsha Deva, and Shiláditya) was a king, who reigned from 606 to 647 over the kingdom of Kanauj (near modern Kanpur). We have far more information about him than we have about most kings of this period, largely due to three witnesses. His court poet, Bana, wrote a prose poem about him, 'The Deeds of Harsha' (*Harṣa/carita*), which offers, hidden between the layers of fulsome praise and literary display, quite a lot of information about life as it was lived at Harsha's court. And the Chinese Buddhist traveler Hsuan Tsang, who visited the region between 630 and 647, gives a detailed eyewitness description of Harsha's administration. Since both Bana and Hsuan Tsang were under Harsha's patronage, we must take their testimonies with a grain of salt, but much of what each says is confirmed by the other, as well as by the third witness, Harsha himself, who wrote three plays, two of which—the two translated in this volume—describe life at court. For instance, Hsuan Tsang reports that when Harsha was meeting with the king of Kama·rupa (Assam), a group of dissidents set fire to a tower in which the Buddha image was placed. Harsha rushed headlong into the flames and saved the image. This scene is dramatically reflected in one of Harsha's plays, 'The Lady of the Jewel Necklace,' when the Harsha-figure, King Údayana, rushes into the fire to save princess Ratnávali.

Harsha came of a powerful ruling family and ruled over the fertile land between the Ganges and Yámuna rivers, a kingdom that he extended into most of Bengal, Bihar, and Malwa, until he ruled the whole of the Ganges basin (including Nepal and Assam), from the Himalayas to the Nármada river, besides Malwa, Gujarat, and Sauráshtra (the modern Kathiawar). He shifted the center of power from Ujjain in the west to Kanauj farther east. He was said to be able to field 60,000 war elephants and 100,000 cavalry. But when, in 620, he tried to cross the Nármada and extend his territory southward into the Deccan, he was stopped by king Pula·keshin II, the Chalúkyan ruler of a Deccan kingdom. After his initial conquests, there was peace in his empire.

In light of the court intrigues in the two plays attributed to him, the details of Harsha's political connections are highly suggestive. Harsha was descended through his grandmother from the second Gupta line, and through his father from the Pushya·bhutis. His sister, Rajyáshri, was married to the Máukhari king at Kanauj. According to Bana, after her husband was killed in battle, Rajyáshri was taken hostage. She escaped and fled to the Vindhyas where she was about to throw herself on her husband's funeral pyre, but Harsha snatched her from the pyre. She then hoped to become a Buddhist nun, but Harsha dissuaded her, as through her he could control the Máukhari kingdom. According to a second tradition, Harsha succeeded to both the Pushya·bhuti and Máukhari thrones, after his elder brother, Rajya·várdhana, the crown prince, and his sister's husband (the Máukhari king) were killed in battle with the Guptas (Robb 2002: 42). A third tradition holds that Rajya·várdhana was treacherously murdered by the king of Bengal, whom he had sought as an ally in an expedition against the Raja of Malwa (Kale 1921: xxi; Smith 1914: 335–9), and a fourth, that Rajya·várdhana retired to a hermitage after their father's death.

Harsha died without leaving an heir. On his death, one of his ministers usurped the throne. His empire did not survive him.

He was a cosmopolitan king, known as a patron of the arts and of all religions. Besides the poet Bana and another famous poet, Mayúra, he also kept at his court a man named Matánga Divákara, a critic and dramatist who came from one of the excluded, Dalit castes, a *caṇḍāla*. (The Kashmiri historian Raja·shékhara first made this assertion in the ninth century. SYLVAIN LÉVI identifies him as a Jain, but his name indicates his low caste origin (1963: 184–95)). Harsha was also a religious eclectic; two of his three plays (the ones translated in this volume) are dedicated to the Hindu god Shiva, while the third, 'How the Nagas were Pleased' (*Nāgānanda*), invokes the Buddha. Such eclecticism is unprecedented in Sanskrit drama, D. DEVAHUTI claims; she continues: "Harsha's quinquennial assemblies further confirm his allegiance to both Hinduism and Buddhism, which were beginning to show increasing signs of convergence. The assemblies were in the Buddhist tradition but were held at the holy Hindu site of Prayāga. Donations distributed on the occasion benefited followers of all sects" (DEVAHUTI 1970: 154–7). Harsha may have became a convert to Buddhism in his later life; we know that he sent a mission to China.

Did Harsha Write These Plays?

Tradition ascribes both 'The Lady of the Jewel Necklace' (*Ratnāvalī*) and 'The Lady who Shows her Love' (*Priya/darśikā*), as well as 'How the Nagas were Pleased,' to Harsha (KALE 1921: xvii). But Mámmata's 'Illumination of Poetry' (*Kāvya/prakāśa*), in the early eleventh century, notes that Harsha gave a great deal of money to Bana, and this is the source of the long-standing rumor that Harsha paid Bana to ghost-write the plays for him (LÉVI 1963: 184–95). Further complications are added by the tendency to confuse this Harsha with either or both of two other Harshas, one of whom was a king (ruler of Kashmir between 1113 and 1124) and the other a poet (the author of the twelfth-century *Naiṣadhīya/carita*)—or could these be a single twelfth-century person, another poet-king named Harsha?

I am persuaded, however, that king Harsha really wrote the plays in this volume himself. After all, ancient India had a great many kings, and many of them employed first-rate poets at their courts. Yet Harsha is almost unique in claiming that he himself, rather than his court poet (in his case, Bana), wrote the three fine plays composed at his court. Moreover, 'The Lady of the Jewel Necklace' and 'The Lady who Shows her Love' are the sorts of plays a king might well write: the plots are full of political intrigue (which involve mistaken identities, both political and erotic, that are mirrored in the frequent use of paronomasia, extended double entendre). And though some of the poetry is quite good, refreshingly simple and straightforward (might one say commanding, or martial?), some of it—let's be frank—is pretty dreadful (take a look at 'The Lady of the Jewel Necklace' 3.87 (verse

11)—worse than anything that Bana or any court poet of the first order would produce for the sake of the seventh-century equivalent of a MacArthur grant. But there is another, better argument for the royal author.

I have said he was *almost* unique, because another poet king, the Pállava ruler Mahéndra·varman, wrote a delightful satire called the 'The Comedy of the Madman's Antics' (*Matta/vilāsa/prahasana*). These two are the only kings who wrote Sanskrit plays good enough to be frequently cited within the tradition or, as far as we know, to survive at all. (Other kings, of course, may have written plays, perhaps in vernaculars as well as in Sanskrit, but no one cared to preserve them by having them copied over and over again; in a climate like India's, only the fittest texts survive.) Oddly enough, Mahéndra·varman was a contemporary of Harsha and was defeated by the same Pula·keshin II who defeated Harsha. Mahéndra·varman ruled Kanchi, on the other side, the southern side, of the same Vindhya stronghold that formed the southern border of the empire of Harsha as well as of the hero of his plays, the mythical King Údayana of Kaushámbi. Pula·keshin II, therefore, surely appears in the Harsha plays as the king of Kósala/Vindhya·ketu, whom Údayana, unlike his author, succeeds in conquering in the battles of the Vindhyas. Pula·keshin II did not, apparently, write any plays worth keeping.

And if we assume that a ruling king really wrote these two plays, we gain access to certain suggestive insights into their plots. Clearly they owe a great deal to the 'Kama Sutra' (*Kāma/sūtra*), the ancient Indian textbook of eroticism, but the 'Kama Sutra' itself is closely based on the 'Artha·

shastra' (*Artha/śāstra*), the ancient Indian textbook of politics. The fantasy of sneaking into the harem, for example, is part of a broader mythology of intrigue that the 'Kama Sutra' presents, a whole new erotic mythology that it creates by applying to sex the Machiavellian politics of the 'Artha·shastra,' composed perhaps a century, or less, before the 'Kama Sutra' (DONIGER AND KAKAR 2002: xi–xiii). The 'Kama Sutra' explicitly refers to the 'Artha·shastra,' and the two texts have much in common. The 'Kama Sutra' tells you how to test married women, to detect a woman likely to commit adultery, in precisely the way that the 'Artha·shastra' tells you to test potential defectors, assassins, and so forth, how to detect suspicious characters. The list (in 'Artha·shastra' 1.14.2) of people in the enemy's territory who are dissatisfied and can be seduced politically is the model for the lists (in 'Kama Sutra' 5.1.52–54) of women in their husband's territory, as it were, who can be seduced sexually.

The 'Artha·shastra' advises the king to test his potential ministers of various departments to make sure they are impervious to the temptations of each of the three goals of life: *dharma* (religion), *artha* (power) and *kāma* (desire) (1.10.3); he also tells him to test the candidate against a fourth power, fear. This then appears in the 'Kama Sutra' as just one test, the test of the guard for the harem, a four-fold test that also includes fear (5.6.40–42). The use of messengers in the 'Kama Sutra' parallels the employment of ambassadors and spies in the 'Artha·shastra' (1.16); the same word (*dūta*) designates both messengers and spies. The internal debate of potential adulterers in the 'Kama Sutra,' persuading themselves of the moral justice of their actions (1.5.4–20), mirrors the similar meditations of spies in the 'Artha·shastra' and the self-persuasions and justifications for seizing power (1.16.29 and 6.2.38). Indeed, the list of reasons that justify adultery in the 'Kama Sutra' include many that are far more political than erotic (1.5.8–21). And surely the obsessively detailed timetable for the man-about-town's day in the 'Kama Sutra' ("He gets up in the morning, relieves himself, cleans his teeth, applies fragrant oils in small quantities, as well as incense, garlands, bees' wax and red lac, looks at his face in a mirror, takes some mouth-wash and betel," etc., 1.4.5) is a satire on the equally detailed plans for the king's day in the 'Artha·shastra' (judge cases, receive embassies, relax in the women's quarters, etc., 1.19.33).

The 'Kama Sutra' shares with the 'Artha·shastra' (1.6, 1.17.35–8) its emphasis on the need for the control of the senses: both Vatsyáyana and Kautílya would have loved Nixon, hated Clinton. The two texts tell the same myths about the same sinners in this regard: Dandákya, Rávana, Indra ('Artha·shastra' 1.15.55; 'Kama Sutra' 1.2.35–36). It is surely significant that the author of the best extant English translation of the 'Artha·shastra,' R. P. Kangle, also translated 'The Lady who Shows her Love.'

Bearing this in mind as we return to the question of Harsha's identity, we can see the coterminous influence of these two great textbooks that justify Henry Kissinger's notorious insistence that power is the greatest aphrodisiac. Take, for instance, the mysterious prediction that is mentioned at the start of 'The Lady of the Jewel Necklace' but not explained until the end, the prediction that anyone who married Ratnávali would conquer the earth. Now consider the map of India. A king in Kanauj who gets, first, nearby Avánti (from Vásava·datta) and then Símhala (from Ratnávali) doesn't need a magic prediction to tell him what he will have: these two dowries *are* the whole world, the whole of India. (Consider, too, the political alliances formed by Harsha's parents and siblings.) A marriage alliance with the ruler of Sri Lanka (Símhala) might not matter so much for, say, the king of Madras/Chennai, but for a north Indian king, Símhala is the end of the world.

Údayana's conquest of another woman (Ságarika or Arányika) is actually the conquest of another country, though he doesn't know it at the time; he wants everything, of course, and he gets it. The jester, as usual saying more than he knows, explicitly compares an erotic conquest with a political one, when he says that the news of a forthcoming rendezvous with Ratnávali will give the king even more pleasure than "his acquisition of the kingdom of Kaushámbi gave." Appeasement is the key to both sex and politics; the same word is used for talking around an offended woman and conciliating a nervous potential enemy. The extreme instance of this comes in Act Four of 'The Lady who Shows her Love,' when the king is trying to find a way to get his girlfriend out of the prison that his wife has put her in, and the jester suggests that he simply attack the harem with his elephants and horses and footsoldiers. The king scorns this plan, preferring to do something that will appease the queen rather than, perhaps, kill her, but the jester is simply urging the king to use all the means at his disposal; all's fair in love and total war. At the start of Act Three of 'The Lady of the Jewel Necklace,' Kánchana·mala remarks of the jester, with bitter sarcasm: "Bravo, Prime Minister Vasántaka, bravo! You have surpassed even Prime Minister Yaugándharáyana with this plot for war and peace." The jester's playful erotic machinations are a direct parallel to the serious political schemes of the real Prime Minister. The jester is the shadow not of the king but of the Machiavellian minister.

A final clue, I think, to the royal nature of the poet lies in the amazing final stanza of both plays, in which Harsha speaks so bitterly about slanderers, a *rasa*-sentiment of *ressentiment* coming out of nowhere. What could the slander be? Is it, perhaps, the rumor that the king did not write the plays himself?

History of the Plot

A complex cycle of classical Sanskrit texts surrounds the mythical figures of king Údayana, his queen, Vásava·datta, and a series of co-wives (DONIGER 1999: 74–84). A version of the story was also told in Pali in the *Dhamma/pad'/aṭṭha/kathā*, in the fifth century CE. Three episodes are told in the 'Ocean of the Rivers of Story' (*Kathā/sarit/sāgara*), a text probably composed in the eleventh or twelfth century in Kashmir but based on a much earlier collection of stories, the no longer extant 'Great Story' (*Bṛhat/kathā*), which was almost certainly known to all of the Sanskrit playwrights. One of these three episodes tells of a celestial magician who disguised himself as Údayana and seduced a woman whom Údayana had intended to take as his co-wife [text 1, 'Ocean of the Rivers of Story' (31), in which the co-wife is Kalínga·sena]; another tells us that Queen Vásava·datta magically disguised herself and served the woman whom the king intended to make his co-wife, until the king saw through the disguise by means of her skill in the art of garland-making [text 2, 'Ocean of the Rivers of Story' (15–16), the co-wife Padmávati]; and, in a third, Údayana became unfaithful and inadvertently called Vásava·datta by the name of her rival, and, later, secretly seduced—while the queen watched in hiding—yet another rival that she had tried in vain to conceal from him [text 3, 'Ocean of the Rivers of Story' (14), Vírachita]. This cycle of stories was taken up in three Sanskrit dramas, one by Bhasa, who replaced the magic transformations and disguises with a dream sequence [text 4, 'Vásava·datta in a Dream,' Padmávati again], and two by Harsha, who replaced them with a portrait of a co-wife, a magic plant fertilizer and a magic show [text 5, 'The Lady of the Jewel Necklace'], and with a play within a play [text 6, 'The Lady who Shows her Love']. We may represent the basic plots of these six texts on a chart:

Text	Genre	What conceals	Who is disguised	What reveals
1. Ocean of the Rivers of Story	narrative	magic	magician	sleep
2. Ocean of the Rivers of Story	narrative	magic	queen	garland/ portrait
3. Ocean of the Rivers of Story	narrative	disguise	co-wife	slip of the tongue
4. Vásava·datta in a Dream	play	disguise	queen	dream/ portrait
5. The Lady of the Jewel Necklace	play	disguise	co-wife	necklace/ portrait/magic
6. The Lady who Shows her Love	play	disguise	co-wife	play/magic

The Story in the 'Ocean of the Rivers of Stories' (*Kathā/sarit/sāgara*)

Let us begin with the story of:

Kalínga·sena and the Magician

King Údayana wanted to make an alliance with a king whose daughter, Kalínga·sena, came to Údayana's kingdom of Kaushámbi and asked him to marry her, which he agreed to do. But Údayana's prime minister, who did not want this marriage to happen (because he had promised the king's first wife that she would have no co-wife), intrigued with the astrologers to delay the date of the wedding for six months, during which Kalínga·sena lived in the kingdom. The prime minister mentally summoned a demon (*rākṣasa*) named Yogéshvara and told him to watch over Kalínga·sena night and day in order to catch her doing something that would prove her unfit to wed the king. In particular, he advised, "If she were to have an affair with a celestial magician (*vidyā/dhara*) or someone like that, that would be very fortunate. And you must observe the divine lover when he is asleep, even if he comes in a different form, for divine beings assume their own forms when they fall asleep."

Now, a celestial magician named Mádana·vega had fallen in love with Kalínga·sena; he used his magic to come to her room in the form of the king and seduce her. The demon found the magician in his own form, asleep on the bed of the sleeping Kalínga·sena; for he was a divine man and had lost his false form because his magic power to take such a form vanished when he was asleep. The demon called the prime minister, who brought the king to Kalínga·sena's room; he saw her asleep and the magician asleep beside her in his own form. The king wanted to kill him, but just then the magician was awakened by his magic and he went out and flew away to the sky. In a moment, Kalínga·sena woke up too; she said to the king, "Why did you go away a moment ago and come back with your minister?" The minister explained to her, "Someone who took the form of the king magically deluded you and married you; it wasn't the king." And they left. The minister told everything to Vásava·datta, who thanked him.

Údayana kept thinking about Kalínga·sena's beauty, and one night when he was full of lust he went to her room alone, with a sword in his hand, and asked her to become his wife. But she rejected him, saying, "You should regard me as another man's wife." The king withdrew and eventually forgot about her. But the magician, who had overheard the conversation, praised his wife and continued to visit her, though he added, "Even though you are a virtuous woman, you have gotten the reputation of a whore" ('Ocean of the Rivers of Stories' 31–34 [6.5–8]).

The magician is revealed in his post-coital repose, the sleep that both allows possession and reveals it. For the Hindus believe that a god or demon who masquerades as someone else in bed is compelled to take his own true form when he loses mental control and hence inadvertently turns off the current from the magic projector in his mind; this happens when he sleeps, gets drunk, dies, gets angry—or makes love, when sexual passion strips away the final illusion, the curse or disguise, and reveals the true identity (DONIGER 2000). But in this case the unmasking takes place after the damage has been done, and Kalínga·sena is punished, and calumniated, for not seeing through the trick sooner. Vásava·datta plays no active role; the prime minister, assisted by the demon and, inadvertently, the magician, intervenes to get rid of the feared co-wife—who must, even at the end, still defend herself from the lustful Údayana.

But Vásava·datta plays an active role in other episodes in the cycle about Údayana, which begin with the same premise as the story of Kalínga·sena: for political reasons, Údayana must take a second wife (or wives). Before the encounter with Kalínga·sena, Údayana had become involved with:

Padmávati, the Lady with the Lotus

King Údayana, King of Vatsa, married to Vásava·datta, daughter of the king of Avánti, was so in love with her that he neglected his royal duties. His ministers decided to save him from himself by getting the King of Mágadha, their enemy, to give his daughter Padmávati ("the Lady with the Lotus") to the king and to make the king believe that Vásava·datta was dead. The ministers gave the queen a charm that enabled her to change her shape, and she disguised herself as a Brahmin woman, under the name of Avántika ("The Woman from the City of Avánti," Vásava·datta's kingdom), and went to serve Padmávati at the court of Mágadha.

When the king of Mágadha offered Padmávati to Údayana, he accepted her. Vásava·datta made garlands for Padmávati, using a special technique that the king had taught her. The bridal couple returned to Vatsa, and Vásava·datta followed in the rear. The king asked Padmávati where she had gotten the garlands; she said she had gotten them from Avántika, and then the king knew that Avántika must be Vásava·datta. The minister told the king all, and the king and his two wives were reconciled ('Ocean of the Rivers of Stories' 15–16 [3.1–2]).

Údayana recognizes Vásava·datta by recognizing himself in her—through the art of making garlands that he had taught her.

But before Padmávati (and, therefore, before Kalínga·sena), there had been:

Vírachita and the Slip of the Tongue

King Údayana married Vásava·datta, but after a while, Údayana became unfaithful and made love with a woman in the harem named Vírachita, with whom he had had an affair before. One day he called the queen by the wrong name, Vírachita, and had to appease her by falling at her feet. Later, a beautiful princess named Bándhumati was sent as a present to the queen. The queen concealed her under the name of Mánjulika, but the king saw her and secretly seduced her. Vásava·datta, who was hidden, witnessed this act; furious at first, she eventually relented and accepted Bándhumati, for she had a tender heart ('Ocean of the Rivers of Stories' 14 [2.60].64–75).

The king mistakes one woman for another, mistaking not the person but the name; when the queen conceals first the rival and then herself, the king finds the secret woman and the queen watches the secret act. In the end, all is revealed and all is accepted.

The Story in Bhasa's 'Vásava·datta in a Dream' and Subándhu's 'Vásava·datta'

Bhasa's 'The Drama of Vásava·datta [who meets her husband] in a Dream' (*Svapna/vāsavadattā*), was composed early in the fourth century CE. This play shares with the first text from the 'Ocean of the Rivers of Story' the revealing sleep/dream; with the second, much of the plot and the name of the co-wife, Padmávati; and, with the third, more of the plot and the slip of the tongue:

Vásava·datta in a Dream

King Údayana was married to Vásava·datta and loved her too much to take a second wife, but there was a prediction that for the good of the kingdom he should marry Padmávati, the sister of Dárshaka, the king of Mágadha. To gain Dárshaka as an ally when Údayana's throne had been usurped, the king's minister, Yaugándharáyana, spread the rumor that Vásava·datta had perished in a fire at Lavánaka, but secretly he put Vásava·datta in the care of Padmávati, giving her the name of Avántika. Údayana married Padmávati, and Vásava·datta made a garland for her husband's bride.

Padmávati was stricken with a headache and lay down in a room different from her own room. The king and the jester went to her own room to conciliate her, but the jester, seeing the garland that Vásava·datta had made, mistook it for a cobra and fled. The king, finding that Padmávati was not in fact there, fell asleep in Padmávati's bed. Vásava·datta came in and, thinking that Padmávati was in the bed, sat on it and said, "I wonder why my heart rejoices so as I sit beside her. And by lying on one side of the bed she seems to invite me to embrace her. I will lie down there." And she lay down.

Then the king, dreaming, called out, "O Vásava·datta," and the queen stood up and said, "It's the king, not Padmávati! Has he seen me?" Again the king called out, "O, princess of Avánti!" and she realized, "Good, the king is just talking in his sleep. There's no one here, so I will stay here for a moment and satisfy my eyes and my heart." Údayana (continuing in his sleep): "My darling, answer me. Are you angry with me?"

V: "No, no, but I am unhappy."

U: "Is it because you are remembering Vírachika [*sic*]?"

V (angrily): "Go away; is Vírachika here too?"

U: "Then let me ask you to forgive me for Vírachika."

V: "I've stayed here for a long time. Someone might see. I'd better go. . . "

As soon as she had left, the king stood up and cried out, "Vásava·datta! Stay, stay!" And then, not sure if he had dreamt it or not, he said, "If it's a dream, it would have been good never to wake up. But if it is a delusion, let me keep it for a long time."

Messengers brought a portrait of Vásava·datta with Údayana, sent by Vásava·datta's mother. The identity of Vásava·datta was revealed through the portrait.

There are three mistaken identities in this play: Vásava·datta masquerades as the minister's sister; Vásava·datta at first mistakes the king for Padmávati in the bed; and the king mistakes the real Vásava·datta for the Vásava·datta in his dream. The content of the dream is most revealing: the king, asleep (innocently) in the rival's bed, remembers another occasion on which he behaved less innocently in another rival's bed and was revealed by the shameful slip of the tongue (a subconscious act, just like a dream, hence a kind of dream within a dream). (Indeed, it is not clear whether the king in the play or the author himself has yet another slip of the tongue about the slip of the tongue, substituting Víra·chika for Vírachita.) This conversation within the dream is particularly noteworthy because the traditional dream books usually analyze only the visual images of dreams, never the words (Doniger O'Flaherty 1984: 25).

In both of these stories about the co-wife Padmávati, the king loves Vásava·datta more than the other woman, and merely takes a second wife for political reasons. But in Harsha's plays, the king prefers the second wife erotically as well as politically, and Vásava·datta's quandary is not merely political, nor is it so easily resolved. Significantly, these co-wives do not have political pseudonyms, as Vásava·datta does when she calls herself Avántika, but, rather, natural pseudonyms, like Padmávati ("the Lady with the Lotus," who is briefly mentioned as another co-wife in 'The Lady who Shows her Love'): they are called "Ságarika" and "Arányika," the ladies of the ocean and the jungle. In Harsha's plays, moreover, as in the third narrative text, it is the identity of the co-wife, not of Vásava·datta, that is concealed for political reasons, and the co-wife therefore suffers much of the loss of status and identity that Vásava·datta suffers in the other versions. To this extent, our sympathy is with the co-wife; but we also empathize with Vásava·datta, who suffers the loss of the king's love.

A final version, that omits the co-wife but reshuffles other familiar elements of the plot, is Subándhu's Sanskrit prose romance, 'Vásava·datta,' composed c. 600 CE:

Prince Kandárpa·ketu saw Vásava·datta in a dream and set out with his friend Makaránda to find her. Resting under a tree at night, he overheard a parrot tell his mate that Vásava·datta, daughter of king Shringára·shékhara of Kúsuma·pura, had dreamt of a young man so handsome that she would not choose any of the several princes who had come to her marriage-choice ceremony. Kandárpa·ketu found Vásava·datta and they eloped secretly. But on their way, an angry sage cursed Vásava·datta to become a lifeless statue until she felt the touch of her lover Kandárpa·ketu. Kandárpa·ketu searched for her until he happened upon the statue and, moved by its likeness to Vásava·datta, embraced it, thus bringing Vásava·datta back to life.

The theme of mutual dreaming comes from the story literature that the 'Ocean of Story' shares with the 'Thousand and One Nights,' but the overheard bird is a touch that Harsha will employ, and the woman mistaken for a statue made from a woman introduces yet another artform into our list:

Text	Genre	What conceals	Who is disguised	What reveals
7. 'Vásava·datta'	narrative	curse	queen	sculpture/ embrace

Thus desire and the embrace is assimilated to the themes of the magic curse and artistic creation as forces that reveal true love.

Harsha's Dramas

We do not know which of the two plays Harsha wrote first. The fact that the speech describing the Spring festival is appropriate to 'The Lady of the Jewel Necklace' but is repeated verbatim in 'The Lady who Shows her Love,' where it is inappropriate, suggests that Harsha wrote 'The Lady of the Jewel Necklace' first and modified it to produce 'The Lady who Shows her Love.' 'The Lady of the Jewel Necklace' is also considerably longer than 'The Lady who Shows her Love,' almost half again as long, and has far more poetry. On the other hand, the puns on *priya* ("dear" or "what is wanted") in the final conversation that is duplicated in both plays make far better sense in 'The Lady who Shows her Love,' and therefore may have been composed for that play and later transferred to the other. As for the plot itself, the action in 'The Lady who Shows her Love' takes place earlier than that of 'The Lady of the Jewel Necklace,' for its first act, set a year or so before the rest of the play, tells us how Údayana first met and married Vásava·datta, an event which is regarded as quite recent (so that Vásava·datta is often referred to as a princess, as well as a queen), whereas in 'The Lady of the Jewel Necklace' it is never described and is presumably more distant in time. Yet Priya·dárshika, but not Ratnávali, mentions Padmávati, the affair with whom took place after Údayana had married Vásava·datta.

We will begin with 'The Lady of the Jewel Necklace,' which Indian tradition regards as the more important play.

The Lady of the Jewel Necklace

Vásava·datta tried to keep the king from seeing Ságarika, but Ságarika saw him and fell in love with him. She painted a portrait of the king as Kama, the god of love, and her friend painted in, beside him, a portrait of Ságarika as Rati, Kama's wife. The king then found the portrait that Ságarika had made of him and declared his passionate love for the unknown maiden who had painted his portrait and hers. Vásava·datta saw the portrait and became suspicious; she bribed Ságarika's friend, by giving her some of her own clothes, to get her to guard Ságarika. This woman, however, dressed Ságarika in the queen's clothes and arranged for the king to meet Ságarika when Ságarika was disguised as Vásava·datta. But Vásava·datta's friend overheard Ságarika's friend talking about it, and the queen went to the place of assignation, the portrait-gallery.

The king mistook her for Ságarika and made love to her with words, addressing her as Ságarika. But when the king attempted to kiss Vásava·datta-as-Ságarika, the queen threw off her veil, in fury. The king begged her to forgive him, but the queen went away. Then Ságarika-as-Vásava·datta started to hang herself with a creeper, in shame that her secret love had been found out. The king, thinking that she was Vásava·datta trying to commit suicide because he had made love to another woman, embraced her. Ságarika, thinking that he knew that she was Ságarika, rejoiced, but then the king realized, with joy, that it was Ságarika, and embraced her again. Just then the queen came back to forgive her husband and accept his apologies. She heard his voice and decided to sneak up on him from behind and put her arms around his neck. But then she overheard the other two and realized that they were in love. The king fell at her feet, but the queen had Ságarika imprisoned—until she was identified (through the necklace) as the princess Ratnávali. Then Vásava·datta adorned Ratnávali with her own ornaments, took her hand, and joined it with the king's.

Here is the plot of:

The Lady who Shows her Love

King Údayana, married to Queen Vásava·datta, was supposed to take as his second wife the princess Priya·dárshika, but before the wedding could take place, Priya·dárshika's father (Vásava·datta's uncle) had been deposed, and in the ensuing chaos Priya·dárshika went into hiding under the name of Aránуika ("The Lady of the Jungle"). Vásava·datta, not knowing who Aránуika was, took her into her service, but the king fell in love with her. The queen, worried that she had lost the king's affections, decided to stage a play about herself and king Údayana.

Aránуika was to play the queen, while their friend Mano·rama was to play the king. But Mano·rama, without Aránуika's knowledge, colluded with the jester so that the king took Mano·rama's place and Aránуika and the king could make love right under the queen's eyes. Vásava·datta gave Aránуika the ornaments from her body, and she gave Mano·rama the ornaments that Vásava·datta's father had given the king at their marriage. The king met Mano·rama, who was dressed like him. She gave him his/her ornaments and he acted in the play.

Vásava·datta walked away and found the jester asleep at the door of the picture gallery. From him she learned that it had been the king playing the part of the king. She imprisoned Arányika but set her free when she discovered that Arányika was Priya·dárshika. She joined the hands of Aráneyika and the king.

Harsha's Treatment of the Conventions of the Narrative

Harsha's 'The Lady of the Jewel Necklace' takes up the story after the events known from the versions of the story that we have seen (the prediction that Údayana must marry Ratnávali, the rumor of Vásava·datta's death by fire) and a few more. While Ratnávali, the daughter of the king of Símhala, was sailing to Kaushámbi, the ship was wrecked and Ratnávali was rescued from the water by a merchant and given to the minister, who recognized her by the jewel necklace that she always wore. He put her in Vásava·datta's service as a handmaid named Ságarika ("the Lady of the Ocean"). And Priya·dárshika has an even more complex prehistory, involving not only Priya·dárshika's father's and step-father's military disasters, as well as her own marital disasters and exile, but the parallel case of Vásava·datta, whom Údayana has not yet married at the start of the play and whose father had captured Údayana. Thus here, in contrast with 'The Lady of the Jewel Necklace,' the two women are on an equal footing at the start: though Priya·dárshika has actually been given to Údayana first, Vásava·datta quickly takes the lead when Údayana takes her physically from her father.

Harsha borrows his plots but expands on them, as he himself says, in the stage director's voice, at the start of both 'The Lady of the Jewel Necklace' and 'The Lady who Shows her Love':

> *His majesty Shri Harsha has composed a play called 'The Lady of the Jewel Necklace'/'The Lady who Shows her Love,' graced by an unprecedented arrangement of the plot.*

Sylvain Lévi criticizes Harsha for stealing his plot(s) from Kali·dasa's 'Málavika and Agni·mitra' (*Mālavikāgnimitra*), though in fact there is a far closer link to Bhasa's 'Vásava·datta in a Dream': where Kali·dasa's play has much the same plot, but different characters, Bhasa's has not only the same plot but the same king and queen. Indeed, by these criteria, Harsha even plagiarized himself, taking the plot of 'The Lady who Shows her Love' from 'The Lady of the Jewel Necklace.' But surely this is the wrong way to think of it. Rather, Harsha was playing new variations on an old theme.

The particular dramatic form of Harsha's plays is that of the minor comedy called a *nāṭikā* (the stage director explicitly identifies it as such), and every *nāṭikā* must follow the same general outline: it is a four act play with many female characters, including a heroine (of royal birth) who is in love with the king and a queen who gives her consent in the end. Its principal mood should be erotic. It most closely corresponds to a romantic comedy in the English theatrical tradition. (The play within a play in 'The Lady who Shows her Love,' by contrast, is identified by all the characters in the play as a *nāṭaka*, a major drama.)

Even LÉVI grudgingly admits that Harsha introduced into the inherited plot a number of original touches: the parrot, the disguise of the maid, the king's playacting, and so forth. It seems to me (and I will argue below) that he also introduced major meditations on self-imitation and artistic representation. The two plays together constitute a kind of variorum edition of the tale with its variants, or, to change the metaphor, a Bach fugue: they go along together for a while on the same path, with the same characters sometimes saying a line that you recognize from the other play, then they part for a while, then meet and part again.

Was the audience in on it from the start, because they knew the story from the earlier sources? Or is it like a murder mystery in which we're in suspense—What was the seer's prediction? Why is Ságarika in disguise?—until Yaugándharáyana explains it all at the end? I think the former situation is far more likely than the latter. JAMES THURBER (1942) wrote a satirical essay called 'The Macbeth Murder Mystery,' in which he imagines a woman who doesn't know the plot of Shakespeare's 'Macbeth' but is addicted to murder mysteries, seeing the play for the first time and wondering all through who did it. We would be just as foolish as she was, if we were to assume that Harsha's audiences expected a surprise. The story of Údayana and Vásava·datta was already a myth in Harsha's day, and originality is not an essential ingredient of a good myth. The voice of myth is predictable, one that the storyteller knows and the audience expects. The audience has an expectation of what the story should say, and the storyteller imitates that paradigm, fulfills that expectation; the audience takes pleasure in predicting what will happen, and satisfaction in seeing it happen, rather than in being surprised or shocked.

In addition to the general convention of the well-known Indian tale of Údayana and Vásava·datta, 'The Lady of the Jewel Necklace' also follows the cross-cultural convention of what literary critics call the recognition narrative, the ultimate revelation of the identity of someone who has been in disguise for much of the story. The recognition narrative served, like the theme of the Pietà or the Madonna and Child for medieval European sculptors, as a classical, shared theme that challenged the artist to use it as a foil for individual originality—for tellers of myths can, in fact, be highly original, as long as they also take pains to touch all the bases that their audiences expect. The recognition scene in narratives is a cliché, which has led literary critics and cultural snobs (two often intersecting groups) commonly to regard such stories with contempt and suspicion. But the audience enjoys the way that, as the story unfolds, we see through the disguise of the new superficial details—a different character, a different country—to realize that it is, in fact, our old friend the finally revealed heroine. When the victim in a masquerade narrative finally recognizes the masquerader ("Oh, it's the princess!"), the reader or listener of the story recognizes the plot ("Oh, it's a recognition story!"). And it is precisely this known quality of the cliché plot (plus its intrinsic appeal: clichés endure because they represent truths) that makes it ultimately fulfilling. The moment when the two apparently different characters are revealed to be two aspects of one person brings with it the same satisfaction as the moment when the last piece of the jigsaw puzzle—or the last line connecting the dots—slips in to reveal the total image, or when, in a piece of classical music, the expected final sequence of chords comes into resolution. This accounts for the extraordinary popularity of recognition scenes in all types of literature, a popularity that remains in tension with the contempt of the critics.

Self-impersonation[1]

Several characters in the two plays by Harsha accidentally (or, occasionally, purposefully) imitate themselves, and in both plays, the double disguise frees another self. In 'The Lady who Shows her Love,' Údayana-as-Mano·rama-as-Údayana is able to make love to his new woman—Priya·dárshika-as- Aránika-as-Vásava·datta—under the eyes of his queen and get away with it, as he fails to do in his own persona, the king-as-the-king. And in 'The Lady of the Jewel Necklace,' it is only when the queen inadvertently masquerades as her rival, the queen-as-Ratnávali-as-Ságarika-as-the-queen, that the truth comes out, first in the king's words and then in Vásava·datta's honest expression of her hurt and her anger.

Údayana's impersonation of Údayana in 'The Lady who Shows her Love' is the most explicit instance of self-impersonation, but in 'The Lady of the Jewel Necklace,' the queen says of him, when he behaves in a characteristically adulterous manner, "My husband, this is worthy of you; it's just like you." The word she uses, *sadṛśam*, more specifically refers to something that looks just like something else. She means that he is true to type, but she says that he gives the appearance of being himself. His ultimate resemblance will be not to himself but to his son: Vasu·bhuti greets Vásava·datta, in Act Four of 'The Lady of the Jewel Necklace,' by saying, "Live long and prosper, and may you have a son just like the king of Vatsa." This is the only reminder in either play that the fight between the two women is a matter not merely of sexual jealousy but of succession; and here we may recall that Harsha himself died without an heir.

There are a number of disguises in the involuted plot of 'The Lady of the Jewel Necklace' (DONIGER 2005: 29–35). People constantly accuse one another of imagining things to be other than they are, and they are usually right. Ratnávali is disguised as Ságarika before the play begins. She mistakes Údayana for Kama, the god of love (an understandable mistake, since she sees Vásava·datta simultaneously worshipping Kama and Údayana), and she imaginatively represents herself as the king's lover in the portrait she paints. Then the intentional disguises begin: Ratnávali-as-Ságarika is disguised as Vásava·datta and mistaken for Vásava·datta, and Vásava·datta, not disguised at all, is taken for (Ratnávali-as)-Ságarika-as-Vásava·datta. Vásava·datta begins the masquerade inadvertently when she gives her own clothes to her rival's friend; but then the reins are taken out of her hands when the clothes are used to deceive her and she unconsciously impersonates Ratnávali-as-Ságarika consciously impersonating her. Through a kind of double-double-cross, in which the king mistakes his queen for the Other Woman, and the Other Woman for the queen, he actually makes love to Vásava·datta when she is undisguised, thinking she is someone else pretending to be her. He calls her by the wrong name, "Ságarika," a fatal (and, in Sanskrit literature, conventional) error. The king cannot tell his women apart, but from time to time he drops remarks that indicate his deeper knowledge that, in various ways, Ratnávali-as-Ságarika is replacing his wife.

This idea of the king's self-imitation is taken into new realms of performance in 'The Lady who Shows her Love,' through the play within the play, a genre that the Sanskrit tradition nicely calls an "embryo play" (*garbha/nāṭaka*), a play for which the outer play serves as a womb. For the king, the play within the play is not only a double impersonation but a double change of gender, a double-cross dress, a double drag that cancels itself out: the king pretends to be a woman pretending to be him. The complexities are multiplied when the play is produced by one of those Indian traditions—alluded to in this very play—in which women play the parts of men: at such a moment, one could imagine a woman playing the part of the king playing the part of a woman playing the part of the king.

What did the queen hope to accomplish by having her rival impersonate her? (She stages the play after the king has fallen in love with Arányika.) Did she think the king would transfer back to her the love he had apparently transferred from her to the new woman? Did she hope to rekindle his love, fanning an old flame, as it were? How bitter must her humiliation have been when she realized her ruse had backfired in such a way that she herself had made it possible for the king to make love to her rival, right before her eyes.

The king "outs" Priya·dárshika without her permission or her conscious knowledge, tricking Priya·dárshika-as-Aránayika-as-Vásava·datta into letting him touch her. Priya·dárshika's own body also forces a Cartesian duplicity upon her: her mind thinks she is touching the hand of Mano·rama, but her body knows she is touching the hand of the king. In the end, Údayana's vision overpowers Vásava·datta's, and she sees not what she wants to see (her straying husband making love to her as she was when he loved her) but what she fears to see, actually sees, and allows herself to be talked out of saying that she sees: her husband making love to her rival. She stages her dream, and the king stages her nightmare. The queen moves, and the king checkmates her.

Representation

Who is staging the dream? Who is in control? We might make a distinction between active dreams and passive nightmares, or conscious and unconscious tricksters. The active masqueraders are the manipulators, like Queen Vásava·datta at first both in 'The Lady of the Jewel Necklace' and in 'The Lady who Shows her Love,' and like Údayana later in that play; the passive, unconscious masqueraders would include people who discover that, without willing it, they have been masquerading as themselves, like Vásava·datta later in 'The Lady of the Jewel Necklace.' Yet even (or especially) the active masqueraders tend to get caught up in their own tricks and discover a frame outside (or inside) the one that they themselves construct to impersonate someone else, a frame in which that someone else may be impersonating them, or they themselves may be unknowingly impersonating themselves. This is what happens, in different ways and in different texts, to both Údayana and Vásava·datta.

What is the relationship between the various forms of mental transformation used in all of these retellings of the tale of Údayana and Vásava·datta, both Harsha's and those of his sources? We have magical illusion (used by Kalínga·sena's magician in the 'Ocean of the Rivers of Story' and Vásava·datta's in 'The Lady of the Jewel Necklace,' and by the king himself in both plays—a magic plant fertilizer in 'The Lady of the Jewel Necklace' and a magic snake-venom cure in 'The Lady who Shows her Love'), art (the trick of garland-making and the portrait made by Ságarika), the slip of the tongue (which happens twice), dreaming (experienced by king Údayana in the play by Bhasa and by the jester in 'The Lady who Shows her Love'), masquerading (by the women in 'The Lady of the Jewel Necklace'), and play-acting (by the king in 'The Lady who Shows her Love'). How do these various forms of illusion—magic impersonation, magic disguise and art, portrait, play, slip of the tongue, and dream—work, each in its own way, as roads to the recognition of the true self and the true beloved? What do they tell us about the relationship between dreams, theatre, and personal masquerade? The jester's sleep, in 'The Lady who Shows her Love,' which lets him unconsciously reveal the truth to the queen, a key moment in the plot, is a transformation of the king's dream in 'Vásava·datta in a Dream' (itself a transformation of the revealing sleep in the 'Ocean of Rivers of Story'). The mynah bird in 'The Lady of the Jewel Necklace' (whom the jester mistakes for a ghost, at first) is similarly unconscious of what she says, but she carries the message that is crucial to the plot. Magic takes one form in one play, another form in another, as does portrait-painting. And, ultimately, they replace one another.

The first transformation (magical illusion) differs from the other three in several ways: the illusory form of the magician lies. It prevents rather than facilitates the union of the king and his mistress, and is ended, rather than created, by the suspension of rational thought. In all of the other variants, the illusory form tells the truth, brings about the ultimate union of the king and the mistress, and is created by the suspension of rational thought. The exception highlights, if it does not actually prove, the rule: one can dream by daylight, through masquerade and the theatre, and reach out to the same kind of emotional truth—often a painful truth—that we find in our dreams.

The play within a play (best known to us from 'Hamlet') is a popular device in Sanskrit literature, beginning long before these plays (in Valmíki's 'Ramáyana' (*Rāmāyaṇa*), for instance; Doniger O'Flaherty 1984: 175) and continuing on into other plays (in Bhava·bhuti's 'Rama's Last Act' (*Uttara/rāma/carita*), for instance; Doniger 2005: 66–7). Vásava·datta's play in 'The Lady who Shows her Love,' or the magician's magic illusion in 'The Lady of the Jewel Necklace,' is actually a play within a play within a play, since the level on which Vásava·datta exists is framed, Pirandello-fashion, by the traditional opening remarks of the stage-director, who tells us that we are going to see a play. Indeed, at the start of 'The Lady of the Jewel Necklace' the stage-director is joined by his wife, the actress, who tells us of her concern for her daughter who is to marry a man in a far distant land. This is, of course, the situation of both Ratnávali and Priya·dárshika, so that the actress is putting herself in the position of a person otherwise never mentioned by anyone in either play—the mother of the heroine. (We hear a lot about their fathers, kings, but not their mothers.) Nor do we hear another word about this story of the actress's daughter that presumably plays itself out beyond the fourth wall, in a world parallel to the worlds of the heroines of the plays. We know that the stage director's brother plays Údayana's Prime Minister, Yaugándharáyana, in 'The Lady of the Jewel Necklace' and the equivalent, Údayana's chamberlain, in 'The Lady who Shows her Love.' It is also implied, in 'The Lady who Shows her Love,' that the stage director himself will play the king; so we may conjecture that the actress, in 'The Lady of the Jewel Necklace,' plays Vásava·datta. And the epilogue sends us off with a reminder that the joyous conclusion of the play will bring joy to us, too, beyond the fourth wall.

Finally, there is the fact of the doubling of the plays, mirroring the doubling of the characters in them. Many stanzas, and many elements of the plot, appear in both plays, but then the essential differences skew the mirror images. One might see an overarching paronomasia of the two dramas, each one referring simultaneously to itself and to the other. One could read them as an exploration of a fork in the road, two possible ways in which the same situation could be resolved, as in PETER HOWITT's film 'Sliding Doors' (1998), which follows the two very different plots that result when a woman either catches or misses a departing subway train. I can imagine a performance of both plays in one evening, or of both played simultaneously, like the comedy and tragedy played simultaneously in Richard Strauss's opera *Ariadne auf Naxos*, or, as I once saw 'Hamlet' and 'Rosenkranz and Guildenstern are Dead' performed, first back to back and then, on the next night, interleaved.[2] How very modern these plays are.

'The Lady of the Jewel Necklace' as an Exemplary Play

And they are also very much to ancient Indian tastes. 'The Lady of the Jewel Necklace,' in particular, is frequently cited by the later textbooks on literature and drama, such as the *Daśa/rūpa* and the *Sāhitya/darpaṇa*, as the exemplar of various literary forms. (The earliest of these textbooks, the *Nāṭya/śāstra*, was written before the time of Harsha). Is it that Harsha was writing by the book, as it were, or, rather that the book (that is, the textbooks on playwriting) was written about Harsha, like the archer who displayed targets where he had always hit the bulls-eye—by drawing a target around his arrow after he had shot it? SYLVAIN LÉVI, whose book on the Indian theatre remains the standard work on the subject, suggests that 'The Lady of the Jewel Necklace' is quoted so profusely in the *Daśa/rūpa* and the *Sāhitya/darpaṇa* in part because it is true to type, in both plot and stock characters, the classical example of the small heroic comedy (*nāṭikā*). In any case, LÉVI himself cites 'The Lady of the Jewel Necklace' and Kali·dasa's 'Shakúntala' (*Abhijñāna/śākuntalā*) as his main examples.

Here is a summary of just the beginning of LÉVI's explication of Indian dramatic theory, using examples from 'The Lady of the Jewel Necklace' in all but a few cases. This summary will demonstrate not only how closely 'The Lady of the Jewel Necklace' (*Ratnāvalī*, here cited as R) either follows or inspires the categories of the Indian analysis, but how closely the plot is developed along traditional lines.

LÉVI begins, as the tradition begins, with the five elements, or moral situations, of the drama:

1. The enterprise: Yaugándharáyana wants to conceal Ratnávali's identity and introduce her as a lady-in-waiting in the harem. [R 1.27].
2. The effort: Ságarika: "As long as no one comes here, I'll gaze at a painting of the man I love, and do what I want." [R 2.13].
3. The possibility of success: The king finds Ságarika and says, "My friend, this comes like a bolt out of the blue." Jester: "Yes indeed, unless Queen Vásava·datta comes to play the part of an untimely hurricane." [R 3.137–138].
4. The certainty of success: The king to the jester: "My friend, I see no way of doing this but appeasing the queen." [R 3.122].
5. Success: The king gets, from the hand of the queen, Ratnávali, who has been passing as Ságarika, and achieves by that marriage universal sovereignty [R 4.248 (verse 21)] (SYLVAIN LÉVI 1963: 32–4).

The theory then goes into far more detail, explaining the articulation of the limbs of the plot, starting with the 12 limbs of the beginning of the articulation of the action:

1. The sowing of the seed of the plot: Yaugándharáyana first reveals his plan: "I, too, did the right thing when I placed her in the queen's hands, showing her great respect." [R 1.28].
2. The ripening of the seed of the plot: Yaugándharáyana: "Or else, how could this happen? First, because of my confidence in a seer's prediction, we asked the king of Símhala ('another continent') for the hand of his daughter in marriage. In the ocean ('from the middle of the ocean') she was shipwrecked and fell into the water, but found a board and climbed up onto it. And then a merchant from Kaushámbi who was returning from Símhala met her while she was still in that condition, recognized her from the sign of her jewel necklace, and brought her here! ('what we want')." [R 1.28].
3. Fixing the seed firmly in the ground: Yaugándharáyana:

   "This undertaking will bring prosperity to my master,
   and since it depends upon the helping hand that fate has given,
   success cannot elude us. All this is true. And yet,
   because I have acted of my own accord,
   I am rather afraid of my master." [R 1.29 (verse 7)].
4. Praise of the hero or heroine: The herald compares the king to the rising moon. [R 1.128 (verse 23)].
5. The conception of a plan: Yaugándharáyana: "And I have heard that Babhrávya too, the chamberlain, together with Vasu·bhuti, the minister of the king of Símhala, somehow or other crossed the ocean and

joined up with Rumánvat, who was going to depose the king of Kósala. And so my master's enterprise is almost accomplished." [R 1.28].

6. Winning happiness: "Why, this is the king, Údayana, to whom my father gave me! *(sighing deeply)* Though I thought my life was blighted because I was sent to someone else, now the sight of him has made it precious to me." [R 1.229].
7. The arrival of the seed: from Vásava·datta: "Then bring me the things I need for the ritual," to Ságarika: "I'll watch unobserved." [R 1.98–101].
8. The production of pain or pleasure. [No example from R.]
9. The surprise: Ságarika: "Why, the god of flower-weapons himself, in the flesh, is receiving this worship! In the women's quarters in my father's palace, we worshipped him just in the form of an image. So I, too, will stay here and worship with these flowers the god of flower-weapons." [R 1.123].
10. Penetrating a secret: Ságarika: "Why, this is the king, Údayana, to whom my father gave me!" [R 1.129].
11. Encouragement, excitement. [No example from R.]
12. The beginning of the actual action in question: Ságarika: "Honor to you, lord of the flower-weapons. My vision of you and yours of me now will not be in vain. *(bowing)*. I have seen what I had to see. So I will go away before anyone sees me." [R 1.123]. Lévi remarks: "This is the beginning of the action which will take place in the second act, in which the lovers will see one another without obstacles" (1963: 44–57).

And that is just the first articulation. LÉVI goes on and on, through the secondary articulation of the action, and the third, fourth, fifth, and final articulations, all of them citing examples from 'The Lady of the Jewel Necklace' and, sometimes, 'Shakúntala.'

To my mind, 'Shakúntala' is not nearly as interesting a play as either 'The Lady of the Jewel Necklace' or 'The Lady who Shows her Love,' but it became far more famous in Europe, from the nineteenth century on, in part because Goethe went mad for it (FIGUEIRA 1991) and in part because it suited European tastes in the age of Romanticism. (As I have argued above, I believe that for us, in the post-Pirandello age, Harsha is a much better fit.) 'The Lady of the Jewel Necklace' is quite well known in India. Yet, because the two Harsha plays were not appreciated outside of India, they were not translated so early, so often, or so well as 'Shakúntala,' and because they're not easily available, they're not appreciated. This is an all-too-familiar vicious circle that the present volume hopes to break open.

The Harsha plays were not translated at all until 1858, while Sir William Jones translated 'Shakúntala' in 1789 and several authors soon after translated it into several European languages (FIGUEIRA 1991). Even now English translations of Harsha are not easily available to non-specialists, while 'Shakúntala' is re-translated constantly, almost as often as the 'Bhágavad Gita' (*Bhagavad/gītā*). There is one important exception to the general dismissal of Harsha by the English-speaking world, and that is the case of MICHAEL MADHUSUDAN DUTT (1824–1873), who produced the very first English translation of 'The Lady of the Jewel Necklace,' in 1858. This is how CLINTON SEELY tells the story:

> The first of these English translations, along with the Bangla version from which he did the translation, served as the impetus for Datta to begin his own career as a playwright and poet in Bangla. The incident concerning how Datta came to pen his very first piece of literature in Bangla—the Bangla original of his play "Sermista"—is related by Bysack [Gour Dass Bysack, Dutt's best friend at Hindoo College] in his essay of reminiscences. He had taken Datta to a rehearsal of Ramnarayan Tarkaratna's Bangla rendition of *Ratnavali*, the drama originally composed in Sanskrit by Harshavardhana (606–647 CE). Tarkaratna, an accomplished Sanskrit scholar and also one of the earliest playwrights in Bangla, had translated the Sanskrit drama into Bangla. Tarkaratna's Bangla play was to be performed on the stage of the short-lived but highly influential Belgachia Theatre, a theater founded and supported by the brothers Pratap Chandra and Isvar Chandra Singh. As was the custom at the time, the local British elite would be invited to attend, and for their sake an English translation needed to be prepared. Bysack had persuaded the Singhs, who were known as the rajas of Paikpara, to engage Datta to do the translation, for Datta, Bysack well knew, was a master craftsman with the English language. After attending the first rehearsal and even before he had embarked upon the translation, Datta, according to Bysack, said to him, "What a pity the rajas should have

> spent such a lot of money on such a miserable play. I wish I had known of it before, as I could have given you a piece worthy of your theater." Bysack writes that he laughed at the very idea of his friend, who had never before composed anything in Bangla, now implying that he could produce a play in Bangla. A week later Datta handed Bysack a draft of the first act of what would be a five-act play, utterly Shakespearean in formal characteristics, about the triangular relationship involving the king Yayati, his wife Devayani, and Sermista, daughter of the *asuras*' monarch but also both servant to Devayani and mother, illicitly, of children by Yayati (SEELY 2004: 29–30).

And so this first translation of 'The Lady of the Jewel Necklace' was, in itself, even more dismissive than the previous silence had been. It was, moreover, not a translation of the Sanskrit at all (though some editions claimed that it was), but a translation of someone else's translation of the Sanskrit into Bengali. In the very next year, 1859, DUTT/DATTA published his English translation of his own Bengali play, *Sermista*, based upon a story from the Sanskrit 'Maha·bhárata' (*Mahā/bhārata*), the tale of Deva·yani and Sarmíshtha, a very different sort of a triangle from the ones that Harsha had written about. Even then, the strong parallels with the English theatre (which we, too, have noted) inspired DUTT to recreate the story as it would have been told in English, rather than to lead the English audience back into the world of Sanskrit drama.

Textual Details

Basically, I have used Moreshvan Ramchandra Kale's edition throughout, and made use of Kale's English and Sanskrit commentaries. There is no critical edition of this text, but Kale uses a number of different MSS and published texts, and explains each of his editorial choices. The arguments he makes for editing as he has done are in general convincing and, in any case, always consistent. The main place I differed was in including the fifth verse of the benediction of 'The Lady of the Jewel Necklace,' which seems to me to belong here and in any case is a lovely verse. I have also used some readings that he has rejected (and have always indicated when this is the case) and queried one line in 'The Lady of the Jewel Necklace,' "You'll have cause to remember your words ..." at 3.77. I have, however, also consulted several other editions (see Bibliography), primarily in order to use their commentaries, particularly the commentaries in the editions by Asoknath Bhattacharya and Devendra Misra.

Acknowledgements

I owe much to my students, Ajay Rao and Blake Wentworth, who read much of the 'The Lady of the Jewel Necklace' with me, rounded up numerous versions of both text and commentary, and made very helpful suggestions, and to Anthony Cerulli, who painstakingly transliterated all the Sanskrit for me.

This book is dedicated to David Shulman, once pupil, now master, who has shared and nourished my obsession with dreams, masks, multiple identities, and Sanskrit literature, even for the tale of Údayana and Vásava·datta, for so many years now.

Notes

1 For the complete, extended version of this section, please consult the CSL website.

2 This was a performance by the Court Theatre in Chicago, in the summer of 1979.

Bibliography

WORKS REFERRED TO IN THE INTRODUCTION

Arthaśāstra. Ed. and trans. R P KANGLE. Delhi. 1986.

Kāmasūtra of Vātsyāyana. See DONIGER and KAKAR below.

Kathāsaritsāgara. Bombay. 1930.

Svapnavāsavadattā of Bhāsa. Ed. C R DEVADHAR. Poona. 1946.

DEVAHUTI, D. See DEVAHUTI below.

DONIGER, WENDY. *The Bedtrick: Tales of Sex and Masquerade*. Chicago. 2000.

DONIGER, WENDY. "The Dreams and Dramas of a Jealous Hindu Queen: Vāsavadattā" In *Dream Cultures: Explorations in the Comparative History of Dreaming*. Eds. GUY STROUMSA and DAVID SHULMAN. New York. 1999.

DONIGER, WENDY. *The Woman Who Pretended to Be Who She Was* New York. 2005.

DONIGER, WENDY and SUDHIR KAKAR. *The Kamasutra of Vatsyayana*. Oxford. 2002.

DONIGER O'FLAHERTY, WENDY. *Dreams, Illusion, and Other Realities*. Chicago. 1984.

DUTT, MICHAEL MADHUSUDAN. *Sermista, a drama in four acts*. Trans. from the Bengali by the author. Calcutta. 1859.

FIGUEIRA, DOROTHY MATHILDA. *Translating the Orient: The Reception of Śakuntalā in Nineteenth Century Europe*. Albany, New York. 1991.

LÉVI, SYLVAIN. *La théatre indien*. Vol. 1, 2nd printing. Paris. 1963.

ROBB, PETER. *A History of India*. London. 2002.

KALE, M R. See KALE (1921) below.

SEELY, CLINTON. *The Slaying of Meghanada: A Ramayana from Colonial Bengal by Michael Madhusudan Datta*. Translated with an Introduction by CLINTON B. SEELY. New York. 2004.

SMITH, VINCENT ARTHUR. *Early History of India from 600 B.C. to the Muhammadan Conquest*. 3rd edn. Oxford. 1914.

Thurber, James. "The Macbeth Murder Mystery." In *My World and Welcome to It*. New York. 1942.

ON HARSHA

Bāṇa. *Harṣacaritam.* Varanasi: Chaukhambha Samskrta Samsthana, 1992.

Devahuti, D. *Harsha: A Political Study*. Oxford, Clarendon, 1970.

Goyal, Shankar. *History and Historiography of the Age of Harsha*. Jodhpur: English Book, 1992.

EDITIONS AND TRANSLATIONS OF 'THE LADY OF THE JEWEL NECKLACE'

Bhattacharya, Asoknath, ed. Maheshwar Das. *Ratnāvalī of Emperor Śrī Harṣa.* [Sanskrit, English, and Bengali; notes in Sanskrit; introd. in English.] Calcutta: Modern Book Agency, 1967.

Dutt, Michael Madhusudan. *Ratnāvalī: a drama in four acts*. [English, translated from the Bengali]. Calcutta: G.A. Savielle, 1858.

Kale, Moreshvan Ramchandra. *The Ratnāvalī of Śrī Harṣa-Deva. Edited with an exhaustive introd., a new Sanskrit commentary, various readings, a literal English translation, copious notes and useful appendices, by M.R. Kale.* Delhi: Motilal Banarsidass, 1921.

Misra, Devendra. *Ratnāvalī.* [Hindi and Sanskrit.] Allahabad: Ramanarayanalala Beniprasada, 1964.

Thakur, Ramji. *Ratnāvalī.* [English.] Delhi: Global Vision Publishing House, 2004.

EDITIONS AND TRANSLATIONS OF 'THE LADY WHO SHOWS HER LOVE'

Kale, Moreshvan Ramchandra. *The Priyadarśikā of Śrī Harṣa-Deva. Edited with an exhaustive introduction, a short Sanskrit comm., various readings, a literal English translation, copious notes and useful appendices*. Bombay, Gopal Narayan & Co., 1928.

Kangle, R P. *Priyadarśikā.* [English and Sanskrit.] Ahmedabad: C.M. Parikh, 1928.

NARIMAN, GUSHTASPSHAH KAIKHUSHRO, A.V. WILLIAMS JACKSON, and CHARLES J. OGDEN. *Priyadarśikā: a Sanskrit drama, by Harṣa. Translated into English by G.K. Nariman, A.V. Williams Jackson, and Charles J. Ogden; with an introduction and notes by the two latter, together with the text in transliteration.* New York, Columbia University Press, 1923. New Delhi: Oriental Reprint, Munshiram Manoharlal Publishers, 1984.

India at the Time of Harsha

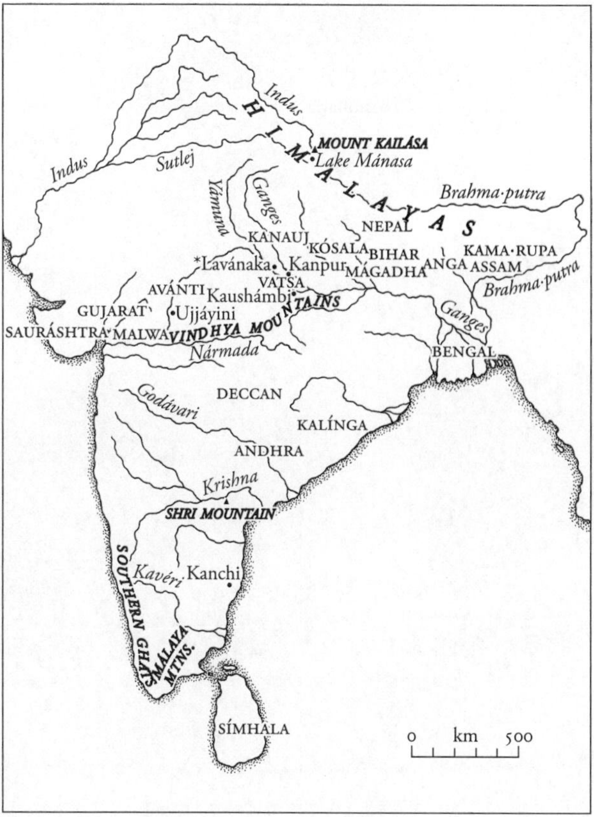

THE LADY OF THE JEWEL NECKLACE

DRAMATIS PERSONÆ

in order of appearance

Characters marked with ⌜corner brackets⌟ speak Prakrit.

⌜ACTRESS⌟	wife of the STAGE DIRECTOR
YAUGÁNDHARÁYANA	the KING's prime minister
KING ÚDAYANA ("Rising")	king of Vatsa (whose capital was Kaushámbi)
⌜VASÁNTAKA⌟ ("Little Spring")	the court jester and confidante, companion, and go-between of the KING; a greedy and lazy Brahmin
⌜CHUTA·LÁTIKA⌟ ("Mango Vine")	palace maid
⌜MÁDANIKA⌟ ("Intoxicating")	palace maid
⌜VÁSAVA·DATTA⌟ ("Given by Indra")	the queen, ÚDAYANA's wife,daughter of PRADYÓTA, the king of Avánti
⌜KÁNCHANA·MALA⌟ ("Golden Garland")	lady-in-waiting to the QUEEN
⌜RATNÁVALI⌟ ("Lady of the Jewel Necklace")	also known as SÁGARIKA, ("Lady of the Ocean"), daughter of VÍKRAMA·BAHU, the king of Símhala (Sri Lanka)
⌜SUSÁNGATA⌟	lady-in-waiting, friend of SÁGARIKA
⌜NÍPUNIKA⌟	lady-in-waiting
MEDHÁVINI ("Ace Reporter")	a talking mynah bird (*sārikā*, *Turdus Salica*)
⌜VASUN·DHARA⌟	gate-keeper
VÍJAYA·VARMAN	nephew of RUMÁNVAT, the commander-in-chief of the king
⌜MAGICIAN⌟	

VASU·BHUTI	minister of state of VÍKRAMA·BAHU, the king of Símhala
BABHRÁVYA	KING ÚDAYANA's chamberlain

People Mentioned

KAUSHÁMBIKA	a woman from Kaushámbi
PRADYÓTA	the king of Avánti (whose capital was Ujjain) and Mágadha
RUMÁNVAT	commander-in-chief of KING ÚDAYANA
VÍKRAMA·BAHU	king of Símhala
THE KING OF KÓSALA	

The Scene

Kaushámbi, the capital city of King Údayana.

Time*

Act One, The Festival of Passion: Late afternoon on a full-moon day in the month of Chaitra (late March to early April).
Act Two, The Banana Bower: The next day, late afternoon.
Act Three, The Rendezvous: A day later, dusk.
Act Four, The Magician: A day later.

* The Sanskrit text does not specify the times, but it is not difficult to tease them out of the data given in the play.

BENEDICTION

PĀD'|ÂGRA|STHITAYĀ muhuḥ stana|bhara-
ṇ'|ānītayā namratāṃ
Śambhoḥ sa|spṛha|locana|traya|pathaṃ
yāntyā tad|ārādhane
hrīmatyā śiras'|īhitaḥ sa|pulaka|
sved'|ôdgam'|ôtkampayā
viśliṣyan kusum'|âñjalir Giri|jayā
kṣipto 'ntare pātu vaḥ! [1]

1.5 api ca,

autsukyena kṛta|tvarā, saha|bhuvā
vyāvartamānā hriyā,
tais tair bandhu|vadhū|janasya vacanair
nīt" ābhimukhyaṃ punaḥ,
dṛṣṭv" âgre varam ātta|sādhvasa|rasā
Gaurī nave saṃgame
saṃrohat|pulakā Hareṇa hasatā
śliṣṭā, śivāy' âstu vaḥ! [2]

[Scene: Kaushámbi, the capital city of king ÚDAYANA*]*

[Time: Late afternoon on a full-moon day in the month of Chaitra (late March to early April)]

[Enter STAGE DIRECTOR.*]**

THE DAUGHTER OF the Mountain
stood on her toes,
but the weight of her breasts kept forcing her
to bow low again and again.
As she brought her offering to Shambhu,
she came within the range
of his three eyes full of desire,
which so embarrassed her that her skin thrilled
and she trembled and broke out in a sweat,
and so the handful of flowers
meant for the top of his head
slipped and fell between them,
and may they protect you.*

And 1.5

At their first meeting, Gauri's eager longing
made her hurry,
but then her innate shyness held her back.
Her kinswomen led her back to face him,
urging her on with all sorts of words,
but when she saw her bridegroom in front of her
such a turmoil of emotion overwhelmed her
that the hair on her body began to stir.
Shiva laughed and embraced her,
and may this be good for you.*

api ca,

«saṃprāptaṃ *makara|dhvajena mathanaṃ*
tvatto mad|arthe purā,
tad yuktaṃ *bahu|mārga|gāṃ* mama puro,
nirlajja, voḍhuṃ tava!
tām ev' ânunayasva *bhāva|kuṭilāṃ*,
he, *kṛṣṇa|kaṇṭha|grahaṃ*
muñc' êty» āha ruṣā yam Adri|tanayā
Lakṣmīś ca, pāyāt sa vaḥ! [2a]

api ca,

1.10 «krodh'|êddhair dṛṣṭi|pātais tribhir upaśamitā
vahnayo 'mī trayo 'pi,
trās'|ārtā ṛtv|ijo 'dhaś capala|gaṇa|hṛt'|ôṣ-
ṇīṣa|paṭṭāḥ patanti,
Dakṣaḥ stauty, asya patnī vilapati karuṇaṃ,
vidrutaṃ c' âpi devaiḥ»
śaṃsann ity aṭṭa|hāso Makha|mathana|vidhau
pātu devyai Śivo vaḥ! [3]

And

Lakshmi and the Daughter of the Mountain
addressed him in anger:
"Long ago, for my sake,
you *churned : destroyed the one who has*
a sea-serpent on : as his banner,
and so it is only fair that you should shamelessly
hold, right in front of me,
a woman who has gone down many an alley :
the river who flows on many paths.
She is the one, *crooked by her very nature :*
with her devious mind,
whom you should sweet-talk,
Krishna, and let go of my neck :
you with your dark neck, and let go of me."
May he protect you!*

And

"Three glances from eyes kindled with anger I.10
put out all three fires;
the mischievous mob stole
the cloths of the turbans
of the terrified sacrificial priests, who fell down;
Daksha sang hymns of praise,
his wife wept piteously,
and the gods ran away."
As Shiva told the goddess this story
of how he ravaged the sacrifice,
he roared with laughter,
and may that protect you.*

api ca,

jitam uḍu|patinā; namaḥ surebhyo;
dvi|ja|vṛṣabhā nir|upadravā bhavantu;
bhavantu ca pṛthivī samṛddha|sasyā;
pratapatu candra|vapur|nar'|êndra|candraḥ! [4]

And

Triumph to the lord of the stars,
  reverence to the gods.
May no calamity befall the bulls of the twice-born.
May the earth yield abundant harvests.
And may the moon of kings shine forth
  like the moon.*

PROLOGUE

nāndy|ante

SŪTRADHĀRAḤ: alam ati|vistareṇa! ady' âhaṃ Vasant'|ôtsave sa|bahu|mānam āhūya nānā|dig|deś'|āgatena rājñaḥ Śrī|Harṣa|devasya pāda|padm'|ôpajīvinā rāja|samūhen' ôkto yathā—«asmat|svāminā Śrī|Harṣa|deven' â|pūrva|vastu|racan"|âlaṃ|kṛtā Ratnāvalī nāma nāṭikā kṛtā. sā c' âsmābhiḥ śrotra|paraṃparayā śrutā, na tu prayogato dṛṣṭā. tat tasy' âiva rājñaḥ sakala|jana|hṛday'|āhlādino bahu|mānād asmāsu c' ânugraha|buddhyā yathāvat prayogeṇa tvayā nāṭayitavy" êti.» tad, yāvad idānīṃ nepathya|racanāṃ kṛtvā, yath"|âbhilaṣitaṃ saṃpādayāmi. *(parikramy' âvalokya ca)* aye! āvarjitāni sakala|sāmājikānāṃ manāṃs' îti me niścayaḥ. kutaḥ:

1.15 Śrī|Harṣo nipuṇaḥ kaviḥ, pariṣad apy
eṣā guṇa|grāhiṇī,
loke hāri ca Vatsa|rāja|caritaṃ,
nāṭye ca dakṣā vayam.
vastv ek'|âikam ap' îha vāñchita|phala|
prāpteḥ padaṃ, kiṃ punar,
mad|bhāgy'|ôpacayād ayaṃ samuditaḥ
sarvo guṇānāṃ gaṇaḥ. [5]

At the end of the benediction

STAGE DIRECTOR: Enough of that. Too many words! Today, in the Spring festival,* the crowd of kings who have come from many directions and live off the lotus feet of his majesty Shri Harsha summoned me respectfully and said, "Our ruler, his majesty Shri Harsha, has composed a play* called 'The Lady of the Jewel Necklace,' graced by an unprecedented arrangement of the plot. We've heard about it from word of mouth, from one to another, but we've never seen it produced. You should therefore produce it and have it properly performed, both to honor this king who gladdens the hearts of all the people and with the thought of doing a favor for us." So, now I'll prepare the stage and do what they wanted. *(walking around and looking around)* Ah, I'm quite sure that the minds of all the assembled people are well-inclined. For:

The poet, Shri Harsha, is talented; 1.15
  this audience appreciates quality;
the story of the king of Vatsa is a crowd-pleaser;
  and we're very good at acting.
Since each one of these factors by itself
  is enough to achieve the desired result,
how much more will this be true
  of the entire combined cluster of qualities
that my good fortune has piled up
  all together here!*

tad yāvad gṛhaṃ gatvā gṛhiṇīm āhūya saṃgītakam anutiṣṭhāmi. *(parikramya, nepathy'|âbhimukham avalokya ca)* idam asmadīyaṃ gṛham. yāvat praviśāmi. *(praviśya)* ārye! itas tāvat.

NAṬĪ: *(praviśya)* ⌜ajja|utta, ia mhi. āṇavedu ajjo ko ṇioo aṇuciṭṭhīadi tti.⌟

SŪTRADHĀRAḤ: ārye, Ratnāvalī|darśan'|ôtsuko 'yaṃ rāja|lokaḥ. tad gṛhyatāṃ nepathyam!

NAṬĪ: *(niḥśvasya, s'|ôdvegam)* ⌜ajja|utta, ṇic|cinto dāṇiṃ si tumaṃ, tā kīsa ṇa ṇaccasi? maha uṇa manda|bhāāe ekkā jjeva duhidā. sā vi tue kahiṃ pi des'|antare diṇṇā. kahaṃ evvaṃ dūra|desa|ṭṭhideṇa bhattuṇā saha se pāṇi|ggahaṇaṃ bhavissadi tti imāe cintāe appā vi me ṇa paḍihādi. kiṃ puṇa ṇaccidavvam!⌟

1.20 SŪTRADHĀRAḤ: ārye dūra|sthiten' êty alam udvegena! paśya:

dvīpād anyasmād api,
  madhyād api jala|nidher, diśo 'py antāt
ānīya jhaṭ|iti ghaṭayati
  vidhir abhimatam abhimukhī|bhūtaḥ. [6]

So I'll go home and call my wife and practice the music. *(walking around and looking at the stage)* This is our house, so I'll just go in. *(entering)* Wife, come here a moment.

ACTRESS: *(entering)* Husband, here I am. Tell me what task is to be done.

STAGE DIRECTOR: Wife, this society of kings is eager to see a performance of 'The Lady of the Jewel Necklace.' So get into costume.

ACTRESS: *(sighing, upset)* Husband, you have nothing to worry about now, so why shouldn't you perform in a play? But I, on the other hand, am very unlucky: I have only one daughter. And you gave even her away to be married in some foreign land or other. How, just how, will she be able to get married to a husband who lives in a land far, far away? When I worry about that, I can't even resemble my own self. How, then, could I act someone else?

STAGE DIRECTOR: Wife, I've had enough of this fuss about 1.20
someone "who lives in a land far, far away" and so forth. Look:

> Even from another continent,
> even from the middle of the ocean,
> even from the end of the quarters of the sky,
> when fate turns toward us
>   it brings us what we want,
> and makes it happen, suddenly, just like that.*

NEPATHYE: sādhu, Bharata|putra, sādhu! evam etat. kaḥ saṃdehaḥ? *(«dvīpād anyasmād» iti paṭhati.)*

SŪTRADHĀRAḤ: *(ākarṇya, nepathy'|âbhimukham avalokya, sa|harṣam)* ārye, eṣa mama kanīyān bhrātā gṛhīta|Yaugandharāyaṇa|bhūmikaḥ prāpta eva. tad ehi. āvām api nepathya|grahaṇāya sajjī|bhavāvaḥ.

iti niṣkrāntau.

1.25 *prastāvanā.*

VOICE OFF: Bravo! Bravo, you son of an actor!* That's right. No doubt about it. *(He repeats "Even from another continent. . . ")*

STAGE DIRECTOR: *(listening, looking off-stage, joyously)* Wife, here's my younger brother, just arrived, to play the part of Yaugándharáyana. Now, come. We too must prepare to get into costume.

They exit.

End of Prelude. 1.25

INTERLUDE

tataḥ praviśati YAUGANDHARĀYAṆAḤ.

YAUGANDHARĀYAṆAḤ: evam etat. kaḥ saṃdehaḥ? *(«dvīpād anyasmād» iti punaḥ paṭhitvā)*

anyathā kva siddh'|ādeśa|pratyaya|prārthitāyāḥ Siṃhal'|ēśvara|duhituḥ samudre yāna|bhaṅga|magn'|ôtthitāyāḥ phalak'|āsādanaṃ, kva ca Kauśāmbīyena vaṇijā Siṃhalebhyaḥ pratyāgacchatā tad|avasthāyāḥ saṃbhāvanaṃ ratna|mālā|cihnāyāḥ pratyabhijñānād ih' ānayanaṃ ca? *(sa|harṣam)* sarvathā spṛśanti naḥ svāminam abhyudayāḥ. *(vicintya)* may" âpi c' âināṃ devī|haste sa|gauravaṃ nikṣipatā yuktam ev' ânuṣṭhitam. śrutaṃ ca mayā: Bābhravyo 'pi kañcukī Siṃhal'|ēśvar'|âmatyena Vasubhūtinā saha kathaṃ katham api samudrād uttīrya, Kośal'|ôcchittaye gatavatā Rumaṇvatā milita iti. tad evaṃ niṣpanna|prāyam api prabhu|prayojanaṃ, na me dhṛtim āvahat' îti kaṣṭo 'yaṃ khalu bhṛtya|bhāvaḥ. kutaḥ?

prārambhe 'smin svāmino vṛddhi|hetau
  daiven' êtthaṃ datta|hast'|âvalambe
siddher bhrāntir n' âsti, satyaṃ. tath" âpi
  sv'|êcch"|ācārī bhīta ev' âsmi bhartuḥ. [7]

Enter YAUGÁNDHARÁYANA.

YAUGÁNDHARÁYANA: That's right. No doubt about it. *(He repeats "Even from another continent. . . ")*

Or else, how could this happen? First, because of my confidence in a seer's prediction, we asked the king of Símhala ("another continent") for the hand of his daughter in marriage. In the ocean ("from the middle of the ocean") she was shipwrecked and fell into the water, but found a board and climbed up onto it. And then a merchant from Kaushámbi who was returning from Símhala met her while she was still in that condition, recognized her from the sign of her jewel necklace, and brought her here! ("what we want") *(joyously)* Our master succeeds in everything he touches. *(reflecting)* I, too, did the right thing when I placed her in the queen's hands, showing her great respect. And I've heard that Babhrávya too, the chamberlain, together with Vasu·bhuti, the minister of the king of Símhala, somehow or other crossed the ocean and joined up with Rumánvat, who was going to depose the king of Kósala. And so my master's enterprise is almost accomplished. Yet this doesn't make me secure. A servant's existence is no good. For:

> This undertaking will bring prosperity
> to my master,
> and since it depends upon the helping hand
> that fate has given,
> success can't elude us. All this is true. And yet,
> because I've acted of my own accord,
> I'm rather afraid of my master.

1.30 *nepathye kalakalaḥ.*

YAUGANDHARĀYAṆAḤ: *(ākarṇya)* aye! yath" âyam abhihanyamāna|mṛdu|mṛdaṅg'|ânugata|gīta|madhuraḥ puraḥ paurāṇāṃ samuccarati carcarī|dhvanis, tathā tarkayāmi Madana|maha|mahīyāṃsaṃ pura|jana|pramodam avalokayituṃ prāsād'|âbhimukhaṃ prasthito deva iti. *(ūrdhvam avalokya)* aye! katham, adhirūḍha eva devaḥ prāsādam. ya eṣa:

viśrānta|*vigraha*|katho, *Ratimāñ* janasya
  citte vasan, priya|*Vasantaka* eva sākṣāt
paryutsuko nija|mah"|ôtsava|darśanāya
  Vats'|ēśvaraḥ Kusuma|cāpa iv' âbhyupaiti. [8]

tad yāvad gṛhaṃ gatvā kārya|śeṣaṃ cintayāmi. *(iti niṣkrāntaḥ.)*

viṣkambhakaḥ.

A clamor off stage. 1.30

YAUGÁNDHARÁYANA: *(listening)* Ah! From the sound of the rhythmic striking of the palms of the hands of the city people beating time, and, in front of them, the sweet sound of the drum beaten in response to the singing, I can guess that the king has set out to climb to the roof-balcony to watch the joy of the people of the city burst its bounds in the Festival of Passion.* *(looking up)* Why, the king has climbed up to the palace roof:

> The Lord of Vatsa draws near,
> like the god of the flower bow in the flesh.
> He has exhausted all talk of *war : the body*,
> lives with *love : Rati* in the mind of the people,
> is fond of *Vasántaka : Spring*
> and is eager to see his own festival.*

Well, I'll go home and think about the rest of what has to be done. *(Exit.)*

End of the interlude.

ACT I
THE FESTIVAL OF PASSION

1.35 *tataḥ praviśaty āsana|stho gṛhīta|Vasant'|ôtsava|veṣo* RĀJĀ VIDŪṢAKAŚ *ca.*

RĀJĀ: *(sa|harṣam avalokya)* sakhe, Vasantaka!

VIDŪṢAKAḤ: ⌜āṇavedu bhavaṃ!⌟

RĀJĀ:

> rājyaṃ nirjita|śatru; yogya|sacive
> nyastaḥ samasto bharaḥ;
> samyak|pālana|lālitāḥ praśamit'|â|
> śeṣ'|ôpasargāḥ prajāḥ;
> Pradyotasya sutā, Vasanta|samayas,
> tvaṃ c' êti nāmrā dhṛtiṃ
> Kāmaḥ kāmam upaitv, ayaṃ punar mama
> manye mahān utsavaḥ. [9]

1.40 VIDŪṢAKAḤ: *(sa|harṣam)* ⌜bho vaassa! evvaṃ ṇṇedam. ahaṃ puṇa jāṇāmi: ṇa bhavado, ṇa Kāma|deassa, mama jjeva ekassa bamhaṇassa aaṃ Maaṇa|mah"|ûsavo, jassa pia|vaasseṇa evaṃ mantīadi.⌟ *(vilokya)* ⌜tā kiṃ imiṇā? pekkha dāva imassa mahu|matta|kāmiṇī|jana|saaṃ|gāha|gahida|siṅgaka|jala|ppahāra|ṇaccanta|ṇāara|jaṇa|jaṇida|kodūhalassa samantado ghummanta|maddal'|uddāma|caccarī|sadda|muhara|racchā|muha|sohiṇo païṇṇa|paḍa|vāsa|puñja|piñjarijjanta|dasa|disā|muhassa sa|ssirīadaṃ maaṇa|mah"|ûsavassa.⌟

Enter the KING, *on a seat,* wearing the clothes for the Spring festival, and the* JESTER *too.* 1.35

KING: *(looking with joy)* Vasántaka, my friend.

JESTER: Sir, command me.*

KING:

> The kingdom has conquered all its enemies;
> the entire burden of the country
>   has been placed on a worthy minister;
> my subjects are well protected
>   to the point of indulgence,
> and their troubles, without exception,
>   have been remedied.
> I have Pradyóta's daughter, the season of Spring,
>   and you.
> Therefore let Kama have just the name
>   as much as he desires,
> but I rather think that this great festival is mine.*

JESTER: *(joyously)* You're right, my friend. But I know that 1.40
this Festival of Passion is neither yours nor the god Kama's, but belongs to me, the one Brahmin whom my dear friend has spoken of in this way. *(looking around)* But what's this? Look at the glory of the Festival of Passion, which has excited the desire of the men of the city; they're dancing, while passionate women, intoxicated by wine, spray water on them from the syringes made of horn that they've taken up in their hands. The gates of the chariot roads resound everywhere with the sound of the clapping of hands magnified by the sounding drums.

RĀJĀ: *(samantād avalokya)* aho, parāṃ koṭim adhirohati pramodaḥ paurāṇām. tathā hi:

kīrṇaiḥ piṣṭātak'|âughaiḥ kṛta|divasa|mukhaiḥ
 kuṅkuma|kṣoda|gaurair
hem'|âlaṃ|kāra|bhābhir bhara|namita|śikhaiḥ
 śekharaiḥ kaiṅkirātaiḥ
eṣā veṣ'|âbhilakṣya|sva|vibhava|vijit'|â|
 śeṣa|Vitt'|ēśa|kośā
Kauśāmbī śātakumbha|drava|khacita|jan" ê-
 v' âika|pītā vibhāti. [10]

api ca,

dhārā|yantra|vimukta|saṃtata|payaḥ|
 pūra|plate sarvataḥ
sadyaḥ sāndra|vimarda|kardama|kṛta|
 krīḍe kṣaṇaṃ prāṅgaṇe
uddāma|pramadā|kapola|nipatat|
 sindūra|rāg'|âruṇaiḥ
saindūrī|kriyate janena caraṇa|
 nyāsaiḥ puraḥ kuṭṭimam. [11]

And the heaps of ochre powder strewn about* make all the quarters of the sky yellow.

KING: *(looking around on all sides)* The joy of the city-dwellers is reaching its climax. For:

> Floods of ochre powder,
> tawny with fine particles of saffron,
> strewn all about, make it dawn.
> Tiaras made of red *ashóka* flowers
> shining with golden ornaments
> are so heavy that the people who wear them
> must bow their heads.
> Their garments tell of a splendor that surpasses
> even the entire treasure of the god of wealth.
> All of this makes Kaushámbi seem solid yellow,
> as if its people were plated with liquid gold.*

And

> In the courtyard where people play,
> the constant, dense poundings of their feet
> immediately trample down
> the steady streams of water
> shot from the horn syringes, and it turns to mud.
> And when vermilion powder falls into it
> from the cheeks of passionate,
> unrestrained women,
> peoples' footprints make red as rouge
> the paved and inlaid floor before us.

1.45 VIDŪṢAKAḤ: *(vilokya)* ⌜imaṃ pi dāva su|viaddha|jaṇa|bharida|siṅgaka|jala|ppahāra|mukka|sik|kāra|maṇo|haraṃ vāra|vilāsiṇī|jaṇa|vilasidaṃ āloedu pia|vaasso!⌟

RĀJĀ: *(vilokya)* vayasya! samyag dṛṣṭaṃ tvayā. kutaḥ:

asmin prakīrṇa|paṭa|vāsa|kṛt'|ândha|kāre
  dṛṣṭo manāṅ maṇi|vibhūṣaṇa|raśmi|jālaiḥ
pātālam udyata|phaṇ'|ākṛti|śṛṅgako 'yaṃ
  mām adya saṃsmarayat' îha *bhujaṅ|ga*|lokaḥ. [12]

VIDŪṢAKAḤ: *(vilokya)* ⌜bho, esā kkhu Maaṇiā maaṇa|vasa|visaṃṣṭhulaṃ Vasant'|âbhiṇaaṃ ṇaccantī Cūaladiāe saha ido jjeva āacchadi. tā avaloedu edaṃ pia|vaasso!⌟

tataḥ praviśato madana|līlāṃ nāṭayantyau Dvi|padī|khaṇḍaṃ gāyantyau CEṬYAU.

1.50 CEṬYAU:

⌜Kusum'|āuha|pia|dūao maülīkida|bahu|cūao
sidhilia|māṇa|ggahaṇao vāadi dāhiṇa|pavaṇao.⌟ [13]

JESTER: *(looking around)* My dear friend should also look at the grace of these courtesans, who make a charming hissing sound as they are struck by the water that sophisticated men shoot from horn syringes. 1.45

KING: *(looking around)* Yes, my friend. For:

This world of *lounge-lizards : serpents*
reminds me of the watery netherworld
of the serpent people.
For, in this darkness
that the densely strewn powder makes,
their horn syringes,
shaped like the raised hoods of cobras,
can just barely be made out by the net of rays
cast by the jewels of the ornaments on them*

JESTER: *(looking around)* Here comes Mádanika, with Chuta·látika, staggering under the influence of passion and dancing the dance of Spring. Look at her, my dear friend!

Enter two PALACE MAIDS, *miming erotic play and singing the Two-feet Suite.**

MÁDANIKA AND CHUTA·LÁTIKA: 1.50

The wind from the south blows,
the beloved messenger
of the god with flower-weapons,
making many mango trees burst into bud
and loosening the grip of the pride of
offended women.*

⌜viasia|baül'|âsoao kaṅkhia|pia|jaṇa|melao
paḍibālaṇ'|â|samatthao tammaï juvaī|satthao.⌟ [14]

⌜iha paḍhamaṃ Mahu|māso
 jaṇassa hiaāiṃ kuṇaï miulāiṃ,
pacchā viddhaï Kāmo
 laddha|ppasarehiṃ kusuma|bāṇehiṃ.⌟ [15]

RĀJĀ: *(nirvarṇya, sa|vismayam)* aho, nirbharaḥ krīḍā|rasaḥ parijanasya! tathā hi:

1.55 srastaḥ srag|dāma|śobhāṃ tyajati viracitām
  ākulaḥ keśa|pāśaḥ,
 kṣībāyā nūpurau ca dvi|guṇataram imau
  krandataḥ pāda|lagnau,
vyastaḥ kamp'|ânubandhād an|avaratam uro
  hanti hāro 'yam asyāḥ
 krīḍantyāḥ pīḍay" êva stana|bhara|vinaman|
  madhya|bhaṅg'|ân|apekṣam. [16]

VIDŪṢAKAḤ: ⌜bho vaassa! ahaṃ pi etāṇaṃ majjhe gadua ṇaccanto gāantao Maaṇa|mah"|ûsavaṃ māṇaïssam.⌟

RĀJĀ: *(sa|smitam)* vayasya, evaṃ kriyatām!

VIDŪṢAKAḤ: *(utthāya,* CEṬYOR *madhye nṛtyan)* ⌜bhodi Maaṇie, bhodi Cūaladie! maṃ pi edaṃ Caccarīṃ sikkhāvehi!⌟

Throngs of young women have made the *bákula*
and *ashóka* trees blossom.
Now they long to be with their lovers
and are pining away, unable to wait.*

First this month of Spring softens peoples' hearts,
and then Kama pierces them with flower arrows
that take advantage of the openings.

KING: *(observing it closely, with astonishment)* My! What an excessive taste for playing servants have. For:

As she plays, a little drunk, 1.55
the mass of her hair, all messed up
and falling down,
gives up, as if with pain, its splendid,
carefully made garland of flowers;
and the two anklets clinging to her feet cry out
doubly, as if in pain;
this pearl necklace of hers, tossed about
by her incessant trembling,
beats ceaselessly against her breast, as if in pain;
and she does not notice that she is bending
at the waist
under the burden of her breasts, as if in pain.*

JESTER: My friend, I too will go between these two and honor the Festival of Passion by dancing and singing.

KING: *(smiling)* You do that, my friend.

JESTER: *(getting up and dancing between the two* PALACE MAIDS*)* Miss Mádanika, Miss Chuta·látika, teach, me, too, the Hand-clapping Song.

UBHE: *(vihasya)* ⌜had'|āsa! ṇa kkhu esā Caccarī.⌟

1.60 VIDŪṢAKAḤ: ⌜tā kiṃ kkhu edaṃ?⌟

MADANIKĀ: ⌜Du|aī|khaṇḍaṃ kkhu edaṃ.⌟

VIDŪṢAKAḤ: *(sa|harṣam)* ⌜kiṃ ediṇā khaṇḍeṇa modaā karīandi?⌟

CEṬYAU: *(vihasya)* ⌜ṇa hi, ṇa hi! paḍhīadi kkhu edaṃ.⌟

VIDŪṢAKAḤ: *(sa|viṣādam)* ⌜jaï paḍhīadi, tā alaṃ mama ediṇā! vaassassa saāsaṃ jevva gamissam.⌟ *(gantum icchati.)*

1.65 UBHE: *(haste gṛhītvā)* ⌜ehi, kīlamha. Vasantaa, kahiṃ gacchasi?⌟ *(iti bahu|vidhaṃ* VASANTAKAM *ākarṣataḥ.)*

VIDŪṢAKAḤ: *(ākṛṣya hastaṃ, prapalāyya,* RĀJĀNAM *upasṛtya)* ⌜vaassa, ṇaccida mhi. ṇa hi, ṇa hi. kīlia palāido mhi.⌟

RĀJĀ: sādhu kṛtam.

CŪTALATIKĀ: ⌜hañje Maaṇie! ciraṃ kkhu amhehiṃ kīlidam. tā ehi. ṇivedamha dāva bhaṭṭiṇīe saṃdesaṃ mahā|rāassa.⌟

MADANIKĀ: ⌜sahi, evaṃ karimha.⌟

1.70 UBHE: *(parikramy' ôpasṛtya ca)* ⌜jaadu, jaadu bhaṭṭā! bhaṭṭā, devī āṇavedi—⌟ *(ity ardh'|ôkte lajjāṃ nāṭayantyau)* ⌜ṇa hi, ṇa hi! viṇṇavedi.⌟

MÁDANIKA AND CHUTA·LÁTIKA: *(laughing)* You damn fool! This is not a Hand-clapping Song.

JESTER: Then what is it? 1.60

MÁDANIKA: This is a piece from the Two-feet Suite.

JESTER: *(joyously)* Sweets? Can I have a piece?*

MÁDANIKA AND CHUTA·LÁTIKA: *(laughing)* No, no! Of course this is the kind of suite that is sung.

JESTER: *(sadly)* If it's just sung, then I've had my fill of it. I'll go to my friend. *(He starts to go.)*

MÁDANIKA AND CHUTA·LÁTIKA: *(grabbing his hands)* Come, 1.65
let's play. Where are you going, Vasántaka? *(They pull him in various ways.)*

JESTER: *(pulling away his hand, running away to the* KING*)* My friend, they made me dance! But enough is enough. I ran away after playing.

KING: Good for you.

CHUTA·LÁTIKA: Mádanika, we've played for a long time. So, come. Let us report the queen's message to the king.

MÁDANIKA: Let's do just that, my friend.

BOTH: *(walking around and approaching)* Victory, victory 1.70
to your majesty. Your majesty, the queen *commands*— *(having said this half, they indicate their embarrassment)* No, no! She *reports*. . . *

RĀJĀ: *(vihasya, s'|ādaram)* Madanike, nanv «ājñāpayat' îty» eva ramaṇīyam, viśeṣato 'dya Madana|mah''|ôtsave. tat kathaya, kim ājñāpayati devī?

VIDŪṢAKAḤ: ⌜āḥ, dāsīe dhīe. kiṃ devī āṇavedi?⌟

UBHE: ⌜evaṃ devī viṇṇavedi: «ajja kkhu mae Maarand'|ôj-jāṇe gadua ratt'|âsoa|pāa|va|tale saṃṭhāvidassa bhaavado kusum'|āuhassa pūā ṇivvattaïdavvā. tahiṃ ajja|utteṇa saṃṇihideṇa hodavvam.»⌟

RĀJĀ: *(s'|ānandam)* vayasya, nanu vaktavyam: utsavād ut-sav'|ântaram āpatitam iti.

I.75 VIDŪṢAKAḤ: ⌜bho vassa, tā uṭṭhehi. tahiṃ jjeva gacchamha, jeṇa tahiṃ gadassa mam' âvi bamhaṇassa sotthi|vāaṇaṃ kiṃ vi bhavissadi.⌟

RĀJĀ: Madanike! gamyatāṃ devyai nivedayitum: ayam aham āgata eva Makarand'|ôdyānam iti.

UBHE: ⌜jaṃ bhaṭṭā āṇavedi.⌟ *(iti niṣkrānte.)*

RĀJĀ: vayasya! ehi, avatarāvaḥ. *(ubhau prāsād'|âvataraṇaṃ nāṭayataḥ.)* vayasya, ādeśaya Makarand'|ôdyānasya mār-gam.

VIDŪṢAKAḤ: ⌜jaṃ bhavaṃ āṇavedi. edu, edu bhavaṃ.⌟

I.80 *ubhau parikrāmataḥ.*

VIDŪṢAKAḤ: *(agrato 'valokya)* ⌜bho, edaṃ taṃ Maarand|uj-jāṇam. tā ehi. pavisamha.⌟ *(iti praviśataḥ.)*

KING: *(laughing respectfully)* Mádanika, "She commands" is quite charming. Especially today, on the Festival of Passion. So tell me, what does the queen command?

JESTER: You daughter of a slave girl, what does the queen *command*?

BOTH: This is what the queen *reports*: "Today, I will go to the Garden of Nectar and place the god of flower-weapons at the foot of the red *ashóka* tree and worship him. This should be done there in the presence of my husband."

KING: *(ecstatically)* My friend, you could say that one festival follows right after another festival.

JESTER: Then, get up, my friend. Let's go there, so that I 1.75
too can get some sort of auspicious present when I get there, since I'm a Brahmin.*

KING: Mádanika, go and *announce* to the queen that I am just coming to the Garden of Nectar.

BOTH: As the king *commands*. *(Exit the* TWO MAIDS.*)*

KING: Come, my friend, let's go down. *(They mime descending from the roof-balcony.)* My friend, show me the path to the Garden of Nectar.

JESTER: As you command, sir. Come, please, sir, come.

They both walk around. 1.80

JESTER: *(looking ahead)* Look, here is the Garden of Nectar. Come, let's go inside it. *(They go into the garden.)*

VIDŪṢAKAḤ: *(avalokya, sa|vismayam)* ⌜bho, vaassa! pekkha, pekkha! edaṃ kkhu taṃ Malaa|mārud'|āndolaṇa|pahullanta|sahaāra|mañjarī|reṇu|paṭala|paḍibaddha|paḍa|vitānaṃ matta|mahu|ara|mutta|jhaṅ|kāra|milida|mahura|koil'|ārāva|saṃgīda|sudi|suhaṃ tuh' āgamaṇa|daṃsit'|ādaraṃ via Maarand|ujjāṇaṃ lakkhīadi. tā pekkhadu bhavaṃ.⌟

RĀJĀ: *(samantād avalokya)* aho, ramyatā Makarand'|ôdyānasya. iha hi:

udyad|vidruma|kāntibhiḥ kisalayais
  tāmrāṃ tviṣaṃ bibhrato,
 bhṛṅg'|ālī|virutaiḥ kalair a|viśada|
  vyāhāra|līlā|bhṛtaḥ,
ghūrṇanto Malay'|ânil'|āhita|calaiḥ
  śākhā|samūhair muhur
 bhānti prāpya *Madhu*|prasaṅgam adhunā
  mattā iv' âmī drumāḥ. [17]

JESTER: *(looking with amazement)* Look, look, my friend! This Garden of Nectar, as if to honor you when it saw you arrive, has made a canopy out of the mass of pollen from the full-blown blossoms that the wind from the Málaya mountains* shook down when it made the mango tree sway. And to please your ear it provides the music of the cries of the cuckoos blended with the humming of the drunken bees. You should see it, sir.

KING: *(looking around)* Ah, the loveliness of the Garden of Nectar! For here:

These trees seem now to be drunk with
spring : wine,
for the sprouts that have the loveliness of
growing coral
give them a flushed complexion,
they play at making blurred, unclear utterances
(the sounds made by rows of bees),
and they reel again and again
when the Málaya wind shakes their
clustered branches.

1.85 api ca,

mūle gaṇḍūṣa|sek'|āsava iva bakulair
vāsyate puṣpa|vṛṣṭyā,
madhv|ātāmre taruṇyā mukha|śaśini cirāc
campakāny adya bhānti,
ākarṇy' âśoka|pād'|āhatiṣu ca raṇatāṃ
nirbharaṃ nūpurāṇāṃ
jhaṅ|kārasy' ânu|gītair anu|raṇanam iv' ā-
rabhyate bhṛṅga|sārthaiḥ. [18]

VIDŪṢAKAḤ: *(ākarṇya)* ⌜bho vaassa! ṇa ede mahu|arā ṇeura| saddaṃ aṇuharanti. ṇeura|saddo jjevva eso devīe pariaṇassa.⌟

RĀJĀ: vayasya, samyag upalakṣitam.

tataḥ praviśati VĀSAVADATTĀ, KĀÑCANAMĀLĀ, *pūj"|ôpakaraṇa|hastā* SĀGARIKĀ, *vibhavataś ca parivāraḥ.*

1.90 VĀSAVADATTĀ: ⌜hañje Kañcaṇamāle! ādeśehi me Maarand| ujjāṇassa maggaṃ.⌟

KĀÑCANAMĀLĀ: ⌜edu, edu bhaṭṭiṇī.⌟

VĀSAVADATTĀ: *(parikramya)* ⌜hañje Kañcaṇamāle! adha ke-ttia dūre so ratt'|âsoa|pāda|vo jahiṃ mae bhaavado ku-sum'|āuhassa pūā ṇivvattaïdavvā?⌟

And 1.85

The *bákula* trees that send down showers
of their flowers
seem to perfume the wine sprinkled in mouthfuls
at their roots.
Today, after a long time, the *chámpaka* trees
shine on
a young woman's moonlike face,
flushed with wine.
And the humming of the bees seems to begin to
echo in an answering song
the loud ringing that they hear from the anklets
resounding on feet that kick the *ashóka* tree.*

JESTER: *(listening)* My friend, it's not the bees that are echoing the sound of the anklets. It's the sound of anklets of the queen's entourage.

KING: My friend, you're right.

Enter VÁSAVA·DATTA, KÁNCHANA·MALA, *and* SÁGARIKA *with the materials of ritual offerings in her hands, and their attendants according to their rank.*

VÁSAVA·DATTA: Kánchana·mala, show me the path to the 1.90
Garden of Nectar.

KÁNCHANA·MALA: Come, please, ma'am, come.

VÁSAVA·DATTA: *(walking about)* Kánchana·mala, how far is that red *ashóka* tree where I am to worship the god of flower-weapons?

KĀÑCANAMĀLĀ: ⌜bhaṭṭiṇi, āsaṇṇo jjeva. kiṃ ṇa pekkhadi bhaṭṭiṇī? iaṃ kkhu sā nirantar'|ubbhiṇṇa|kusuma|sohiṇī bhaṭṭiṇīe parigahidā māhavī|ladā. esā vi avarā ṇomāliā ladā, jāe a|āla|kusuma|samuggama|saddhāluṇā bhaṭṭiṇā aṇu|diṇaṃ āāsīadi appā. tā edaṃ atikkamia dīsadi jjeva so ratt'|âsoa|pāa|vo, jahiṃ devī pūāṃ ṇivvattaïssadi.⌟

VĀSAVADATTĀ: ⌜tā ehi, tahiṃ jjevva lahu gacchamha.⌟

1.95 KĀÑCANAMĀLĀ: ⌜edu, edu bhaṭṭiṇī.⌟

sarvāḥ parikrāmanti.

KĀÑCANAMĀLĀ: ⌜bhaṭṭiṇi, aaṃ khu so ratt'|âsoa|pāa|vo, jahiṃ devī pūāṃ ṇivvattaïssadi.⌟

VĀSAVADATTĀ: ⌜teṇa hi me pūā|ṇimittāiṃ uvaaraṇāiṃ uvaṇehi.⌟

SĀGARIKĀ: *(upasṛtya)* ⌜bhaṭṭiṇi, edaṃ savvaṃ sajjam.⌟

1.100 VĀSAVADATTĀ: *(nirūpya, ātma|gatam)* ⌜aho, pamāo pariaṇassa! jassa jjeva daṃsaṇa|padhādo paatteṇa rakkhīadi, tassa jjeva diṭṭhi|goare paḍidā bhave. bhodu, evaṃ tāva bhaṇissam:⌟ *(prakāśam)* ⌜hañje Sāarie! kīsa tumaṃ ajja Maaṇa|mah"|ûssava|parāhīṇe pariaṇe sāriaṃ ujjhia ih' āgadā? tā tahiṃ jjeva lahuṃ gaccha. edaṃ vi savvaṃ pū"|ôbaaraṇaṃ Kañcaṇamālāe hatthe samappehi.⌟

KÁNCHANA·MALA: It's quite close, ma'am. Doesn't your highness see it? Here's the *mádhavi* vine, shining with constantly produced flowers, which your highness adopted.* And this other is the new jasmine vine that the king himself takes pains with day after day, because he believes it will flower out of season.* Right beyond it you can actually see the red *ashóka* tree where your highness will perform the ritual.

VÁSAVA·DATTA: Then, come, let's go right there quickly.

KÁNCHANA·MALA: Come, please, ma'am, come. 1.95

They all walk around.

KÁNCHANA·MALA: Your highness, right here is the red *ashóka* tree where your highness will perform the ritual.

VÁSAVA·DATTA: Then bring me the things I need for the ritual.*

SÁGARIKA: *(approaching)* Everything is ready here, your highness.

VÁSAVA·DATTA: *(watching, to herself)* Ah, the carelessness of 1.100
servants.* She'll come right into the path of vision of the very man from whose range of sight I have made great efforts to keep her. All right. I'll just say this. *(out loud)* Ságarika, how is it that you've come here, leaving the mynah bird behind, when all the servants are busily preoccupied with the Festival of Passion? Now, go right back there quickly. Put all these materials for the ritual in Kánchana·mala's hands.

SĀGARIKĀ: ⌜jaṃ bhaṭṭiṇī āṇavedi.⌟ *(iti tathā kṛtvā, kati cit padāni gatvā, ātma|gatam)* ⌜sāriā mae uṇa Susaṃgadāe hatthe samappidā. edaṃ vi atthi me pekkhiduṃ kodūhalaṃ: kiṃ jahā tādassa ante|ure bhaavaṃ Aṇaṅgo accīadi iha vi taha jjeva, kiṃ aṇṇah" êtti. tā a|lakkhidā bhavia pekkhissam. jāva iha pūā|samao hoi, tāva ahaṃ pi bhaavantaṃ Aṇaṅgaṃ jjeva pūaïduṃ kusumāiṃ avaciṇissam.⌟ *(iti kusum'|âvacayaṃ nāṭayati.)*

VĀSAVADATTĀ: ⌜Kañcaṇamāle, paḍiṭṭhāvehi asoa|mūle bhaavantaṃ Pajjuṇṇam.⌟

KĀÑCANAMĀLĀ: ⌜jaṃ bhaṭṭiṇī āṇavedi.⌟ *(tathā karoti.)*

VIDŪṢAKAḤ: ⌜bho, vaassa! jadhā vīsanto ṇeura|saddo, tahā takkemi: āadā devī asoa|mūlaṃ tti.⌟

I.105 RĀJĀ: *(avalokya)* vayasya, samyag avadhāritam. paśy' êyaṃ devī yā kil' âiṣā:

Kusuma|su|kumāra|mūrtir
 dadhatī niyamena tanutaraṃ madhyam
ābhāti makara|ketoḥ
 pārśva|sthā cāpa|yaṣṭir iva. [19]

tad ehi. upasarpāvaḥ. *(upasṛtya)* priye Vāsavadatte!

VĀSAVADATTĀ: *(vilokya)* ⌜kadhaṃ, ajja|utto! jaadu, jaadu ajja|utto! edaṃ āsaṇaṃ. ettha uvavisadu ajja|utto.⌟

SÁGARIKA: As your highness commands. *(doing this, walking a few steps, and saying to herself)* I already put the mynah bird back in Susángata's hands. I'm very curious to see if the bodiless god is worshipped here too just as in the women's quarters in my father's palace, or differently. I'll watch unobserved. As long as the ritual lasts, I too will gather flowers to worship the bodiless god.* *(She mimes gathering flowers.)**

VÁSAVA·DATTA: Kánchana·mala, set up the god Pradyúmna at the foot of the *ashóka* tree.*

KÁNCHANA·MALA: As your highness commands. *(She does this.)*

JESTER: Since the sound of the anklets has died down, my friend, I guess the queen has come to the foot of the *ashóka* tree.

KING: *(looking)* You're right, my friend. Look, here's the queen: 1.105

She seems like the staff of
 the bow standing at the side
of the god who has a sea-serpent on his banner,
for she has a form delicate as a flower
and a waist made thinner by her vow.*

So come, let's go up to her. *(approaching)* Dearest Vásava·datta!

VÁSAVA·DATTA: *(looking)* Why, it's my husband! Victory, victory to my husband! Here is a seat. Please sit down on it, my husband.

RĀJĀ *nāṭyen' ôpaviśati.*

I.110 KĀÑCANAMĀLĀ: ⌜bhaṭṭiṇi, sa|hattha|diṇṇa|kuṅkuma|cacciā|sohidaṃ kadua, ratt'|âsoa|pāa|vaṃ accīadu bhaavaṃ Pajjuṇṇo.⌟

VĀSAVADATTĀ: ⌜uvaṇehi me pūj"|ôvaaraṇāiṃ.⌟

KĀÑCANAMĀL" *ôpanayati.* VĀSAVADATTĀ *tathā karoti.*

RĀJĀ: priye,

pratyagra|*majjana*|viśeṣa|vivikta|kāntiḥ,
  kausumbha|*rāga*|rucira|*sphurad*|*aṃśukāntā*
vibhrājase Makara|ketanam arcayantī,
  bāla|pravāla|viṭapi|prabhavā lat" êva. [20]

I.115 api ca,

spṛṣṭas tvay" âiṣa, dayite,
  Smara|pūjā|vyāpṛtena hastena
udbhinn'|âpara|mṛdutara|
  kisalaya iva lakṣyate 'śokaḥ. [21]

The KING *mimes sitting down.*

KÁNCHANA·MALA: Your majesty, it is time to worship the god Pradyúmna, adorning the red *ashóka* tree with saffron powder, with your own hand. I.110

VÁSAVA·DATTA: Bring me the ritual materials.

KÁNCHANA·MALA *brings them.* VÁSAVA·DATTA *does the ritual.*

KING: My dearest,

As you worship the god with a sea-serpent
on his banner,
you seem like a vine growing on a tree covered
with young shoots,
looking especially bright and refreshed by a recent
bath : sprinkling,
and *the ends of your garment shining with :
made beautiful by*
the *red dye made from : pollen of
kusúmbha* flowers.*

And: I.115

This *ashóka* tree, touched, my darling, by
your hand
engaged in worshipping Memory,
seems to have sprouted another even
softer shoot.*

api ca,

Anaṅgo 'yam an|aṅgatvam adya nindiṣyati dhruvam,
yad anena na samprāptaḥ pāṇi|sparś'|ôtsavas tava. [22]

KĀÑCANAMĀLĀ: ⌜bhaṭṭiṇi, accido bhaavaṃ Pajjuṇṇo. tā karehi bhattuṇo uiddaṃ pūā|sak|kāam.⌟

I.120 VĀSAVADATTĀ: ⌜teṇa hi uvaṇehi me kusumāiṃ vilebaṇaṃ ca.⌟

KĀÑCANAMĀLĀ: ⌜bhaṭṭiṇi, edaṃ savvaṃ sajjaṃ.⌟

VĀSAVADATTĀ *nāṭyena* RĀJĀNAṂ *pūjayati.*

SĀGARIKĀ: *(gṛhīta/kusumā)* ⌜ha ddhī! ha ddhī! kahaṃ, kusuma|loh'|ôkkhitta|hiaāe adi|ciraṃ jevva mae kidam! tā jāva imiṇā sinduvāra|viḍaveṇa ovāria|sarīrā bhavia pekkhāmi.⌟ *(tathā kṛtvā, vilokya, sa/vismayam)* ⌜kahaṃ, paccakkho evva bhaavaṃ Kusum'|āuho iha pūāṃ paḍicchadi. amhāṇaṃ tādassa ante|ure uṇa citta|gado accīadi. tā ahaṃ vi iha tthidā jjevva imehiṃ kusumehiṃ bhaavandaṃ Kusum'|āuhaṃ pūaïssaṃ.⌟ *(kusumāni prakṣipya)* ⌜ṇamo de bhaavaṃ Kusum'|āuha! a|moha|daṃsaṇo me dāṇiṃ tumaṃ bhavissasi.⌟ *(iti praṇamya)* ⌜diṭṭhaṃ jaṃ diṭṭhavvam. tā jāva ṇa ke vi maṃ pekkhadi, tāva jjeva gamissam.⌟ *(iti kati cit padāni gacchati.)*

And:

> The bodiless god will certainly curse
> being bodiless today,
> because the joy of the touch of your hand
> in the festival
> cannot reach him.*

KÁNCHANA·MALA: Your highness, the god Pradyúmna has been worshipped. Now do the appropriate ritual of reverence to your husband.

VÁSAVA·DATTA: Then bring me the flowers and the oils. 1.120

KÁNCHANA·MALA: Everything is ready here, your highness.

VÁSAVA·DATTA *mimes worshipping the* KING.

SÁGARIKA: *(holding flowers)* Oh no! How did I manage to waste so much time? My greed for flowers carried my heart away. Well, I will watch, concealing my body behind the clustered lower branches of this *sinduvára* tree.* *(doing this and looking, with amazement)* Why, the god of flower-weapons himself, in the flesh, is receiving this worship! In the women's quarters in my father's palace, we worshipped him just in the form of an image. So I, too, will stay here and worship with these flowers the god of flower-weapons. *(throwing flowers)* Honor to you, lord of the flower-weapons. My sight of you now will not be in vain.* *(bowing)* I have seen what I had to see. So I will go away before anyone sees me. *(She takes a few steps.)*

KĀÑCANAMĀLĀ: ⌜ajja|Vasantaa, ehi! saṃpadaṃ tumaṃ vi sotthi|vāaṇaṃ paḍiccha.⌟ *(*VIDŪṢAKA *upasarpati.)*

I.125 VĀSAVADATTĀ: *(vilepana|kusum'|ābharaṇa|dāna|pūrvakam)* ⌜ajja, sotthi|vāaṇaṃ paḍiccha.⌟ *(ity arpayati.)*

VIDŪṢAKAḤ: *(sa|harṣaṃ gṛhītvā)* ⌜sotthi bhodīe.⌟

nepathye VAITĀLIKAḤ *paṭhati.*

ast'|âpāsta|samasta|bhāsi nabhasaḥ
pāraṃ prayāte ravāv
āsthānīṃ samaye samaṃ nṛ|pa|janaḥ
sāyaṃtane saṃpatan
saṃpraty eṣa saro|ruha|dyuti|muṣaḥ
pādāṃs tav' āsevituṃ
prīty|utkarṣa|kṛto dṛśām *Udayanasy'*
êndor iv' ôdvīkṣate. [23]

SĀGARIKĀ: *(śrutvā, sa|harṣaṃ parivṛtya,* RĀJĀNAṂ *sa|spṛhaṃ paśyantī)* ⌜kahaṃ, aaṃ so rāā Udaaṇo, jassa ahaṃ tādeṇa diṇṇā.⌟ *(dīrghaṃ niḥśvasya)* ⌜tā para|ppessaṇa|dūsidaṃ pi me jīvidaṃ edassa daṃsaṇeṇa dāṇiṃ bahu|mataṃ saṃvuttam.⌟

I.130 RĀJĀ: aye! katham, utsav'|âpahṛta|cetobhiḥ saṃdhy"|âtikramo 'py asmābhir n' ôpalakṣitaḥ. saṃprati pariṇatam ahaḥ. devi, paśya:

KÁNCHANA·MALA: Good Vasántaka, come, you too should now accept the auspicious offering. *(The* JESTER *approaches.)*

VÁSAVA·DATTA: *(after offering sandal paste, flowers, and or-* 1.125
naments) Good sir, accept this auspicious offering. *(She gives it to him.)*

JESTER: *(taking it joyously)* Thank you, my lady.

Offstage, a ROYAL HERALD *recites:*

> Now at the time of evening, when the sun has gone
> to the far bank of the sky,
> and its light is entirely cast off onto the mountain
> where the sun goes home,
> this company of kings all coming together
> to the assembly hall
> look forward to serving the *feet of Údayana,*
> which, like the *rays of the rising* moon,
> steal the lustre of the day-lotuses
> and give overflowing pleasure to the eyes.*

SÁGARIKA: *(hearing with joy, looking with desire at the* KING*)* Why, this is the king, Údayana, to whom my father gave me! *(sighing deeply)* Though I thought my life was blighted because I was sent to someone else, now the sight of him has made it precious to me.

KING: Oh! How is it that our minds were so carried away 1.130
by the festival that we did not notice that the sunset had passed. Now the day is bent low with age. See, my queen:

udaya|taṭ'|ântaritam iyaṃ
prācī sūcayati diṅ niśā|nātham
paripāṇḍunā mukhena,
priyam iva hṛdaya|sthitaṃ ramaṇī. [24]

devi, tad uttiṣṭha. āvās'|âbhyantaram eva praviśāvaḥ. *(sarva utthāya parikrāmanti.)*

SĀGARIKĀ: ⌜kadhaṃ, patthidā devī. bhodu. tā ahaṃ vi turidaṃ gamissam.⌟ *(*RĀJĀNAṂ *sa/spṛhaṃ dṛṣṭvā, niḥśvasya)* ⌜ha ddhī! ha ddhī! manda|bhāiṇīe mae pekkhidum api ciraṃ na pārido aaṃ jaṇo.⌟ *(iti* RĀJĀNAṂ *paśyantī niṣkrāntā.)*

RĀJĀ: *(parikrāman)*

I.135 devi! tvan|mukha|paṅka|jena śaśinaḥ
śobhā|tiras|kāriṇā,
paśy' âb|jāni vinirjitāni sahasā
gacchanti vicchāyatām.
śrutvā tvat|parivāra|vāra|vanitā|
gītāni bhṛṅg'|âṅganā
līyante mukul'|ântareṣu śanakaiḥ
saṃjāta|lajjā iva. [25]

iti niṣkrāntāḥ sarve.

iti «Madana/mah"/ôtsavo» nāma prathamo 'ṅkaḥ.

This eastern quarter of the sky reveals, *with her*
very pale face,
the lord of the night, hidden by the sloping curtain
of the mountain where he rises,
just as a beautiful woman shows, *by her very*
pale face,
her lover hidden in her heart.*

So get up, my queen. Let's go into the palace. *(They all get up and walk around.)*

SÁGARIKA: Oh, the queen is leaving. All right. Then I too will go quickly. *(looking at the* KING *with desire, sighing)* Oh dear! How unlucky I am. For a long time I couldn't even see this man. *(Exit, looking at the* KING*.)*

KING: *(walking around)*

Look, my queen! Your lotus face eclipses 1.135
the splendor of the moon,
and vanquishes the lotuses,
which suddenly lose their lustre.
The female bees, hearing the songs of
the courtesans of your entourage,
hide slowly inside the buds,
as if suddenly ashamed.*

Exit all.

The end of Act One, called "The Festival of Passion."

PRELUDE TO ACT II

tataḥ praviśati sārikā|pañjara|vyagra|hastā SUSAṂGATĀ.

SUSAṂGATĀ: ⌜ha ddhī, ha ddhī! kahiṃ dāṇiṃ mama hatthe sāriā|pañjaraṃ ṇikkhivia gadā me pia|sahī Sāariā? tā kahiṃ puṇa eṇaṃ pekkhissam?⌟ *(agrato 'valokya)* ⌜kahaṃ, esā khu Ṇiuṇiā ido jjeva āacchadi. tā jāva edaṃ pucchissam.⌟

tataḥ praviśati NIPUṆIKĀ.

2.5 NIPUṆIKĀ: *(sa|vismayam)* ⌜accariaṃ, accariaṃ! aṇ|aṇṇa|sa|diso pabhāvo maṇṇe devadāe. uvaladdho khu mae bhaṭṭiṇo vutt'|anto. tā gadua bhaṭṭiṇīe ṇivedaïssam.⌟ *(iti parikrāmati.)*

SUSAṂGATĀ: *(upasṛtya)* ⌜sahi Ṇiuṇie! kahiṃ dāṇiṃ tumaṃ vimha'|ôkkhitta|hiaā via iha ṭṭhidaṃ maṃ avadhīria ido adikkāmasi?⌟

NIPUṆIKĀ: ⌜kadhaṃ, Susaṃgadā! halā Susaṃgade! su|ṭṭhu tue jāṇidaṃ. edaṃ kkhu mama vimhaassa kāaṇam: ajja kila bhaṭṭā Siri|pavvatādo āadassa Sirikhaṇḍadāsa|ṇāma|dheassa dhammiassa saāsādo a|kāla|kusuma|saṃjaṇaṇa|dohalaaṃ sikkhia attaṇo paḍigihīdaṃ ṇomāliaṃ kusuma|samiddhi|sohidaṃ karissadi tti. tahiṃ edaṃ vutt'|antaṃ jāṇiduṃ devīe pesida mhi. tumaṃ uṇa kahiṃ patthidā?⌟

[Time: The next day, late afternoon.]

Enter SUSÁNGATA, *busying her hands with a cage holding a mynah bird.*

SUSÁNGATA: Oh dear, Oh dear! Where did my dear friend Ságarika go now, after she put the mynah bird cage in my hands? Where will I see her again? *(looking in front of her)* Why, here's Nípunika, coming right here. I'll ask her.

Enter NÍPUNIKA.

NÍPUNIKA: *(with astonishment)* Amazing, amazing. I think 2.5
the power of a divinity must be unlike anything else. I have news of the king, which I'll go and report to my mistress. *(She walks about.)*

SUSÁNGATA: *(approaching)* My friend Nípunika, where are you going now, passing me by as I stand here, ignoring me as if your heart has been carried away by amazement?

NÍPUNIKA: Why, it's Susángata! Susángata, you have understood the situation perfectly. This is the reason for my astonishment. Just today, a pious person named Shri·khanda·dasa has come from the Shri mountain,* and he taught the king what plants want,* so that he can make them flower out of season. And so the king will use this to beautify the new jasmine—which he himself married*—with a profusion of blossoms. The queen sent me there to find out the news about this. But where are you heading?

SUSAṂGATĀ: ⌜pia|sahiṃ Sāariaṃ aṇṇesidum.⌟

NIPUṆIKĀ: ⌜sahi, diṭṭhā mae de pia|sahī Sāariā gahida|citta| phalaka|vattiā|samuggaā samuviggā via kadalī|gharaaṃ pavisantī. tā gaccha tumaṃ. ahaṃ pi devīe saāsaṃ gamissam.⌟

2.10 *niṣkrānte.*

praveśakaḥ

SUSÁNGATA: To look for my dear friend Ságarika.

NÍPUNIKA: My friend, I saw your dear friend Ságarika entering the banana bower. She seemed upset, and was carrying a painting board, brushes, and paint box. That's where you should go. I'll go to the queen.

Exit the two women. 2.10

End of Interlude

ACT II
THE BANANA BOWER

tataḥ praviśati gṛhīta|citra|phalaka|vartikā madan'|âvasthāṃ nāṭayantī SĀGARIKĀ.

SĀGARIKĀ: *(niḥśvasya)* ⌜hiaa, pasīda, pasīda! kiṃ imiṇā āāsa|metta|phaleṇa dul|laha|jaṇa|ppatthaṇ'|âṇubandheṇa? aṇṇaṃ ca: jeṇa evva diṭṭheṇa de īdiso saṃtāvo ṇu vaḍḍhadi, taṃ evva puṇo vi pekkhiduṃ ahilasasi tti, aho de mūḍhadā! kahaṃ a adi|nisaṃsa jammado pahudi saha|saṃvaḍḍhidaṃ imaṃ jaṇaṃ pariccaïa, khaṇa|metta|daṃsaṇa|paricidaṃ jaṇaṃ aṇugacchanto ṇa lajjasi? aha vā ko tuha doso! Aṇaṅga|sara|paḍaṇa|bhīdeṇa tue evvaṃ ajja vvavasidaṃ.⌟ *(s'|âsram)* ⌜bhodu. Aṇaṅgaṃ dāva ubālahissaṃ.⌟ *(añjaliṃ baddhvā)* ⌜bhaavaṃ Kusum'|āuha! nijjia|saala|sur'|âsuro bhavia itthiā|jaṇaṃ paharanto kadhaṃ ṇa lajjasi?⌟ *(vicintya)* ⌜adha vā aṇ|aṅgo si.⌟ *(dīrghaṃ niḥśvasya)* ⌜savvahā mama manda|bhāinīe maraṇaṃ evva imiṇā duṇ|ṇimitteṇa uvatthidaṃ.⌟ *(phalakam avalokya)* ⌜tā jāva ṇa ko vi iha āacchadi, tāva ālekkha|samappidaṃ taṃ ahimadaṃ jaṇaṃ pekkhia jahā|samīhidaṃ karissaṃ.⌟ *(s'|âvaṣṭambham eka|manā bhūtvā, nāṭyena phalakaṃ gṛhītvā, niḥśvasya)* ⌜jaï vi me adi|saddhaseṇa vevadi aaṃ ati|mettaṃ agga|hattho, tahā vi ṇa tthi tassa jaṇassa aṇṇo daṃsaṇ'|ôvāo tti jahā|tahā ālihia ṇaṃ pekkhissaṃ.⌟ *(iti nāṭyena likhati.)*

Enter SÁGARIKA, *miming love-sickness, holding a painting board and a brush.*

SÁGARIKA: *(sighing)* Be still, my heart, be still. What's the use of this obsessive longing for a person impossible to get? Nothing will come of it but wasted effort. And besides: What a fool you are, to long to see again the very man who, when you see him, makes you all the more miserable. How is it, cruelest of hearts, that you're not ashamed to run after a person you've only seen for a moment, abandoning this person—me!—you've grown up with from birth? But perhaps this is not your fault. Perhaps you've done this today because you're afraid the arrows of the bodiless god will hit you. *(in tears)* I'll tell the bodiless god a thing or two. *(joining her palms in reverence)* Lord of the flower-weapons, you've conquered all the gods and anti-gods, so why aren't you ashamed to attack a mere woman? *(thinking)* But, of course, you have no body.* *(sighing deeply)* This bad omen* foretells my approaching death altogether, unlucky as I am. *(looking at the painting board)* As long as no one comes here, I'll gaze at a painting of the man I love, and do what I want to do.* *(miming concentrating her mind resolutely and taking up the board, sighing)* Even though my great nervousness makes my fingers tremble too much, nevertheless, there's no other way for me to see him. So I'll draw him however I can and then look at him. *(She mimes drawing.)*

tataḥ praviśati SUSAṂGATĀ.

2.15 SUSAṂGATĀ: ⌜edaṃ taṃ kadalī|haraaṃ. tā pavisāmi.⌟ *(praviśy' âgrato vilokya, sa|vismayam)* ⌜esā me pia|sahī Sāariā. kiṃ uṇa esā guru'|âṇurā'|ôkkhitta|hiaā via kiṃ vi ālihantī ṇa maṃ pekkhadi? bhodu. tā jāva se diṭṭhi|pahaṃ pariharia ṇirūaïssaṃ kiṃ esā ālihadi tti.⌟ *(svairaṃ pṛṣṭhato 'syāḥ sthitvā, dṛṣṭvā, sa|harṣam)* ⌜kahaṃ, bhaṭṭā ālihido! sādhu, Sāarie, sādhu! aha vā ṇa kamal'|āaraṃ vajjia rāa|haṃsī aṇṇassiṃ ahiramadi!⌟

SĀGARIKĀ: ⌜ālihido khu mae eso. kiṃ uṇa aṇ|avarada|ṇivaḍanta|bāppha|salileṇa ṇa me diṭṭhī pekkhiduṃ pabhavati.⌟ *(mukham uttānī|kṛty' âśrūṇi nivārayantī,* SUSAṂGATĀṂ *dṛṣṭv" ôttarīyeṇa phalakaṃ pracchādayantī, sa|vilakṣa|smitam)* ⌜kahaṃ, pia|sahī Susaṃgadā! sahi, ido uvaviśa.⌟

SUSAṂGATĀ: *(upaviśya, balāt phalakam ākṛṣya)* ⌜sahi, ko eso tue ettha ālihido?⌟

SĀGARIKĀ: *(sa|lajjam)* ⌜sahi, paütta|Maaṇa|mah"|ûsave bhaavaṃ Aṇaṅgo.⌟

SUSAṂGATĀ: *(sa|smitam)* ⌜aho de ṇiuṇattaṇam. kiṃ puṇa, suṇṇaṃ via edaṃ cittaṃ paḍibhādi. tā ahaṃ pi ālihia Rati|sa|ṇāhaṃ karissam.⌟ *(vartikāṃ gṛhitvā, nāṭyena* RATI/ *vyapadeśena* SĀGARIKĀṂ *likhati.)*

2.20 SĀGARIKĀ: *(vilokya, s'|âsūyam)* ⌜Susaṃgade, kīsa tue ahaṃ ettha ālihidā?⌟

Enter SUSÁNGATA

SUSÁNGATA: [*(to herself)**] Here's the banana bower. I'll go inside. *(She enters and looks again with amazement.)* Here's my dear friend Ságarika. Why is she drawing with a heart so carried away by heavy passion that she doesn't see me? All right. As long as I can avoid the path of her gaze, I'll find out what she's drawing. *(standing cautiously behind her, seeing, with joy)* What's this? She's drawn the king! Bravo, Ságarika, bravo! But, of course, a female royal swan wouldn't be happy anywhere but in a lotus pond.* 2.15

SÁGARIKA: [*(to herself)*] I've drawn him, but my eyes can't look at him because my tears won't stop flowing. *(lifting up her face and stopping her tears, seeing* SUSÁNGATA, *hiding the painting board with her upper garment, with a forced smile)* Why, it's my dear friend Susángata! Sit down here, my friend.

SUSÁNGATA: *(sitting down and taking the painting board by force)* My friend, who's this that you have drawn?

SÁGARIKA: *(with embarrassment)* My friend, it's the bodiless god in the festival of love that's just begun.

SUSÁNGATA: *(smiling)* My, how clever you are.* But something is missing in this picture. I too will draw, and I'll put Rati beside her husband. *(Taking the brush, she mimes drawing* SÁGARIKA *while pretending to draw* RATI.*)*

SÁGARIKA: *(looking at it with indignation)* Susángata, why have you drawn me here? 2.20

SUSAṂGATĀ: *(vihasya)* ⸢sahi, kiṃ a|āraṇaṃ kuppasi? jādiso tue Kāma|devo ālihido, tādisī mae Raï ālihidā. tā aṇṇadhā|sambhāviṇi, kiṃ tue ediṇā ālabideṇa? kahehiṃ dāva savvaṃ vutt'|antam.⸥

SĀGARIKĀ: *(sa|lajjā, sva|gatam)* ⸢ṇaṃ jānida mhi pia|sahīe.⸥ *(*SUSAṂGATĀṂ *haste gṛhītvā, prakāśam)* ⸢pia|sahi, mahadī khu me lajjā. tā tahā karesu, jahā ṇa ko vi avaro edaṃ vutt'|antaṃ jāṇedi.⸥

SUSAṂGATĀ: ⸢sahi, mā lajja. īdisassa kaṇṇā|raaṇassa avassaṃ evva īdisse vare ahilāseṇa hodavvam. taha vi, jahā ṇa ko vi avaro edaṃ vutt'|antaṃ jāṇissadi, taha karemi. edāe uṇa medhāviṇīe sāriāe ettha kāaṇeṇa hodavvam. kadā vi esā imassa ālāvassa gahid'|akkharā bhavia kassa vi purao mantaïssadi.⸥

SĀGARIKĀ: ⸢tā kiṃ dāṇiṃ ettha karaïssam? ado vi ahiadaraṃ me saṃtāvo vaṭṭhadi.⸥

2.25 *madan'|âvasthāṃ nāṭayati.*

SUSAṂGATĀ: *(*SĀGARIKĀYĀ *hṛdaye hastaṃ dattvā)* ⸢sahi, samassasa, samassasa. jāva imāo digghiāo ṇaliṇī|vattāiṃ muṇāliāo a giṇhia lahuṃ āacchāmi.⸥ *(niṣkramya punaḥ praviśya ca, nāṭyena nalinī|patraiḥ śayanīyaṃ mṛṇālair valayāni ca racayitvā, pariśiṣṭāni nalinī|patrāṇi* SĀGARIKĀYĀ *hṛdaye nikṣipati.)*

SĀGARIKĀ: ⸢sahi, avaṇehi imāiṃ ṇaliṇī|vattāiṃ muṇāla|valaāiṃ a. alaṃ edehiṃ. kīsa a|āraṇe attāṇaṃ āāsesi? ṇaṃ bhaṇāmi—⸥

SUSÁNGATA: *(laughing)* My friend, why are you getting angry for no reason? I've drawn Rati, too, just as you painted Kama. So why are you babbling about something that you imagine to be other than it is? Now, tell me the whole story.

SÁGARIKA: *(embarrassed, to herself)* So my dear friend has found me out. *(taking* SUSÁNGATA *by the hand, out loud)* My dear friend, I'm so ashamed. So do make sure that no one else knows this story.

SUSÁNGATA: My friend, don't be ashamed. Such a jewel of a girl must, inevitably, long for such a bridegroom. Nevertheless, I will make sure that no one else knows the story. But they may find out anyway through this mynah bird, rightly called "Ace Reporter."* For she may pick up the syllables of this little chat and blurt it out in front of someone, sooner or later.

SÁGARIKA: But what can I do about that now? This makes me even more miserable.

She mimes love-sickness. 2.25

SUSÁNGATA: *(putting her hand on* SÁGARIKA*'s heart)* Courage, my friend, courage. I'll go quickly and gather lotus leaves and stalks from this long pond. *(She goes away and comes back. She mimes making a bed out of lotus leaves and bracelets out of lotus stalks; she scatters the rest of the lotus leaves on* SÁGARIKA*'s heart.)*

SÁGARIKA: My friend, take away these lotus leaves and lotus stalks. I've had enough of them. Why do you go to such trouble for nothing? For I'm telling you:

⌜dul|laha|jaṇ'|âṇurāo,
lajjā guruī, para|vvaso appā—
pia|sahi, vi|samaṃ pemmaṃ,
maraṇaṃ saraṇaṃ na varam ekkam?⌟ [1]

iti mūrcchati.

2.30 SUSAṂGATĀ: *(sa|karuṇam)* ⌜sahi Sāarie, samassasa, samassasa.⌟

NEPATHYE:

kaṇṭhe kṛtt'|âvaśeṣaṃ kanaka|mayam adhaḥ
śṛṅkhalā|dāma karṣan,
krāntvā dvārāṇi helā|cala|caraṇa|raṇat|
kiṃkiṇī|cakra|vālaḥ,
datt'|ātaṅko 'ṅganānām anusṛta|sariṇaḥ
saṃbhramād aśva|pālaiḥ
prabhraṣṭo 'yaṃ plavaṅgaḥ praviśati nṛ|pater
mandiraṃ mandurāyāḥ. [2]

api ca,

naṣṭaṃ varṣa|varair manuṣya|gaṇan"|â|
bhāvād apāsya trapām,
antaḥ kañcuki|kañcukasya viśati
trāsād ayaṃ vāmanaḥ,
paryant'|āśrayibhir nijasya sa|dṛśaṃ
nāmnaḥ kirātaiḥ kṛtaṃ,
kubjā nīcatay" âiva yānti śanakair
ātm"|ēkṣaṇā|śaṅkinaḥ. [3]

I love someone out of reach,
shyness weighs me down,
I'm in the power of someone else—
my dear friend, this love is unequal,
and death is the only and the best refuge.*

She faints.

SUSÁNGATA: *(with pity)* Courage, Ságarika, my friend, courage! 2.30

VOICE OFF:

A monkey has broken out of the horse-stables
  and gone into the king's palace,
frightening the women. The grooms in confusion
  follow his path as he crosses the gates,
dragging under him the dangling remaining half
of the garland of golden chains broken off
  from his neck
and wearing anklets of bells that tinkle
with the playful movements of his feet.

And

The people of the third sex, casting off all shame
because they are not counted among men,
  have fled;
the dwarf, in terror, goes inside the skirts of
  the chamberlain;
the tribesmen called Scattered Wanderers
  have acted according to their names,
taking refuge in the outlying areas;
and the hunchbacks, fearing that they may be seen,
creep along, bending low.*

2.35 SUSAMGATĀ: *(ākarṇy' âgrato 'valokya, sa|saṃbhramam utthāya,* SĀGARIKĀṂ *haste gṛhītvā)* ⌜sahi, uṭṭhehi uṭṭhehi. eso kkhu duṭṭha|vāṇaro ido jjeva āacchadi. tā a|lakkhidaṃ tamāla|viḍav'|ândha|āre pavisia imaṃ adivāhema.⌟ *(tathā kṛtvā, ubhe sa|bhayaṃ paśyantau sthite.)*

SĀGARIKĀ: ⌜Susaṃgade! kahaṃ, tue citta|phalahao ujjido. kadā vi ko vi taṃ pekkhadi.⌟

SUSAṂGATĀ: ⌜aï, su|tthide, kiṃ ajja vi citta|phalaeṇa karissasi? eso kkhu dadhi|bhatta|lampaḍo sāriā|pañjaraṃ ugghāḍia avakkando duṭṭha|vāṇaro. mehāviṇī vi uḍḍīṇā esā gacchadi. tā ehi. lahuṃ aṇusaramha. imassa ālāvassa gahid'|akkharā kassa vi purado mantaïssadi.⌟

SĀGARIKĀ: ⌜sahi, evvaṃ karemha.⌟ *(iti parikrāmataḥ.)*

NEPATHYE: ⌜hī hī, bho! accariaṃ, accariaṃ!⌟

2.40 SĀGARIKĀ: *(vilokya, sa|bhayam)* ⌜Susaṃgade, jāṇiadi puṇo vi so duṭṭha|vāṇaro āacchadi tti.⌟

SUSAṂGATĀ: *(*VIDŪṢAKAṂ *dṛṣṭvā, vihasya)* ⌜aï kāare, mā bhehi. bhaṭṭuṇo pāsa|vattī ajja|Vasantao kkhu eso.⌟

SĀGARIKĀ: *(sa|spṛham avalokya)* ⌜sahi Susaṃgade, daṃsaṇīyo kkhu aaṃ jaṇo.⌟

SUSÁNGATA: *(hearing, looking ahead, getting up in haste and confusion, grabbing* SÁGARIKA *by the hand)* Stand up, my friend, stand up. That horrid monkey is coming right here. Let's ignore him and go into the dark thicket of *tamála* trees and let him pass us by.* *(They do this and stand there and watch with fear.)* 2.35

SÁGARIKA: Susángata! You left the paint board behind! Someone, sooner or later, will see it.

SUSÁNGATA: O, you stubborn girl, what use is a paint board to you now? This horrid monkey, greedy for some yogurt to eat, opened the mynah bird's cage and went away. And so "Ace Reporter" flew up and went. So come. Let's follow quickly. Surely she's picked up the syllables of this little chat and will blurt it out in front of someone.

SÁGARIKA: Let's do that, my friend. *(They walk around.)*

JESTER (OFFSTAGE): Wow! Wow! How amazing, absolutely amazing!

SÁGARIKA: *(looking around with fear)* Susángata, I bet that horrid monkey is coming again! 2.40

SUSÁNGATA: *(seeing the* JESTER, *and smiling)* O you coward, don't be afraid. This is just the good Vasántaka, the king's side-kick.

SÁGARIKA: *(looking with longing)* Susángata, my friend, this man is worth looking at.

SUSAṂGATĀ: ⌜aï, su|tthide, kiṃ imiṇā diṭṭheṇa? dūre bhodi khu sāriā. tā ehi. aṇusaramha.⌟

ubhe niṣkrānte.

2.45 *tataḥ praviśati prahṛṣṭo* VIDŪṢAKAḤ.

VIDŪṢAKAḤ: ⌜hī hī, bho! accariaṃ, accariaṃ! sāhu re Sirikhaṇḍadāsa dhammia, sāhu! jeṇa diṇṇa|metteṇa jjeva teṇa dohaeṇa īdisī ṇomāliā saṃvuttā jeṇa nir|antar|ubbhiṇṇa|kusuma|guccha|śobhia|viḍavā ubahasantī via lakkhiadi devī|parigahidaṃ mādhavī|ladaṃ. tā jāva gadua pia|vaassaṃ vaḍḍhāvaïssam.⌟ *(parikramy' âvalokya ca)* ⌜eso kkhu pia|vaasso tassaṃ dohadassa laddha|pacchaadāe parokkhaṃ vi taṃ ṇomāliaṃ paccakkhaṃ via kusumidaṃ pekkhanto haris'|upphulla|loaṇo ido jjeva āacchadi. tā jāva ṇaṃ uvasappāmi.⌟

tataḥ praviśati yathā|nirdiṣṭo RĀJĀ.

RĀJĀ: *(sa|harṣam)*

uddām'|ôtkalikāṃ, vipāṇḍura|*rucaṃ*,
prārabdha|jṛmbhāṃ kṣaṇād
āyāsaṃ śvasan'|ôdgamair a|viratair
ātanvatīm ātmanaḥ,
ady' ôdyāna|latām imāṃ *sa|madanāṃ*
nārīm iv' ânyāṃ dhruvaṃ
paśyan kopa|vipāṭala|dyuti mukhaṃ
devyāḥ kariṣyāmy aham. [4]

SUSÁNGATA: O you stubborn girl, what use is looking? The mynah bird must be getting far away. So come, let's follow him.

Exit the two women.

Enter the JESTER, *joyously.* 2.45

JESTER: Wow! Wow! How amazing, absolutely amazing! Bravo, pious Shri·khanda·dasa, bravo! The mere touch of the stuff that plants want immediately made the new jasmine sprout shoots gorgeous with clumps of constantly opening flowers, as if it was laughing at the *mádhavi* creeper that the queen had adopted. Let me go and congratulate my dear friend. *(walking around and looking)* Here's my dear friend coming right here. He has such confidence in that stuff that plants want that he sees the new jasmine flowering as if it were right before his eyes, even though it's out of his sight, and his own eyes seem to blossom with joy. I'll go to meet him.

Enter the KING, *as described.*

KING: *(with joy)*

Today I'll surely make the queen's face glow red
with anger,
when I regard this vine in the garden as
another woman,
on the Passion tree : full of passion,
with *luxuriant buds : sudden violent longing*
and a pale *hue : complexion*,
just beginning to *blossom : yawn*,
and revealing *the trouble caused by the ceaseless*
rising of the winds : her exhaustion with the

2.50 tad vṛtt'|ântam upalabdhuṃ gato Vasantako 'dy' âpi n' āyāti.

VIDŪṢAKAḤ: *(sahas" ôpasṛtya)* ⌜jaadu, jaadu pia|vaasso! bho vaassa, diṭṭhiā vaḍḍasi.⌟ *(«jeṇa diṇṇa|metteṇa jjeva teṇa dohaeṇa īdisī ṇomāliā saṃvutt" êty» ādi paṭhati.)*

RĀJĀ: vayasya, kaḥ saṃdehaḥ? a|cintyo hi maṇi|mantr'|âuṣadhīnāṃ prabhāvaḥ. paśya:

kaṇṭhe Śrī|puruṣ'|ôttamasya samare
 dṛṣṭvā maṇiṃ śatrubhir
naṣṭaṃ, mantra|balād vasanti vasu|dhā|
 mūle bhujaṅ|gā hatāḥ.
pūrvaṃ Lakṣmaṇa|vīra|vānara|bhaṭā
 ye Meghanād'|āhatāḥ
pītvā te 'pi mah"|âuṣadher guṇa|nidher
 gandhaṃ punar jivītāḥ. [5]

tad ādeśaya mārgaṃ, yena vayam api tad|avalokena cakṣuṣaḥ phalam anubhavāmaḥ.

2.55 VIDŪṢAKAḤ: *(s'|āṭopam)* ⌜edu, edu bhavaṃ.⌟

RĀJĀ: gacch' âgrataḥ.

ubhau sa|garvaṃ parikrāmataḥ.

*ceaseless rising of her sighs.**

But Vasántaka, who went to find out news of this, hasn't come back yet. 2.50

JESTER: *(suddenly approaching)* Victory, victory, my dear friend. Good fortune smiles on you, my friend! *(He repeats: "The mere touch of the stuff that plants want immediately made the new jasmine sprout shoots. . . ")*

KING: My friend, what doubt can there be? For the power of jewels, mantras, and herbs is beyond imagining. Look:

> When they saw the jewel on the throat of
> the best of men,
> his enemies in the battle were destroyed.
> The serpents live at the base of the earth,
> kept down by the power of mantras.
> Lákshmana and the heroic monkey soldiers
> had been struck down by Megha·nada,
> but when they drank just the perfume of the great
> herb that was an ocean of medicinal powers,
> they came back to life.*

So show me the path, so that we too can look at it, the apple of my eye.

JESTER: *(with pride)* Come, please, sir, come. 2.55

KING: Lead the way.

They walk around proudly.

VIDŪṢAKAḤ: *(ākarṇya, sa|bhayaṃ parāvṛtya,* RĀJĀNAṂ *gṛhītvā, sa|saṃbhramam)* ⌜bho vaassa, ehi, palāamha.⌟

RĀJĀ: kim artham?

2.60 VIDŪṢAKAḤ: ⌜eassiṃ vaüla|pāa|ve ko vi bhūdo paḍivasadi.⌟

RĀJĀ: dhiṅ murkha! viśrabdhaṃ gamyatām. kuta īdṛg|vidhānām atra saṃbhavaḥ?

VIDŪṢAKAḤ: ⌜bho, eso kkhu phuḍ'|akkharaṃ eva mantedi. tā jaï mama vaaṇaṃ na pattiāasi, tā aggado bhavia saaṃ evva dāva āaṇṇehi.⌟

RĀJĀ: *(tathā kṛtvā, śrutvā ca)*

spaṣṭ'|âkṣaram idaṃ yasmān
  madhuraṃ strī|sva|bhāvataḥ,
alp'|âṅgatvād a|nirhrādi,
  manye, vadati sārikā. [6]

2.65 *(ūrdhvaṃ nirūpya)* kathaṃ, sārik" âiv' êyam!

VIDŪṢAKAḤ: *(ūrdhvam avalokya)* ⌜āḥ, kathaṃ, saccaṃ evva sāriā.⌟ *(sa|roṣaṃ daṇḍa|kāṣṭham udyamya)* ⌜āḥ, dāsīe dhīe, kiṃ tue jāṇidaṃ saccaṃ jjeva Vasantao bhāadi tti? tā ciṭṭha muhuttaam, jāva imiṇā pisuṇa|jaṇa|hiaa|kuḍileṇa daṇḍa|kaṭṭheṇa paripakkaṃ via kaïttha|phalaṃ imādo baüla|pāa|vādo āhaṇia bhūmīe tumaṃ pāḍayissam.⌟ *(iti hantum udyataḥ.)*

RĀJĀ: *(nivārayan)* murkha, kim apy eṣā ramaṇīyaṃ vyāharati. tat kim enāṃ trāsayasi? śṛṇuvas tāvat.

JESTER: *(listening, turning back in fright, grabbing the* KING, *in agitation)* Oh my friend, come, let's run away.

KING: What for?

JESTER: Some ghost lives in this *bákula* tree. 2.60

KING: You idiot. Go on, and don't be afraid. How could such a thing be possible here?

JESTER: Oh! It's talking with distinct syllables. If you don't believe what I'm saying, then get in front and listen to it yourself.

KING: *(doing this, and listening)*

Because its feminine nature
makes this speech sweet, with clear syllables,
and because its body is so small that its voice
doesn't carry far,
I think it must be a mynah bird.

(looking up) Why, yes, it is indeed a mynah. 2.65

JESTER: *(looking up)* Why, it really is a mynah. *(angrily raising his cane)* You daughter of a slave girl, did you think that Vasántaka was really afraid? Just stay there for a minute, while I strike you with my cane—it's as crooked as the heart of a villain—and make you fall to the ground from this *bákula* tree like an overripe wood apple fruit. *(He gets ready to strike.)*

KING: *(restraining him)* You idiot, she's saying something charming. So why are you frightening her? Let's listen for a while.

ubhāv ākarṇayataḥ.

VIDŪṢAKAḤ: *(ākarṇya)* ⌜bho vaassa, sudaṃ tue jaṃ edāe mantidaṃ? esā bhaṇādi: «sahi, ko eso tue ettha ālihido?» «sahi, paütta|Maaṇa|mah"|ûssave bhaavaṃ Aṇaṅgo tti.» puṇo vi esā bhaṇādi: «sahi, kīsa tue ahaṃ ettha ālihidā?» «sahi, kiṃ a|āraṇaṃ kuppasi? jādiso tue Kāma|deo ālihido, tādisī mae Raï ālihid" êtti. tā aṇṇadhā|sambhāviṇi, kiṃ tue ediṇā ālavideṇa? kahehi savvaṃ vutt'|antam!» bho vaassa, kiṃ ṇṇedam?⌟

2.70 RĀJĀ: vayasy' âivaṃ tarkayāmi: kay" âpi hṛdaya|vallabho 'nurāgād ālikhya Kāma|deva|vyapadeśena sakhī purato 'pahnutaḥ. tat sakhy" âpi pratyabhijñāya vaidagdhyād asāv api tatr' âiva Rati|vyapadeśen' ālikhit" êti.

VIDŪṢAKAḤ: *(choṭikāṃ dattvā)* ⌜bho vaassa, jujjadi. evvaṃ kkhu edaṃ.⌟

RĀJĀ: vayasya, tūṣṇīṃ bhava. punar apy eṣā vyāharati.

VIDŪṢAKAḤ: ⌜bho, esā bhaṇādi: «sahi, mā lajja. īdisassa kaṇṇā|raaṇassa avassaṃ evva īdise vare ahilāseṇa hodavvam.» bho vaassa, jā esā ālihidā, sā kkhu kaṇṇā daṃsaṇīā.⌟

RĀJĀ: yadi evam, avahitau śṛṇuvas tāvat. asty atr' âvakāśo naḥ kutūhalasya. *(ity ubhāv ākarṇayataḥ.)*

They listen.

JESTER: *(listening)* My friend, did you hear what she said? She says: "My friend, who is this that you have drawn?" "My friend, it's the bodiless god in the festival of love that has just begun." Then she says, "My friend, why have you drawn me?" "My friend, why are you angry for no reason? I've drawn Rati, too, just as you painted Kama. So why are you babbling about something that you imagine to be other than it is? Now, tell me the whole story." My friend, what's all this?

KING: My friend, this is what I deduce. Some woman 2.70
sketched the darling of her heart, because she was in love with him, and then passed him off in front of her friend under the pretext that it was the god Kama. But that friend was worldly enough to see through this trick and sketched her, too, in that picture, under the pretext of Rati.

JESTER: *(snapping his fingers)* My friend, that sounds right. That must be it.

KING: My friend, be quiet. She's speaking again.

JESTER: She's saying: "My friend, don't be ashamed. Such a jewel of a girl must, inevitably, long for such a groom." My friend, the young girl who is sketched must be worth looking at.

KING: If so, let's listen carefully. This is a good opportunity for our curiosity. *(They listen.)*

2.75 VIDŪṢAKAḤ: ⌜bho vaassa, sudaṃ tue jaṃ edāe mantidam? «sahi, avaṇehi imāiṃ ṇaliṇī|vattāiṃ muṇāla|valaāiṃ a. alaṃ ediṇā. kīsa a|āraṇe attāṇaṃ āāsesi?»⌟

RĀJĀ: vayasya, na kevalaṃ śrutam, abhiprāyo 'pi lakṣitaḥ.

VIDŪṢAKAḤ: ⌜bho, mā tumaṃ paṇḍiavva|gavvaṃ uvvaha. ahaṃ de edāe muhādo suṇia savvaṃ vakkhāṇaïssam. tā suṇamha. ajja vi kurakurāadi evva esā sāriā dāsīe dhīā.⌟

RĀJĀ: yuktam abhihitam. *(punar ākarṇayataḥ.)*

VIDŪṢAKAḤ: ⌜bho vaassa, esā kkhu sārikā dāsīe duhidā catuv|vedī bamhaṇo via ricāiṃ paṭhiduṃ pavuttā.⌟

2.80 RĀJĀ: vayasya, kathaya, kim apy anya cetasyā mayā n' âvadhāritaṃ kim anay" ôktam iti.

VIDŪṢAKAḤ: ⌜bho, edaṃ edāe paḍhidaṃ:⌟

⌜dul|laha|jaṇ'|âṇurāo,
   lajjā guruī, para|vvaso appā—
pia|sahi, vi|samaṃ pemmaṃ,
   maraṇaṃ saraṇaṃ na varam ekkam?⌟ [7]

RĀJĀ: *(sa|smitam)* sādhu bhavantaṃ! mahā|brāhmaṇaṃ muktvā ko 'nya evam ṛcām abhijñaḥ?

VIDŪṢAKAḤ: ⌜tado kiṃ ṇu kkhu edam?⌟

JESTER: My friend, did you hear what she said? "My friend, 2.75
take away these lotus leaves and lotus stalks. I've had enough of them. Why do you go to such trouble for nothing?"

KING: My friend, not only have I heard, I've also noted the implications.

JESTER: Don't show off your pride in interpretation. When I've heard it all from her mouth, I'll analyze it all for you. So let's listen. This daughter of a slave mynah is jabbering even now.

KING: Rightly said. *(They listen again.)*

JESTER: My friend, this mynah, daughter of a slave girl, is beginning to chant Rig Veda verses as if she were a Brahmin who knows all four Vedas.

KING: Tell me, my friend. My mind wandered a bit to 2.80
something else and I didn't catch it. What did she say?

JESTER: This is what she recited:

> I love someone out of reach,
> shyness weighs me down,
> I'm in the power of someone else—
> my friend, this love is unequal,
> and death is the only and the best refuge.

KING: *(smiling)* Bravo! Who other than some big-shot Brahmin like you would be familiar with Rig Vedic verses like those?

JESTER: All right, then, what is it?

2.85 RĀJĀ: nanu gāth" êyam.

VIDŪṢAKAḤ: ⌜kiṃ gāthā?⌟

RĀJĀ: kay" âpi ślāghya|yauvanayā priyatamam an|āsādayantyā jīvita|nirapekṣay" ôktam.

VIDŪṢAKAḤ: *(uccair vihasya)* ⌜bho, kiṃ edehiṃ vakka|bhaṇidehiṃ? ujju evva kiṃ ṇa bhaṇāsi jahā: «maṃ aṇ|āsādayantīe tti.» aṇṇahā ko aṇṇo Kusuma|cāva|vvavadeseṇa evaṃ ṇiṇhavīadi?⌟ *(hasta|tālaṃ dattv" ôccair vihasati.)*

RĀJĀ: *(ūrdhvam avalokya)* dhiṅ mūrkha! kim uccair hasatā tvay" êyam uttrāsitā, yen' ôḍḍīy' ânyatra kv' âpi gatā.

2.90 *ubhau nirūpayataḥ.*

VIDŪṢAKAḤ: *(vilokya)* ⌜bho, esā kkhu kaalī|gharaṃ evva gadā. tā ehi, lahuṃ aṇusaramha.⌟

RĀJĀ:

dur|vārāṃ kusuma|śara|vyathāṃ vahantyā
kāminyā yad abhihitaṃ puraḥ sakhīnām,
tad bhūyaḥ śiśu|śuka|sārikābhir uktaṃ
dhanyānām śravaṇa|path'|âtithitvam eti. [8]

VIDŪṢAKAḤ: ⌜edu, edu bhavaṃ.⌟ *(parikrāmataḥ.)* ⌜bho, edaṃ kkhu kaalī|gharaaṃ. jāva pavisamha.⌟

2.95 *ubhau praviśataḥ.*

KING: It's a song.

JESTER: A song?

KING: Yes, and recited by some woman in the pride of her youth who has failed to win the man she loves most and does not value her life.

JESTER: *(laughing loudly)* What's the use of these words that twist and turn back? Why don't you talk straight and say that she means, "who has failed to win *me*"? For who else would have been passed off as the god with the flower bow? *(He claps his hands and laughs loudly.)*

KING: *(looking up)* Shut up, you fool. You've laughed so loudly that you've frightened the bird and she's taken flight and gone somewhere else.

They look around.

JESTER: *(looking about)* Oh, she's gone to the banana bower. So come, let's follow, quickly.

KING:

> When a woman in love, suffering the irresistible
> anguish of the flower arrows,
> says something in front of her woman friends,
> and children, parrots, or mynah birds repeat it,
> fortunate are the people whose ears it visits.

JESTER: Come, please, sir, come. *(They walk around.)* Here's the banana bower. Let's go in.

They go inside.

VIDŪṢAKAḤ: ⌜bho, gadā dāsīe dhīā. ettha dāva manda|mārud'|uvvellanta|bāla|kaalī|dala|sīdale silā|tale upavisia muhuttaaṃ vīsamha.⌟

RĀJĀ: yad abhirucitaṃ bhavate.

ity upaviśantaḥ.

RĀJĀ: *(niḥśvasya, «durvārām ity» ādi punaḥ paṭhati.)*

2.100 VIDŪṢAKAḤ: *(pārśvato 'valokya)* ⌜bho! edeṇa kkhu ugghāḍia|duvāreṇa tāe sāriāe pañjareṇa hodavvam. eso vi so citta|phalao. jāva ṇaṃ geṇhāmi.⌟ *(phalakaṃ gṛhītvā, nirūpya ca, sa|harṣam)* ⌜bho vaassa, diṭṭhiā vaḍḍhasi!⌟

RĀJĀ: *(sa|kautukam)* vayasya, kiṃ etat?

VIDŪṢAKAḤ: ⌜bho, edaṃ kkhu taṃ, jaṃ mae bhaṇidam: «tumaṃ jjeva ettha ālihido. ko aṇṇo kusuma|cāva|vvavadeseṇa ṇihṇīadi tti?»⌟

RĀJĀ: *(sa|harṣaṃ hastau prasārya)* sakhe, darśaya, darśaya.

VIDŪṢAKAḤ: ⌜ṇa de daṃsaïssaṃ. sā vi kaṇṇaā ettha jjeva ālihidā ciṭṭhadi. tā kiṃ pāritosieṇa viṇā īdisaṃ kaṇṇā|raaṇaṃ daṃsīadi?⌟

2.105 RĀJĀ: *(kaṭakam arpayann eva balād gṛhītvā, vilokya, sa|vismayam)*

līl"|âvadhūta|padmā,
  kathayantī *pakṣa|pātam* adhikaṃ naḥ,
mānasam upaiti: k" êyaṃ
  citra|gatā rāja|haṃs" îva? [9]

JESTER: That daughter of a slave girl has gone. Let's rest for a moment, sitting on this stone bench that's been cooled by the young banana leaves waving in the gentle wind.

KING: As you like.

They sit.

KING: *(sighing, repeats the verse: "When a woman in love. . . ")*

JESTER: *(looking to the side)* This must be the mynah bird's 2.100
cage, with its door busted open. And this is the painting board. I'll take it. *(taking the painting board, and inspecting it, with joy)* Oh, my friend! Good fortune smiles on you!

KING: *(with curiosity)* What's that, my friend?

JESTER: It's just as I told you. *You* yourself are sketched here. For who else would have been passed off as the god with the flower bow?

KING: *(reaching out his hands with joy)* Show me! Show me!

JESTER: I will not show you. The girl herself is also sketched here. Why should I show this gem of a woman without getting a reward?

KING: *(taking it by force while giving him his golden bracelet,* 2.105
looking at it with amazement)

> Who is this, *painted in a picture* ⁝
> *with a graceful gait* like a swan,
> who has *captivated my heart* ⁝
> *flown off to Lake Mánasa,*
> who *puts Lakshmi to shame with her grace* ⁝
> *shakes down lotuses in her play,*

api ca,

vidhāy' â|pūrva|pūrṇ'|êndum
asyā mukham, abhūd dhruvam
dhātā nij'|āsan'|âmbho|ja|
vinimīlana|duḥ|sthitaḥ. [10]

tataḥ praviśati SĀGARIKĀ SUSAṂGATĀ *ca.*

2.110 SUSAṂGATĀ: ⌈sahi, ṇa samāsādidā amhehiṃ sāriā. tā citta|phalaaṃ pi dāva imādo kadalī|gharādo geṇhia lahuṃ āgacchamha.⌋

SĀGARIKĀ: ⌈sahi, evaṃ karemha.⌋

ubhe parikrāmataḥ.

VIDŪṢAKAḤ: ⌈bho vaassa, kīsa uṇa esā avaṇada|muhī ālihidā?⌋

SUSAṂGATĀ: *(ākarṇya)* ⌈sahi, jahā Vasantao mantedi, tahā takkemi bhaṭṭiṇā vi ettha jjeva hodavvam. tā kadalī|gumm|antaridāo bhavia pekkhamha dāva.⌋

2.115 *ubhe paśyataḥ.*

RĀJĀ: vayasya, paśya paśya. *(«vidhāy' â/pūrva/pūrṇ'/êndum ity» ādi punaḥ paṭhati.)*

SUSAṂGATĀ: ⌈sahi, diṭṭhiā vaḍḍhasi! eso de hiaa|vallaho tumaṃ jjevva ṇivaṇṇaanto ciṭṭhadi.⌋

SĀGARIKĀ: *(sa/lajjam)* ⌈kīsa parihāsa|sīladāe imaṃ jaṇaṃ lahuṃ karesi?⌋

and shows her great *partiality : beating of wings*
to us.*

And

When the creator had set the moon, like none
before, firmly in her face,
he became unsettled, because the lotuses that were
his own seat closed.*

Enter SÁGARIKA *and* SUSÁNGATA.

SUSÁNGATA: My friend, we haven't caught the mynah. So 2.110
let's at least get the painting board from this banana bower and get out of here fast.

SÁGARIKA: Let's do that, my friend.

They walk around.

JESTER: My friend, why is this girl painted with her face downcast?

SUSÁNGATA: *(hearing)* Since the jester is talking, my friend, I deduce that the king must also be here. So let's conceal ourselves inside the banana bower and watch.

They watch. 2.115

KING: Look, my friend, look! *(He recites the verse again: "When the creator had set. . .")*

SUSÁNGATA: My friend, good fortune smiles on you! This darling of your heart stands staring at *you.*

SÁGARIKA: *(embarrassed)* Why do you make light of this person just because you're so fond of teasing?*

VIDŪṢAKAḤ: *(RĀJĀNAṂ cālayitvā)* ⌜ṇaṃ bhaṇāmi: kīsa esā avaṇada|muhī ālihid" êtti?⌟

2.120 RĀJĀ: nanu sārikay" âiva sakalam āveditam.

SUSAṂGATĀ: ⌜sahi, daṃsidaṃ kkhu Mehāviṇīe attaṇo mehāvittaṇam.⌟

VIDŪṢAKAḤ: ⌜bho vaassa, avi suhāadi de loaṇam?⌟

SĀGARIKĀ: *(sa|sādhvasam, ātma|gatam)* ⌜kiṃ eso bhaṇissadi tti jaṃ saccaṃ jīvida|maraṇāṇaṃ antare vaṭṭhāmi.⌟

RĀJĀ: sukhayat' îti kim ucyate? paśya:

2.125 kṛcchrād ūru|yugaṃ vyatītya, su|ciraṃ
bhrāntvā nitamba|sthale,
madhye 'syās tri|valī|taraṅga|viṣame
nispandatām āgatā
mad|dṛṣṭis tṛṣit" êva saṃprati śanair
āruhya tuṅgau stanau,
s'|ākāṅkṣaṃ muhur īkṣate jala|lava|
prasyandinī locane. [11]

SUSAṂGATĀ: ⌜sahi, sudaṃ tue.⌟

SĀGARIKĀ: *(vihasya)* ⌜tumaṃ evva suṇu, jāe āleha|viṇṇāṇaṃ evaṃ vaṇṇīadi.⌟

VIDŪṢAKAḤ: ⌜bho vaassa, jassa uṇa īdisīo vi evaṃ samāgamaṃ bahu maṇṇanti, tassa vi attaṇo uvari ko parāhavo, jeṇa ettha evva tāe ālihidaṃ attāṇaaṃ ṇa pekkhasi?⌟

JESTER: *(shaking the* KING*)* Hey! I'm talking. Why is this girl painted with her face downcast?

KING: Why, it was the mynah who explained all of this. 2.120

SUSÁNGATA: My friend, the Ace Reporter reported like an ace.

JESTER: My friend, does this delight your eye?

SÁGARIKA: *(to herself, anxiously)* What will he say? I wonder, and truly I stand between life and death.

KING: How can you ask, "Does it delight?" See:

> My gaze, as if thirsty, passed beyond her pair of thighs with difficulty, 2.125
> and wandered for a long time over her broad hips,
> coming to a stop in her midsection,
> a bumpy ride because of the waves of the triple folds.
> Now it has gently climbed the peaks of her breasts
> and looks again and again with desire
> at her eyes, which are shedding drops of water.*

SUSÁNGATA: My friend, did you hear that?

SÁGARIKA: *(laughing)* You're the one who should hear, since it's your skill in drawing that's being described in this way.

JESTER: My friend, when women like this think highly of getting together with you, how can you have so little self-esteem that you don't see that this woman has sketched you right here?

RĀJĀ: *(nirvarṇya)* vayasya! anayā likhito 'ham iti yat satyaṃ, mam' ātmany eva bahu|mānas tat kathaṃ na paśyāmi? paśya:

2.130 bhāti patito likhantyās
tasyā bāṣp'|âmbu|śīkara|kaṇ'|âughaḥ,
sved'|ôdgama iva kara|tala|
saṃsparśād eṣa me vapuṣi. [12]

SĀGARIKĀ: *(ātma|gatam)* ⌜hiaa, samassasa samassasa. maṇo|ratho vi de ettiaṃ bhūmiṃ ṇa gado.⌟

SUSAṂGATĀ: ⌜sahi, tumaṃ evva ekā salāhaṇīā, jāe bhaṭṭā vi evaṃ mantīadi.⌟

VIDŪṢAKAḤ: *(pārśvato 'valokya)* ⌜bho vaassa, edaṃ sa|rasa|kamalinī|dala|muṇāla|viraïdaṃ tāe evva maaṇ'|âvatthā|sūaaṃ saaṇīaṃ lakkhīadi.⌟

RĀJĀ: vayasya, nipuṇam upalakṣitam. tathā hi:

2.135 parimlānaṃ pīna|
stana|jaghana|saṅgād ubhayatas
tanor madhyasy' ântaḥ
parimilanam a|prāpya haritam,
idaṃ vyasta|nyāsaṃ
ślatha|bhuja|lat"|ākṣepa|valanaiḥ
kṛś'|âṅgyāḥ saṃtāpaṃ
vadati nalinī|patra|śayanam. [13]

KING: *(looking carefully)* My friend, if it's true that she has sketched me, then I would certainly think highly of myself. And how could I not see it? See:

> The flood of spraying tear-drops 2.130
> that fell from her as she sketched
> seems like sweat breaking out on my body
> from the touch of the palm of her hand.

SÁGARIKA: *(to herself)* Courage, my heart, courage. Even your wildest wish could not reach such a place.

SUSÁNGATA: My friend, you alone are the one who should be praised, since the king is talking like this about you.

JESTER: *(looking to the side)* My friend, this bed seems to be a sign of her love-sickness, for it's made of lotus stalks and juicy lotus petals.

KING: Cleverly observed, my friend. For:

> This bed made of lotus leaves tells of the heat 2.135
> of her slender body,
> since it's badly parched on both sides
> from the contact with her full breasts and buttocks,
> but still green in the innermost part
> where it didn't touch her slender waist,
> and it's in disarray because of the tossing
> and turnings
> of her limp, vine-like arms.

api ca,

sthitam urasi viśālaṃ padminī|patram etat
kathayati na tath" ântar manmath'|ôtthāṃ avasthām
ati|guru|paritāpa|mlāpitābhyāṃ yath" âsyāḥ
stana|yuga|pariṇāhaṃ maṇḍalābhyāṃ bravīti. [14]

VIDŪṢAKAḤ: *(nāṭyena mṛṇālikāṃ gṛhītvā)* ⌜bho vaassa, aaṃ avaro tāe evva pīṇa|tthaṇ'|umhā|kilisanta|komala|muṇā-la|hāro. tā pekkhadu bhavaṃ.⌟

RĀJĀ: *(gṛhītv" ôrasi vinyasya)* ayi, jaḍa|prakṛte,

2.140 paricyutas tat|kuca|kumbha|madhyāt
kiṃ śoṣam āyāsi, mṛṇāla|hāra?
na sūkṣma|tantor api tāvakasya
tatr' âvakāśo, bhavataḥ kim u syāt? [15]

SUSAṂGATĀ: *(sva|gatam)* ⌜ha ddhī! ha ddhī! guru'|âṇurā'|ôk-khita|hiao bhaṭṭā a|saṃbaddhaṃ pi manteduṃ paütto. tā ṇa juttaṃ ado varaṃ uvekkhidum. bhodu. evvaṃ dā-va.⌟ *(prakāśam)* ⌜sahi, jassa kide tumaṃ āgadā, so aaṃ te purado ciṭṭhadi.⌟

SĀGARIKĀ: *(s'|âsūyam)* ⌜Susaṃgade, kassa kide ahaṃ ettha āgadā?⌟

SUSAṂGATĀ: *(vihasya)* ⌜aï aṇṇa|saṅkide, ṇaṃ citta|phalaassa. tā geṇha edam.⌟

And:

This large lotus leaf that was on her chest,
with two circles parched by intense heat,
speaks not so much of the state of the rising desire
within her,
as of the circumferences of her breasts.

JESTER: *(miming picking up a lotus shoot)* My friend, here's another necklace of tender lotus stalks withered by the steam from her large breasts. Sir, look at it!

KING: *(taking it and placing it on his chest)* You are numb by nature,

necklace of lotus filaments, so why did you wither 2.140
when you fell from between her breasts that are
like pitchers?
There's not even enough space there for a thin
thread of you,
so how could there be room for all of you?

SUSÁNGATA: *(to herself)* Oh dear, oh dear. His heart is so carried away by his heavy love for her that the king has even begun to speak incoherently. It wouldn't be right to go on ignoring him after this. All right. Let's try this. *(aloud)* My friend, the one that you came here for is right there in front of you.

SÁGARIKA: *(with irritation)* Susángata, for whom did I come here?

SUSÁNGATA: *(laughing)* You keep imagining that things are other than they are. You came for the painting board. So take it.

SĀGARIKĀ: *(sa|roṣam)* ⌜a|usala mhi tuha īdisāṇāṃ ālāvāṇāṃ. tā aṇṇado gamissam.⌟ *(iti gantum icchati.)*

2.145 SUSAṂGATĀ: (SĀGARIKĀṂ *haste gṛhītvā)* ⌜aï a|sahaṇe, iha ciṭṭha dāva muhuttaaṃ, jāva imādo kadalī|gharādo citta|phalahaṃ geṇhia āacchāmi.⌟

SĀGARIKĀ: ⌜sahi, evvaṃ karehi.⌟

SUSAṂGATĀ *kadalī|gṛh'|āmukhaṃ parikrāmati.*

VIDŪṢAKAḤ: (SUSAṂGATĀṂ *dṛṣṭvā, sa|saṃbhramam)* ⌜bho vaassa, pacchādehi edaṃ citta|phalaaṃ. esā kkhu devīe paricāriā Susaṃgadā āgadā.⌟

RĀJĀ *paṭ'|ântena phalakaṃ pracchādayati.*

2.150 SUSAṂGATĀ: *(apasṛtya)* ⌜jaadu, jaadu bhaṭṭā!⌟

RĀJĀ: Susaṃgate, sv|āgatam. ih' ôpaviśyatām.

SUSAṂGAT" *ôpaviśati.*

RĀJĀ: Susaṃgate, katham aham iha|stho bhavatyā jñātaḥ?

SUSAṂGATĀ: *(vihasya)* ⌜bhaṭṭā, ṇa kevalaṃ tumaṃ, aaṃ pi citta|phalaeṇa saha savvo vutt'|anto mae viṇṇādo. tā gadua devīe ṇivedaïssaṃ.⌟

2.155 VIDŪṢAKAḤ: *(apavārya, sa|bhayam)* ⌜bho vaassa, savvaṃ saṃbhāvīadi. muharā kkhu esā gabbha|dāsī. tā pāritosieṇa saṃpīṇehi ṇaṃ.⌟

SÁGARIKA: *(angrily)* I'm not clever enough for this sort of banter of yours. I'll go somewhere else. *(She starts to go.)*

SUSÁNGATA: *(grabbing* SÁGARIKA *by the hand)* Oh, you impa- 2.145
tient girl, stay here for a moment while I get the painting board from this banana bower and come back.

SÁGARIKA: All right, my friend.

SUSÁNGATA *walks around toward the banana bower.*

JESTER: *(seeing* SUSÁNGATA, *in haste and confusion)* Oh, my friend! Hide the painting board. Here comes the queen's lady-in-waiting, Susángata.

The KING *hides the board with the end of his shirt.*

SUSÁNGATA: *(approaching)* Victory, victory to the king. 2.150

KING: Welcome, Susángata. Please sit here.

SUSÁNGATA *sits.*

KING: Susángata, how did you know that I was here?

SUSÁNGATA: *(laughing)* Your majesty, I knew not just about you, but about him and the whole affair with the painting board. And now I'm going to go and report to the queen.

JESTER: *(aside, with fear)* My friend, all of this could happen. 2.155
This girl, born to be a slave girl, is a blabbermouth. Bribe her with a present.

RĀJĀ: yuktam uktaṃ bhavatā. (SUSAṂGATĀṂ *haste gṛhītvā)* Susaṃgate, krīḍā|mātram ev' âitat. a|kāraṇe tvayā devī na khedayitavyā. idaṃ te paritoṣikam. *(karṇ'|ābharaṇaṃ prayacchati.)*

SUSAṂGATĀ: *(praṇamya, sa|smitam)* ⌜bhaṭṭā, alaṃ saṅkāe. mae vi bhaṭṭiṇo pasāeṇa kīlidaṃ evva. tā kiṃ kaṇṇ'|ābharaṇeṇa? eso jjeva me guruo pasāo jaṃ «kīsa tue ahaṃ ettha citta|phalae ālihida tti?» kuvidā me pia|sahī Sāariā. tā gadua pasādedu ṇaṃ bhaṭṭā.⌟

RĀJĀ: *(sa|saṃbhramam utthāya)* kv' âsau, kv' âsau?

SUSAṂGATĀ: ⌜ido, ido bhaṭṭā.⌟

2.160 VIDŪṢAKAḤ: ⌜bho, geṇhāmi edaṃ citta|phalam. kadā vi puṇo vi ediṇā kajjaṃ bhavissadi.⌟

SUSAṂGATĀ: ⌜bhaṭṭā! iaṃ sā.⌟

sarve kadalī|gṛhān niṣkrāmanti.

SĀGARIKĀ: (RĀJĀNAṂ *dṛṣṭvā, sa|harṣaṃ, sa|sādhvasaṃ sa|kampaṃ ca, sva|gatam)* ⌜ha ddhī! ha ddhī! edaṃ pekkhia ati|saddhaseṇa na sakkaṇomi padādo padaṃ vi gantum. tā kiṃ dāṇiṃ ettha karissam?⌟

VIDŪṢAKAḤ: (SĀGARIKĀṂ *dṛṣṭvā)* ⌜hī hī, bhoḥ! accariaṃ, accariaṃ! īdisaṃ rūvaṃ māṇusa|loe ṇa puṇo dīsadi. tā takkemi Paāvaïṇo vi edaṃ ṇimmāvia vimhao samuppaṇṇo tti.⌟

2.165 RĀJĀ: vayasya, mam' âpy evaṃ manasi vartate.

KING: Right you are. *(taking* SUSÁNGATA *by the hand)* Susángata, this was just a joke. You shouldn't trouble the queen for nothing. Here is a present for you. *(He gives her an ear ornament.)*

SUSÁNGATA: *(bowing with a smile)* Don't worry, your majesty. I too was joking, with your majesty's indulgence. So there's no need for the ear ornament. But you could do me this great favor. My dear friend Ságarika got angry with me and said, "Why did you draw me on this painting board?" So please, your majesty, go and appease her.

KING: *(quickly standing up)* Where is she, where is she?

SUSÁNGATA: This way please, your majesty, this way.

JESTER: You know, I'll take this picture board along. There 2.160
may still be some use for it again sometime.

SUSÁNGATA: Here she is, your majesty.

They all come out of the banana bower.

SÁGARIKA: *(seeing the* KING, *with joy, trembling and nervous, to herself)* Oh dear, oh dear! When I see him I'm so overanxious that I can't take one step after another. What can I do about this now?

JESTER: *(seeing* SÁGARIKA*)* Wow! Wow! How amazing, absolutely amazing! Such beauty can't be seen anywhere else in the mortal world. I bet even the Creator was struck with astonishment when he made this!

KING: My friend, the same thought was in my mind. 2.165

dṛśaḥ pṛthutarī|kṛtā
jita|nij'|âb|ja|patra|tviṣaś,
caturbhir api «sādhu sādhv»
iti mukhaiḥ samaṃ vyāhṛtam,
śirāṃsi calitāni vis-
maya|vaśād dhruvaṃ vedhasā
vidhāya lalanāṃ jagat|
traya|lalāma|bhūtām imām. [16]

SĀGARIKĀ: *(s'|âsūyaṃ* SUSAṂGATĀM *ālokya)* ⌜sahi, īdiso citta|phalao tue āṇīdo.⌟ *(iti gacchati.)*

RĀJĀ:

dṛṣṭiṃ ruṣā kṣipasi, bhāmini, yady ap' îmāṃ,
snigdh" êyam eṣyati tath" âpi na rūkṣa|bhāvam.
tyaktvā tvarāṃ vraja, pada|skhalitair ayaṃ te
khedaṃ kariṣyati gurur nitarāṃ nitambaḥ. [17]

2.170 SUSAṂGATĀ: ⌜bhaṭṭā, adi|kovaṇā kkhu esā. tā hatthe geṇhia pasādehi ṇam.⌟

RĀJĀ: *(s'|ānandam)* yath" āha bhavatī. (SĀGARIKĀṂ *haste gṛhītvā, sparśa|sukhaṃ nāṭayati.)*

VIDŪṢAKAḤ: ⌜bho, esā kkhu tue a|puvvā Siri samāsādidā.⌟

RĀJĀ: vayasya, satyam.

Surely when the Creator made this woman,
the ornament of the triple world,
he was so amazed that his eyes,
whose lustre surpassed even that of the petals
  of his own lotus,
grew even wider; and his four mouths cried,
  "Bravo! Bravo!"
all together, in chorus,
and all his heads nodded in assent.*

SÁGARIKA: *(looking at* SUSÁNGATA *with irritation)* That's quite a painting board you brought, my friend. *(She moves away.)*

KING:

Even though you cast this glance in fury,
  angry woman,
it's so affectionate that it can't become harsh.
Go, but forget your haste, for your heavy hips
will make your feet stumble
and exhaust you entirely.

SUSÁNGATA: Your majesty, she gets awfully angry. But take her hand and appease her. 2.170

KING: *(ecstatically)* Whatever you say, ma'am. *(Taking* SÁGARIKA *by the hand, he mimes his pleasure in her touch.)*

JESTER: So, you've won this Goddess of Fortune, like none before.

KING: That's the truth, my friend.

Śrīr eṣā, pāṇir apy asyāḥ
 pārijātasya pallavaḥ.
kato 'nyathā sravaty eṣa
 sveda|cchadm'|âmṛta|dravaḥ? [18]

2.175 SUSAṂGATĀ: ⌜sahi, adi|niṣṭhurā dāṇiṃ si tumaṃ, jā evaṃ bhaṭṭiṇā hatthe gihīdā vi kovaṃ ṇa muñcasi.⌟

SĀGARIKĀ: *(sa/bhrū/bhaṅgam)* ⌜aï Susaṃgade, ajja vi ṇa viramesi?⌟

RĀJĀ: ayi, prasīda! na khalu yuktaḥ sakhī|jana evaṃ|vidhaḥ kop'|ânubandhaḥ.

VIDŪṢAKAḤ: ⌜esā kkhu avarā devī Vāsavadattā.⌟

RĀJĀ *sa/cakitaṃ* SĀGARIKĀYĀ *hastaṃ muñcati.*

2.180 SĀGARIKĀ: *(sa/saṃbhramam)* ⌜Susaṃgade, kiṃ dāṇiṃ ettha karissam?⌟

SUSAṂGATĀ: ⌜sahi, edaṃ tamāla|vīthiaṃ antaria ṇikkamamha.⌟

niṣkrānte.

RĀJĀ: *(pārśvato 'valokya)* vayasya, kva sā devī Vāsavadattā?

VIDŪṢAKAḤ: ⌜bho! ṇa jāṇāmi kva sā. mae «esā kkhu avarā devī Vāsavadattā adi|dīha|rosadāe ti» bhaṇidaṃ.⌟

2.185 RĀJĀ: dhiṅ mūrkha!

This is the Goddess of Fortune,
and her hand is a branch of the tree of paradise.
How else could this ambrosia be flowing,
pretending to be sweat?*

SUSÁNGATA: My friend, you're too hard-hearted, not to let 2.175
go of your anger even when the king is holding your hand.

SÁGARIKA: *(frowning)* For goodness sake, Susángata, won't you stop even now?

KING: Oh, do relent! It's not right to hold on to such anger toward a friend.

JESTER: Here is Queen Vásava·datta all over again.*

The KING *nervously lets go of* SÁGARIKA*'s hand.*

SÁGARIKA: *(in agitation)* Susángata, what do I do about this 2.180
now?

SUSÁNGATA: My friend, let's get out of here, screening ourselves behind this alley of dark *tamála* trees.

Exit the two women.

KING: *(looking to the side)* My friend, where is Queen Vásava·datta?

JESTER: Goodness, I don't know where she is. I just said, "Here is Queen Vásava·datta, all over again—because she's staying angry for so long."

KING: Damn it, you idiot! 2.185

prāptā katham api daivāt
kaṇṭham *a|nīt"* âiva sā prakaṭa|*rāgā*
ratnāval" îva kāntā
mama hastād bhraṃśitā bhavatā. [19]

tataḥ praviśati VĀSAVADATTĀ KĀÑCANAMĀLĀ *ca.*

VĀSAVADATTĀ: ⌈hañje Kañcaṇamāle, adha kettia dūre dāṇiṃ sā ajja|utteṇa parigihīdā ṇomāliā?⌋

KĀÑCANAMĀLĀ: ⌈bhaṭṭiṇi, edaṃ kadalī|gharaaṃ adikkamia dīsadi evva.⌋

2.190 VĀSAVADATTĀ: ⌈tā ādesehi maggam.⌋

KĀÑCANAMĀLĀ: ⌈edu, edu bhaṭṭiṇī.⌋

RĀJĀ: vayasya, kv' êdānīṃ priyā draṣṭavyā?

KĀÑCANAMĀLĀ: ⌈bhaṭṭiṇi, jahā samīve bhaṭṭā mantedi, taha takkemi bhaṭṭiṇīṃ evva paḍivālaanto ciṭṭhadi tti. tā uvasappadu bhaṭṭiṇī.⌋

VĀSAVADATTĀ: *(upasṛtya)* ⌈jaadu, jaadu ajja|utto!⌋

2.195 RĀJĀ: *(apavārya)* vayasya, pracchādaya citra|phalakam.

VIDŪṢAKAḤ *kakṣāyāṃ phalakaṃ prakṣipy' ôttarīyeṇa pracchādayati.*

VĀSAVADATTĀ: ⌈ajja|utta, aha kusumidā ṇomāliā?⌋

> Somehow, by chance, I found my beloved
> *Ratnávali : like a jeweled necklace*,
> revealing her *passion : brilliance*
> but not yet *embracing : placed around* my neck,
> and you made her fall out of my hands.*

Enter VÁSAVA·DATTA, *with* KÁNCHANA·MALA.

VÁSAVA·DATTA: Kánchana·mala, how far is it now to the new jasmine that my husband married?

KÁNCHANA·MALA: Your highness, you'll see it as soon as we pass this banana bower.

VÁSAVA·DATTA: Then show me the path. 2.190

KÁNCHANA·MALA: Come, please, ma'am, come.

KING: My friend, where can I see my dear one now?

KÁNCHANA·MALA: Your highness, since the king is talking nearby, I think he must be waiting for your highness. Your highness should go to him.

VÁSAVA·DATTA: *(approaching)* Victory, victory to my husband!

KING: *(aside)* My friend, hide the painting board. 2.195

The JESTER *throws the painting board under his arm and hides it with his shirt.*

VÁSAVA·DATTA: My husband, has the new jasmine flowered?

RĀJĀ: devi, prathamam ih' āgatair apy asmābhis tvaṃ cira-yas' îti n' âiva dṛṣṭā. tad ehi. sahitāv eva tāṃ paśyāvaḥ.

VĀSAVADATTĀ: *(nirvarṇya)* ⌜ajja|utta, muha|rāgādo evva mae jāṇidaṃ jahā kusumidā ṇomāliā tti. tā ṇa gamissam.⌟

2.200 VIDŪṢAKAḤ: ⌜hī hī, bho! jidaṃ, jidaṃ amhehiṃ.⌟

iti bāhū prasārya nṛtyati. nṛtyataḥ kakṣ"|ântarāt phalakaḥ patati. RĀJ" *âpavārya* VIDŪṢAKAM *aṅgulyā tarjayati.*

VIDŪṢAKAḤ: *(apavārya)* ⌜bho, mā kuppa. tūṇhīo ciṭṭha. ahaṃ evva ettha jāṇissam.⌟

KĀÑCANAMĀLĀ: *(phalakaṃ gṛhītvā, nirūpy' âpavārya)* ⌜bhaṭ-ṭiṇi, pekkha dāva kim ettha citta|phalae ālihidaṃ.⌟

VĀSAVADATTĀ: *(nirūpy' âpavārya)* ⌜Kañcaṇamāle, aaṃ ajja|utto. iaṃ uṇa Sāariā. kiṃ ṇṇedam?⌟

2.205 KĀÑCANAMĀLĀ: ⌜bhaṭṭiṇi, ahaṃ pi edaṃ evva cintemi.⌟

VĀSAVADATTĀ: *(sa|kopa|hāsam)* ⌜ajja|utta, keṇa edaṃ ālihi-dam?⌟

RĀJĀ: *(sa|vailakṣya|smitam, apavārya)* vayasya, kiṃ bravīmi?

VIDŪṢAKAḤ: *(apavārya)* ⌜bho, mā cintehi. ahaṃ uttaraṃ dāissam.⌟ *(prakāśaṃ,* VĀSAVADATTĀṂ *prati)* ⌜bhodi, mā aṇ-ṇathā saṃbhāvehi. «appā kila dukkheṇa ālihīadi tti» mama vaaṇaṃ suṇia pia|vaasseṇa edaṃ ālekkha|viṇṇāṇaṃ daṃsidam.⌟

KING: My queen, although we got here first, we didn't see it, thinking that you were delayed. So let's go together to see it, the two of us.

VÁSAVA·DATTA: *(looking closely at him)* My husband, from the fact that your face is flushed I know that the new jasmine has flowered. So I will not go.

JESTER: Hurrah, hurrah, we've won, we've won! 2.200

As he says this, he stretches out his two arms and dances, and as he dances, the painting board falls from under his arm. The KING, *aside, threatens the* JESTER *with his finger.*

JESTER: *(aside)* Hey, don't get mad. Keep quiet. I'll manage this all by myself.

KÁNCHANA·MALA: *(picking up the painting board, looking at it closely; aside)* Your highness, look what is sketched on this painting board.

VÁSAVA·DATTA: *(looking at it closely; aside)* Kánchana·mala, this is my husband. And this, here, is Ságarika. What is this?

KÁNCHANA·MALA: Your highness, I too was wondering about 2.205
that.

VÁSAVA·DATTA: *(smiling in anger)* My husband, who sketched this?

KING: *(with a forced smile, aside)* My friend, what can I say?

JESTER: *(aside)* Don't worry. I'll give them an answer. *(aloud, to* VÁSAVA·DATTA*)* Ma'am, don't imagine things to be other than they are. When my dear friend heard me say, "It's difficult to draw yourself," he demonstrated his skill in drawing.

RĀJĀ: yath" āha Vasantakas, tath" âiv' âitat.

2.210 VĀSAVADATTĀ: *(phalakaṃ nirdiśya)* ⌜ajja|utta, esā vi jā avarā tuha samīve ālihidā, tā kiṃ ajja|Vasantaassa viṇṇāṇam?⌟

RĀJĀ: *(s'|â|smitam)* devi, alam anyathā śaṅkayā. iyaṃ hi k" âpi kanyakā sva|cetas" âiva parikalpy' ālikhitā. na tu dṛṣṭa|pūrvā.

VIDŪṢAKAḤ: ⌜bhodi, saccaṃ saccam. savāmi bamha|sūtteṇa jaï īdiśī kadā vi amhehiṃ diṭṭha|puvvā.⌟

KĀÑCANAMĀLĀ: *(apavārya)* ⌜bhaṭṭiṇi, ghuṇ'|akkharaṃ pi kadā vi saṃbhavadi jjeva.⌟

VĀSAVADATTĀ: *(apavārya)* ⌜aï ujue, Vasantao kkhu eso. ṇa jāṇāsi tumaṃ eassa vakka|bhaṇidāiṃ.⌟ *(prakāśam)* ⌜ajja|utta, mama uṇa edaṃ citta|phalaaṃ pekkhantīe sīsa|veaṇā samuppaṇṇā. tā gamissaṃ aham.⌟ *(prasthitā.)*

2.215 RĀJĀ: *(paṭ'|ântena gṛhītvā)* devi,

«prasīd' êti» brūyām
idam a|sati kope na ghaṭate;
«kariṣyāmy evaṃ n' ô
punar iti» bhaved abhyupagamaḥ;
«na me doṣo 'st' îti»
tvam idam api ca jñāsyasi mṛṣā;
kim etasmin vaktuṃ
kṣamam? iti na vedmi, priyatame! [20]

KING: Yes, it's just as Vasántaka said.

VÁSAVA·DATTA: *(pointing to the painting board)* And this other woman drawn near you, my husband, is that the good Vasántaka's skill? 2.210

KING: *(with a forced smile)* My queen, that's enough of this worrying about things that aren't so. For this woman is some girl or other that I thought up purely in my imagination and then sketched. I never saw her before.*

JESTER: It's true, ma'am, it's true. I swear by my sacred thread, we never ever saw such a girl before.*

KÁNCHANA·MALA: *(aside)* Your highness, such a coincidence does sometimes happen.*

VÁSAVA·DATTA: *(aside)* How simple you are! This is Vasántaka. You have no idea how he twists words around. *(aloud)* My husband, I've gotten a headache from staring at this painting board. So I'm leaving. *(She starts to go.)*

KING: *(grabbing her by the hem of her garment)* My queen, 2.215

If I say, "Relent," it wouldn't be right,
  because you show no anger;
if, "I won't do it again,"
  it would be an admission of guilt;
if, "It's not my fault," you would know that this,
  too, was false.
What can I say in this situation? My dearest,
I do not know.

VĀSAVADATTĀ: *(sa/vinayaṃ paṭ'/ântam ākarṣantī)* ⌜ajja|utta, mā aṇṇadhā saṃbhāvehi. saccaṃ jjeva maṃ sīsa|veaṇā bādhedi. tā gamissam.⌟

ubhe niṣkrānte.

VIDŪṢAKAḤ: *(pārśvāny avalokya)* ⌜bho, diṭṭhiā vaḍḍhasi! kkhemeṇa amhāṇaṃ adikkantā a|āla|vād'|āvalī.⌟

2.220 RĀJĀ: dhiṅ mūrkha! kṛtaṃ paritoṣeṇa! yāntyā ābhijātyān nigūḍho na lakṣitas tvayā devyāḥ kop'|ânubandhaḥ.

bhrū|bhaṅge sahas" ôdgate 'pi vadanaṃ
nītaṃ parāṃ namratām;
īṣan māṃ prati bheda|kāri hasitaṃ
n' ôktaṃ vaco niṣṭhuram;
antar|bāṣpa|jaḍī|kṛtaṃ prabhutayā
cakṣur na visphāritaṃ;
kopaś ca prakaṭī|kṛto dayitayā
muktaś ca na praśrayaḥ. [21]

tad ehi. devīm eva prasādayituṃ gacchāvaḥ.

iti niṣkrāntāḥ sarve.

iti «Kadalī/gṛho» nāma dvitīyo 'ṅkaḥ.

VÁSAVA·DATTA: *(politely pulling free the end of her garment)* My husband, don't imagine things to be other than they are. It's absolutely true that this headache is tormenting me. So I'm leaving.

Exit the two women.

JESTER: *(looking to the sides)* Good fortune smiles on you! The untimely hurricane has passed us by, and we're safe.

KING: Damn you, you idiot, and your gloating. Because she 2.220
is well-bred, the queen concealed her persistent anger as she left, and you didn't notice it.

Though she suddenly frowned,
she bowed her face very low;
she shot a small, piercing smile at me
but spoke no harsh word;
her eyes were glazed with suppressed tears,
but did not open wide.
My darling clearly showed her anger
but did not let go of her dignity,
because of her self-control.

Come, then, let's go to appease the queen.

Exit all.

The end of Act Two, called "The Banana Bower."

PRELUDE TO ACT III

tataḥ praviṣati MADANIKĀ.

MADANIKĀ: *(ākāśe)* ⌜Kosambie! Kosambie! avi diṭṭhā tue bhaṭṭiṇo saāse Kañcaṇamālā ṇa vā?⌟ *(karṇaṃ dattvā)* ⌜kiṃ bhaṇāsi? «ko vi kālo tāe āacchia gadāe tti?» tā kahiṃ dāṇiṃ pekkhissam?⌟ *(agrato 'valokya)* ⌜kahaṃ, esā khu Kañcaṇamālā ido evva āgacchadi. tā jāva ṇaṃ uvasappāmi.⌟

tataḥ praviśati KĀÑCANAMĀLĀ.

3.5 KĀÑCANAMĀLĀ: *(s'|ôtprāsam)* ⌜sāhu, re amacca|Vasantaa, sāahu! adisaïdo tue amacca|Jogandharāaṇo imāe saṃdhi|viggaha|cintāe.⌟

MADANIKĀ: *(upasṛtya, sa|smitam)* ⌜halā Kañcaṇamāle, kiṃ ajja|Vasantaeṇa kidaṃ, jeṇa so evaṃ salāhiadi?⌟

KĀÑCANAMĀLĀ: ⌜halā Maaṇie, kiṃ tava ediṇā jāṇideṇa? tumaṃ imaṃ rahassaṃ rakkhiduṃ ṇa pāresi.⌟

MADANIKĀ: ⌜save devīe calaṇehiṃ, jadi kassa vi purado paāsemi.⌟

KĀÑCANAMĀLĀ: ⌜jaï evaṃ, tā suṇu. ajja kkhu mae rāa|ulāo paḍiṇiuttamāṇāe citta|sāliā|duāre Vasantaassa Susaṃgadāe samaṃ ālāvo sudo.⌟

[Time: A day later, dusk]

Enter MÁDANIKA.

MÁDANIKA: *(calling aloud)* Kaushámbika! Kaushámbika! Did you or did you not see Kánchana·mala with the king? *(cocking an ear)* What are you saying? "She came and went some time ago." Then, where can I find her now? *(looking in front of her)* Why, here comes Kánchana·mala right here. I'll go up to her.

Enter KÁNCHANA·MALA.

KÁNCHANA·MALA: *(sarcastically)* Bravo, Prime Minister Va- 3.5
sántaka, bravo! You have surpassed even Prime Minister Yaugándharáyana with this plot for war and peace.

MÁDANIKA: *(approaching, smiling)* Kánchana·mala, what has the noble Vasántaka done that you should praise him like that?

KÁNCHANA·MALA: Mádanika, what use will it be to you to know this? You won't be able to keep the secret.

MÁDANIKA: I swear by the feet of the queen, if I reveal it to anyone at all.

KÁNCHANA·MALA: In that case, listen. Just today, as I was returning from the royal palace, at the door of the picture gallery I overheard a conversation between Vasántaka and Susángata.

3.10 MADANIKĀ: *(sa|kautukam)* ⌜sahi, kīdiso?⌟

KĀÑCANAMĀLĀ: ⌜jaha: «Susaṃgade, ṇa kkhu Sāariaṃ vajjia aṇṇaṃ kiṃ pi pia|vaassassa a|sacchadāe kāraṇaṃ. tā cintehi ettha paḍiāraṃ tti.»⌟

MADANIKĀ: ⌜tado Susaṃgadāe kiṃ bhaṇidam?⌟

KĀÑCANAMĀLĀ: ⌜evaṃ tāe bhaṇidam: «ajja khu devīe citta|phalaa|vutt'|anta|saṅkidāe Sāariaṃ rakkhiduṃ mama hatthe samappantīe jaṃ ṇevatthaṃ me pasādī|kidaṃ teṇa jjeva viracida|bhaṭṭiṇī|vesaṃ Sāariaṃ giṇhia ahaṃ pi Kañcaṇamālā|vesa|dhāriṇī bhavia paose iha āgamissam. tumaṃ pi iha evva citta|sāliā|duāre maṃ paḍivālaïssasi. tado māhavī|ladā|maṇḍave tāe saha bhaṭṭiṇo samāgamo bhavissadi tti.»⌟

MADANIKĀ: *(sa|roṣam)* ⌜Susaṃgade, hadā asi kkhu tumaṃ, jā evaṃ pariaaṇa|vacchalaṃ deviṃ vañcesi.⌟

3.15 KĀÑCANAMĀLĀ: ⌜halā, tumaṃ dāṇiṃ kahiṃ patthidā?⌟

MADANIKĀ: ⌜ahaṃ khu a|ssattha|sarīrassa bhaṭṭiṇo kusala|vutt'|antaṃ jāṇiduṃ gadā tumaṃ ciraas' îti uttamantīe devīe tuha saāsaṃ pesida mhi.⌟

MÁDANIKA: *(with curiosity)* What sort of conversation, my 3.10
friend?

KÁNCHANA·MALA: This sort: "Susángata, there's no other cause of my dear friend's illness but Ságarika. So think of some remedy for it."

MÁDANIKA: And what did Susángata say to that?

KÁNCHANA·MALA: This is what she said: "When the queen got the wind up about the affair of the painting board, she put Ságarika into my hands to guard and gave me some of her own costume to appease me. I'll dress Ságarika in that to make her an imitation queen, and I myself will dress as Kánchana·mala and come here with her at dusk today. Now, you wait for me right here at the door of the picture gallery. Then she can get together with the king in the pavilion of *mádhavi* vines."

MÁDANIKA: *(angrily)* Damn you, Susángata, for betraying the queen, who has always treated her servants like daughters.

KÁNCHANA·MALA: But where are you heading now? 3.15

MÁDANIKA: The queen sent me to you because she had begun to worry when you took so long, going to find out news of the king's recovery from his serious illness.

KĀÑCANAMĀLĀ: ⌜adi|ujjuā dāṇiṃ sā devī, jā evaṃ pattīadi! eso kkhu bhaṭṭā a|ssatthadā|miseṇa attaṇo maaṇ'|âvatthaṃ pacchādaanto danta|toraṇa|valabhīe ciṭṭhadi. tā ehi. edaṃ vutt'|antaṃ bhaṭṭiṇīe ṇivedamha.⌟

iti niṣkrānte.

praveśakaḥ.

KÁNCHANA·MALA: How very simple the queen must be if she believes that now! The king is staying in his roof-garden with the ivory gates, concealing his love-sickness under the pretext of physical illness. Well, come along. Let's report this news to the queen.

Exit the two women.

End of Interlude

ACT III
THE RENDEZVOUS

tataḥ praviśati madan'|âvasthāṃ nāṭayann upaviṣṭo RĀJĀ.

RĀJĀ: *(niḥśvasya)*

saṃtāpo, hṛdaya, Smar'|ânala|kṛtaḥ
saṃpraty ayaṃ sahyatāṃ!
n' âsty ev' ôpaśamo 'sya, tāṃ prati punaḥ
kiṃ tvaṃ mudhā tāmyasi?
yan mūḍhena mayā tadā katham api
prāpto gṛhītvā ciraṃ
vinyastas tvayi sāndra|candana|rasa|
sparśo na tasyāḥ karaḥ. [1]

aho, mahad āścaryam!

manaś calaṃ prakṛty" âiva,
dur|lakṣyaṃ ca. tath" âpi me
Kāmen' âitat kathaṃ viddhaṃ
samaṃ sarvaiḥ śilī|mukhaiḥ? [2]

(ūrdhvam avalokya) Kusuma|dhanvan,

bāṇāḥ pañca mano|bhavasya, niyatās
teṣām a|saṃkhyo janaḥ
prāyo 'smad|vidha eva lakṣya iti yal
loke prasiddhiṃ gatam.
dṛṣṭaṃ tat tvayi vipratīpam adhunā
yasmād a|saṃkhyair ayaṃ
viddhaḥ kāmi|janaḥ śarair a|śaraṇo
nītas tvayā pañcatām. [3]

Enter the KING, *seated, miming love-sickness.* 3.20

KING: *(sighing)*

> Endure now, my heart, this fever kindled by the
> fire of Memory.
> There is absolutely no way to put it out.
> Then why are you suffocating on her account,
> all in vain?
> What a fool I was, when I managed somehow
> to grasp her hand,
> whose touch was like rich sandalwood salve,
> not to hold it to you for a long, long time.

And this is most amazing:

> The heart is by nature a moving target, hard to hit.
> And yet
> Kama managed somehow to hit mine
> with all of his stone-tipped arrows, all at once.

(looking up) O God whose bow is made of flowers, 3.25

> The arrows of the god born in the heart are fixed
> in number—five—
> though countless people, most of them precisely
> my type,
> have been their targets. All of this has become
> a popular cliché.
> But now your ratio appears to be just the opposite,
> for you pierced this helpless tribe of lovers with
> innumerable arrows
> and reduced them to the five elements.*

(vicintya) na tath" âham evaṃ|vidh'|âvastham ātmānam anucintayāmi yath" ântar|nigūḍha|kopa|saṃrambhāyā devyā locana|gocara|gatāṃ tapasvinīṃ Sāgarikām. tathā hi:

hriyā sarvasy' âsau
    harati «vidit" âsm' îti» vadanaṃ.
  dvayor dṛṣṭv" ālāpaṃ
    kalayati kathām ātma|viṣayām.
sakhīṣu smerāsu
    prakaṭayati vailakṣyam adhikaṃ.
  priyā prāyeṇ' āste
    hṛdaya|nihit'|ātaṅka|vidhurā. [4]

tad|vārtt"|ânveṣaṇāya gataḥ kathaṃ cirayati Vasantakaḥ?

3.30 *tataḥ praviśati hṛṣṭo* VASANTAKAḤ.

VIDŪṢAKAḤ: *(sa|paritoṣam)* ⌜hī hī, bhoḥ! Kausambī|rajja|lāheṇ' âvi ṇa tādiso pia|vaassassa paritoso āsi, jādiso ajja maha saāsādo pia|vaaṇaṃ suṇia bhavissadi tti takkemi. tā jāva gadua pia|vaassassa ṇivedaïssam.⌟ *(parikramy' âvalokya ca)* ⌜kadhaṃ, eso pia|vaasso imaṃ jjeva disaṃ avalokaanto ciṭṭhadi, tahā takkemi maṃ evva paḍivāledi tti. tā uvasappāmi ṇam.⌟ *(upasṛtya)* ⌜jaadu, jaadu pia|vaasso! bho vaassa, diṭṭhiā vaḍḍhasi samīhid'|abbhadhikāe kajja|siddhīe.⌟

(thinking) I'm not worried so much about myself, though I've been reduced to this sorry state, as about poor Ságarika, if she comes within the queen's range of vision, for the queen is possessed by a rage that she has hidden deep inside her. Indeed:

> She turns her face away from everyone,
> embarrassed by the thought,
> "They know about me." When she sees
> two people talking together,
> she reckons that they're talking about her.
> And when her women friends smile, she becomes
> even more uncomfortable.
> My dear one suffers most of the time from a heart
> oppressed by apprehension.*

I sent Vasántaka to get some news about her; why is he taking so long?

Enter VASÁNTAKA, *rejoicing.* 3.30

JESTER: *(with satisfaction)* Hurrah! Not even his acquisition of the kingdom of Kaushámbi gave my dear friend such satisfaction as I bet he'll have today when he hears the delightful news that I bring him. I'll go to my dear friend and report it to him. *(walking around and looking around)* Why, here is my dear friend looking in this very direction. I bet he's waiting just for me. I'll go up to him. *(approaching)* Victory, victory to my dear friend. Good fortune smiles on you, my friend, with this success in your undertaking, far beyond your expectations.

RĀJĀ: *(sa|harṣam)* vayasya, api kuśalaṃ priyāyāḥ?

VIDŪṢAKAḤ: *(sa|garvam)* ⌜bho, a|cireṇa saaṃ jjeva pekkhia jāṇissasi.⌟

RĀJĀ: *(sa|paritoṣam)* vayasya, darśanam api bhaviṣyati priyāyāḥ?

VIDŪṢAKAḤ: *(s'|âhaṃkāram)* ⌜bho, kīsa ṇa bhavissadi jassa de uvahasida|Vihappadi|buddhi|vihavo ahaṃ amacco!⌟

RĀJĀ: *(vihasya)* na khalu citram. kiṃ na saṃbhāvyate tvayi? tat kathaya. vistarataḥ śrotum icchāmi.

VIDŪṢAKAḤ: *(karṇe)* ⌜evaṃ evaṃ.⌟

RĀJĀ: *(sa|harṣam)* sādhu, vayasya, sādhu! idaṃ te pāritoṣikam. *(iti hastād apanīya kaṭakaṃ dadāti.)*

VIDŪṢAKAḤ: *(kaṭakaṃ paridhāy' ātmānaṃ nirvarṇya)* ⌜bho, imaṃ tāva suddha|suvaṇṇa|kaḍaa|maṇḍia|hatthaṃ attaṇo bamhaṇīe gadua daṃsaïssam.⌟

RĀJĀ: *(haste gṛhītvā nivārayan)* sakhe, paścād darśayiṣyasi. jñāyatāṃ tāvat kim avaśiṣṭam ahna iti.

VIDŪṢAKAḤ: *(vilokya)* ⌜bho, pekkha pekkha! eso kkhu guru'|âṇurā'|ôkkhitta|hiao saṃjjhā|vadhū|diṇṇa|saṃkedo via attha|giri|sihara|kāṇaṇaṃ aṇusaradi bhaavaṃ sahassa|rassī.⌟

KING: *(with joy)* My friend, is my dear one doing well?

JESTER: *(with pride)* Before long, you yourself can determine that, because you'll see her.

KING: *(with satisfaction)* My friend, will I actually get to see my dear one?

JESTER: *(with egotistical pride)* Why not? Since you have me 3.35
as your prime minister, and I make a laughing-stock of Brihas·pati's brain-power.*

KING: *(laughing)* I'm not at all surprised. Is there nothing you can't do? Now, tell me. I want to hear all the details.

JESTER: *(in his ear)* Like this, like that. . . .

KING: *(with joy)* Bravo, my friend, bravo! Here's a reward for you. *(He takes a gold bracelet from his hand and gives it to him.)*

JESTER: *(putting on the bracelet and admiring himself)* I'll go and show the Brahmin lady, my wife, how my hand looks with this pure gold bracelet adorning it.

KING: *(holding him back by the hand)* You'll show it to her 3.40
later, my friend. For now, find out how much remains of the day.

JESTER: *(observing)* Look, look! The Lord of a Thousand Rays is slipping away to the woods on the peak of the mountain where he goes home, as if he were keeping a rendezvous with his bride the sunset, with a heart carried away by heavy love for her.

RĀJĀ: *(vilokya, sa|harṣam)* sakhe, samyag upalakṣitam! paryavasitam ahaḥ. tathā hi:

«adhvānaṃ n' âika|cakraḥ prabhavati bhuvana|
bhrānti|dīrghaṃ vilaṅghya
prātaḥ prāptuṃ ratho me punar iti» manasi
nyasta|cint"|âti|bhāraḥ
sandhy"|āmṛṣṭ'|âvaśiṣṭa|sva|kara|parikara|
spaṣṭa|hem'|âra|paṅkti
vyākṛṣy' âvasthito 'sta|kṣiti|bhṛti nayat' îv'
âiṣa dik|cakram arkaḥ. [5]

api ca,

3.45 «yāto 'smi, padma|nayane, *samayo* mam' âiṣa,
suptā may" âiva bhavatī pratibodhanīyā.»
pratyāyanām ayam it' îva *saro|ruhiṇyāḥ*
sūryo 'sta|mastaka|niviṣṭa|*karaḥ* karoti. [6]

tad uttiṣṭha, mādhavī|latā|maṇḍapaṃ gatvā priyatamā|saṃket'|âvasaraṃ pratipālayāvaḥ.

VIDŪṢAKAḤ: ⌈bho, sohaṇaṃ bhaṇidaṃ.⌋ *(ity uttiṣṭhataḥ.)*

KING: *(observing, with joy)* Rightly observed, my friend. The day has wound down. For:

The sun bears a heavy load of anxiety in his mind,
thinking,
"My one-wheeled chariot will not be able to
rise again, tomorrow morning,
after it has traversed the long road of wandering
over the whole earth."
And so, as he settles down on the mountain
where he goes home,
and the sunset wipes out his rays,
a cluster of those that remain
form a wheel in the sky, with clearly outlined
spokes of golden rays,
and he seems to pull that down and lead it away.*

And

"I've gone, Lotus-eyes; my *time : rendezvous* 3.45
has come.
You're asleep, and I'll wake you."
The sun : a lover says this to reassure the
day-lotus : woman holding a lotus,
placing his *rays : hands* on the top of
the home mountain : her lowered head.*

So, stand up. Let's go to the pavilion of *mádhavi* vines and wait for the moment of my rendezvous with my dearest.

JESTER: How beautifully said. *(They stand up.)*

VIDŪṢAKAḤ: *(vilokya)* ⌜bho vaassa, pekkha pekkha. eso kkhu bahalī|kida|virala|vaṇa|rāi|saṃniveso gahīda|ghaṇa|paṅka|pīvara|vana|varāha|mahisa|kisiṇa|cchavī pasaradi puvva|disaṃ pacchādaanto timira|saṃghāo.⌟

RĀJĀ: *(samantād vilokya)* sakhe, sādhu dṛṣṭam. tathā hi:

3.50 puraḥ pūrvām eva
sthagayati, tato 'nyām api diśaṃ.
kramāt krāmann adri|
druma|pura|vibhāgāṃs tirayati.
upetaḥ pīnatvaṃ
tad|anu bhuvanasy' ēkṣaṇa|phalaṃ
tamaḥ|saṃghāto 'yaṃ
harati Hara|kaṇṭha|dyuti|haraḥ. [7]

tad ādeśaya mārgam.

VIDŪṢAKAḤ: ⌜edu, edu pia|vaasso.⌟

parikrāmataḥ.

VIDŪṢAKAḤ: *(nirūpya)* ⌜bho vaassa, edaṃ kkhu samāsaṇṇaṃ saṃsatta|bahala|patta|pāda|va|ladāhiṃ piṇḍī|kid'|ândha|āraṃ via Maarand'|ujjāṇam. tā kahaṃ ettha maggo lakkhīadi?⌟

3.55 RĀJĀ: *(gandham āghrāya)* vayasya, gacch' âgrataḥ. nanu su|parijñāta ev' âtra mārgaḥ. tathā hi:

JESTER: *(looking around)* Look, my friend, look. The mass of darkness is black as the hide of fat forest boars and buffalo covered with thick mud. As it moves on, covering the eastern quarter, it makes the spacing of the sparse rows of forest trees become dense.*

KING: *(looking all around)* Well observed, my friend. For:

> The mass of darkness obscures first the east and 3.50
> then the other quarters,
> and then, moving on by gradual degrees,
> hides the distinctions between hills, trees and
> town buildings.
> It steals the color of Shiva's neck and then,
> becoming swollen,
> steals the very faculty of sight of all the world.*

So, show me the path.

JESTER: Come, dear friend, come.

They walk around.

JESTER: *(observing closely)* My friend, we're near the Garden of Nectar, whose trees and vines with their entwined thick foliage seem to have rolled the darkness up into a ball. How can we spot the path here?

KING: *(smelling the perfume)* You go in front, my friend. 3.55
The path here is actually quite easy to make out. For

pāl" îyaṃ campakānāṃ niyatam, ayam asau
sundaraḥ sinduvāraḥ.
sāndrā vīthī tath" êyaṃ bakula|viṭapināṃ,
pāṭalā|paṅktir eṣā.
āghrāy' āghrāya gandhaṃ vividham adhigataiḥ
pāda|pair evam asmin
vyaktiṃ panthāḥ prayāti dvi|guṇatara|tamo|
nihnuto 'py eṣa cihnaiḥ. [8]

iti parikrāmataḥ.

VIDŪṢAKAḤ: ⌜bho, edaṃ kkhu ṇivaḍanta|matta|mahu|araṃ kusum'|āmoda|vāsida|dasa|disaṃ masiṇa|maraada|maṇi|silā|kuṭṭima|suhāanta|calaṇa|saṃcāra|sūcidaṃ taṃ evva māhavī|ladā|maṇḍapaṃ saṃpatta mha. tā iha jjevva ciṭṭhadu bhavaṃ, jāva ahaṃ devī|vesa|dhāriṇaṃ Sāariaṃ geṇhia lahuṃ āacchāmi.⌟

RĀJĀ: vayasya, tena hi tvaryatāṃ tvaryatām.

3.60 VIDŪṢAKAḤ: ⌜bho, mā uttamma. esa āgado mhi.⌟ *(iti niṣkrāntaḥ.)*

RĀJĀ: yāvad aham apy asyāṃ marakata|śilā|vedikāyām upaviśya priyāyāḥ saṃketa|samayaṃ pratipālayāmi. *(upaviśya sa|cintam)* aho, ko 'pi kāmi|janasya sva|gṛhiṇī|samāgama|paribhāvino janam abhinavaṃ prati pakṣa|pātaḥ. tathā hi:

This is certainly the row of *chámpaka* trees, and
that is the beautiful *sinduvára*.
And this is the dense avenue of *bákula* trees,
and that the row of trumpet flowers.
Even though the path is veiled by twice as much
darkness in this garden,
you can clearly discern it by the signs of
the trees that you can identify
simply by smelling and smelling
each different perfume.

They walk around.

JESTER: Now we've reached the pavilion of *mádhavi* vines. I can tell, because intoxicated bees swarm around it, the fragrance of its flowers perfumes the air in all the quarters of the sky, and its stone floors paved with smooth emeralds feel so good when my feet walk on them. So wait here, please, sir, while I get Ságarika, who'll be wearing the queen's clothes, and come back right away.

KING: Hurry, please, my friend, hurry.

JESTER: Oh don't be so impatient! I'll be back. *(Exit.)* 3.60

KING: Meanwhile, I'll sit on this altar made of stone inlaid with emeralds and wait for the moment of the rendezvous with my dear one. *(sitting down and thinking)* Strange that a lover, scorning the embrace of his own wife, should be so partial to a new person. For:

praṇaya|viśadāṃ
  dṛṣṭiṃ vaktre dadāti na śaṅkitā.
ghaṭayati ghanaṃ
  kaṇṭh'|āśleṣe rasān na payo|dharau.
vadati bahuśo
  «gacchām' îti» prayatna|dhṛt" âpy, aho,
ramayatitarāṃ
  saṃketa|sthā tath" âpi hi kāminī. [9]

aye, kathaṃ cirayati Vasantakaḥ? tat kiṃ nu khalu viditaḥ syād ayaṃ vṛtt'|ânto devyā?

tataḥ praviśati VĀSAVADATTĀ KĀÑCANAMĀLĀ *ca.*

3.65 VĀSAVADATTĀ: ⌜hañje Kañcaṇamāle, saccaṃ jjevva maha vesaṃ kadua Sāariā ajja|uttaṃ ahisarissadi?⌟

KĀÑCANAMĀLĀ: ⌜kahaṃ aṇṇadhā bhaṭṭiṇīe ṇivedīadi? adha vā citta|sāliā|duāre ṭṭhido Vasantao jjevva de paccaaṃ uppādaïssadi.⌟

VĀSAVADATTĀ: ⌜teṇa hi tahiṃ jjevva gacchamha.⌟

KĀÑCANAMĀLĀ: ⌜edu, edu bhaṭṭinī.⌟ *(ubhe parikrāmataḥ.)*

tataḥ praviśati kṛt'|âvaguṇṭhano VASANTAKAḤ.

3.70 VASANTAKAḤ: *(karṇaṃ dattvā)* ⌜jadhā citta|sāliā|duāre pada|saddo suṇīadi, tadhā takkemi āgadā Sāaria tti.⌟

She is too nervous to cast a cheerful, loving glance
upon his face.
When she embraces him with her arms
around his neck,
she doesn't press her breasts hard against him
in passion.
She keeps saying, "I must go," even though he
holds onto her with great effort.
And yet a lover at a rendezvous gives him
the most intense pleasure.

Oh, why is Vasántaka taking so long? Could the queen have gotten wind of this affair?

Enter VÁSAVA·DATTA, *with* KÁNCHANA·MALA.

VÁSAVA·DATTA: Kánchana·mala, is it true that Ságarika is go- 3.65
ing to keep a tryst with my husband wearing my clothes?

KÁNCHANA·MALA: How could your highness have been given a report of things other than they are? But Vasántaka himself, standing at the door of the picture gallery, will convince you.

VÁSAVA·DATTA: Then let's go there.

KÁNCHANA·MALA: Come, please, ma'am, come. *(They walk around.)*

Enter VASÁNTAKA, *veiled.*

VASÁNTAKA: *(cocking an ear)* Since I heard the sound of 3.70
footsteps at the door of the picture gallery, I think Ságarika has arrived.

KĀÑCANAMĀLĀ: ⌜bhaṭṭini, iaṃ sā citta|sāliā. tā jāva Vasantaassa saṇṇaṃ karemi.⌟ *(iti choṭikāṃ dadāti.)*

VIDŪṢAKAḤ: *(sa|harṣam upasṛtya, sa|smitam)* ⌜Susaṃgade, su|ṭṭhu kkhu kido tue eso Kañcaṇamālāe veso. adha Sāariā dāṇiṃ kahiṃ?⌟

KĀÑCANAMĀLĀ: *(aṅgulyā darśayantī)* ⌜ṇaṃ esā.⌟

VIDŪṢAKAḤ: *(dṛṣṭvā, sa|vismayam)* ⌜esā phuḍaṃ evva devī Vāsavadattā!⌟

3.75 VĀSAVADATTĀ: *(s'|āśaṅkam, ātma|gatam)* ⌜kadhaṃ, jāṇida mhi!⌟

VIDŪṢAKAḤ: *(choṭikāṃ dadāti)* ⌜bhodi Sāarie, ido āaccha.⌟ *(VĀSAVADATTĀ vihasya KĀÑCANAMĀLĀM avalokayati.)*

KĀÑCANAMĀLĀ: *(apavāry' âṅgulyā tarjayantī)* ⌜ha'|āsa, sumarissasi edaṃ attaṇo vaaṇam.⌟

VIDŪṢAKAḤ: ⌜turaadu, turaadu Sāariā. eso kkhu puvva|disādo uggacchadi bhaavaṃ mia|lañchaṇo.⌟ *(parikrāmati.)*

RĀJĀ: aye! upasthita|priyā|samāgamasy' âpi kim idam aty|artham uttāmyati me cetaḥ? atha vā:

3.80 tīvraḥ Smara|saṃtāpo
na tath" ādau bādhate, yath" āsanne.
tapati prāvṛṣi nitarām
abhyarṇa|jal'|āgamo divasaḥ. [10]

KÁNCHANA·MALA: Your highness, here is the picture gallery. I'll just give Vasántaka a signal. *(She snaps her fingers.)*

JESTER: *(approaching with joy, and smiling)* Susángata, you've done a great job of disguising yourself as Kánchana·mala. But where's Ságarika?

KÁNCHANA·MALA: *(pointing with her finger)* There she is.

JESTER: *(looking, with astonishment)* This really is Queen Vásava·datta!

VÁSAVA·DATTA: *(worried, to herself)* Why, he's recognized 3.75
me!

JESTER: *(snapping his fingers)* My lady Ságarika, come this way. *(*VÁSAVA·DATTA *smiles and gives* KÁNCHANA·MALA *a look.)*

KÁNCHANA·MALA: *(aside, threatening with her finger)* You damn fool, you'll have cause to remember these words of yours.*

JESTER: Hurry up, Ságarika, please, ma'am, hurry up. Look, the moon, the god with the mark of a hare, is rising in the east.* *(He walks around.)*

KING: What is this extreme longing that my mind feels even now that the meeting with my dear one is so close? Or is it that:

> The sharp heat of Memory is not so oppressive 3.80
> in the beginning as when it draws near.
> The days are hottest when the downpour
> is about to come, in the monsoon.*

VIDŪṢAKAḤ: *(karṇaṃ dattvā)* ⌜bhodi Sāarie, eso khu pia|vaasso tumaṃ jjeva uddisia ukkaṇṭha|ṇibbharaṃ mantedi. tā ṇivedemi se tuh' āgamaṇam.⌟

VĀSAVADATTĀ: *(śiraḥ|saṃjñāṃ dadāti.)*

VIDŪṢAKAḤ: *(*RĀJĀNAM *upasṛtya)* ⌜bho vaassa, diṭṭhiā vaḍḍhasi! esā kkhu mae ānīdā Sāariā.⌟

RĀJĀ: *(sa|harṣaṃ, sahas" ôtthāya)* vayasya, kv' âsau?

3.85 VIDŪṢAKAḤ: ⌜ṇaṃ esā.⌟

RĀJĀ: *(upasṛtya)* priye Sāgarike,

śīt'|âṃśur mukham, utpale tava dṛśau,
padm'|ânukārau karau,
rambhā|garbha|nibhaṃ tath" ōru|yugalaṃ,
bāhū mṛṇāl'|ôpamau
ity, āhlāda|kar'|âkhil'|âṅgi, rabhasān
niḥ|śaṅkam āliṅgya mām
aṅgāni tvam Anaṅga|tāpa|vidhurāṇy
ehy, ehi, nirvāpaya! [11]

VĀSAVADATTĀ: *(sa|bāṣpam, apavārya)* ⌜Kañcaṇamāle, evvaṃ pi mantia ajja|utto puṇo vi maṃ ālavissadi tti, aho, accariaṃ!⌟

KĀÑCANAMĀLĀ: *(apavārya)* ⌜bhaṭṭiṇi, evvaṃ ṇṇedam. kiṃ uṇa sāhasiāṇaṃ puruṣāṇaṃ ṇa sambhāvīadi?⌟

JESTER: *(cocking an ear)* My lady Ságarika, here is my dear friend speaking words laden with longing, and all about you. I'll tell him that you have arrived.

VÁSAVA·DATTA: *(gives a sign of assent by nodding her head.)*

JESTER: *(approaching the* KING*)* Good fortune smiles on you, my friend! I've brought Ságarika here.

KING: *(suddenly standing up, with joy)* My friend, where is she, where is she?

JESTER: Here she is. 3.85

KING: *(approaching)* My dear Ságarika,

> Your face is the moon with its cool rays,
> your eyes two blue lotuses,
> your hands are like day-lotuses, your two thighs
> like the inner surface of plantains,
> and your arms are like lotus filaments.
> All of your limbs are a source of delight.
> But my limbs are wasting away in the fever
> of the god who has no limbs.
> So come, come, embrace me fiercely,
> without hesitation, and soothe them.*

VÁSAVA·DATTA: *(in tears, aside)* Kánchana·mala, how amazing it is, that after talking like this, my husband will speak intimately with me again.

KÁNCHANA·MALA: *(aside)* Exactly so, your highness. Indeed, rash, violent men are capable of anything.

3.90 VIDŪṢAKAḤ: ⌜bhodi Sāarie, vīsaddhā bhavia pia|vaassaṃ ālāvehi. ajja vi dāva se ṇicca|ruṭṭhāe devīe Vāsavadattāe duṭṭha|vaaṇehiṃ kaṭuidāiṃ sottāiṃ sampadaṃ suhāvedu tuha mahura|vaaṇ'|ôvaṇṇāso.⌟

VĀSAVADATTĀ: *(apavārya, sa|roṣa|smitam)* ⌜Kañcaṇamāle, ahaṃ īdisī kaḍua|bhāsiṇī. ajja|Vasantao uṇa piaṃ|vado.⌟

KĀÑCANAMĀLĀ: *(apavārya)* ⌜had'|āsa, sumarissasi edaṃ vaaṇam.⌟

VIDŪṢAKAḤ: *(vilokya)* ⌜bho vaassa, pekkha pekkha. eso kkhu kuvida|kāmiṇī|kapola|saṇṇiho puvva|disaṃ paāsanto udido bhaavaṃ mia|lañchaṇo.⌟

RĀJĀ: priye Sāgarike, paśya:

3.95 āruhya śaila|śikharaṃ
tvad|vadan'|âpahṛta|kānti|sarvasvaḥ
pratikartum iv' ōrdhva|*karaḥ*
sthitaḥ purastān niśā|nāthaḥ. [12]

api ca, darśitam anen' ôdgacchatā prakṛti|jaḍatvam. kutaḥ:

JESTER: My lady Ságarika, trust my dear friend and speak intimately with him. Just today his ears were burnt by the acid words of that perennially bad-tempered Queen Vásava·datta. Soothe them now with the balm of your sweet words. 3.90

VÁSAVA·DATTA: *(aside, smiling with fury)* So, Kánchana·mala, my words are caustic, and the good Vasántaka's are sycophantic.

KÁNCHANA·MALA: *(aside)* You damn fool, you'll have cause to remember these words of yours.

JESTER: *(looking around)* Look, my friend, look. The moon, the god with the mark of a hare, now red as the cheek of an offended mistress, has risen, illuminating the east.

KING: Look, my dear Ságarika:

> Your face has robbed the moon, lord of the night, 3.95
> of all that he has, his beauty.
> Now he has climbed the peak of a mountain and
> stands facing you,
> raising his *rays : hands* as if to retaliate.

And as he rises, he reveals his natural dullness. For:

kiṃ padmasya rucaṃ na hanti? nayan'|ā-
    nandaṃ vidhatte kiṃ?
  vṛddhiṃ vā *jhaṣa|ketanasya* kurute
    n' āloka|mātreṇa kim?
vaktr'|êndau tava saty ayaṃ yad aparaḥ
    śīt'|âṃśur abhyudgato
  darpaḥ syād amṛtena ced, iha tad apy
    ev' âsti *bimb'|âdhare*. [13]

VĀSAVADATTĀ: *(sa|roṣam avaguṇṭhanam apanīya)* ⌜ajja|utta, saccaṃ evva ahaṃ Sāariā. tumaṃ uṇa Sāari"|ôkkhita|hiao savvaṃ evva Sāariā|maaṃ pekkhasi.⌟

RĀJĀ: *(sa|vailakṣyam apavārya)* kathaṃ, devī Vāsavadattā? vayasya, kim etat?

3.100 VIDŪṢAKAḤ: *(sa|viṣādam)* ⌜bho vaassa, kiṃ avaram? amhāṇaṃ jīvia|saṃsao jādo eso.⌟

RĀJĀ: *(upaviśy' âñjaliṃ baddhvā)* priye Vāsavadatte, prasīda prasīda.

VĀSAVADATTĀ: *(tan mukh'|âbhimukhaṃ hastau prasāry' âśruṇi vidhārayantī)* ⌜ajja|utta, mā evaṃ bhaṇa. aṇṇa|gadāiṃ imāiṃ akkharāiṃ.⌟

VIDŪṢAKAḤ: *(ātma|gatam)* ⌜kiṃ dāṇiṃ ettha karissaṃ? bhodu evaṃ dāva.⌟ *(prakāśam)* ⌜bhodi, mah"|âṇubhāvā kkhu tumam. tā khamīadu dāva ekko avarāho pia|vaassassa.⌟

VĀSAVADATTĀ: ⌜ajja|Vasantaa, ṇaṃ paḍhama|saṃgame vigghaṃ karantīe mae evva edassa avaraddham.⌟

The moon of your face eclipses the beauty of
the lotus
and delights the eye. Merely by appearing,
it makes the one who has a big fish *on : as* its banner
swell, because, despite its presence, another
cool-rayed moon has risen.
And if he takes pride in the ambrosia,
that, too, is in your lower lip that is like
a *bimba fruit : lunar disk*.*

VÁSAVA·DATTA: *(in fury, taking off her veil)* My husband, I am truly Ságarika. For your heart is so entirely carried away by Ságarika that you see *everything* as made of Ságarika.

KING: *(discomfited, aside)* Why, it's Queen Vásava·datta! What is this, my friend?

JESTER: *(in despair)* What else, my friend? Our very lives 3.100
are suddenly at risk here.

KING: *(sitting down and joining his palms in supplication)* My dear Vásava·datta, relent, oh please relent.

VÁSAVA·DATTA: *(turning her face toward his, stretching out her hands and holding back her tears)* My husband, don't talk like that. Those syllables are meant for someone else.

JESTER: *(to himself)* What can I do about this now? All right. Here goes. *(aloud)* My lady, you are so generous. So please forgive my dear friend this first offense.

VÁSAVA·DATTA: Good Vasántaka, it is I who have offended him, by posing an obstacle to his first rendezvous.

3.105 RĀJĀ: devi, evaṃ pratyakṣa|dṛṣṭa|vyalīkaḥ kiṃ bravīmi? tath" âpi vijñāpayāmi: *(pādayoḥ patati.)*

ātāmratām apanayāmi vilakṣa eṣa
lākṣā|kṛtāṃ caraṇayos tava, devi, mūrdhnā
kop'|ôparāga|janitāṃ tu mukh'|êndu|bimbe
hartuṃ kṣamo, yadi paraṃ karuṇā mayi syāt. [14]

VĀSAVADATTĀ: *(hastena vārayantī)* ⌜ajja|utta, uṭṭhehi uṭṭhehi. ṇil|lajjo khu so jaṇo jo ajja|uttassa īdisaṃ hiaaṃ jānia puṇo vi kuppadi. tā suhaṃ ciṭṭhadu ajja|utto. gamissaṃ aham.⌟ *(iti gantum icchati.)*

KĀÑCANAMĀLĀ: ⌜bhaṭṭiṇi, karehi pasādam. evaṃ caraṇa|paḍidaṃ mahā|rāaṃ ujjia gadāe devīe avassaṃ pacchā|dāveṇa hodavvam.⌟

VĀSAVADATTĀ: ⌜avehi a|paṇḍide! kudo ettha pasādassa paccā|dāvassa vā kāraṇam? tā ehi, gacchamha.⌟

3.110 RĀJĀ: devi, prasīda prasīda. *(«ātāmratām apanayām' îty» ādi punaḥ paṭhati.)*

VIDŪṢAKAḤ: ⌜bho, uṭṭhehi! gadā devī. tā kiṃ ettha araṇṇa|rudidaṃ karesi?⌟

RĀJĀ: *(mukham unnamayya, dṛṣṭvā)* katham, a|kṛtv" âiva prasādaṃ gatā devī?

KING: My queen, what can I say? My cheating has been exposed right before your eyes. Yet I would argue: *(He falls at her feet.)* 3.105

> Blushing with shame, my queen, I will wipe away
> with my head
> the redness that lac has painted on your feet.
> But I can remove the flush of the angry eclipse
> on your moon-face
> only if you show great compassion toward me.*

VÁSAVA·DATTA: *(restraining him with her hand)* My husband, get up, get up. Only a shameless person would get angry again, knowing her husband's heart to be like this. So be at ease, my husband. I'm leaving. *(She starts to go.)*

KÁNCHANA·MALA: Your highness, do relent. If the queen just goes away and leaves the great king fallen at her feet like that, she'll certainly regret it later.

VÁSAVA·DATTA: Get away! You understand nothing. There is no cause here for relenting or regretting. Come, let's go.

KING: Relent, my queen, relent. *(He repeats the verse: "Blushing with shame...")* 3.110

*[Exit the two women.]**

JESTER: Stand up. The queen has gone. So why are you crying in the wilderness here?

KING: *(raising his head and seeing)* How could the queen have left without relenting?

VIDŪṢAKAḤ: ⌜kahaṃ na kido pasādo, jaṃ ajja vi a|kkhada|sarīrā ciṭṭhamha?⌟

3.115 RĀJĀ: dhiṅ mūrkha! kim eva mām apahasasi? nanu tvat|kṛta ev' âyam āpatito 'smākaṃ mahān an|arthaḥ. kutaḥ:

samārūḍhā prītiḥ
 praṇaya|bahu|mānād anu|dinaṃ
 vyalīkaṃ vīkṣy' êdaṃ
 kṛtam a|kṛta|pūrvaṃ khalu mayā,
priyā muñcaty adya
 sphuṭam a|sahanā jīvitam asau;
 prakṛṣṭasya premṇaḥ
 skhalitam a|viṣahyaṃ hi bhavati. [15]

VIDŪṢAKAḤ: ⌜bho, ruṭṭhā devī kiṃ karaïssadi tti na jāṇāmi. Sāariā uṇa duk|karaṃ jīvissadi tti takkemi.⌟

RĀJĀ: vayasya, aham apy evaṃ cintayāmi. hā, priye Sāgarike!

tataḥ praviśati VĀSAVADATTĀ/*veṣa/dhāriṇī* SĀGARIKĀ.

3.120 SĀGARIKĀ: *(s'/ôdvegam)* ⌜diṭṭhiā ṇ' âhaṃ imiṇā viraïda|devī|veseṇa imādo citta|sālīādo ṇikkamantī keṇ' âvi lakkhida mhi. tā idāṇiṃ kiṃ karaïssam?⌟ *(s'/âsraṃ cintayati.)*

VIDŪṢAKAḤ: ⌜bhoḥ! kiṃ mūḍho via ciṭṭhasi? cintehi ettha paḍiāraṃ!⌟

RĀJĀ: nanu tam eva cintayāmi. vayasya, devī|prasādanaṃ muktvā n' ânyam atr' ôpāyaṃ paśyāmi. tad ehi, gacchāvaḥ.

JESTER: How can you say she didn't relent, when we're standing here without a single wound on our bodies?

KING: Damn you, you idiot. Why are you making fun of 3.115
me like this? It's all because of your doings that this great disaster has struck us. For:

Mutual respect for our affection made our love
grow stronger day by day,
but when my dear one sees that I have cheated
like this,
as I have never done before,
she'll be unable to bear it,
and she'll surely throw away her life today.
For when love is lofty, a slip is unbearable.*

JESTER: I don't know what the queen, in her fury, will do, but I bet Ságarika will find it very hard to stay alive.

KING: My friend, I, too, am worried about that very same thing. Oh, my dear Ságarika!

Enter SÁGARIKA, *wearing the clothes of* VÁSAVA·DATTA.

SÁGARIKA: *(upset)* Luckily, nobody noticed me as I came out 3.120
of the painting gallery wearing Vásava·datta's clothes. But what shall I do now? *(She thinks, tearfully.)*

JESTER: Why are you standing there like an idiot? Think of some remedy for this.

KING: I *am* thinking about that very thing. My friend, I see no way of doing this but appeasing the queen. So, come along. Let's go there.

iti parikrāmataḥ.

SĀGARIKĀ: *(vimṛśya)* ⌜varaṃ dāṇiṃ saaṃ jjeva appāṇaṃ ubbandhia uvaradā, na uṇa jāṇida|saṃketa|vutt'|antāe devīe paribhuda mhi. tā jāva ahaṃ asoa|pāda|vaṃ gadua jahā|samīhidaṃ karissam.⌟

3.125 VIDŪṢAKAḤ: *(ākarṇya)* ⌜ciṭṭha dāva, ciṭṭha bho! pada|saddo suṇīadi. jāṇāmi kadā vi gahida|pacchā|dābā puṇo vi devī āgadā bhave.⌟

RĀJĀ: vayasya, mah"|ânubhāvā khalu devī. kadā cid evam api syāt. tat tvaritaṃ nirūpyatām.

VIDŪṢAKAḤ: ⌜jaṃ bhavaṃ āṇavedi.⌟ *(iti parikrāmati.)*

SĀGARIKĀ: *(upasṛtya)* ⌜tā jāva imāe māhavī|ladāe pāsaṃ viraïa asoa|pāda|ve appāṇaaṃ ubbandhia vāvādemi.⌟ *(iti latā|pāśaṃ racayantī)* ⌜hā tāda, hā amba, esā dāṇiṃ ahaṃ a|ṇādhā a|saraṇā vivajjāmi manda|bhāiṇī.⌟ *(iti kaṇṭhe latā|pāśam arpayati.)*

VIDŪṢAKAḤ: *(vilokya)* ⌜kā puṇa esā? kahaṃ, devī Vāsavadattā!⌟ *(sa|saṃbhramam, uccaiḥ)* ⌜bho vaassa, parittāhi parittāhi! esā kkhu devī Vāsavadattā ubbandhia attāṇaaṃ vāvādedi.⌟

3.130 RĀJĀ: *(sa|saṃbhramam upasṛtya)* kv' âsau, kv' âsau?

VIDŪṢAKAḤ: ⌜ṇaṃ esā!⌟

RĀJĀ: *(upasṛtya, kaṇṭhāt pāśam apanayan)* ayi, sāhasa|kariṇi! kim idam a|kāryaṃ kriyate?

They walk around.

SÁGARIKA: *(considering)* It would be better for me to end my life now, myself, by hanging myself, than to be disgraced by the queen when she finds out about the affair of the rendezvous. So I will go to the *ashóka* tree and do what I want to do.

JESTER: *(listening)* Wait, wait a minute! I hear the sound 3.125
of footsteps. I think the queen might be coming back again, perhaps feeling remorse.

KING: My friend, the queen is indeed generous. Perhaps that's precisely what's happened. Do find out right away.

JESTER: As your majesty commands. *(He walks around.)*

SÁGARIKA: *(approaching)* I'll make a noose out of this *mádhavi* vine and kill myself by hanging myself from the *ashóka* tree. *(preparing a noose from the vine)* Father! Mother! I'm going to die now, unlucky as I am, with no one to protect me, nowhere to go for refuge. *(She puts the noose around her neck.)*

JESTER: *(looking)* Now, who's this? Why, it's Queen Vásava·datta! *(in haste, loudly)* Help! Friend! Help! Queen Vásava·datta here is committing suicide by hanging herself!

KING: *(running up in haste and confusion)* Where is she? 3.130
Where is she?

JESTER: Here she is!

KING: *(running up, taking the noose from her neck)* Rash woman, how can you do this deed that must not be done!

mama kaṇṭha|gatāḥ prāṇāḥ
  pāśe kaṇṭha|gate tava.
ataḥ sv'|ârthaḥ prayatno 'yaṃ;
  tyajyatāṃ sāhasaṃ, priye! [16]

SĀGARIKĀ: *(*RĀJĀNAṂ *dṛṣṭvā)* ⌜ammo, kathaṃ, eso bhaṭṭā!⌟ *(sa|harṣam, ātma|gatam)* ⌜jaṃ saccaṃ: eṇaṃ pekkhia puṇo vi jīvid'|âhilāso saṃvuttā. aha vā eṇaṃ pekkhia kad'|atthā bhavia suheṇa evva jīvidaṃ paricaïssam.⌟ *(prakāśam)* ⌜muñcadu, muñcadu maṃ bhaṭṭā! parāhīṇo khu aaṃ jaṇo, na uṇa īdisaṃ avasaraṃ mariduṃ pāvehi.⌟ *(iti punaḥ pāśaṃ kaṇṭhe dātum icchati.)*

3.135 RĀJĀ: *(nirvarṇya, sa|harṣam, ātma|gatam)* kathaṃ, priyā me Sāgarikā! *(kaṇṭhāt pāśam ākṣipya)*

alam, alam ati|mātraṃ sāhasen' âmunā te!
  tvaritam, ayi, vimuñca tvaṃ latā|pāśam etam!
calitam api niroddhuṃ jīvitaṃ, jīvit'|ēśe,
  kṣaṇam iha mama kāṇṭhe bāhu|pāśaṃ nidhehi! [17]

(iti bāhum ākṣipya, kaṇṭhe kṛtvā, sparśaṃ nāṭayan) sakhe, iyam an|abhrā vṛṣṭiḥ.

VIDŪṢAKAḤ: ⌜bho, evaṃ ṇṇedaṃ, jadi a|āla|vād'|āvalī bhavia na āādi devī Vāsavadattā.⌟

tataḥ praviśati VĀSAVADATTĀ KĀÑCANAMĀLĀ *ca.*

3.140 VĀSAVADATTĀ: ⌜hañje Kañcaṇamāle, taṃ tahā calaṇa|nivaḍidaṃ ajja|uttaṃ avadhīria āacchantīe mae ati|ṇiṭṭhuraṃ kidam. tā idāṇiṃ saaṃ jevva gadua ajja|uttaṃ aṇuṇaïssam.⌟

My life's breaths come to my throat
ve when the noose is around your throat.
So my effort here is for my own sake;
  dear one, give up this rash intention.

SÁGARIKA: *(seeing the* KING*)* Why, it's the king! *(to herself, with joy)* Truly, when I see him even my love of life returns. Or, rather, when I see him, my life is complete, and I can give it up happily. *(aloud)* Let me go, your majesty, let me go! This person is in the power of another, and will not again get such an opportunity to die. *(She tries to put the noose around her neck again.)*

KING: *(looking at her closely, joyously, to himself)* Why, it's my 3.135
dear Ságarika! *(taking the noose from her neck)*

No more, no more of this too rash act of yours!
Oh, quickly throw away this noose made of a vine.
Ruler of my life, put the noose of your arms,
  for just a moment,
here around my neck to hold in my life,
  though it has set out to go.

(taking her arm and putting it around his neck, miming his joy at her touch) My friend, this comes like a bolt out of the blue.*

JESTER: Yes indeed, unless Queen Vásava·datta comes to play the part of an untimely hurricane.

Enter VÁSAVA·DATTA*, with* KÁNCHANA·MALA.

VÁSAVA·DATTA: Kánchana·mala, it was too cruel of me to go 3.140
off like that, scorning my husband fallen at my feet. So now I myself will go to my husband and win him over.

KĀÑCANAMĀLĀ: ⌜ko aṇṇo devīṃ vajjia evvaṃ bhaṇiduṃ jāṇādi? varaṃ so jjeva devo duj|jaṇo bhodu, ṇa uṇa devī. tā edu, edu bhaṭṭiṇī.⌟

parikrāmataḥ.

RĀJĀ: ayi mugdhe, kim ady' âpi madhya|sthatayā vayaṃ viphala|mano|rathāḥ kriyāmahe?

KĀÑCANAMĀLĀ: *(karṇaṃ dattvā)* ⌜bhaṭṭiṇi, eso khu jahā samīve bhaṭṭā mantedi, tadā takkemi tumaṃ evva aṇuṇeduṃ ido evv' āgacchadi.⌟

3.145 VĀSAVADATTĀ: *(sa|harṣam)* ⌜teṇa hi a|lakkhidā evva puṭṭhado gadua kaṇṭhe geṇhia pasādaïssam.⌟

VIDŪṢAKAḤ: ⌜bhodi Sāarie, vīsatthā bhavia pia|vaassaṃ ālavehi.⌟

VĀSAVADATTĀ: *(ākarṇya, sa | viṣādam)* ⌜Kañcaṇamāle! kadhaṃ, Sāariā ido evv' āgadā? tā suṇissaṃ dāva pacchā upasappissam.⌟ *(tathā karoti.)*

SĀGARIKĀ: ⌜bhaṭṭā, kiṃ ediṇā alīa|dākkhiṇṇeṇa jīviādo vi vallahatarāe devīe appāṇaṃ avarāhiṇaṃ karesi?⌟

RĀJĀ: ayi, mithyā|vādinī khalv asi. kutaḥ:

KÁNCHANA·MALA: Who but the queen would know how to talk like this? Better that the king should behave badly, but not the queen. So come, please, ma'am, come.

They walk around.

KING: You naïve girl, even now your indecision thwarts our desires!

KÁNCHANA·MALA: *(cocking an ear)* Since the king is talking nearby, ma'am, I think he is coming this way to win *you* over.

VÁSAVA·DATTA: *(with joy)* Then I'll go behind him where he can't see me and throw my arms around his neck to appease him. 3.145

JESTER: My lady Ságarika, trust my dear friend and speak with him in confidence.

VÁSAVA·DATTA: *(hearing this, desolated)* Why, Kánchana·mala, Ságarika has come here. I'll just creep up on the side and listen. *(She does this.)*

SÁGARIKA: Your majesty, why are you using this cheating gallantry to be unfaithful to the queen, who is dearer to you than life itself?

KING: What you say is simply not so. For:

3.150 śvās'|ôtkampini kampitaṃ kuca|yuge,
maune priyaṃ bhāṣitaṃ,
vaktre 'syāḥ kuṭilī|kṛta|bhruṇi tathā
yātaṃ mayā pādayoḥ—
itthaṃ naḥ saha|j'|âbhijātya|janitā
sev" âivam devyāḥ paraṃ.
prem'|ābandha|vivardhit'|âdhika|rasā
prītis tu yā, sā tvayi. [18]

VĀSAVADATTĀ: *(sahas" ôpasṛtya, sa|roṣam)* ⌜ajja|utta, juttaṃ edaṃ, sa|risaṃ edam!⌟

RĀJĀ: *(dṛṣṭvā, sa|vailakṣyam)* devi, na khalv a|kāraṇe mām upālabdhum arhasi. satyaṃ tvām eva matvā veṣa|sādṛśya|vipralabdhā vayam ih' āgatāḥ. tat kṣamyatām. *(iti pādayoḥ patati.)*

VĀSAVADATTĀ: *(sa|roṣam)* ⌜ajja|utta, uṭṭhehi uṭṭhehi. kiṃ ajja vi saha|j'|âbhijādāe sevāe dukkhaṃ aṇuhavīadi?⌟

RĀJĀ: *(sva|gatam)* kim etad api śrutaṃ devyā? tat sarvathā devī|prasādanaṃ prati nir|āśī|bhūtāḥ smaḥ. *(adho|mukhas tiṣṭhati.)*

3.155 VIDŪṢAKAḤ: ⌜bhodi, tumaṃ kiṃ ubbandhia attāṇaaṃ vāvādesi tti vesa|sārissa|mohideṇa mae pia|vaasso ittha āṇido. jaï mama vaaṇaṃ ṇa pattiāasi, tā pekkha etaṃ ladā|pāsam.⌟

I trembled when her sighs made her breasts tremble, 3.150
spoke sweet words when she was silent,
and, when the brows on her face bent in a frown,
fell at her feet—in all of these ways we served the queen
because of her inborn good breeding.
But the love whose emotion is heightened by the bonds of affection—
that is for you.

VÁSAVA·DATTA: *(suddenly moving forward, in fury)* My husband, this is worthy of you; it's just like you.

KING: *(seeing her, discomfited)* My queen, you should not accuse me without cause. The truth is that we were misled by the similarity of your clothes and thought she was you, and so we came here. Forgive us. *(He falls at her feet.)*

VÁSAVA·DATTA: *(with fury)* Get up, my husband, get up. Why even now should you suffer the misery of serving someone with "inborn good breeding"?

KING: *(to himself)* Oh no, did the queen hear even that? Then all hopes we had of appeasing her are shattered. *(He stands there with his head lowered.)*

JESTER: I was fooled by the similarity of your clothes, ma'am, 3.155
and thought that you were committing suicide by hanging yourself, and so I brought my dear friend here. If you don't believe what I'm saying, then look at this noose made of a vine.

iti latā|pāśaṃ darśayati.

VĀSAVADATTĀ: *(sa|kopam)* ⌜Kañcaṇamāle, edeṇa jjeva la-dā|pāseṇa bandhia geṇha eṇaṃ bamhaṇam. edaṃ ca duv|viṇīdaṃ kaṇṇakaṃ aggado karehi.⌟

KĀÑCANAMĀLĀ: ⌜jaṃ devī āṇavedi.⌟ *(latā|pāśena* VIDŪṢAKAṂ *badhnatī)* ⌜had'|āsa, aṇuhava dāṇiṃ attaṇo duṇ|ṇaassa phalam. Sāgarie, tumaṃ vi aggado hoi.⌟

SĀGARIKĀ: *(sva|gatam)* ⌜ha ddhī! kadhaṃ a|kida|puṇṇāe mae mariduṃ pi attaṇo icchae na pāridam.⌟

3.160 VIDŪṢAKAḤ: *(sa|viṣādaṃ* RĀJĀNAM *avalokya)* ⌜bho vaassa, sumarehi maṃ a|ṇādhaṃ devīe bandhanādo vivajjantaṃ.⌟

sarvān ādāya niṣkrāntā VĀSAVADATTĀ.

RĀJĀ: *(sa|khedam)* kaṣṭaṃ bhoḥ! kaṣṭam!

kiṃ devyāḥ kṛta|dīrgha|roṣa|muṣita|
snigdha|smitaṃ tan mukhaṃ,
trastāṃ Sāgarikāṃ su|saṃbhṛta|ruṣā
kiṃ tarjyamānāṃ tayā,
baddhvā nītam ito Vasantakam ahaṃ
kiṃ cintayām' îty? aho,
sarv'|ākāra|kṛta|vyathaḥ kṣaṇam api
prāpnomi n' ô nirvṛtim. [19]

He shows her the noose made of a vine.

VÁSAVA·DATTA: *(in anger)* Kánchana·mala, tie this Brahmin up with this noose made of a vine and bring him along. And put this badly brought-up little girl in front.

KÁNCHANA·MALA: As your highness commands. *(tying the* JESTER *up with the noose made of a vine)* You damn fool, now you can experience the fruit of your own wicked plotting. Ságarika, you too, go in front.

SÁGARIKA: *(to herself)* Oh no! I must not have amassed enough merit, for I didn't even get my wish to die.

3.160 JESTER: *(looking at the* KING, *with despair)* My friend, remember me, one who met with disaster when the queen bound me and I had no one to protect me.

Exit VÁSAVA·DATTA, *taking them with her.*

KING: *(suffering)* What a miserable mess! What a debacle!

> Shall I worry about the queen's face,
> its affectionate smile usurped by her
> long-smoldering rage?
> Or Ságarika, terrified, threatened by that
> towering rage?
> Or Vasántaka, bound and led away from here?
> Tormented by every sort of anguish,
> I cannot find peace of mind even for a moment.

tat kim idānīm iha sthitena? devīṃ prasādayitum abhyantaram eva praviśāmi.

3.165 *iti niṣkrāntāḥ sarve.*

iti «Saṃketo» nāma tṛtīyo 'ṅkaḥ.

But what's the use of my staying here? I'll go inside to appease the queen.

Exit all.

The end of Act Three, called "The Rendezvous."

PRELUDE TO ACT IV

tataḥ praviśati gṛhīta|ratna|mālā s'|âsrā SUSAṂGATĀ.

SUSAṂGATĀ: *(sa|karuṇaṃ niḥśvasya)* ⌜hā pia|sahi Sāarie, hā lajjāuṇṇi, hā udāra|śīle, hā sahī|jaṇa|vacchale, hā somma| daṃsaṇe! kahiṃ dāṇiṃ tumaṃ mae pekkhidavvā?⌟ *(iti roditi. ūrdhvam avalokya, niḥśvasya ca)* ⌜aï, devva|hadaa a|aruṇa! a|sāmaṇṇa|rūa|sohā tādisī tue jaï ṇimmidā, tā kīsa uṇa īdisaṃ avatth'|antaraṃ pāvidā? iaṃ a raaṇa|mālā jīvida|ṇir|āsāe tāe «kassa vi bamhaṇassa hatthe paḍivādesu tti» bhaṇia mama hatthe samappidā. tā jāva kiṃ pi bamhaṇaṃ aṇṇesāmi.⌟ *(parikramy' âgrato vilokya ca)* ⌜ae, eso khu ajja|Vasantao ido jjeva āacchadi. tā jāva edassa jjeva edaṃ paḍivādaïssam.⌟

tataḥ praviśati prahṛṣṭo VASANTAKAḤ.

4.5 VASANTAKAḤ: ⌜hī hī, bho! ajja kkhu pia|vaasseṇa pasādidāe tatta|bhodīe Vāsavadattāe bandhaṇādo moāvia sa|hattha|diṇṇehiṃ modaeiṃ cirassa dāva kālassa uaraṃ me su|pūridaṃ kidam. aṇṇaṃ ca edaṃ paṭṭ'|aṃsua|jualaṃ kaṇṇ'|ābharaṇaṃ a diṇṇam. tā jāva dāṇiṃ gadua pia| vaassaṃ pekkhāmi.⌟ *(parikrāmati.)*

SUSAṂGATĀ: *(rudatī, sahas" ôpasṛtya)* ⌜ajja|Vasantaa, ciṭṭha dāva muhuttaam.⌟

VIDŪṢAKAḤ: *(dṛṣṭvā)* ⌜kadhaṃ, Susaṃgadā! Susaṃgade, kiṃ| ṇimittaṃ rodīadi? ṇa kkhu Sāariāe acc|āhidaṃ kiṃ vi saṃvuttam?⌟

[Time: A Day Later]

Enter SUSÁNGATA, *in tears, holding a jewel necklace.*

SUSÁNGATA: *(sighing, with pity)* O my dear friend Ságarika, so modest, so noble in temperament, so beautiful to look at. You always treated your friends like daughters. But where can I see you now? *(She weeps, looking up and sighing.)* Damned, pitiless fate, if you created someone of such uncommon beauty and presence, then why did you condemn her to be reduced to such a sorry state? When she had no hope for her life, she placed this jewel necklace in my hands and said, "Put it in the hands of some Brahmin." So now I'm looking for some Brahmin. *(walking around and looking in front of her)* Why, there's the good Vasántaka coming this very way. He's the one I'll give this to.

Enter VASÁNTAKA, *rejoicing.*

VASÁNTAKA: Hurrah! Today my dear friend appeased her 4.5
highness Vásava·datta and she set me free from prison and gave me sweets with her own hand, enough to keep my belly full for a long time! And she also gave me this pair of silk garments and an ear ornament. Now I'll go to see my dear friend. *(He walks around.)*

SUSÁNGATA: *(weeping, suddenly coming up to him)* Good Vasántaka, wait just a minute!

JESTER: *(seeing her)* Why, it's Susángata. Susángata, why are you crying? Has something disastrous happened to Ságarika? Oh, I hope not!

SUSAMGATĀ: ⌜ajja|Vasantaa, edaṃ jjeva ṇivedaïssam. sā kkhu tavassiṇī devīe Ujjaïṇiṃ ṇiadi tti pavādaṃ kadua uvatthide addha|ratte ṇa jāṇīadi kahiṃ ṇīd" êtti.⌟

VIDŪṢAKAḤ: *(s'|ôdvegam)* ⌜adi|ṇigghiṇaṃ kkhu kidaṃ devīe.⌟

4.10 SUSAMGATĀ: ⌜iaṃ ca raaṇa|mālā tāe jīvida|ṇir|āsāe «ajja| Vasantaassa hatthe paḍivādesu tti» bhaṇia mama hatthe samappidā. tā geṇhadu edaṃ ajjo.⌟

VIDŪṢAKAḤ: *(s'|âsram)* ⌜bhodi, ṇa me īdise patthāve hatthā geṇhiduṃ pasaranti.⌟

ubhau ruditaḥ.

SUSAMGATĀ: *(añjaliṃ baddhvā)* ⌜tāe jjeva aṇuggahaṃ karanto aṅgī|karedu edaṃ ajjo.⌟

VIDŪṢAKAḤ: *(vicintya)* ⌜aha vā uvaṇehi, jeṇa imāe jjevva Sāariā|viraha|dukkhidaṃ pia|vaassaṃ viṇodaïssam.⌟

4.15 SUSAMGAT" *ôpanayati.*

VIDŪṢAKAḤ: *(gṛhītvā, nirvarṇya, sa|vismayam)* ⌜Susaṃgade, kudo uṇa tāe īdisassa alaṃ|kārassa samāgamo?⌟

SUSAMGATĀ: ⌜ajja, mae vi sā kodūhaleṇa pucchidā jjev' âsi.⌟

VIDŪṢAKAḤ: ⌜tado tāe kiṃ bhaṇidaṃ?⌟

SUSÁNGATA: Good Vasántaka, that's precisely what I want to tell you. The queen circulated a rumor that she had sent that poor girl to Ujjain, and then at midnight they took her away—I don't know where.

JESTER: *(upset)* The queen did such an excessively cruel thing?

SUSÁNGATA: And when she had no hope for her life, she placed this jewel necklace in my hands and said, "Put it in the hands of the good Vasántaka." So, good sir, please take it. 4.10

JESTER: *(tearfully)* Under such circumstances, my lady, my hands won't stretch out to receive it.

They weep.

SUSÁNGATA: *(joining her palms in supplication)* Just as a favor to her, good sir, please accept it.

JESTER: *(thinking)* Or bring it, and use it to cheer up my dear friend, who is suffering from his separation from Ságarika.

SUSÁNGATA *presents it to him.* 4.15

JESTER: *(taking it and looking at it closely, with astonishment)* Susángata, where in the world could she have come to possess such an ornament?

SUSÁNGATA: I, too, was curious about that, sir, and asked her.

JESTER: And what did she say?

SUSAMGATĀ: ⌜tado sā ūddhaṃ pekkhia dīhaṃ ṇissasia: «Susaṃgade, kiṃ dāṇiṃ tue edāe kadhāe tti» bhaṇia rodidum paüttā.⌟

4.20 VIDŪṢAKAḤ: ⌜ṇaṃ kahidaṃ jjeva sāmaṇṇa|jaṇa|dul|laheṇa imiṇā paricchadeṇa: savvahā mahā|kula|ppasūdāe tāe hodavvaṃ tti. Susaṃgade, pia|vaasso dāṇiṃ kahiṃ?⌟

SUSAMGATĀ: ⌜ajja, eso khu bhaṭṭā devī|bhavaṇāo ṇikkamia phaḍia|silā|maṇḍavaṃ gado. tā gacchadu ajo. ahaṃ vi devīe pāsa|vattiṇī bhavissam.⌟

VIDŪṢAKAḤ: ⌜evvam.⌟

iti niṣkrāntau.

praveṣakaḥ.

SUSÁNGATA: She looked upward, sighed deeply, said, "Susángata, you don't need to hear that whole story now," and started to weep.

JESTER: Indeed, this ornament, which would be impossible 4.20
for any ordinary person to get, tells the story—that she must come from an altogether great family. Susángata, where is my dear friend now?

SUSÁNGATA: When the king came out of the queen's palace, sir, he went to the crystal pavilion. Please, sir, go there. And I'll stay by the queen's side.

JESTER: Yes.

Exit all.

End of Interlude

ACT IV
THE MAGICIAN

4.25 *tataḥ praviśaty āsana|stho* RĀJĀ.

RĀJĀ: *(vicintya)*

sa|vyājaiḥ śapathaiḥ, priyeṇa vacasā,
citt'|ânuvṛtty" âdhikaṃ,
vailakṣyeṇa pareṇa pāda|patanair,
vākyaiḥ sakhīnāṃ muhuḥ
pratyāpattim upāgatā na hi tathā
devī rudatyā, yathā
prakṣāly' êva tay" âiva bāṣpa|salilaiḥ
kopo 'panītaḥ svayam. [1]

(s'|ôtkaṇṭhaṃ niḥśvasya) idānīṃ devyāṃ prasannāyāṃ Sāgarikā|cint" âiva kevalaṃ māṃ bādhate. kutaḥ:

ambho|ja|garbha|su|kumāra|tanus tath" âsau
kaṇṭha|grahe prathama|rāga|ghane
madhyaḥ patan Madana|mārgaṇa|randhra|mārgair,
manye, mama priyatamā hṛdayaṃ praviṣṭā. [2]

4.30 *(vicintya)* yo 'pi me viśvāsa|sthānaṃ, Vasantakaḥ, so 'pi devyā saṃyatas tiṣṭhati. tat kasy' âgre bāṣpa|mokṣaṃ kariṣye? *(iti niḥśvasiti.)*

Enter the KING, *seated.* 4.25

KING: *(thinking)*

> I swore deceptive oaths, and spoke endearing
> words, and did whatever she fancied,
> and paraded my great shame, and fell at her feet;
> and her women friends spoke to her
> again and again.
> But none of that brought the queen back to herself
> as much as she did, herself, when she wept
> and dispelled her anger
> as if washing it away with the water of her
> own tears.*

(sighing with longing) Now that I've appeased the queen, all that bothers me is my concern for Ságarika. For:

> My dearest one's body is as tender as the inside
> of a lotus,
> and she melted when I embraced her neck
> too hard in that first passion.
> So I think she must have entered my heart
> through the paths of the openings
> made by the Intoxicator's arrows,
> which fell at the same time.*

(thinking) And Vasántaka, in whom I always confide, also 4.30
remains imprisoned by the queen. So whose shoulder is there for me to cry on? *(He sighs.)*

tataḥ praviśati VASANTAKAḤ.

VASANTAKAḤ: *(*RĀJĀNAṂ *dṛṣṭvā)* ⌜eso kkhu ṇibbhar'|ôkkaṇṭhā|parikkhāmaṃ vi salāghaṇijja|lāvaṇṇaṃ taṇuṃ samuvvahanto udio via dudiā|cando ahiaaraṃ sohadi pia|vaasso. tā jāva ṇaṃ uvasappāmi.⌟ *(upasṛtya)* ⌜sotthi bhavade! diṭṭhiā diṭṭho si devī|hattha|gadeṇ' âvi mae puṇo vi edehiṃ acchīhiṃ.⌟

RĀJĀ: *(dṛṣṭvā, sa|harṣam)* aye! Vasantakaḥ prāptaḥ! sakhe, pariṣvajasva mām.

VIDŪṢAKAḤ: *(pariṣvajati.)*

4.35 RĀJĀ: vayasya, veṣeṇ' âiva niveditas te devyāḥ prasādaḥ. tat kathyatām, idānīṃ Sāgarikāyāḥ kā vārt" êti.

VIDŪṢAKAḤ *sa|vailakṣyam adho|mukhas tiṣṭhati.*

RĀJĀ: vayasya, kiṃ na kathayasi?

VIDŪṢAKAḤ: ⌜a|ppiaṃ te ṇivediduṃ na pāremi.⌟

RĀJĀ: *(s'|ôdvegam)* vayasya, katham a|priyam? vyaktam utsṛṣṭaṃ jīvitaṃ tayā. hā! priye Sāgarike. *(iti mūrcchati.)*

4.40 VIDŪṢAKAḤ: *(sa|saṃbhramam)* ⌜samassasadu, samassasadu pia|vaasso.⌟

Enter VASÁNTAKA.

VASÁNTAKA: *(seeing the* KING*)* Violent longing is wasting away my dear friend, yet his beauty inspires more praise than ever, like that of the waxing moon on the second day. I'll just go up to him. *(approaching)* Hello, sir. It's my good fortune to see you again with my own two eyes, after I had fallen into the queen's hands.

KING: *(seeing him, with joy)* Vasántaka has come! Give me a hug, my friend!

JESTER: *(Hugs him.)*

KING: My friend, your clothes alone announce to me that 4.35
you appeased the queen. So tell me now, what news of Ságarika?

The JESTER *looks ashamed, and hangs his head.*

KING: My friend, why don't you tell me?

JESTER: I can't bring myself to tell you bad news.

KING: *(upset)* What do you mean, "bad news," my friend? It's clear, she's given up her life! O, my dear Ságarika! *(He faints.)*

JESTER: *(hastily)* Courage, my dear friend, courage! 4.40

RĀJĀ: *(samāśvasya, s'|âsram)*

prāṇāḥ parityajata kāmam a|dakṣiṇaṃ māṃ!
re, dakṣiṇā bhavata, mad|vacanaṃ kurudhvam!
śīghraṃ na yāta yadi, tan muṣitāḥ stha nūnaṃ
yātā su|dūram adhunā gaja|gāminī sā. [3]

VIDŪṢAKAḤ: ⌜bho vaassa, mā aṇṇadhā saṃbhāvehi. sā kkhu tavassiṇī devīe Ujjeṇiṃ pesid" êti suṇīadi. ado mae «a|ppiaṃ» tti bhaṇidam.⌟

RĀJĀ: katham, Ujjayinīṃ preṣitā! aho, nir|anurodhā mayi devī! vayasya, kena tav' âitad ākhyātam?

VIDŪṢAKAḤ: *(s'|âsraṃ, niḥśvasya)* ⌜bho! Susaṃgadāe. aṇṇaṃ ca, mama hatthe tāe kiṃ vi ṇimittaṃ iaṃ raaṇa|mālā pesidā.⌟

RĀJĀ: kim aparaṃ māṃ samāśvāsayitum? tad vayasy' ôpanaya.

VIDŪṢAKA *upanayati.*

RĀJĀ: *(gṛhītvā ratna|mālāṃ, nirvarṇya, hṛdaye nidhāya)* ahaha!

kaṇṭh'|āśleṣaṃ samāsādya
tasyāḥ prabhraṣṭay" ânayā:
tuly'|âvasthā sakh" îv' êyaṃ
tanur āśvāsyate mama. [4]

vayasya, tvaṃ paridhatsv' âitām, yena vayam enāṃ tāvad dṛṣṭvā dhṛtiṃ kariṣyāmaḥ.

KING: *(reviving, tearfully)*

Breaths of my life, leave me; do what I ask.
Oblige me more than I obliged her.
If you don't leave quickly,
  you'll surely be plundered.
For the woman who walks with the grace of
  an elephant
has already gone far away.*

JESTER: My friend, don't imagine things to be other than they are. I've heard that the queen has sent the poor girl to Ujjain. That's why I said, "bad news."

KING: What, sent to Ujjain? Oh, how unkind the queen is to me! My friend, who told you this?

JESTER: *(tearfully, sighing)* Susángata. And besides, for some 4.45
reason or other, she sent this jewel necklace by my hand.

KING: Why else but to encourage me? Give it to me, my friend.

The JESTER *gives it to him.*

KING: *(taking the jewel necklace, looking at it, placing it on his heart)* Oh!

It comforts my body like a friend,
for it has had the same experience:
first it embraced her neck, and then it fell away.

My friend, put it on, so that we can look at it and find 4.50
strength of mind.

VIDŪṢAKAḤ: ⌜jaṃ bhavaṃ āṇavedi.⌟ *(paridadhāti.)*

RĀJĀ: *(s'|âsram)* vayasya, dur|labhaṃ punar darśanaṃ priyāyāḥ.

VIDŪṢAKAḤ: *(diśo 'valokya, sa|bhayam)* ⌜bho vaassa, mā evvaṃ ucca mantehi. kaā vi ko vi devīe iha saṃcaradi.⌟

tataḥ praviśati vetra|hastā VASUṂDHARĀ.

4.55 VASUṂDHARĀ: *(upasṛtya)* ⌜jaadu, jaadu bhaṭṭā! bhaṭṭā, eso kkhu Rumaṇvado bhāiṇeo Vijayavammā piaṃ kiṃ pi ṇivedidu|kāmo duāre ciṭṭhadi.⌟

RĀJĀ: Vasuṃdhare, a|vilambitaṃ praveśaya.

PRATĪHĀRĪ: ⌜jaṃ devo āṇavedi.⌟ *(iti niṣkramya,* VIJAYAVARMAṆĀ *saha punaḥ praviśya)* ⌜Vijaavammā, eso kkhu bhaṭṭā. tā uvasappadu ajjo.⌟

VIJAYAVARMĀ: *(upasṛtya)* jayatu, jayatu devaḥ! deva, diṣṭyā vardhase Rumaṇvato vijayena.

RĀJĀ: sādhu Rumaṇvan, sādhu! a|cirān mahat|prayojanam anuṣṭhitam. Vijayavarman, ita āsyatām.

4.60 VIJAYAVARM" *ôpaviśati.*

RĀJĀ: Vijayavarman, jitaḥ Kosal'|âdhipatiḥ?

JESTER: As your majesty commands. *(He puts it on.)*

KING: *(tearfully)* My friend, it will be hard to find a way to see my dear one again.

JESTER: *(looking around in all directions, frightened)* My friend, don't talk so loud! Sometime, someone who belongs to the queen may be passing by here.

Enter VASUN·DHARA *[the Gate-keeper] with a cane staff in her hand.*

VASUN·DHARA: *(approaching)* Victory, victory to the king. 4.55
Víjaya·varman, the son of Rumánvat's sister, is waiting here at the door, your majesty, eager to tell you some good news.

KING: Vasun·dhara, bring him in without delay.

GATE-KEEPER: As your majesty commands. *(going out, returning with* VÍJAYA·VARMAN*)* Víjaya·varman, this is the king. You may approach, sir.

VÍJAYA·VARMAN: *(approaching)* Victory, victory to the king. Good fortune smiles on you, sire, for Rumánvat brings you victory.

KING: Bravo, Rumánvat, bravo! You accomplished a great undertaking in a short time. Víjaya·varman, sit down here.

VÍJAYA·VARMAN *sits down.* 4.60

KING: Víjaya·varman, has the king of Kósala been conquered?

VIJAYAVARMĀ: devasya prabhāveṇa.

RĀJĀ: Vijayavarman, tat kathaya, katham iti? vistarataḥ śrotum icchāmi.

VIJAYAVARMĀ: deva, śrūyatām. vayam ito dev'|ādeśāt katipayair ev' âhobhir an|eka|kari|turaga|patti|dur|nivāreṇa mahatā bala|samūhena gatvā Vindhya|durg"|âvasthitasya Kosal'|âdhipater dvāram avaṣṭabhya senāḥ samāveśayitum ārabdhāḥ.

4.65 RĀJĀ: tatas tataḥ?

VIJAYAVARMĀ: tataḥ Kosal'|âdhipatir api darpāt paribhavam a|sahamāno hāstika|prāyam a|śeṣam ātma|sainyaṃ sajjī|kṛtavān.

VIDŪṢAKAḤ: ⌜bho, lahuṃ ācakkha. vevadi via me hiaam.⌟

RĀJĀ: tatas tataḥ?

VIJAYAVARMĀ: deva, kṛta|niścayaś c' âsau

VÍJAYA·VARMAN: By your majesty's power.

KING: Tell me how, Víjaya·varman. I want to hear it in detail.

VÍJAYA·VARMAN: Please listen, your majesty. We set out from here by your majesty's command, and traveled for a few days with a great collected power, well nigh irresistible with its many elephants, horses, and foot soldiers. Then we blocked the passage of the king of Kósala, who was stationed in a fort in the Vindhya mountain, and we began to encamp our armies.

KING: And then? 4.65

VÍJAYA·VARMAN: Then the king of Kósala, too proud to allow himself to be overpowered like that, marshaled his entire army, which consisted principally of elephants.

JESTER: Talk fast! My heart feels as if it's trembling!

KING: And then?

VÍJAYA·VARMAN: When he had made his resolution, your majesty,

4.70 yoddhuṃ nirgatya Vindhyād abhavad abhimukhas
tat|kṣaṇaṃ dig|vibhāgān
Vindhyen' êv' âpareṇa dvipa|pati|pṛtan"|ā-
pīḍa|bandhena rundhan,
vegād bāṇān vimuñcan sa|mada|kari|ghaṭ'|ôt-
piṣṭa|pattir nipatya
pratyaicchad vāñchit'|āpti|dvi|guṇita|rabhasas
taṃ Rumaṇvān kṣaṇena. [5]

api ca:

astra|vyasta|śiras|tra|śastra|kaṣaṇ'|ôt-
kṛtt'|ôttam'|âṅge kṣaṇaṃ
vyūḍh"|âsṛk|sariti svanat|praharaṇe
varm'|ôdvalad|vahnini
āhūy' āji|mukhe sa Kosala|patir
bhaṅga|pratīpī|bhavann
eken' âiva Rumaṇvatā śara|śatair
matta|dvipa|stho hataḥ. [6]

VIDŪṢAKAḤ: ⌜jaadu, jaadu bhavaṃ! jitaṃ amhehiṃ!⌟ *(ity ut-thāya nṛtyati.)*

RĀJĀ: sādhu Kosala|pate, sādhu! mṛtyur api te ślāghyo, yasya śatravo 'py evaṃ puruṣa|kāraṃ varṇayanti. tatas tataḥ?

He went out from the Vindhya mountain to fight 4.70
  and faced us for a moment,
obstructing all the quarters of the sky with his band
  of closely packed bull elephants,
as if it were another Vindhya mountain.
Though the temples of the rutting elephants
  crushed Rumánvat's foot soldiers,
he shot arrows rapidly and stood against him
  in a moment,
for his violent zeal was doubled
  by getting what he desired.

And:

As the battle began, missiles knocked off helmets,
whose sword-like edges struck heads and
  cut them off,
and in a moment a river of blood flooded the field.
Blows rang out and fire blazed up from armor.
The king of Kósala,
  mounted on a rutting elephant,
staving off a rout, challenged Rumánvat,
who killed him with hundreds of arrows
  in single combat.

JESTER: Victory, victory to you, sir! We have won! *(He stands up and dances.)*

KING: Bravo, king of Kósala, bravo! Even your death is worthy of praise, for even your enemies acclaim your manly deeds. And then?

4.75 VIJAYAVARMĀ: deva, tato Rumaṇvān api Kosaleṣu mad|bhrātaraṃ jyāyāṃsaṃ Jayavarmāṇaṃ sthāpayitvā samara|vraṇitam a|śeṣa|balam anuvartamānaḥ śanaiḥ śanair āgacchaty eva.

RĀJĀ: Vasuṃdhare, ucyatāṃ Yaugandharāyaṇa «dīyatāṃ mat|prasādo 'sy' êti.»

VASUṂDHARĀ: ⌜jaṃ devo āṇavedi.⌟ *(iti* VIJAYAVARMAṆĀ *saha niṣkrāntā.)*

tataḥ praviśati KĀÑCANAMĀLĀ.

KĀÑCANAMĀLĀ: ⌜āṇatta mhi devīe jaha «hañje, Kañcaṇamāle, gaccha. edaṃ inda|jāliaṃ ajja|uttassa daṃsehi.»⌟ *(parikramy' âvalokya ca)* ⌜eso kkhu bhaṭṭā. tā jāva ubasappāmi.⌟ *(upasṛtya)* ⌜jaadu, jaadu bhaṭṭā! devī viṇṇavedi: «eso khu Ujjeṇīdo Savvasiddhi ṇāma inda|jālio āgado. tā pekkhadu ṇaṃ ajja|utto tti.»⌟

4.80 RĀJĀ: asti naḥ kautukam indra|jāle. tac chīghraṃ praveśaya.

KĀÑCANAMĀLĀ: ⌜jaṃ devo āṇavedi tti.⌟

niṣkramya, punaḥ picchikā|hasten' āindra|jālikena saha praviśati.

AINDRAJĀLIKAḤ: *(picchikāṃ bhramayan)*

⌜paṇamaha calaṇa Indassa inda|jālaa|piṇaddha|ṇāmassa,
taha jjevva Saṃbarassa, māā|su|pariṭṭhida|jasassa.⌟ [7]

VÍJAYA·VARMAN: Then, your majesty, Rumánvat put my 4.75
older brother Jaya·varman in command of Kósala and is coming here in slow marches, bringing his entire army, bearing their battle-wounds.

KING: Vasun·dhara, tell Yaugándharáyana to give this man a reward from me.

VASUN·DHARA: As your majesty commands. *(Exit, with* VÍJAYA·VARMAN.*)*

Enter KÁNCHANA·MALA.

KÁNCHANA·MALA: The queen commanded me: "Kánchana·mala, go and show this magician to my husband." *(walking around and looking)* Here is the king. I'll approach him. *(approaching)* Victory, victory to the king. The queen reports: "This magician named All-powerful has come from Ujjain.* My husband should see him."

KING: We have some curiosity about magic. Bring him in 4.80
right away.

KÁNCHANA·MALA: As your majesty commands.

She exits and enters again with the MAGICIAN, *who holds a fan of peacock feathers in his hand.*

MAGICIAN: *(waving the peacock fan)*

> Bow to the feet of Indra,
> whose name is closely bound up
> in the very name of magic, "the Net of Indra,"
> and of Shámbara, whose fame in illusion is
> well-established.*

4.85 KĀÑCANAMĀLĀ: *(upasṛtya)* ⌜bhaṭṭā, eso kkhu indi|jālao.⌟

AINDRAJĀLIKAḤ: ⌜jaadu, jaadu devo! deva,⌟

⌜kiṃ dharaṇie miaṅko, āāse mahi|haro, jale jalaṇo,
majjh'|aṇhammi paoso dāvijjaï? dehi āṇattim!⌟ [8]

⌜aha vā kiṃ bahuṇā jappideṇa?⌟

⌜majja païṇṇā esā: jaṃ jaṃ hiaeṇa ihasi saṃdaṭṭuṃ,
taṃ taṃ daṃsemi ahaṃ guruṇo manta|ppabhāveṇa.⌟ [9]

4.90 VIDŪṢAKAḤ: ⌜bho vaassa, avahido hohi. īdiso se avaṭṭambho, jeṇa savvaṃ saṃbhāvīadi.⌟

RĀJĀ: bhadra, tiṣṭha tāvat. Kāñcanamāle! ucyatāṃ devī: «yuṣmadīya ev' âyam aindra|jāliko vijanī|kṛtaś c' âyam uddeśaḥ. tad ehi. sahitāv ev' âinaṃ paśyāva iti.»

KĀÑCANAMĀLĀ: ⌜jaṃ bhaṭṭā āṇavedi.⌟ *(iti niṣkrāntā.)*

tataḥ praviśati VĀSAVADATTĀ KĀÑCANAMĀLĀ *ca.*

VĀSAVADATTĀ: ⌜Kañcaṇamāle, Ujjaïṇīdo āado tti atthi me tassiṃ inda|jālie pakkha|vādo.⌟

4.95 KĀÑCANAMĀLĀ: ⌜ṇṇādi|kula|bahu|māṇo kkhu eso bhaṭṭiṇīe. tā edu, edu bhaṭṭiṇī.⌟ *(iti parikrāmataḥ.)*

KÁNCHANA·MALA: *(approaching)* Your majesty, here is the magician. 4.85

MAGICIAN: Victory, victory to the king! Your majesty:

> The moon, with the mark of the hare, on earth,
> or a mountain in the sky, or fire in water,
> or dusk at noon—
> what would you like to see?
> Just give the command.

But what's the use of so much talk?

> This is my promise: Whatever you wish
> in your heart to see
> I will show you, by the power of my teacher's
> mantra.

JESTER: My friend, pay attention. He has such confidence that he's capable of anything. 4.90

KING: Wait, sir, wait a minute. Kánchana·mala, tell the queen: "This magician is yours. And this place has been emptied of all the people. So come, and we two will see him together."

KÁNCHANA·MALA: As your majesty commands. *(Exit.)*

Enter VÁSAVA·DATTA *and* KÁNCHANA·MALA.

VÁSAVA·DATTA: Kánchana·mala, recalling that the magician has come from Ujjain, I'm well disposed toward him.*

KÁNCHANA·MALA: Your highness of course honors this man of her father's family. So come, please, ma'am, come. *(They walk around.)* 4.95

VĀSAVADATTĀ: *(upasṛtya)* ⌜jedu, jedu ajja|utto.⌟

RĀJĀ: devi, bahutaram anena garjitam. tad ih' ôpaviśyatām. paśyāmas tāvat.

VĀSAVADATT" *ôpaviśati.*

RĀJĀ: bhadra, prastūyatām indra|jālam.

4.100 AINDRAJĀLIKAḤ: ⌜jaṃ devo āṇavedi.⌟ *(iti bahu|vidhaṃ nāṭyaṃ kṛtvā, picchikāṃ bhramayan)*

⌜Hari|Hara|Bamha|ppamuhe
deve daṃsemi deva|rāaṃ ca,
gagaṇammi Siddha|Cāraṇa|
sura|vahū|satthaṃ ca ṇaccantam.⌟ [10]

⌜tā pekkhadu devo.⌟

RĀJĀ: *(ūrdhvam avaloky' āsanād avataran)* āścaryam, āścaryam! devi, paśya:

eṣa Brahmā saro|je, raja|nikara|kalā|
śekharaḥ Śaṅkaro 'yaṃ,
dorbhir daity'|ântako 'sau sa|dhanur|asi|gadā|
cakra|cihnaiś caturbhiḥ.
eṣo 'py Airāvata|sthas tri|daśa|patir, amī,
devi, devās tath" ânye,
nṛtyanti vyomni c' âitaś cala|caraṇa|raṇan|
nūpurā divya|nāryaḥ. [11]

VÁSAVA·DATTA: *(approaching)* Victory, victory to my husband.

KING: My queen, this man has boasted rather a lot. But do sit down here, please, and then let's see.

VÁSAVA·DATTA *sits down.*

KING: My good man, let the magic begin.

MAGICIAN: As your majesty commands. *(He mimes various actions and waves his peacock fan.)* 4.100

I will show you, in the sky,
Vishnu, Shiva, and Brahma,
and all the other gods, and the king of the gods,
and the whole host of *siddhas* and *cháranas*
and the women of the gods, dancing.*

Behold, please, your majesty!

KING: *(looking upward and descending from his throne)* Amazing! Absolutely amazing! Look, my queen:

Here is Brahma on his lotus, and this is Shánkara,
wearing his tiara made of the crescent moon,
and that is the Demon-killer,
with his four signifying arms
holding the bow, sword, mace and discus.
And that is the king of the gods,
seated on his elephant Airávata,
and those, my queen, are the other gods,
and the heavenly women,
their anklets ringing as their feet move,
dancing in the sky.*

4.105 VĀSAVADATTĀ: ⌜accariaṃ, accariaṃ!⌟

VIDŪṢAKAḤ: *(apavārya)* ⌜āḥ, dāsīe putta indajālia! kiṃ edehiṃ devehiṃ acchārāhiṃ ca daṃsidāhiṃ? jaï de imiṇā parituṭṭheṇa kajjaṃ, tā Sāariaṃ daṃsehi.⌟

tataḥ praviśati VASUṂDHARĀ.

VASUṂDHARĀ: *(*RĀJĀNAM *upasṛtya)* ⌜jedu, jedu bhaṭṭā! amacco Jogandharāaṇo viṇṇavedi: «eso kkhu Vikkamabāhuṇo pahāṇ'|âmacco Vasubhūdi Babbhavveṇa kañcuiṇā saha āgado. tā aruhadi devo imassiṃ jjeva sundara|muhuttae pekkhidum. ahaṃ pi kajja|sesaṃ samāpia āgado evva tti.»⌟

VĀSAVADATTĀ: ⌜ajja|utta, ciṭṭhadu dāva inda|ālaṃ. māula|gharādo pahāṇ'|âmacco Vasubhūdi āgado. taṃ dāva pekkhadu ajja|utto.⌟

4.110 RĀJĀ: yath" āha devī. *(aindra|jālikaṃ prati)* bhadra, viśramyatām idānīm.

AINDRAJĀLIKAḤ: ⌜jaṃ devo āṇavedi.⌟ *(punaḥ picchikāṃ bhramayati.)*

(niṣkrāman) ⌜ekko uṇa maha khelao avassaṃ deveṇa pekkhidavvo.⌟

RĀJĀ: bhadra, drakṣyāmaḥ.

VĀSAVADATTĀ: ⌜Kañcaṇamāle, gaccha tumaṃ, dehi se pāritosikam.⌟

VÁSAVA·DATTA: Amazing, absolutely amazing! 4.105

JESTER: *(aside)* You son of a slave girl, you magician, you, what use are all these gods and heavenly courtesans you've displayed? If you want to satisfy him, show him Ságarika.

Enter VASUN·DHARA.

VASUN·DHARA: *(approaching the* KING*)* Victory, victory to your majesty. Prime Minister Yaugándharáyana reports: "Vasu·bhuti, the minister of state of Víkrama·bahu, has arrived with our chamberlain, Babhrávya. Your majesty should, please, see them, at this fine moment. I too am coming as soon as I have finished what remains to be done."

VÁSAVA·DATTA: My husband, let the magic show wait. The minister of state, Vasu·bhuti, has come from the house of my maternal uncle.* So my husband should see him at once.

KING: As the queen says. *(to the* MAGICIAN*)* My good man, 4.110
please stop now.

MAGICIAN: As your majesty commands. *(He waves the peacock fan again.)*

(departing) But your majesty must, without fail, watch one more trick of mine.

KING: My good man, we will see it.

VÁSAVA·DATTA: Kánchana·mala, go and give him a little present.

KĀÑCANAMĀLĀ: ⌜jaṃ devī āṇavedi.⌟ *(*AINDRA|JĀLIKENA *saha niṣkrāntā.)*

4.115 RĀJĀ: Vasantaka, pratyudgamya praveśyatāṃ Vasubhūtiḥ.

VIDŪṢAKAḤ: ⌜jaṃ devo āṇavedi.⌟ *(iti* VASUṂDHARAYĀ *saha niṣkrāntaḥ.)*

tataḥ praviśati VASANTAKEN' *ânugamyamāno* VASUBHŪTIR BĀBHRAVYAŚ *ca.*

VASUBHŪTIḤ: *(samantād avalokya)* aho Vats'|ēśvarasy' ânubhāvaḥ! iha hi:

ākṣipto jaya|kuñjareṇa, tura|gān
nirvarṇayan vallabhān,
saṃgīta|dhvaninā hṛtaḥ, kṣiti|bhṛtāṃ
goṣṭhīṣu tiṣṭhan kṣaṇam,
sadyo vismṛta|Siṃhal'|êndra|vibhavaḥ
kakṣā|pradeṣe 'py, aho,
dvāḥ|sthen' âiva kutūhalena mahatā
grāmyo yath" âhaṃ kṛtaḥ. [12]

4.120 BĀBHRAVYAḤ: Vasubhūte, adya khalu cirāt svāminaṃ drakṣyām' îti yat satyam, ānand'|âtiśayena kim apy avasth"|ântaram anubhavāmi. kutaḥ:

KÁNCHANA·MALA: As your majesty commands. *(Exit with the* MAGICIAN.*)*

KING: Vasántaka, go out and bring Vasu·bhuti in. 4.115

JESTER: As your majesty commands. *(Exit with* VASUN·DHARA.*)*

Enter VASU·BHUTI *and* BABHRÁVYA, *followed by* VASÁNTAKA.

VASU·BHUTI: *(looking around on all sides)* Oh, the magnificence of the king of Vatsa! For here:

> Distracted by the victorious elephant
>   while staring at the priceless horses,
> carried away by the echoes of music
>   while stopping for a moment among
>   the assemblies of kings who rule the earth,
> even as I stood on the threshold of the
> walled courtyard I immediately forgot
> the majesty of the king of Símhala,
> and my great curiosity made me just like
>   a simple country boy.

BABHRÁVYA: Vasu·bhuti, the realization that I will actually 4.120
see my master this very day after such a long time gives me such excessive joy that I am experiencing a kind of transformation. For:

vivṛddhiṃ kampasya
prathayatitarāṃ sādhvasa|vaśād,
a|vispaṣṭāṃ dṛṣṭiṃ
tirayatitarāṃ bāṣpa|paṭalaiḥ,
skhalad|varṇāṃ vāṇīṃ
jaḍayatitarāṃ gadgadatayā,
jarāyāḥ sāhāyyaṃ
mama hi paritoṣo 'dya kurute. [13]

VIDŪṢAKAḤ: *(agre bhūtvā)* ⌜edu, edu amacco.⌟

VASUBHŪTIḤ: *(*VIDŪṢAKASYA *kaṇṭhe ratna|mālāṃ dṛṣṭv" âpavārya)* Bābhravya, jāne s" âiv' êyaṃ ratna|mālā, yā devena rāja|putryai prasthāna|kāle dattā.

BĀBHRAVYAḤ: amātya, asti sādṛśyam. tat kiṃ Vasantakaṃ pṛcchāmi prāptim asyāḥ?

4.125 VASUBHŪTIḤ: Bābhravya, mā m" âivam. mahati rāja|kule ratna|bāhulyān na dur|labho bhūṣaṇānāṃ saṃvādaḥ. *(iti parikrāmati.)*

VIDŪṢAKAḤ: ⌜bho, eso kkhu mahā|rāao. tā upasappadu amacco.⌟

VASUBHŪTIḤ: *(upasṛtya)* vijayatāṃ mahā|rājaḥ!

RĀJĀ: *(utthāya)* ārya, abhivādaye.

VASUBHŪTIḤ: āyuṣmān bhava!

4.130 RĀJĀ: āsanam, āsanam āryāya.

Nervousness has made my trembling worse
and wider ranging;
veils of tears further obscure my eyesight;
because I'm all choked up,
my speech mumbles and stumbles on its syllables
more than ever.
My utter delight is giving a helping hand to
my old age!

JESTER: *(going in front)* Come, please, your Excellency, come.

VASU·BHUTI: *(seeing the jewel necklace on the* JESTER*'s neck, aside)* Babhrávya, I know that necklace! It's the very one that the king gave the princess at the time of her departure.

BABHRÁVYA: Your Excellency, it does look just like it. Shall I ask Vasántaka how he got it?

VASU·BHUTI: No, no, Babhrávya, don't. There are so many 4.125
jewels in a great royal palace that it's not hard to find a correspondence of ornaments.* *(They walk around.)*

JESTER: Here is the great king. Please approach him, your Excellency.

VASU·BHUTI: *(approaching)* Total victory to the great king!

KING: *(rising)* I greet you, good sir.

VASU·BHUTI: Live long and prosper!

KING: A seat, a seat, for the gentleman. 4.130

VIDŪṢAKAḤ: ⌜edaṃ āsaṇam. upavisadu amacco.⌟

VASUBHŪTIR *upaviśati.*

BĀBHRAVYAḤ: deva, Bābhravyaḥ praṇamati.

RĀJĀ: *(pṛṣṭhe hastaṃ dattvā)* Bābhravya, ita āsyatām. *(*BĀBHRAVYA *upaviśati.)*

4.135 VIDŪṢAKAḤ: ⌜amacca, esā devī Vāsavadattā paṇamadi.⌟

VĀSAVADATTĀ: ⌜ajja, paṇamāmi.⌟

VASUBHŪTIḤ: āyuṣmati, Vatsa|rāja|sa|dṛśaṃ putram āpnuhi.

sarve upaviśanti.

RĀJĀ: ārya Vasubhūte, api kuśalaṃ tatra|bhavataḥ Siṃhal'|ēśvarasya?

4.140 VASUBHŪTIḤ: *(ūrdhvam avalokya, niḥśvasya ca)* deva, na jāne kiṃ vijñāpayāmi.

adho|mukhas tiṣṭhati.

VĀSAVADATTĀ: *(sa|viṣādam, ātma|gatam)* ⌜ha ddhī! ha ddhī! kiṃ dāṇiṃ Vasubhūdi kadhaïssadi?⌟

JESTER: Here is a seat. Please be seated, your Excellency.

VASU·BHUTI *sits down.*

BABHRÁVYA: Your majesty, Babhrávya bows to you.

KING: *(placing his hand on* BABHRÁVYA*'s back)* Babhrávya, come and sit over here. *(*BABHRÁVYA *sits down.)*

JESTER: Your Excellency, Queen Vásava·datta here bows to 4.135
you.

VÁSAVA·DATTA: Good sir, I bow to you.

VASU·BHUTI: May you live long and have a son just like the king of Vatsa.

They all sit down.

KING: Good Vasu·bhuti, is all well with His Majesty the king of Símhala?

VASU·BHUTI: *(looking up and sighing)* Your majesty, I don't 4.140
know what to report.

He stands there with his head lowered.

VÁSAVA·DATTA: *(desolated, to herself)* Oh dear! What story is Vasu·bhuti going to tell now?

RĀJĀ: kathaya, kim etat? ārya, ākula iva me 'ntar|ātmā.

BĀBHRAVYAḤ: *(apavārya)* amātya, ciram api sthitvā kathanīyam. tat kathyatām.

4.145 VASUBHŪTIḤ: *(s'|âsram)* deva, na śakyaṃ nivedayituṃ, tath" âpy eṣa kathayāmi manda|bhāgyaḥ. y" âsau Siṃhal'|ēśvareṇa sva|duhitā Ratnāvalī nām' āyuṣmatīṃ Vāsavadattāṃ dagdhām upaśrutya devāya pūrvaṃ prārthitā satī dattā.

RĀJĀ: *(apavārya)* devi, kim etad alīkam eva tvan|mātul'|âmātyaḥ kathayati?

VĀSAVADATTĀ: *(smitvā)* ⌜ajja|utta, ṇa jāṇīadi ko aliaṃ mantedi tti.⌟

VIDŪṢAKAḤ: ⌜tado tāe kiṃ vuttam?⌟

VASUBHŪTIḤ: sā ca yuṣmad|antikam ānīyamānā yāna|bhaṅgāt sāgare nimagnā. *(iti rudann adho|mukhas tiṣṭhati.)*

4.150 VĀSAVADATTĀ: *(s'|âsram)* ⌜hā, hada mhi manda|bhāiṇī! hā, bahiṇi Raaṇāvali, kahiṃ dāṇiṃ si? dehi me paḍivaaṇam.⌟

RĀJĀ: devi, samāśvasihi samāśvasihi! dur|avagāhā gatir daivasya. yāna|bhaṅga|patit'|ôtthitau nanv etāv eva te nidarśanam. *(iti* VASUBHŪTI|BĀBHRAVYAU *darśayati.)*

KING: Tell us what the situation is. Good sir, my inner soul is a bit uneasy.

BABHRÁVYA: *(aside)* Your Excellency, no matter how long you stand there, you're going to have to tell it. So let it be told.

VASU·BHUTI: *(tearfully)* Your majesty, it's not possible to tell 4.145
it, but I'm the unlucky one who has to tell it. When you asked the king of Símhala for the hand of his own daughter, named Ratnávali, he gave her to your majesty, after he heard that queen Vásava·datta had perished in a fire. And—

KING: *(aside)* My queen, what is this lie that the prime minister of your maternal uncle is telling?

VÁSAVA·DATTA: *(smiling)* My husband, one never knows who is telling a lie.

JESTER: What happened to her then?

VASU·BHUTI: He sent her to you, but there was a shipwreck, and she drowned in the ocean. *(He stands there, head bowed, weeping.)*

VÁSAVA·DATTA: *(tearfully)* Oh god, what a wretched, un- 4.150
lucky woman I am. O my sister Ratnávali,* where are you now? Answer me!

KING: Courage, my queen, courage. The ways of fate are unfathomable. After all, these two went down with the shipwreck and came up again; let them be your examples for comparison. *(pointing to* VASU·BHUTI *and* BABHRÁVYA.*)*

VĀSAVADATTĀ: ⌜ajja|utta, jujjadi edaṃ. paraṃ kuto mama ettiaṃ bhāa|heam?⌟

nepathye mahān kalakalaḥ.

harmyāṇāṃ hema|śṛṅga|śriyam iva nicayair
arciṣām ādadhānaḥ
sāndr'|ôdyāna|drum'|âgra|glapana|piśunit'|â-
tyanta|tīvr'|âbhitāpaḥ
kurvan krīḍā|mahī|dhraṃ sa|jala|jala|dhara|
śyāmalaṃ dhūma|pātair
eṣa ploṣ'|ārta|yoṣij|jana iha sahas" âiv'
ôtthito 'ntaḥ|pure 'gniḥ. [14]

4.155 api ca

devī|dāha|pravādo 'sau
yo 'bhūl Lāvāṇake purā,
kariṣyann iva taṃ satyam
ayam agniḥ samutthitaḥ. [15]

sarve saṃbhrāntāḥ paśyanti.

RĀJĀ: *(sa|saṃbhramam utthāya)* katham, antaḥ|pure 'gniḥ? kaṣṭaṃ! devī Vāsavadattā dagdhā! hā, priye Vāsavadatte!

VĀSAVADATTĀ: ⌜ajja|utta, parittāhi parittāhi!⌟

4.160 RĀJĀ: aye! katham, ati|saṃbhramād iha|sth" âpi devī n' ôpalakṣitā! devi, samāśvasihi samāśvasihi.

VÁSAVA·DATTA: My husband, you are right in that. But where would I get such great luck?

A great hubbub off-stage.

A fire has just broken out all of a sudden
  in the women's quarters,
terrifying the women as it flares up.
Its heaps of flames
give the palaces beautiful golden turrets.
The scorched tips of the dense trees
  in the garden show
  how excessively sharp its heat is.
And the clouds of smoke that fall
  on the artificial hill
make it look like a dark cloud full of water.

And 4.155

This fire broke out as if to make
the rumor that was spread in Lavánaka before—
saying that the queen was burnt—
come true.*

All look on in confusion.

KING: *(arising in haste)* What? A fire in the women's quarters? Oh no! What if Queen Vásava·datta has been burnt! Oh, my dear Vásava·datta!

VÁSAVA·DATTA: Help, my husband, help!

KING: Oh! Why, in my extreme haste and confusion, I didn't notice the queen even though she was standing right here beside me. Courage, my queen, courage! 4.160

VĀSAVADATTĀ: ⌈ajja|utta, mae attaṇo kide ṇa bhaṇidam. esā kkhu mae ṇigghiṇāe idha niaḍeṇa saṃjamidā Sāariā vivajjadi. tā taṃ parittāadu ajja|utto.⌋

RĀJĀ: kathaṃ devi, Sāgarikā vipadyate? eṣa gacchāmi.

VASUBHŪTIḤ: deva, kim a|kāraṇam eva pataṅga|vṛttiḥ kriyate?

BĀBHRAVYAḤ: deva, yuktam āha Vasubhūtiḥ.

4.165 VIDŪṢAKAḤ: *(*RĀJĀNAM *uttarīye gṛhītvā)* ⌈vaassa, mā kkhu evaṃ sāhasaṃ karehi!⌋

RĀJĀ: *(uttarīyam utsṛjya)* dhiṅ mūrkha! Sāgarikā vipadyate! kim ady' âpi prāṇā dhāryante? *(iti jvalana|praveśaṃ nāṭayitvā, dhūm'|âbhibhavaṃ nāṭayan)*

virama, virama vahne, muñca dhūm'|ânubandhaṃ!
prakaṭayasi kim uccair arciṣāṃ cakra|vālam?
viraha|huta|bhuj" âhaṃ yo na dagdhaḥ priyāyāḥ
pralaya|dahana|bhāsā, tasya kiṃ tvaṃ karoṣi? [16]

VĀSAVADATTĀ: ⌈kadhaṃ, mama dukkha|bhāiṇīe vaaṇādo evvaṃ ajjhavasidaṃ ajja|utteṇa! tā ahaṃ pi ajja|uttaṃ evva aṇugamissam.⌋

VIDŪṢAKAḤ: *(parikrāmann, agrato bhūtvā)* ⌈bhodi, ahaṃ vi de path'|ôvadesao homi.⌋

VÁSAVA·DATTA: My husband, I didn't speak for my own sake. But Ságarika may die, for in my cruelty I had her chained up here. Save her, please, my husband.

KING: What? Ságarika may die, my queen? I will go!

VASU·BHUTI: Your majesty, why should you go the way of a moth for no real reason?

BABHRÁVYA: Your majesty, what Vasu·bhuti said is right.

JESTER: *(grabbing the* KING *by his shirt)* My friend, don't do 4.165
anything so rash!

KING: *(freeing his shirt)* You idiot! Ságarika may die! Why is the breath of life still in me even now? *(He mimes rushing into the fire and being overcome by smoke.)*

> Stop, fire, stop! Give up
> this unbroken wave of smoke!
> Why do you brandish on high
> this circling mass of flames?
> If I wasn't burnt up by the fire of separation from my dear one,
> that blazed like the doomsday fire, what can you do to me?

VÁSAVA·DATTA: Since my husband has unhesitatingly done this because of what I said—miserably unlucky woman that I am—, I, too, will follow my husband.

JESTER: *(walking around and standing in front of her)* I, too, ma'am, will be your pathfinder.

4.170 VASUBHŪTI: kathaṃ, praviṣṭa eva jvalanaṃ Vatsa|rājaḥ! tan mam' âpi dṛṣṭa|rāja|putrī|vipatter ih' âiva yuktam ātmānam āhutī|kartum.

BĀBHRAVYAḤ: hā deva! kim idam a|kāraṇam eva Bharata|kulaṃ saṃśaya|tulām āropitam? atha vā kiṃ pralāpena? aham api bhakti|sa|dṛśam ācarāmi.

sarve 'gni|praveśaṃ nāṭayanti.

tataḥ praviśati nigaḍa|saṃyatā SĀGARIKĀ.

SĀGARIKĀ: *(diśo 'valokya)* ⌜ha ddhī! samantado pajjalido huta|vaho.⌟ *(vicintya, sa|paritoṣam)* ⌜ajja huta|vaho diṭṭhiā karissadi me duḥkh'|âvasāṇam.⌟

4.175 RĀJĀ: aye! iyam āsanna|huta|vahā vartate Sāgarikā. tat tvaritam enāṃ saṃbhāvayāmi. *(tvaritam upasṛtya)* ayi priye, kim ady' âpi saṃbhrame sva|sthay" âvasthīyate?

SĀGARIKĀ: *(*RĀJĀNAṂ *dṛṣṭvā, sva|gatam)* ⌜kadhaṃ, ajja|utto! tā edaṃ pekkhia puṇo vi me jīvid'|âhilāso saṃvutto.⌟ *(prakāśam)* ⌜parittāadu, parittāadu bhaṭṭā!⌟

RĀJĀ: bhīru, alaṃ bhayena:

muhūrtam api sahyatāṃ
    bahala eṣa dhūm'|ôdgamo! *(agrato 'valokya)*
  hahā, dhig! idam aṃśukaṃ
    jvalati te stanāt pracyutam!
(vilokya) muhuḥ skhalasi kiṃ? kathaṃ,
    nigaḍa|saṃyat" âsi! *(parikaraṃ baddhvā)* drutaṃ
  nayāmi bhavatīm itaḥ.
    priyatame, 'valambasva mām! [17]

VASU·BHUTI: Why, the king of Vatsa has already entered the fire! Then it is proper that I, too, who saw the princess die, should offer myself as an oblation into the fire here. 4.170

BABHRÁVYA: Your majesty, why jeopardize the race descended from Bharata for no good reason?* But what's the use of idle talk? I too will act in accordance with my devotion.

All mime entering the fire.

Enter SÁGARIKA, *in chains.*

SÁGARIKA: *(looking in all directions)* Oh no! The fire is blazing up on all sides! *(thinking, with satisfaction)* Fortunately, the fire, carrier of oblations, will put an end to my suffering today.

KING: Ságarika is here near the fire! I'll help her right away. 4.175
(approaching her in haste) My dear, how can you remain so self-possessed even now in this haste and confusion?

SÁGARIKA: *(seeing the* KING, *to herself)* Why, it's my husband! When I see him, my love of life comes back again. *(aloud)* Save me, your majesty! Save me,

KING: Don't be afraid, my timid one:

> Put up with this thick outpouring of smoke for
> just a moment. *(looking forward)*
> Oh no! This silk garment has fallen from your
> breast and caught fire.
> *(looking)* Why do you keep stumbling?
> Why, you're in chains! *(tying up his dhoti)*
> I will quickly take you away from here, my dearest.
> Hold on to me!

(kaṇṭhe gṛhītvā, nimīlit'|âkṣaḥ sparśa|sukhaṃ nāṭayan) aho! kṣaṇān me 'pagato 'yaṃ saṃtāpaḥ. priye, samāśvasihi samāśvasihi.

4.180 vyaktaṃ lagno 'pi bhavatīṃ
na dahaty eva pāvakaḥ,
yataḥ saṃtāpam ev' âyaṃ
sparśas te harati, priye! [18]

(unmīly' âkṣiṇī, diśo 'valokya, SĀGARIKĀṂ *ca muktvā)* aho, mahad āścaryam!

kv' âsau gato huta|vahas?
tad|avastham etad antaḥ|puraṃ.

*(*VĀSAVADATTĀṂ *dṛṣṭvā)* katham, Avanti|nṛ|p'|ātma|j" êyam!

VĀSAVADATTĀ: *(*RĀJÑAḤ *śarīraṃ parāmṛśya, sa|harṣam)* ⌜diṭṭhiā a|kkhata|sarīro ajja|utto.⌟

RĀJĀ:

4.185 Bābhravya eṣa—

BĀBHRAVYAḤ: deva, idānīṃ pratyujjīvitāḥ smaḥ.

RĀJĀ:

—Vasubhūtir ayaṃ!—

VASUBHŪTIḤ: vijayatāṃ mahā|rājaḥ!

(holding her around her neck, he closes his eyes and mimes his pleasure at her touch) Ah! For a moment, the burning anguish has left me. Courage, my darling, courage!

> Clearly the fire does not really burn you, 4.180
> even though it has caught you,
> for your touch now, darling, takes away
> even my burning anguish.

(opening his eyes, looking in all directions, and letting go of SÁGARIKA*)* How absolutely amazing!

> Where has the fire gone? The women's quarters are
> just as they were before.

> *(seeing* VÁSAVA·DATTA*)* And here is the daughter
> of the king of Avánti.

VÁSAVA·DATTA: *(touching the* KING*'s body, with joy)* Thank goodness, my husband's body is unhurt.

KING:

> This is Babhrávya— 4.185

BABHRÁVYA: We've been brought back to life, your majesty.

KING:

> —and this Vasu·bhuti!—

VASU·BHUTI: Total victory to the great king!

4.190 RĀJĀ:

—vayasyaḥ!

VIDŪṢAKAḤ: ⌜jaadu, jaadu bhavaṃ!⌟

RĀJĀ:

svapne matir bhramati, kiṃ nv idam indra|jālam?

4.195 VIDŪṢAKAḤ: ⌜bho, mā saṃdehaṃ karehi. inda|jālaṃ evva edam. bhaṇidaṃ teṇa dāsīe putteṇa inda|jālieṇa jahā «ekko uṇa maha khelao avassaṃ deveṇa pekkhidavva tti.» tā taṃ jjeva edam.⌟

RĀJĀ: devi, iyaṃ tvad|vacanād asmābhir ih' ānītā Sāgarikā.

VĀSAVADATTĀ: *(sa/smitam)* ⌜ajja|utta, jāṇidaṃ mae.⌟

VASUBHŪTIḤ: *(SĀGARIKĀṂ dṛṣṭv" âpavārya)* Bābhravya, sa|dṛś" îyaṃ rāja|putryā!

BĀBHRAVYAḤ: amātya, mam' âpy etad eva manasi vartate.

4.200 VASUBHŪTIḤ: *(RĀJĀNAM uddiśya)* deva, kuta iyaṃ kanyakā?

RĀJĀ: devī jānāti.

KING: 4.190

—my friend!

JESTER: Victory, victory to you, sir!

KING:

Is my mind wandering in a dream, or is this magic?

JESTER: Have no doubt; this is magic, all right. That son of 4.195
a slave girl, the magician, said, "But your majesty must, without fail, watch one more trick of mine." Well, this was it.

KING: My queen, because of what you said, we brought Ságarika here, and here she is.

VÁSAVA·DATTA: *(smiling)* I know, my husband.

VASU·BHUTI: *(seeing* SÁGARIKA, *aside)* Babhrávya, she looks just like the princess!

BABHRÁVYA: Your Excellency, the very same thought is in my mind, too.

VASU·BHUTI: *(to the* KING*)* Your majesty, where does this girl 4.200
come from?

KING: The queen knows.

VASUBHŪTIḤ: devi, kutaḥ punar iyaṃ kanyakā?

VASAVADATTĀ: ⌜amacca, «esā kkhu sāgarādo pāvid” êti» bhaṇia amacca|Joandharāaeṇa mama hatthe ṇikkhidā. ado evva Sāariā tti saddāvīadi.⌟

RĀJĀ: *(sva/gatam)* Yaugandharāyaṇena nyastā! katham asau mām a|nivedya kiṃ cit kariṣyati?

4.205 VASUBHŪTIḤ: *(apavārya)* Bābhravya, yathā su|sa|dṛśī Vasantakasya kaṇṭhe ratna|mālā, asyāś ca sāgarāt prāptiḥ, tathā vyaktaṃ Siṃhal’|ēśvarasya duhitā Ratnāval” îyam. *(prakāśam)* āyuṣmati, na khalu rāja|putrī Ratnāvalī tvam, enām avasthām upagatā?

SĀGARIKĀ: *(*VASUBHŪTIṂ *vilokya, s’/âsram)* ⌜kahaṃ, amacco Vasubhūdi!⌟

VASUBHŪTIḤ: *(s’/âsram)* hā, hato ’smi manda|bhāgyaḥ!

bhūmau nipatati.

SĀGARIKĀ: ⌜hā tāda, hā amba! kahiṃ si? dehi me paḍivaaṇaṃ.⌟

4.210 *iti* VASUBHŪTER *upari patantī, moham upagatā.*

VĀSAVADATTĀ: *(sa/saṃbhramam)* ⌜ajja|kañcuiṃ, iaṃ sā mama bahiṇī Raaṇāvalī?⌟

BĀBHRAVYAḤ: devi, iyam eva sā.

VĀSAVADATTĀ: *(*RATNĀVALĪM *āliṅgya)* ⌜bahiṇī, samassassa samassassa.⌟

VASU·BHUTI: Your highness, ma'am, where, again, does this girl come from?

VÁSAVA·DATTA: Your Excellency, Prime Minister Yaugándharáyana put her into my hands, saying, "She came from the ocean." And so she is called Ságarika, the Lady of the Ocean.

KING: *(to himself)* Yaugándharáyana placed her! How can he do anything without reporting to me?

VASU·BHUTI: *(aside)* Babhrávya, since the necklace on Vasá- 4.205
ntaka's neck bears such a strong resemblance, and since this girl came from the ocean, it's clear that this is Ratnávali, the daughter of the king of Símhala. *(aloud)* Princess Ratnávali! But what a sorry state you've been reduced to!

SÁGARIKA: *(looking at* VASU·BHUTI, *tearfully)* Why, it's prime minister Vasu·bhuti!

VASU·BHUTI: *(tearfully)* Oh! How wretched and unlucky I am.

He falls on the ground.

SÁGARIKA: Father! Mother! Where are you? Answer me!

She falls on top of VASU·BHUTI *and faints.* 4.210

VÁSAVA·DATTA: *(in confusion)* Good chamberlain, this woman. She is my sister Ratnávali?

BABHRÁVYA: That is indeed who this woman is, your highness.

VÁSAVA·DATTA: *(embracing* RATNÁVALI*)* Courage, my sister, courage!

RĀJĀ: katham, udātta|vaṃśasya Siṃhal'|ēśvarasya Vikrama-bāhor ātma|j" êyam.

4.215 VIDŪṢAKAḤ: *(ratna/mālā spṛśan, sva/gatam)* ⌜paḍhamaṃ jevva mae jāṇidaṃ: ṇa kkhu sāmaṇṇa|jaṇassa īdiso paricchao hodi tti.⌟

VASUBHŪTIḤ: *(utthāya)* āyuṣmati, samāśvasihi samāśvasihi! nanv iyaṃ jyāyasī te bhaginī duḥkham āste. tat pariṣvajasv' âinām.

SĀGARIKĀ: *(samāśvasya,* VĀSAVADATTĀṂ *dṛṣṭvā, sva/gatam)* ⌜kid'|âvarāhā kkhu ahaṃ devīe ṇa sakkuṇomi muhaṃ daṃsidum.⌟

ity adho/mukhī tiṣṭhati.

VĀSAVADATTĀ: *(s'/âsraṃ bāhū prasārya)* ⌜ehi, ehi adi|ṇiṭṭhure! idāṇiṃ pi dāva siṇehaṃ daṃsehi.⌟ *(iti kaṇṭhe gṛhṇāti.* RATNĀVALĪ *skhalitaṃ nāṭayati. apavārya)* ⌜ajja|utta, lajjemi kkhu imiṇā attaṇo ṇisaṃsatteṇa. tā avaṇehi de bandhanam.⌟

4.220 RĀJĀ: *(sa/paritoṣam)* yath" āha devī. *(iti tathā karoti.)*

VĀSAVADATTĀ: ⌜ajja|utta, amacca|Yaugandharāaṇeṇa ettiaṃ kkhu kālaṃ duj|jaṇī|kida mhi, jeṇa jāṇiteṇa vi ṇa ṇivedidam.⌟

tataḥ praviśati YAUGANDHARĀYAṆAḤ.

KING: Why, she is the daughter of Víkrama·bahu, the king of Símhala, and he has an exalted lineage.

JESTER: *(touching the necklace, to himself)* Right from the very start, I knew that such an ornament could not belong to any ordinary person. 4.215

VASU·BHUTI: *(standing up)* Courage, your highness, courage! Your older sister here is so unhappy. Embrace her.

SÁGARIKA: *(reviving, seeing* VÁSAVA·DATTA*, to herself)* I have certainly committed an offense against the queen. I can't look her in the eye.

She stands there, head down.

VÁSAVA·DATTA: *(tearfully stretching out her arms)* Come, stubborn girl, come! Now, at least, you should show some affection. *(She embraces her around the neck.* RATNÁVALI *mimes stumbling. Aside)* My husband, I'm so ashamed of this cruel thing that I've done. Take off her chains.

KING: *(with satisfaction)* As the queen says. *(He does this.)* 4.220

VÁSAVA·DATTA: It was Yaugándharáyana who made me behave so badly, all this time, because he knew but did not let me know.*

Enter YAUGÁNDHARÁYANA.

YAUGANDHARĀYAṆAḤ:

devyā mad|vacanād yad" âbhyupagataḥ
patyur viyogas, tadā
sā devasya kalatra|saṃghaṭanayā
duḥkhaṃ mayā sthāpitā.
tasyāḥ prītim ayaṃ kariṣyati jagat|
svāmitva|lābhaḥ prabhoḥ—
satyaṃ, darśayituṃ tath" âpi vadanaṃ
śaknomi n' ô lajjayā. [20]

4.225 *(kṣaṇaṃ vicintya)* atha vā kiṃ kriyate? īdṛśam atyanta|mānanīyeṣv api nir|anurodha|vṛtti svāmi|bhakti|vratam. *(vilokya)* ayaṃ devaḥ. yāvad upasarpāmi. *(upasṛtya)* jayatu, jayatu devaḥ! deva, kṣamyatāṃ yan mayā devasy' â|nivedya kṛtam.

RĀJĀ: Yaugandarāyaṇa, kathaya, kim a|nivedya kṛtam?

YAUGANDHARĀYAṆAḤ: karotv āsana|parigrahaṃ devaḥ. sarvaṃ vijñāpayāmi.

sarve yathā|sthānam upaviśanti.

YAUGANDHARĀYAṆAḤ: *(kṛt'|âñjaliḥ)* deva, śrūyatām. iyaṃ Siṃhal'|ēśvara|duhitā siddhen' ādiṣṭā yathā: yo 'syāḥ pāṇiṃ grahīṣyati, sa sārva|bhaumo rājā bhaviṣyati. tatas tat|pratyayād asmābhiḥ svāmy|arthaṃ bahuṣaḥ prārthyamānen' âpi Siṃhal'|ēśvareṇa devyā Vāsavadattāyāś citta|khedaṃ pariharatā yadā na dattā—

YAUGÁNDHARÁYANA:

> At my request, the queen consented to
> a separation from her husband,
> but the king's plan to merge with another wife
> made her miserable.
> True, it will give her pleasure to see the king
> become master of the universe,
> but, still, I'm ashamed to look her in the eye.*

(thinking for a moment) But what's to be done? Such is the vow of devotion to one's master that it will not swerve even for people who deserve the greatest respect. *(looking)* Here's the king. I'll just approach him. *(approaching)* Victory, victory to your majesty. I hope your majesty will forgive me for what I did without reporting to your majesty. 4.225

KING: Yaugándharáyana, tell the story of what you did without reporting to me.

YAUGÁNDHARÁYANA: Your majesty, please take a seat. I will explain everything.

They all sit down, according to their rank.

YAUGÁNDHARÁYANA: *(folding his palms together)* Listen, please, your majesty. A seer made a prediction about this daughter of the king of Símhala, that whoever took her hand in marriage would become king of all the world. And because I believed that, we asked him for her on your majesty's behalf many times. But when the king of Símhala refused to give her, because he didn't want to distress the mind of Queen Vásava·datta—

4.230 RĀJĀ: tadā kim?

YAUGANDHARĀYAṆAḤ: tadā «Lāvāṇakena vahninā devī dagdh" êti» prasiddhim utpādya tad|antikaṃ Bābhravyaḥ prahitaḥ.

RĀJĀ: tataḥ paraṃ śrutaṃ mayā. ath' êyaṃ devyā haste kim anucintya sthāpitā?

VIDŪṢAKAḤ: ⌜bho, aṇ|ācakkhidaṃ vi edaṃ jāṇīadi jjeva, jadhā: ante|ura|gadā suheṇa de ṇaaṇa|padhaṃ gamissadi tti.⌟

RĀJĀ: *(vihasya)* Yaugandharāyaṇa, gṛhīt'|âbhiprāyo 'si Vasantakena?

4.235 YAUGANDHARĀYAṆAḤ: yad ājñāpayati devaḥ.

RĀJĀ: aindra|jālika|vṛtt'|ânto 'pi, manye, tvat|prayoga eva.

YAUGANDHARĀYAṆAḤ: deva! evam. anyath" ântaḥ|pure baddhāyā asyāḥ kuto devena darśanam? a|dṛṣṭāyāś ca Vasubhūtinā kutaḥ parijñānam? *(vihasya)* parijñātāyāś ca bhaginyāḥ samprati yathā karaṇīyaṃ, tatra devī pramāṇam.

VĀSAVADATTĀ: *(sa|smitam)* ⌜ajja, phuḍaṃ jjeva kiṃ ṇa bhaṇasi, jahā: paḍivādehi de Raaṇāvaliṃ tti.⌟

VIDŪṢAKAḤ: ⌜bhodi, su|ṭṭhu tue jāṇido amaccass' âbhippāo.⌟

KING: What then? 4.230

YAUGÁNDHARÁYANA: Then we circulated a rumor—"The queen has been burnt by a fire at Lavánaka"—and sent Babhrávya to him.

KING: I've heard what came next. But what were you thinking of when you had this girl placed in the hands of the queen?

JESTER: I can figure that out even without being told: that when she was in the women's quarters she could easily come into your line of vision.

KING: *(laughing)* Yaugándharáyana, did Vasántaka grasp your intention?

YAUGÁNDHARÁYANA: As your majesty says. 4.235

KING: And that magic business was also nothing but a part of your plot, I think?

YAUGÁNDHARÁYANA: Just so, your majesty. How else could your majesty have seen her, when she was imprisoned in the women's quarters? And if she was not seen, then how could Vasu·bhuti have recognized her? *(laughing)* And now that the queen has recognized her sister, she has the authority over what should be done with her.

VÁSAVA·DATTA: *(smiling)* My dear sir, why don't you say it clearly? "Give Ratnávali to him."

JESTER: Your highness, you have well understood the Prime Minister's intention.

4.240 VĀSAVADATTĀ: *(hastaṃ prasārya)* ⌜ehi Raaṇāvali, ehi. ettiaṃ vi dāva me bahiṇi"|âṇurūpaṃ bhodu.⌟ *(*RATNĀVALĪṂ *svair ābharaṇair alaṃ|kṛtya, gṛhītvā,* RĀJĀNAM *upasṛtya)* ⌜ajja|utta, paḍiccha edam.⌟

RĀJĀ: *(sa|paritoṣaṃ hastau prasārya)* ko devyāḥ prasādo na bahu manyate?

VĀSAVADATTĀ: ⌜ajja|utta, dūre kkhu edāe pidu|kulam. tā tadhā karehi, jadhā na bandhu|jaṇaṃ sumaredi.⌟ *(iti samarpayati.)*

RĀJĀ: yath" ājñāpayati devī. *(*RATNĀVALĪṂ *gṛhṇāti.)*

VIDŪṢAKAḤ: *(nṛtyan)* ⌜hī hī, bho! puhavī kkhu dāṇi hattha|gadā pia|vaassassa.⌟

4.245 VASUBHŪTIḤ: āyuṣmati, sthāne devī|śabdam udvahasi!

YAUGANDHARĀYAṆAḤ: idānīṃ sa|phala|pariśramo 'smi saṃvṛttaḥ. deva, tad ucyatāṃ: kiṃ te bhūyaḥ priyam upakaromi?

RĀJĀ: kim ataḥ param api priyam asti? yataḥ:

VÁSAVA·DATTA: *(stretching out her hand)* Come, Ratnávali, come. Let me at least do this much, as befits a sister. *(adorning* RATNÁVALI *with her own ornaments, taking her by the hand, and approaching the* KING*)* My husband, accept this woman. 4.240

KING: *(stretching forth his hands, with satisfaction)* What favor from the queen would not be received as a great honor?

VÁSAVA·DATTA: My husband, her father's family is quite far away. So make sure that she does not miss her friends and relations. *(She gives her to him.)*

KING: As the queen commands. *(He takes* RATNÁVALI.*)*

JESTER: *(dancing)* Hurrah! The whole earth has now come into my dear friend's hands!

VASU·BHUTI: Truly, your highness, you deserve the title of queen. 4.245

YAUGÁNDHARÁYANA: Now my labors have borne fruit. Tell me, your majesty, what more do you want me to do?

KING: What more could anyone want? For:

nīto Vikramabāhur ātma|samatāṃ,
prāpt" êyam urvī|tale
sāraṃ Sāgarikā sa|sāgara|mahī|
prāpty eka|hetuḥ priyā,
devī prītim upāgatā ca bhaginī|
lābhāj, jitāḥ Kosalāḥ,
kiṃ n' âsti tvayi saty, amātya|vṛṣabhe,
yasmai karomi spṛhām? [21]

tath" âp' îdam astu:

4.250 *bharata/vākyam.*

urvīm uddāma|sasyāṃ janayatu visṛjan
Vāsavo vṛṣṭim iṣṭām.
iṣṭais trai|viṣṭapānāṃ vidadhatu vidhivat
prīṇanaṃ vipra|mukhyāḥ.
ā|kalp'|ântaṃ ca bhūyāt samupacita|sukhaḥ
saṃgamaḥ saj|janānāṃ.
niḥ|śeṣaṃ yāntu śāntiṃ piśuna|jana|giro
dur|jayā vajra|lepāḥ. [22]

iti niṣkrāntāḥ sarve.

ity «Aindra/jāliko» nāma caturtho 'ṅkaḥ.

iti Śrī/Harṣadevasya kṛtiḥ samāpt" êyaṃ Ratnāvalī nāma nāṭikā.

Víkrama·bahu is now my second self.
I have won Ságarika,
the very essence of all that there is
   on the surface of the earth,
and the means of gaining the earth
   bounded by the ocean.
The queen is pleased because she's gotten a sister.
I've conquered Kósala. And as long as you,
   a bull among ministers,
are there, what could I long for that I do not have?

And in addition, this:

The actors' epilogue. 4.250

May Indra, sending down the desired rain,
make the earth bring forth abundant crops.
May the leading Brahmins please the gods
with sacrifices properly done.
May good people live together 'til
   the end of the eon,
heaping up happiness.
And may the words of slanderers,
   so hard to overcome because
   their stain is as permanent as diamonds,
rest in peace.*

Exit all.

End of Act Four, called "The Magician."

End of the play called 'The Lady of the Jewel Necklace,' the work of Shri Harsha·deva.

THE LADY WHO SHOWS HER LOVE

DRAMATIS PERSONÆ

in order of appearance

Characters marked with ⌜corner brackets⌟ speak Prakrit.

STAGE DIRECTOR	
VÍNAYA·VASU	the chamberlain of KING DRIDHA·VARMAN
KING ÚDAYANA ("Rising")	king of Vatsa
⌜VASÁNTAKA⌟ ("Little Spring")	the court jester
⌜YASHO·DHARA⌟	gate-keeper
RUMÁNVAT	ÚDAYANA's minister of state (his general in 'The Lady of the Jewel Necklace')
VÍJAYA·SENA	commander-in-chief of KING ÚDAYANA (VÍJAYA·VARMAN in 'The Lady of the Jewel Necklace')
⌜INDÍVARIKA⌟	palace maid
⌜PRIYA·DÁRSHIKA⌟ ("The Lady Who Shows Her Love")	also known as ARÁNYIKA, "The Lady of the Jungle," daughter of KING DRIDHA·VARMAN
⌜MANO·RAMA⌟	lady-in-waiting, friend of ARÁNYIKA
⌜VÁSAVA·DATTA⌟ ("Given by Indra")	the queen, ÚDAYANA's wife
SANKRITYÁYANI	an elderly holy woman and playwright, who speaks Sanskrit
⌜KÁNCHANA·MALA⌟ ("Golden Garland")	lady-in-waiting to the QUEEN

People Mentioned

KING DRIDHA·VARMAN	king of the Anga country and father of PRIYA·DÁRSHIKA; married to the sister of VÁSAVA·DATTA's mother
VINDHYA·KETU	ally of DRIDHA·VARMAN, king of the wilderness
PRADYÓTA	also called MAHA·SENA, king of Avánti, father of VÁSAVA·DATTA
YAUGÁNDHARÁYANA	ÚDAYANA's Prime Minister
⌜QUEEN ANGÁRAVATI⌟	mother of VÁSAVA·DATTA, wife of MAHA·SENA

The Scene

All but the first interlude takes place in Kaushámbi, the capital city of King Údayana.

The first interlude takes place somewhere in the Vindhyas.

Time

Act One: Autumn, shortly before noon.
Act Two: A year later. Late afternoon.
Act Three: A few days later. Late afternoon.
Act Four: A few days later.

BENEDICTION

Dhūma|vyākula|dṛṣṭir, indu|kiraṇair
āhlādit'|âkṣī punaḥ,
paśyantī varam utsuk", ānata|mukhī,
bhūyo hriyā Brahmaṇaḥ,
s'|ērṣyā pāda|nakh'|êndu|darpaṇa|gate
Gaṅgāṃ dadhāne Hare,
sparśād utpulakā kara|graha|vidhau
Gaurī śivāy' âstu vaḥ. [1]

api ca

Kailās'|âdrāv udaste paricalati gaṇeṣ'
ûllasat|kautukeṣu,
kroḍaṃ mātuḥ Kumāre viśati, viṣa|muci
prekṣamāṇe saroṣam,
pād'|âvaṣṭambha|sīdad|vapuṣi Daśa|mukhe
yāti Pātāla|mūlaṃ,
kruddho 'py āśliṣṭa|mūrtir bhaya|ghanam Umayā
pātu tuṣṭaḥ Śivo naḥ. [2]

[Enter STAGE DIRECTOR.*]*

When smoke got in her eyes,
  the rays of the moon refreshed them.
When she looked up at her bridegroom
  with longing, she lowered her head again
because she was shy in front of Brahma.
Jealousy washed over her when she saw
Hara holding the Ganges,
reflected in the moon-mirrors of her toes,
but her skin thrilled at his touch when he took her
  hand in the ceremony.
May that Gauri be good for you!*

And:

Mount Kailása was uprooted and began to quake.
That made the gang of goblins pop out
  with curiosity.
That made Kumára dash under his mother's skirts,
and that made the venomous snake look around
  in fury.
And when Ten-heads sank under the weight
  of the foot
pressing him down to the very roots of the
  underworld,
Shiva became angry, but when Uma embraced him
  in terror
he was pleased, and may he protect us.*

PROLOGUE

1.5 *nāndy|ante*

SŪTRADHĀRAḤ: *(parikramya)* ady' âhaṃ Vasant'|ôtsave sa|bahumānam āhūya nānā|dig|deśād āgatena rājñaḥ Śrī|Harṣadevasya pāda|padm'|ôpajīvinā rāja|samūhen' ôktaḥ: «yath" âsmat|svāminā Śrī|Harṣadeven' âpūrva|vastu|racan"|âlaṃkṛtā ‹Priyadarśikā› nāma nāṭikā kṛt", êty asmābhiḥ śrotra|paraṃparayā śrutam. na tu prayogato dṛṣṭā. tat tasy' âiva rājñaḥ sarva|jana|hṛday'|āhlādino bahumānād, asmāsu c' ânugraha|buddhyā yathāvat prayogeṇa tvayā nāṭayitavy" êti.» tad yāvan nepathya|racanāṃ kṛtvā yath" âbhilaṣitaṃ saṃpādayāmi. *(parito 'valokya)* āvarjitāni sāmājika|manāṃs' îti me niścayaḥ. kutaḥ:

Śrī|Harṣo nipuṇaḥ kaviḥ, pariṣad apy
    eṣā guṇa|grāhiṇī,
  loke hāri ca Vatsa|rāja|caritaṃ,
    nāṭye ca dakṣā vayam,
vastv ek'|âikam ap' îha vāñchita|phala|
    prāpteḥ padaṃ, kiṃ punar
  mad|bhāgy'|ôpacayād ayaṃ samuditaḥ
    sarvo guṇānāṃ guṇaḥ. [3]

At the end of the benediction 1.5

STAGE DIRECTOR: *(walking around)* Today, in the Spring festival,* the crowd of kings who have come from many directions and live off the lotus feet of his majesty Shri Harsha summoned me respectfully and said, "Our ruler, his majesty Shri Harsha, has composed a play called 'The Lady Who Shows her Love,' graced by an unprecedented arrangement of the plot. We've heard about it by word of mouth, from one to another, but we've never seen it produced. You should therefore produce it and have it properly performed, both to honor this king who gladdens the hearts of all the people and with the thought of doing a favor for us." So, now I'll prepare the theatre and do what they wanted. *(walking about and looking around)* I'm quite sure that the minds of the assembled people are well-inclined. For:

> The poet, Shri Harsha, is talented;
> this audience appreciates quality;
> the story of the king of Vatsa* is a crowd-pleaser;
> and we're very good at acting.
> Since each one of these factors by itself
> is enough to achieve the desired result,
> how much more will this be true
> of the entire combined cluster of qualities
> that my good fortune has piled up
> all together here!

(nepathy'|âbhimukham avalokya) aye! katham, prastāvan"|âbhyudyate mayi vidit'|âsmad|abhiprāyo 'ṅg'|âdhipater Dṛḍhavarmaṇaḥ kañcukino bhūmikāṃ kṛtv" âsmad|bhrāt" êta ev' âbhivartate. tad yāvad aham apy anantara|bhūmikāṃ saṃpādayāmi.

iti niṣkrāntaḥ.

1.10 *iti prastāvanā.*

(looking toward the stage area) Oh! As I was beginning the prelude, my brother, who knew what I intended to do, put on the costume of the chamberlain of Dridha·varman, king of the Anga country, and now he's coming right this way. So I, too, will put on the costume of the very next character.*

Exit.

End of the Prelude. 1.10

INTERLUDE

tataḥ praviśati KAÑCUKĪ.

KAÑCUKĪ: *(sa|śoka|śramam nāṭayan, niḥśvasya)* kaṣṭaṃ bhoḥ kaṣṭam!

rājño vipad, bandhu|viyoga|duḥkhaṃ,
deśa|cyutir, durgama|mārga|khedaḥ
āsvādyate 'syāḥ kaṭu|niṣphalāyāḥ
phalaṃ may" âitac cira|jīvitāyāḥ. [4]

1.15 *(sa|śokaṃ sa|vismayaṃ ca)* tādṛśasy' âpi nām' â|pratihata|śakti|trayasya Raghu|Dilīpa|Nala|tulyasya devasya Dṛḍhavarmaṇo mat|prārthyamān" âpy anena sva|duhitā Vatsa|rājāya datt", êti baddh'|ânuśayena Vatsa|rājo bandhanān na nivartata, iti ca labdha|randhreṇa sahas"|āgatya Kaliṅga|hatakena vipattir īdṛśī kriyata, iti yat satyam upapannam api na śraddadhe. katham ek'|ânta|niṣṭhuram īdṛśaṃ ca daivam asmāsu! yena s" âpi rāja|putrī yathā kathaṃ cid enāṃ Vatsa|rājāy' ôpanīya svāminam an|ṛṇaṃ kariṣyām', îti matvā mayā tādṛśād api pralaya|kāla|dāruṇād avaskanda|saṃbhramād apavāhya devasya Dṛḍhavarmaṇo mitra|bhāv'|ânvitasy' âiv' âṭavikasya nṛpater Vindhyaketor gṛhe sthāpitā satī, snānāya «n' âtidūram, ity» Agastya|tīrthaṃ gate mayi kṣaṇāt kair api nipatya, hate Vindhyaketau, rakṣobhir iva nirmānuṣī|kṛte, dagdhe sthāne, na

[Somewhere in the Vindhyas]

Enter the CHAMBERLAIN.*

CHAMBERLAIN: *(miming sorrow and exhaustion, sighing)* How dreadful, how dismal!

The king's disaster;
  my misery in being separated from my family;
exile from my country;
  fatigue from traveling a rough road—
this is the bitter fruit that I must taste
at the end of my long, fruitless life.

(in sorrow and astonishment) I can't believe that such a catas- 1.15
trophe has truly happened to king Dridha·varman, such a king that his triple powers went unchallenged, for he was the equal of great kings like Raghu, Dilípa, and Nala.* But he had promised his daughter to the king of Vatsa even though that vile king of Kalínga had asked for her, and for that reason the king of Kalínga nursed a grudge against him, and, when he learned that the king of Vatsa had been captured and had not returned, he seized the opportunity and suddenly attacked Dridha·varman.* Why has cruel fate targeted us like this? For I thought, "I'll manage somehow to bring that princess to the king of Vatsa and so free my master from his debt to him." And so I carried her away from the chaos of that assault, which was as terrible as the time of doomsday, and placed her in the house of Vindhya·ketu, king of the jungle, who was connected to king Dridha·varman by a bond of friendship. But when I had gone off to bathe at the shrine of Agástya ("It's not very far off," I thought),

jñāyate kasyām avasthāyāṃ vartata iti. nipuṇaṃ ca vicitam etan mayā sarvaṃ sthānam. na ca jñātaṃ kiṃ tair eva dasyubhir nīt" âtha vā dagdh" êti. tat kiṃ karomi manda|bhāgyaḥ?

(vicintya) aye! śrutaṃ mayā bandhanāt paribhraṣṭaḥ Pradyota|tanayām apahṛtya Vatsa|rājaḥ Kauśāmbīm āgata iti. kiṃ tatr' âiva gacchāmi? *(niḥśvasy' ātmano 'vasthāṃ paśyan)* kim iva hi rāja|putryā vinā tatra gatvā kathayiṣyāmi? aye! kathitaṃ c' âdya mama Vindhyaketunā, «mā bhaiṣīḥ. jīvati tatra|bhavān mahā|rājo Dṛḍhavarmā, gāḍha|prahāra|jarjarī|kṛto baddhas tiṣṭhati iti.» tad adhunā svāminam eva gatvā pāda|paricaryayā jīvita|śeṣam ātmanaḥ saphalayiṣyāmi. *(parikramy' ōrdhvam avalokya)* aho atidāruṇatā śarad|ātapasya! yad evam aneka|duḥkha|saṃtāpiten' âpi mayā tīkṣṇo 'vagamyate.

instantly some people attacked like demons, killed Vindhya·ketu, and burnt the place so that there was no human left alive. And no one knows what happened to her. I searched the entire area carefully, but couldn't find out if those bandits took her away or burnt her. Oh what shall I do, unlucky as I am?

(thinking) Ah! I've heard that the king of Vatsa broke out of prison and returned to Kaushámbi, taking Pradyóta's daughter away with him.* Shall I go there? *(sighing, considering his own situation)* But what tale can I tell, if I go there without the princess? I know. Just today,* Vindhya·ketu said to me, "Don't be afraid. For his majesty the great king Dridha·varman is alive, though he has been cut to pieces by deep wounds and is in prison." So I'll go now to him, for he's my master, and make the rest of my life fruitful by serving at his feet. *(walking around and looking up)* Oh my, how terrible the autumn sun is. For I feel it sharply even though I'm already heated up by so many sorrows.

ghana/bandha/mukto 'yaṃ

kany''/āgrahaṇāt parāṃ tulāṃ prāpya

ravir *adhigata/sva/dhāmā*

pratapati khalu Vatsārāja iva. [5]

iti niṣkrāntaḥ.

iti viṣkambhakaḥ.

This sun, *freed from the prison of the clouds,*
has reached the constellation of Libra
after leaving the Virgin,
and now blazes fiercely, with his glory restored, :
just like the king of Vatsa
who, freed from close imprisonment,
outweighs all others since he has taken the princess,
and now shines forth in his own home
*that he has regained.**

Exit.

End of the Interlude.

ACT I

tataḥ praviśati RĀJĀ VIDŪṢAKAŚ *ca.*

RĀJĀ:

bhṛtyānām a|vikāritā parigatā,
dṛṣṭā matir mantriṇāṃ,
mitrāṇy apy upalakṣitāni, viditaḥ
paur'|ânurāgo 'dhikam.
nirvyūḍhā raṇa|sāhasa|vyasanitā,
strī|ratnam āsāditaṃ.
nirvyājād iva dharmataḥ, kim iva na
prāptaṃ mayā bandhanāt? [6]

1.25 VIDŪṢAKAḤ: *(sa|roṣam)* ⌜bho vaassa! kahaṃ taṃ evva dāsīe uttaṃ bandhaṇa|hadaaṃ pasaṃsesi? taṃ dāṇiṃ visumaridaṃ? jaṃ taha ṇava|ggaho via gaa|vaī khalakhalāamāṇa|loha|siṅkhalā|bandhana|paḍikkhalanta|calaṇo, suṇṇa|duk|khara|pisuṇida|hiaa|saṃdāvo, rosa|vas|uttambhida|diṭṭhī, *gurua|kara*|phoḍia|dharaṇi|maggo, raaṇīsu vi a|ṇiddā|suhaṃ aṇūhudo si.⌟

[Time: Autumn, late morning.] 1.20

[Scene: Kaushámbi, the capital city of king ÚDAYANA*]*

Enter the KING, *with the* JESTER.

KING:

I learned how steadfast my servants were,
  and how wise my ministers;
I found out who my friends were, too,
  and discovered that the people of the town
  were more devoted than ever.
I fully indulged my passion
  for the violence of battle
and won the jewel of women.
Was there anything I did not get from
  my imprisonment,
as from dharma that is free from hypocrisy?

JESTER: *(in fury)* My friend, how can you praise prison, that 1.25
damn son of a slave girl? Have you forgotten it now? How you felt like a newly captured bull elephant—the clanking iron chains shackled to your feet made you stumble at every step, the burning of your heart was revealed only by the blankness of your lotus face, your eyes rolled upwards in the grip of your rage, and your *heavy arms : great trunk* cleared the ground along your path. You didn't even have the comfort of sleep in the nights.

RĀJĀ: Vasantaka, durjanaḥ khalv asi. paśya:

dṛṣṭaṃ cārakam andhakāra|gahanaṃ,
tan|mukh'|êndu|dyuti.
pīḍā te nigala|svanena, madhurās
tasyā giro na śrutāḥ.
krūrā bandhana|rakṣiṇo 'dya manasi,
snigdhāḥ kaṭ'|âkṣā na te,
doṣān paśyasi bandhanasya, na punaḥ
Pradyota|putryā guṇān. [7]

VIDŪṢAKAḤ: *(sa|garvam)* ⌜bho! jaï dāva bandhaṇaṃ suha|ṇibandhaṇaṃ hoi, tā kīsa tumaṃ, diḍhavammā baddho, tti Kaliṅga|raṇṇo uvari rosaṃ bandhesi?⌟

RĀJĀ: *(vihasya)* dhiṅ mūrkha! na khalu sarvo Vatsa|rājo, ya evaṃ Vāsavadattām avāpya bandhanān niryāsyati. tad āstāṃ tāvad iyaṃ kathā. Vindhyaketor upari bahūny ahāni Vijayasenasya preṣitasya. na c' âdy' âpi tat|sakāśāt kaś cid āgataḥ. tad āhūyatāṃ tāvad amātyo Rumaṇvān. tena saha kiṃ cid ālapitum icchāmi.

1.30 *praviśya*

PRATĪHĀRĪ: ⌜jedu, jedu devvo! eso kkhu Vijaaseṇo amacco, Rumaṇṇo vi paḍihāra|bhūmiṃ uvaṭṭhio.⌟

RĀJĀ: tvaritaṃ praveṣaya tau.

PRATĪHĀRĪ: ⌜jaṃ devo āṇavedi.⌟

KING: Vasántaka, you really are no good. Look:

> You saw the prison plunged into darkness,
> but not the light of her moon-face.
> You hated the clanking sound of the chains,
> but you didn't hear her sweet words.
> Even now, you see in your mind's eye
> the cruel prison guards,
> but not her affectionate sidelong glances.
> You note the faults of prison,
> but not the virtues of Pradyóta's daughter.

JESTER: *(with pride)* Yeah? Well, if prison brings such happiness, then why do you harbour such fury against the king of Kalínga, knowing that he has imprisoned Dridha·varman?

KING: *(laughing)* You idiot. Not everyone is a king of Vatsa who can get a Vásava·datta like that and break out of prison. So let's have no more of this talk. Many days have passed since we sent Víjaya·sena against Vindhya·ketu, and even today no one has come back from him. So summon Minister Rumánvat right away. I want to have a little talk with him.*

Enter the GATE-KEEPER. 1.30

GATE-KEEPER: Victory, victory to your majesty. Víjaya·sena and Minister Rumánvat are here by the door.

KING: Have them come in right away.

GATE-KEEPER: As your majesty commands.

iti niṣkrāntā.

1.35 *tataḥ praviśati* RUMAṆVĀN VIJAYASENAŚ *ca.*

RUMAṆVĀN: *(vicintya)*

tat|kṣaṇam api niṣkrāntāḥ
kṛta|doṣā iva vin" âpi doṣeṇa
praviśanti śaṅkamānā
rāja|kulaṃ prāyaśo bhṛtyāḥ. [8]

(upasṛtya) jayatu devaḥ!

RĀJĀ: *(āsanaṃ nirdiśya)* Rumaṇvan, ita āsyatām.

1.40 RUMAṆVĀN: *(sa|smitam upaviśya)* eṣa khalu jita|Vindhyaketur Vijayasenaḥ praṇamati.

VIJAYASENAS *tathā karoti.*

RĀJĀ: *(s'|ādaraṃ pariṣvajya)* api kuśalī bhavān?

VIJAYASENAḤ: adya svāminaḥ prasādāt.

RĀJĀ: Vijayasena, upaviśyatām.

1.45 VIJAYASENA *upaviśati.*

Exit.

Enter RUMÁNVAT *and* VÍJAYA·SENA.

RUMÁNVAT: *(thinking)*

> Even when they've just gone out a moment ago,
> and have done nothing wrong,
> servants generally enter the royal palace
> worrying that
> they've done something wrong.

(approaching) Victory to your majesty.

KING: *(indicating a seat)* Rumánvat, please be seated here.

RUMÁNVAT: *(sitting down with a smile)* Here is Víjaya·sena, who has conquered Vindhya·ketu and bows to you.

VÍJAYA·SENA *does so.*

KING: *(embracing him with esteem)* Are you well, sir?

VÍJAYA·SENA: I am now, by my master's favor.

KING: Víjaya·sena, please sit down.

VÍJAYA·SENA *sits down.*

RĀJĀ: Vijayasena, kathaya Vindhyaketor vṛttāntam.

VIJAYASENAḤ: deva kim aparaṃ kathayāmi? yādṛśaḥ svāmini kupite.

RĀJĀ: tath" âpi vistarataḥ śrotum icchāmi.

VIJAYASENAḤ: deva, śrūyatām. ito vayaṃ deva|pād'|ādeśād yath"|ādiṣṭena kari|turaga|padāti|sainyena mahāntam apy adhvānaṃ divasa|trayeṇ' ôllaṅghya prabhāta|velāyām a|tarkitā eva Vindhyaketor upari nipatitāḥ smaḥ.

1.50 RĀJĀ: tatas tataḥ?

VIJAYASENAḤ: tataḥ so 'py asmad|bala|tumula|kalakal'|ākarṇanena pratibuddhaḥ kesar" îva Vindhya|kandarān nirgatya Vindhyaketur an|apekṣita|bala|vāhano, yathā|saṃnihita|katipaya|sahāyaḥ, sahasā sva|nām' ôdghoṣayann asmān abhiyoddhuṃ pravṛttaḥ.

RĀJĀ: *(*RUMAṆVANTAM *avalokya, sa|smitam.)* śobhitaṃ Vindhyaketunā. tatas tataḥ?

VIJAYASENAḤ: tato 'smābhir, «ayam asāv! iti» dviguṇatara|baddha|matsar'|ôtsāhair vimardena niḥśeṣita|sahāya eka vimardit'|âdhika|bala|krodha|vego dāruṇataraṃ samprahāram akarot.

RĀJĀ: sādhu Vindhyaketo! sādhu sādhu!

KING: Víjaya·sena, tell me what happened to Vindhya·ketu.

VÍJAYA·SENA: Your majesty, can I tell something else? It's the sort of thing that makes my master angry.

KING: Nevertheless, I want to hear it, in full detail.

VÍJAYA·SENA: Then listen, please, your majesty. We set out from here by your majesty's command, with an army of elephants, horses, and foot soldiers, and traveled a long road in three days. Then, at dawn, we made a surprise attack on Vindhya·ketu.

KING: And then? 1.50

VÍJAYA·SENA: Then Vindhya·ketu, too, was awakened by hearing the clamor of the tumult of our armies, and he rushed out like a lion from a cave in the Vindhyas. Without waiting for his army and its wagons, with just a few aides who were nearby, he began suddenly to fight against us, proclaiming his name aloud.

KING: *(looking at* RUMÁNVAT *and smiling)* That was fine of Vindhya·ketu. And then?

VÍJAYA·SENA: Then our envy and our energy were doubled when we realized, "There he is!" And with a great crushing slaughter we killed all his aides so that he was quite alone. But the slaughter just increased the onslaught of his power and anger, and he exchanged blows even more fiercely.

KING: Bravo, Vindhya·ketu, Bravo, Bravo!

1.55 VIJAYASENAḤ: kiṃ vā varṇyate, deva? saṃkṣepato vijñāpayāmi.

pādātaṃ pattir eva prathamataram uraḥ|
peṣa|mātrena piṣṭvā,
dūrān nītvā śar'|âughair hariṇa|kulam iva
trastam aśvīyam āśāḥ,
sarvatr' ôtsṛṣṭa|sarva|praharaṇa|nivahas,
tūrṇam utkhāya khaḍgaṃ,
paścāt kartuṃ pravṛttaḥ kari|kara|kadalī|
kānana|ccheda|līlām. [9]

evaṃ bala|tritayam ākulam eka eva
kurvan kṛpāṇa|kiraṇa|cchurit'|âṃsa|kūṭaḥ,
śastra|prahāra|śata|jarajarit'|ôru|vakṣāḥ
śrāntaś cirād vinihato yudhi Vindhyaketuḥ. [10]

RĀJĀ: Rumaṇvan, sat|puruṣ'|ôcitaṃ mārgam anugacchato yat satyam vrīḍitā eva vayaṃ Vindhyaketor maraṇena.

RUMAṆVĀN: deva, tvad|vidhānām eva guṇ'|âika|pakṣa|pātināṃ ripor api guṇāḥ prītiṃ janayanti.

VÍJAYA·SENA: How can I describe it, your majesty? Let me report it briefly: 1.55

First, fighting on foot himself,
he crushed the foot-soldiers
merely by striking them with his own chest.
With floods of arrows shot from afar, he scattered
the terrified cavalry in all directions,
  like a herd of antelope.
He shot his entire bolt of weapons all around him,
and then, at the finish,
he quickly unsheathed his sword and began
the game of cutting off the banana-grove of
  elephants' trunks.

When he had, all alone,
routed our three-fold army,*
his sword flashing its rays on his
  mountainous shoulders,
hundreds of blows from our blades splintered
  his broad chest,
and after a long time, exhausted,
Vindhya·ketu died in battle.

KING: Rumánvat, to tell the truth, the death of Vindhya·ketu, who followed the traditional path of a good man, puts us to shame.

RUMÁNVAT: Your majesty, only someone like you, who side so entirely with virtue alone, would take pleasure even in an enemy's virtues.

1.60 RĀJĀ: Vijayasena, apy asti Vindhyaketor apatyaṃ, yatr' âsya paritoṣasya phalaṃ darśayāmi?

VIJAYASENAḤ: deva, idam api vijñāpayāmi. evaṃ sa|bandhu|parivāre hate Vindhyaketau, tam anusṛtāsu saha|dharma|cāriṇīṣu Vindhya|śikhar'|āśriteṣu jana|padeṣu, śunyībhūte tat|sthāne, «hā tāta, hā mātaḥ! iti» kṛta|kṛpaṇa|pralāpā Vindhyaketor veśmany ābhijāty'|ânurūpā kanyakā «tad|duhit", êty» asmābhir ānītā dvāri tiṣṭhati. tāṃ prati devaḥ pramāṇam.

RĀJĀ: Yaśodhare, gaccha. tvam eva Vāsavadattāyāḥ samarpaya. vaktavyā ca devī, «bhaginī|buddhyā tvay" âiva sarvadā draṣṭavyā. gīta|nṛtta|vādy'|ādiṣu viśiṣṭa|kany"|ôcitaṃ sarvaṃ śikṣayitavyā. yadā vara|yogyā bhaviṣyati tadā māṃ smāray' êti.»

PRATĪHĀRĪ: ⌈jaṃ devo āṇavedi.⌋

iti niṣkrāntā.

1.65 *nepathye* VAITĀLIKAḤ

līlā|majjana|maṅgal'|ôpakaraṇa|
 snānīya|sampādinaḥ
sarv'|ântaḥpura|vāra|vibhramavatī|
 lokasya te saṃprati
āyāsa|skhalad|aṃśuk'|âvyavahita|

KING: Víjaya·sena, does Vindhya·ketu have any child, to whom I could show my pleasure with a reward? 1.60

VÍJAYA·SENA: Your majesty, I'll report this too. When Vindhya·ketu had been killed, and his relatives and entourage with him, his wives—following their duty always to share his dharma—followed him, and the people of the countryside all took refuge on the peaks of the Vindhya mountains. The whole place was deserted. "Father! Mother!"—piteous cries rang out in Vindhya·ketu's house, from a young girl whose beauty spoke of her good breeding. "She must be Vindhya·ketu's daughter," we thought, and brought her here. She's standing there at the door now. Your majesty has the authority over her.

KING: Yasho·dhara, go yourself and hand her over to Vásava·datta and say to the queen, "Regard her always as your own sister, and teach her everything that a distinguished young girl should know—singing and dancing and playing musical instruments and so forth. And when she's ready to take a husband, remind me."

GATE-KEEPER: As your majesty commands.

Exit.

Off stage, the ROYAL HERALD *recites:* 1.65

The little world of courtesans
  in the women's quarters,
in their haste and effort to prepare
  the towels and oils
that make bathing both auspicious and fun,
have let slip their silken upper garments, revealing

cchāy"|âvadātaiḥ stanair
utkṣipt'|âpara|śātakumbha|kalaś" êv'
âlaṃkṛtā snāna|bhūḥ. [11]

RĀJĀ: *(ūrdhvam avalokya)* aye! kathaṃ, nabho|madhyam adhyāste bhagavān sahasra|dīdhitiḥ. saṃprati hi.

ābhāty ark'|âṃśu|tāpa|kvathad iva śaphar'|ôd-
vartanair dīrghik"|āmbhaś.
chatr'|ābhaṃ nṛtta|līlā|śithilam api śikhī
barha|bhāraṃ tanoti.
chāyā|cakraṃ tarūṇāṃ hariṇa|śiśur upaity
ālavāl'|âmbu|lubdhaḥ.
sadyas tyaktvā kapolaṃ viśati madhu|karaḥ
karṇa|pālīṃ gajasya. [12]

Rumaṇvan, uttiṣṭh' ôttiṣṭha. praviśy' ābhyāntaram eva kṛta|yath"|ôcita|kriyāḥ sat|kṛtya Vijayasenaṃ Kaliṅg'|ôcchittaye preṣayāmaḥ.

1.70 *iti niṣkrāntāḥ sarve.*

iti prathamo 'ṅkaḥ.

the golden gleam of breasts that outshine
the other golden pots that adorn your royal bath.

KING: *(looking upward)* Why, the god of a thousand rays is in the middle of the sky. For now:

The darting of the minnows makes
the water in the long ponds look as if
it were boiling in the heat of the sun's rays.
The peacock spreads his tail like an umbrella,
slackened a bit during his graceful dancing.
The fawns steal into the circle of shade made by
the trees,
hoping to drink from the water of the pools around
their trunks.
And the bee quickly leaves the elephant's cheek
and goes under his ear.*

Rumánvat, get up, get up! Let's go right into the women's quarters and do the usual rituals and honor Víjaya·sena and send him to wipe out the king of Kalínga.

Exit all. 1.70

End of Act One.

ACT II

tataḥ praviśati VIDŪṢAKAḤ.

VIDŪṢAKAḤ: ⌜ṇaṃ bhaṇido mhi Indīvariāe jaha, «ajja, uvavāsa|ṇiama|ṭṭhiā devī Vāsavadattā sotthi|vāaṇa|ṇimittaṃ saddāvedi tti.» tā jāva dhārā|ghar|ujjāṇa|digghiāe ṇhāia devī|pāsaṃ gadua kukkuṭa|vādaṃ karissaṃ. aṇṇahā kahaṃ amhāṇaṃ sarisā brahmaṇā rāa|kule paḍiggahaṃ karenti?⌟ *(nepaty'|âbhimukham avalokya)* ⌜kahaṃ, eso pia|vaasso ajja devīe virah|ukkaṇṭha|viṇodaṇā|ṇimittaṃ dhārā|ghar|ujjāṇaṃ evva patthido. tā jāva vaasseṇa saha evva gadua jah'|ôdidaṃ aṇuciṭṭhissaṃ.⌟

tataḥ praviśati s'|ôtkaṇṭho RĀJĀ.

2.5 RĀJĀ:

> kṣāmāṃ, maṇgala|mātra|maṇḍana|bhṛtaṃ,
> mand'|ôdyam'|ālāpinīm,
> āpāṇḍu|cchavinā mukhena vijita|
> prātastan'|êndu|dyutim,
> s'|ôtkaṇṭhāṃ niyam'|ôpavāsa|vidhinā
> ceto mam' ôtkaṇṭhate
> tāṃ draṣṭuṃ, pratham'|ânurāga|janit'|â-
> vasthām iv' âdya priyām. [1]

VIDŪṢAKAḤ: *(upasṛtya)* ⌜sotthi hode! vaḍḍhadu bhavaṃ!⌟

RĀJĀ: *(vilokya)* Vasantaka, kasmāt prahṛṣṭa iva lakṣyase?

[A year later. Late afternoon.]

Enter the JESTER.

JESTER: Indívarika said to me, "Good sir, Queen Vásava·datta, who has been observing the vow of a fast, may call on you to receive the auspicious present." And so I'll bathe in the long pond in the garden beside the fountain-house, go to the queen, and crow like a rooster.* How else can Brahmins like us accept presents in the palace? *(looking offstage)* Why, my dear friend here is just setting out now to go to the garden by the fountain-house, to divert the longing caused by his separation from the queen. I'll go with my friend and do as I said.

Enter the KING, *full of longing.*

KING: 2.5

My mind longs to see today my beloved,
who is full of longing
because of the regimen of fasting in her vow.
She is thin, wears only auspicious ornaments,
speaks slowly and haltingly,
and the pale complexion of her face outdoes the
moonlight of the morning—
quite as if she were falling in love for the first time.

JESTER: *(approaching)* Hello, sir! I hope you're doing well, sir!

KING: *(looking at him)* Vasántaka, why do you seem so elated?

VIDŪṢAKAḤ: ⌜accadi kkhu devī bamhaṇaṃ.⌟

2.10 RĀJĀ: yady evaṃ tataḥ kim?

VIDŪṢAKAḤ: *(sa|garvam)* ⌜bho! īriso kkhu bamhaṇo, jo caü|vveda|pañca|veda|chaṭṭha|veda|bamhaṇa|sahassa|pajjāule rāa|ule puḍhamaṃ ahaṃ devī|saāsādo sotthi|vāāṇaṃ lahemi.⌟

RĀJĀ: *(vihasya)* veda|saṃkhyay" âiv' āveditaṃ brāhmaṇyam. tad āgaccha, mahā|brāhmaṇa. dhārā|gṛh'|ôdyānam eva gacchāvaḥ.

VIDŪṢAKAḤ: ⌜jaṃ devo āṇavedi.⌟

RĀJĀ: gacch' âgrataḥ.

2.15 VIDŪṢAKAḤ: ⌜bho ehi, gacchamha.⌟ *(parikramy'|âvalokya ca)* ⌜bho vaassa, pekkha pekkha a|virada|paḍanta|viviha|kusuma|suumāla|silā|al|ucchaṅgassa, parimala|ṇilīṇa|mahuara|bhara|bhagga|baüla|māladī|ladā|jālaassa, kamala|gandha|gahaṇ|uddāma|māruda|parjavabuddha|bandhūa|bandhaṇassa, a|virala|tamāla|taru|pihid'|ātapa|ppaāsassa assa dhārā|ghar|ujjāṇassa sa|ssarīaaṃ.⌟

RĀJĀ: vayasya, sādhv abhihitam. atra hi.

vṛntaiḥ kṣudra|pravāla|sthagitam iva talaṃ
bhāti Śephālikānāṃ.
gandhaḥ Sapta|cchadānāṃ sapadi gajamad'|ā-
moda|mohaṃ karoti.
ete c' ônnidra|padma|cyuta|bahala|rajaḥ|

JESTER: The queen is going to honor a Brahmin.

KING: So, what about it? 2.10

JESTER: *(with pride)* Why, a Brahmin such as I am will be the first to receive the auspicious present from the queen herself, in the palace in a mob of thousands of Brahmins who know four Vedas, five Vedas, six Vedas.*

KING: *(laughing)* The number of Vedas you mention does indeed reveal what sort of a Brahmin you are. Come then, great Brahmin. Let's go to the fountain-house.

JESTER: As your majesty commands.

KING: Lead the way.

JESTER: Come, let's go! *(walking around and looking)* Look, 2.15
my friend, look how wonderful the garden of the fountain-house is. The various flowers that fall continuously on the surfaces of the stone slabs make them soft. The bees that swarm to the perfume of the *bákula* and jasmine vines and cling to their fragrance are so heavy that they break off networks of their flowers. Unchecked winds steal the perfume of the lotuses and force open the *bandhúka* stalks.* And the dense *tamála* trees hide the light of the sun.

KING: Well observed, my friend. For here:

The stalks of the flowers of the Sad Tree
make the ground look as if
it were inlaid with tiny pieces of coral.
The perfume of the flowers of the Seven-leaved
  Tree for a moment
is mistaken for the strong odor of elephants' ichor.

puñja|piṅg'|âṅgarāgā
gāyanty a|vyakta|vācaḥ kim api madhuliho
vāruṇī|pāna|mattāḥ. [2]

VIDŪṢAKAḤ: ⌜bho vaassa! edaṃ pi dāva pekkha, pekkha! jo eso a|virala|paḍanta|kusuma|ṇiaro ajja vi patt|antara|gala-nta|varis'|âvasāṇa|salila|bindū via lakkhīadi satta|vaṇṇa|pāavo.⌟

RĀJĀ: vayasya, samyag utpreksitam. bahv eva sadṛśaṃ jala-da|samayasya. tathā hi:

2.20 bibhrāṇā mṛdutāṃ śirīṣa|kusuma|
śrī|hāribhiḥ śādvalaiḥ,
sadyaḥ kalpita|kuṭṭimā marakata|
kṣodair iva kṣālitaiḥ,
eṣā saṃprati bandhanād vigalitair
bandhūka|puṣp"|ôtkarair
ady'|âpi kṣitir indragopaka|śataiś
chann" êva saṃlakṣyate. [3]

tataḥ praviśati CEṬĪ.

CEṬĪ: ⌜āṇatta mhi devīe Vāsavadattāe: «hañje Indīvarie, ajja mae Agatthi|mah"|êsiṇo aggho dādavvo. tā gaccha tu-maṃ. sehāliā|kusuma|mālaṃ lahu geṇhia āacch' êtti. esā

The masses of pollen fallen from the newly
awakened lotuses
make the bodies of these honey-making bees
quite yellow,
and drinking the wine of the flowers has made
them so high
that they seem to be singing some song with
blurred words.*

JESTER: And look at this, too, my friend, look! Right now the ceaseless showers of flowers from the Seven-leaved Tree seem like so many drops of water dripping between its leaves at the end of a rain.

KING: My friend, you've seen it just as it is. It's very much like the rainy season. For:

The patches of grass that out-shine 2.20
shirísha blossoms
make the ground here soft and seem suddenly
to pave it with pieces of wet emeralds.
And right now, with the piles of *bandhúka* flowers
fallen from the stem,
it looks as if it were covered with hundreds of
fire-flies.*

*Enter a palace maid [*INDÍVARIKA*].*

INDÍVARIKA: Queen Vásava·datta commanded me, saying: "Indívarika, today I must give an offering to the great sage Agástya. So you must go and get a garland of Sad Tree flowers and come back right away. And this Aránvika must go, too, and quickly gather and bring here the

vi āraṇṇiā dhārā|ghar|ujjāṇa|dīhiāe jāva evva viasiāiṃ kamalāiṃ ṇa atth'|âhilāsiṇā sujjeṇa maülāvijjanti, tāva evva lahuaṃ avaciṇua āacchadu tti.» esā tavassiṇī taṃ dīhiaṃ ṇa jāṇādi. tā geṇhia taṃ gamissaṃ.⌋ *(nepathy'|âbhimukham avalokya)* ⌈ido ido, Āraṇṇie, ehi!⌋

tataḥ praviṣaty ĀRAṆYIKĀ.

ĀRAṆYIKĀ: *(sa|bāṣp'|ôdvegam, ātma|gatam)* ⌈taha ṇāma tārise vaṃse uppaṇṇāe, aṇṇa|jaṇaṃ āṇāvia ṭṭhidāe, saṃpadaṃ parassa mae āṇattī kādavv', êtti ṇa tthi kkhu duk|kharaṃ devassa. aha vā maha evva eso doso, jeṇa jāṇantīe vi ṇa vāvādio appā. tā kiṃ saṃpadaṃ karissaṃ? aha vā duk|kharaṃ dāṇiṃ mae cintidaṃ. varaṃ evva edaṃ vi. ṇa uṇa appaṇo mah'|agghaṃ vaṃsaṃ paāsaantīe mae lahū|kido appā. tā kā gaī? jaha|bhaṇidaṃ aṇuciṭṭhissaṃ.⌋

2.25 CEṬĪ: ⌈ido ehi, Āraṇṇie.⌋

ĀRAṆYIKĀ: ⌈iaṃ āacchāmi.⌋ *(śramaṃ nāṭayantī)* ⌈hañje, dūre kiṃ ajja vi digghiā?⌋

CEṬĪ: ⌈esā sehāliā|gumm|antariā. tā ehi, odaramha.⌋

avataraṇaṃ nāṭayataḥ.

fully opened lotuses from the long pond in the garden of the fountain-house, before the sun, longing to go home in the west, makes them close up into buds." Now, this poor girl doesn't know the long pond. So I'll take her with me and go there. *(looking offstage)* Come this way, over here, Arányika.

Enter ARÁNYIKA.

ARÁNYIKA: *(in tears, upset, to herself)* That I, born in such a lineage, born to command other people, should now have come to such a state as this, and have to carry out someone else's commands—truly there's nothing that fate can't do. Or, rather, it's my own fault, since even when I knew this I didn't do away with myself. And so what shall I do now? Or, rather, it's hard to do now what I was thinking of. Even this is better than that. But, on the other hand, I must not dishonor myself by revealing my exalted lineage. What recourse do I have? I'll do as I'm told.

INDÍVARIKA: Come on, Arányika, this way. 2.25

ARÁNYIKA: I'm coming. *(miming exhaustion)* Gosh, how far away can that long pond still be?

INDÍVARIKA: It's here, hidden by a thicket of Sad Trees. So come, let's go down to it.

The two of them mime going down.

RĀJĀ: vayasya, kim anyad iva cintayasi? nanu bravīmi: «bahv eva sadṛśaṃ jalada|samayasy' êti.» *(«bibhrāṇā mṛdutām» ity ādi punaḥ paṭhati.)*

2.30 VIDŪṢAKAḤ: *(sa|krodham)* ⌜bho, tumaṃ dāva edaṃ aṇṇaṃ a pekkhanto ukkaṇṭhā|ṇibbharaṃ viṇodesi appāṇaṃ. mama uṇa bamhaṇassa sotthi|vāaṇa|velā adikkamadi. tā jāva ahaṃ tuvariaṃ dīhiāe ṇhāia devīe saāsaṃ gamissaṃ.⌟

RĀJĀ: nanu mūrkha, pāraṃ gatā eva vayaṃ dīrghikāyāḥ. evam an|ek'|êndriya|sukh'|âtiśayam anubhavann api n' ôpalakṣayasi? paśya:

śrotraṃ haṃsa|svano 'yaṃ sukhayati dayitā|
  nūpura|hrāda|kārī.
 dṛṣṭi|prītiṃ vidhatte taṭa|taru|vivar''|ā-
  lakṣitā saudha|pālī.
gandhen' âmbho|ruhāṇāṃ parimala|paṭunā
  jāyate ghrāṇa|saukhyaṃ.
 gātrāṇāṃ hlādam ete vidadhati maruto
  vāri|saṃparka|śītāḥ. [4]

tad ehi, dīrghikā|taṭam upasarpāvaḥ. *(parikramy' âvalokya ca)* vayasya, paśya, paśya!

udyāna|devatāyāḥ
 sphuṭa|paṅkaja|kānti|hāriṇī svacchā
dṛṣṭir iva dīrghik'' êyaṃ
 ramayati māṃ *darśanen'* âiva. [5]

KING: My friend, why do you seem to be worrying about something else? I said: "It's very much like the rainy season." *(he recites again: "The patches of grass. . . ")*

JESTER: *(angrily)* It's all right for you to look at this and look at that to distract yourself from the burden of your longing. But I'm a Brahmin, and the moment when I can receive the auspicious present is going by. So I'll bathe quickly in the long pond and go to the queen. 2.30

KING: You idiot, we've already arrived right on the bank of the pond. How can you feel such an extremely pleasant sensation in several of your senses, and still not notice it? Look:

> The honking of the geese, making the sound of
> my darling's anklets, delights the ear.
> The line of white plastered houses, seen through
> the spaces
> between the trees on the bank, pleases the eye.
> The perfume, intense with the fragrance of lotuses,
> pleasures the nose.
> And these breezes, cool from the touch
> of the water,
> gladden the limbs.

Come, then. Let's go up to the bank of the long pond. *(walking around and looking)* Look, my friend, look!

> This long pond is like the eye
> of the goddess of the garden,
> crystal clear, charming *with many a :*
> *as a full-blown* lotus,
> captivating me by the mere *sight : darshan* of it.*

2.35 VIDŪṢAKAḤ: *(sa|kautukam)* ⌜bho vaassa, pekkha pekkha. kā esā kusuma|parimala|suandha|veṇī|mahuar'|āvalī, vidduma|la"|âruṇa|hattha|pallavā, ujjalanta|taṇu|komala|bāhu|ladā saccaṃ paccakkha|carī via ujjāṇa|devadā itthiā dīsaï?⌟

RĀJĀ: *(sa|kautukaṃ vilokya)* vayasya, niratiśaya|svarūpa|śobhā|janita|bahu|vikalp" êyam. yat satyam aham api n' âvagacchāmi. paśya:

pātālād bhuvan'|âvalokana|parā
kiṃ nāga|kany"|ôtthitā?
mithyā tat khalu, dṛṣṭam eva hi mayā,
tasmin kuto 'st' īdṛśī?
mūrtā syād iha kaumudī, na ghaṭate
tasyā divā darśanaṃ.
k" êyaṃ hasta|tala|sthitena kamalen'
ālokyate Śrīr iva? [6]

VIDŪṢAKAḤ: *(nirūpya)* ⌜esā kkhu devīe pariāriā Indīvariā. tā gumm|antariā bhavia pekkhamha.⌟

ubhau tathā kurutaḥ.

2.40 CEṬĪ: *(kamalinī|patra|grahaṇaṃ nāṭayantī)* ⌜Āraṇṇie, avaïṇuṃ tumaṃ padumāiṃ. ahaṃ vi edassiṃ ṇalinī|pattammi sehāliā|kusumāiṃ avaïṇua devī|saāsaṃ gamissaṃ.⌟

JESTER: *(with curiosity)* Look, my friend, look! Who is that woman? She looks like the goddess of the garden incarnate, walking before our eyes: A line of bees cluster around her braid that smells sweet with the fragrance of flowers. Her hands are like sprays of blossoms, and red as coral vines. And her arms are shining, slender, and delicate as vines. 2.35

KING: *(looking, with curiosity)* My friend, her unsurpassed beauty and grace inspire many imaginings. But even I don't know the truth. Look:

> Is she a serpent princess who has come up from
> the netherworld,
> determined to look at the earth?
> No, for I've seen it, and where could such a woman
> live in it?
> Perhaps she's the moonlight, incarnate here.
> But we can't see that during the day.
> Who is she?
> With that lotus held in the palm of her hand,
> she looks just like the goddess Shri.*

JESTER: *(looking closely)* Why, that's the queen's maid, Indívarika. Let's hide behind this thicket and watch.

The two of them do this.

INDÍVARIKA: *(miming picking a lotus leaf)* Arányika, you gather the lotuses. I'll gather the Sad Tree flowers in this lotus leaf and go to the queen. 2.40

RĀJĀ: vayasya, saṃlāpa iva vartate. tad avahitāḥ śṛṇumaḥ. kadā cid ita eva vyaktī|bhaviṣyati.

CEṬĪ *gamanaṃ nāṭayati.*

ĀRAṆYIKĀ: ⌈halā Indīvarie! ṇa sakkuṇomi tue viṇā muhuttaṃ vi ettha āsiduṃ.⌋

CEṬĪ: *(vihasya)* ⌈jādisaṃ ajja mae devīe mantidaṃ sudaṃ, tāriseṇa ciraṃ evva mae viṇā tue āsidavvaṃ.⌋

2.45 ĀRAṆYIKĀ: *(sa|viṣādam)* ⌈kiṃ devīe mantidaṃ?⌋

CEṬĪ: ⌈evaṃ. «tadā esā ahaṃ mahā|rāeṇa bhaṇidā jaha: ‹jadā esā Viñjhakedu|duhidā vara|joggā bhavissadi, tadā ahaṃ sumarāidavvo tti.› tā saṃpadaṃ mahā|rāaṃ sumarāvemi jeṇa se vara|cintā|pajjāulo bhavissadi.»⌋

RĀJĀ: *(sa|harṣam)* iyaṃ sā Vindhyaketor duhitā. *(s'|ânutāpam)* ciraṃ muṣitāḥ smo vayam. vayasya, nirdoṣa|darśanā kanyakā khalv ayam. viśrabdham idānīṃ paśyāmaḥ.

ĀRAṆYIKĀ: *(sa|roṣaṃ karṇau pidhāya)* ⌈tā gaccha tumaṃ. ṇa maha tue a|saṃbaddha|ppalāviṇīe paoaṇaṃ.⌋

CEṬY *apasṛtya puṣp'|âvacayaṃ nāṭayati.*

2.50 RĀJĀ: aho sutarāṃ prakaṭī|kṛtam ābhijātyaṃ dhīratayā. vayasya, dhanyaḥ khalv asau ya etad|aṅga|sparśa|sukha|bhājanaṃ bhaviṣyati.

ĀRAṆYIKĀ *kamal'|âvacayaṃ nāṭayati.*

KING: My friend, they seem to be talking together. Let's listen carefully. Perhaps it will make everything clear.

The MAID *mimes going.*

ARÁNYIKA: Indívarika! I can't stay here even for a moment without you.

INDÍVARIKA: *(laughing)* According to what I heard the queen say today, you're going to have to stay for a very long time indeed without me.

ARÁNYIKA: *(crestfallen)* What did the queen say? 2.45

INDÍVARIKA: This. "The great king said this to me: 'When the daughter of Vindhya·ketu is ready to take a husband, remind me.' Well, now I will remind the great king so that he will begin to preoccupy himself with thoughts of a bridegroom for her."

KING: *(with joy)* This woman is Vindhya·ketu's daughter! *(with regret)* We have been robbed of a sight of her for too long. My friend, this is certainly a woman whom it is no sin to look at. We can watch her now quite confidently.

ARÁNYIKA: *(angrily covering her ears)* Oh, go away! I have no use for you when you babble such nonsense.

The MAID *moves away and mimes gathering flowers.*

KING: Ah, her firmness quite clearly indicates her good 2.50
breeding. My friend, whoever gets to enjoy the pleasure of touching that body will be a privileged man indeed.

ARÁNYIKA *mimes gathering lotuses.*

VIDŪṢAKAḤ: ⌜bho vaassa! pekkha pekkha. accarīaṃ accarīaṃ. esā salila|calanta|kara|pallava|ppahā|vitthideṇa ohasia|sohaṃ karedi kamala|vaṇaṃ avaciṇantī.⌟

RĀJĀ: vayasya, satyam ev' âitat. paśya:

a|cchinn'|âmṛta|bindu|vṛṣṭi|sadṛśīṃ
   prītiṃ dadatyā dṛśāṃ,
yātāyā vigalat|*payodhara|paṭād*
   draṣṭavyatāṃ kām api,
asyāś, candramasas tanor iva, *kara|*
   sparś"|āspadatvaṃ gatā
n' âite yan mukulī|bhavanti sahasā
   padmās, tad ev' âdbhutam. [7]

2.55 ĀRAṆYIKĀ: *(bhramara|bādhāṃ nāṭayantī)* ⌜ha ddhi! ha ddhi! ede kkhu avare pariccaïa kamaliṇīṃ ṇīl|uppala|vaṇāiṃ samāpaḍantā ṇiuṇaaraṃ bādhantā āāsaanti maṃ duṭṭha|mahuarā.⌟ *(uttarīyeṇa mukhaṃ pidhāya, sa|bhayam)* ⌜halā Indīvarie, parittāehi maṃ, parittāehi maṃ! ede kkhu duṭṭha|mahuarā paribhavissanti.⌟

VIDŪṢAKAḤ: ⌜bho vaassa, puṇṇā de maṇo|rahā. jāva evva gabbha|dāsīe sudā ṇa āacchadi, dāva evva tumaṃ vi tuṇhīko bhavia uvasappa. esā vi salila|sadda|sūideṇa paa|saṃcāreṇa, Indīvariā āacchadi tti jāṇia tumaṃ evva olambissadi.⌟

RĀJĀ: sādhu vayasya, sādhu! kāl'|ânurūpam upadiṣṭam.

JESTER: Look, my friend, look! Amazing, quite amazing! The spray of her hand as it moves through the water, spreading its glow, seems to mock the beauty of the bed of lotuses that she's gathering.

KING: My friend, that is the absolute truth. Look:

> It's a wonder that these lotuses do not immediately
> close up into buds when
> they are touched by the *fingers : rays*
> of that woman, who, like the moon,
> casts glances that give delight like
> a continuous shower of drops of ambrosia,
> and who has become particularly beautiful because
> *the silken garment on her breasts : the veil of clouds*
> has slipped away.

ARÁNYIKA: *(miming an onslaught of bees)* Oh no! Oh no! 2.55
These other, horrid bees have left the lotus plant and settled on the beds of blue lotuses, and now they're assaulting me quite sharply and tormenting me. *(covering her face with her upper garment, in fear)* Indívarika, save me, save me! For these horrid bees will overpower me!

JESTER: My friend, your wishes have come true! Go to her, without a word, before that daughter of a born slave girl comes. This girl, here, will know from the sound in the water that feet are moving through it, and, thinking that Indívarika has come, she will cling to you!

KING: Bravo, my friend, bravo! Your advice is quite timely.

ity ĀRAṆYIKĀ/*samīpam upasarpati.*

ĀRAṆYIKĀ: *(pada/śabd'/ākarṇanaṃ nāṭayantī)* ⌜Indīvarie! lahu uvasappa, lahu uvasappa! āulī|kida mhi duṭṭha|mahuarehiṃ.⌟

2.60 RĀJĀNAM *avalambate.* RĀJĀ *kaṇṭhe gṛhṇāti.* ĀRAṆYIK" *ôttarīyaṃ mukhād apanīya,* RĀJĀNAM *a/paśyantī bhramar'/âvalokanaṃ nāṭayati.*

RĀJĀ: *(sv'/ôttarīyeṇa bhramarān nivārayan)*

> ayi visṛja viṣādaṃ, bhīru, bhṛṅgās tav' âite
> parimala|rasa|lubdhā vaktra|padme patanti.
> vikirasi yadi bhūyas trāsa|lolāyat'|âkṣī
> kuvalaya|vana|lakṣmīṃ, tat kutas tvāṃ tyajanti? [8]

ĀRAṆYIKĀ: (RĀJĀNAṂ *dṛṣṭvā sādhvasaṃ nāṭayantī)* ⌜kahaṃ, ṇa esā Indīvariā!⌟ *(sa/bhayaṃ* RĀJĀNAṂ *tyaktv" âpasarantī)* ⌜Indīvarie! lahu āaccha, lahu āaccha! parittāehi maṃ!⌟

VIDŪṢAKAḤ: ⌜hodi, saala|puḍavī|parittāṇa|samattheṇa Vaccha|rāeṇa parittāantī ceḍiṃ Indīvariaṃ akkandasi!⌟

2.65 RĀJĀ: *(«ayi visṛja» ity ādi punaḥ paṭhati.)*

ĀRAṆYIKĀ: (RĀJĀNAM *avalokya, sa/spṛhaṃ sa/lajjaṃ c' ātma/gatam)* ⌜aaṃ kkhu so mahā|rāo jassa ahaṃ tādeṇa diṇṇā. ṭhāṇe kkhu tādassa pakkha|vādo.⌟

He goes close to ARÁNYIKA.

ARÁNYIKA: *(miming hearing the sound of footsteps)* Indívarika, come to me quickly, come to me quickly! These horrid bees are driving me mad!

She clings to the KING. *The* KING *clasps her around the neck.* ARÁNYIKA *removes her upper garment from her face but does not see the* KING, *as she mimes looking at the bees.* 2.60

KING: *(driving the bees away with his own upper garment)*

> Oh, do not despair, timorous woman!
> These bees, greedy for a taste of perfume,
> are alighting on your lotus face.
> If your eyes, wide with terror, scatter about
> the beauty of a bed of water lilies even more,
> how will they ever leave you?

ARÁNYIKA: *(miming alarm on seeing the* KING*)* Why, this is not Indívarika! *(leaving the* KING *and moving away in fear)* Indívarika! Come quickly, come quickly! Save me!

JESTER: My lady, you're being saved by the king of Vatsa, who is capable of saving the entire world, and you're crying for a maid named Indívarika!

KING: *(repeats "Oh, do not despair...")* 2.65

ARÁNYIKA: *(looking at the* KING *with longing and shyness, to herself)* So this man is the great king to whom my father gave me. My father was certainly partial to the right side here.

ākulatāṃ nāṭayati.

CEṬĪ: ⌜āāsiā kkhu Āraṇṇiā duṭṭha|mahuarehiṃ. tā jāva uvasappia samassāsemi. Ārāṇṇie, mā bhaāhi. esā uvaada mhi.⌟

VIDŪṢAKAḤ: ⌜bho, osara, osara. esā kkhu Indīvariā āadā. edaṃ uttantaṃ pekkhia devīe ṇivedaïssadi.⌟ *(aṅgulyā nirdiśya)* ⌜tā imaṃ evva kadalī|gharaṃ pavisia muhuttaṃ ciṭṭhamha.⌟

2.70 *ubhau tathā kurutaḥ.*

CEṬĪ: *(upasṛtya, kapolau spṛśantī)* ⌜hañje Āraṇṇie, kamala|sarisassa tuha vaaṇassa aaṃ doso, jaṃ mahu|arā evvaṃ avarajjhanti.⌟ *(haste gṛhītvā)* ⌜tā ehi, gacchamha. pariṇado diaho.⌟

gamanaṃ nāṭayataḥ.

ĀRAṆYIKĀ: *(kadalī|gṛh'|âbhimukham avalokya)* ⌜hañje Indīvarie adisisiradāe salilassa ūru|tthambho via samuppaṇṇo. tā saṇiaṃ saṇiaṃ gacchamha.⌟

CEṬĪ: ⌜taha.⌟

2.75 *iti niṣkrānte.*

VIDŪṢAKAḤ: ⌜bho, ehi, ṇikkamamha. taṃ geṇhia esā dāsīe sudā Indīvariā gadā.⌟

RĀJĀ: *(niḥśvasya)* kathaṃ gatā! sakhe Vasantaka, na khalv a|vighnam abhilaṣitam a|dhanyaiḥ prāpyate. *(vilokya)* sakhe, paśya, paśya:

She mimes high emotion.

INDÍVARIKA: These horrid bees are certainly annoying Arányika. I'll go up to her and comfort her. Aránvika, don't be afraid. I'm coming!

JESTER: Oh, go away, go away. Here comes Indívarika. If she sees what's happening here, she'll tell it to the queen. *(pointing with his finger)* Let's go into this banana bower and wait for a moment.

The two of them do that. 2.70

INDÍVARIKA: *(approaching* ARÁNYIKA *and touching her cheeks)* Aránvika, it's your own fault. It's because your face is like a lotus that the bees bother you. *(taking her by the hand)* Come then, let's go. The day is bent low with age.

They mime going.

ARÁNYIKA: *(looking toward the banana bower)* Indívarika, the water was so extremely cold that my thighs seem to be numb.* So let's go slowly, slowly.

INDÍVARIKA: All right.

Exit the two women. 2.75

JESTER: Come, we can come out now. That daughter of a slave girl, Indívarika, has taken her and gone.

KING: *(sighing)* What, gone? My friend Vasántaka, unfortunate people do not get what they want without obstacles. *(looking)* See, my friend, see:

ābaddha|mukham ap' îdaṃ
  kaṇṭakitāṃ kamala|kānanaṃ tasyāḥ
sukumāra|pāṇi|pallava|
  saṃsparśa|sukhaṃ kathayat' îva. [9]

(niḥśvasya) sakhe, ka idānīm upāyaḥ punas tāṃ draṣṭum?

2.80 VIDŪṢAKAḤ: ⌜bho, tume evva puttaliaṃ bhañjia dāṇiṃ rodisi. ṇa maha kkhu bamhaṇassa vaaṇaṃ karesi.⌟

RĀJĀ: kiṃ mayā na kṛtam?

VIDŪṢAKAḤ: ⌜taṃ dāṇiṃ visumaridaṃ. jaha «tuṇhīko bhavia uvasapp êtti» mae bhaṇidaṃ. adisaṃkaḍe jaṃ bhavaṃ pavisia alia|paṇḍicca|duv|vidaddhadāe «aï visija visād' êtti» edehiṃ aṇṇehiṃ a kahua|vaaṇehiṃ ṇibbhaccia sampadaṃ kiṃ rodisi. puṇo vi uvāaṃ pucchasi.⌟

RĀJĀ: kathaṃ, samāśvāsanam api nirbhartsanam iti bhaṇitaṃ mūrkheṇa!

VIDŪṢAKAḤ: ⌜jāṇidaṃ evva ko ettha mukkho tti. tā kiṃ edeṇa? attham|a'|âhilāsī bhaavaṃ sahassa|rassī. tā ehi abbhantaraṃ evva pavisamha.⌟

2.85 RĀJĀ: *(vilokya)* aye pariṇata|prāyo divasaḥ. ahaha, samprati hi:

hṛtvā padma|vana|dyutiṃ, priyatam" êv',
  êyaṃ dina|śrīr gatā.
 rāgo 'smin, mama cetas' îva, savitur
  bimbe 'dhikaṃ lakṣyate.
cakrāhvo, 'ham iva, sthitaḥ saha|carīṃ

> This bed of lotuses has closed its faces,
> but still their prickles are raised,
> as if telling of the pleasure of the touch
> of the tender spray that is her hand.*

(sighing) My friend, what means can we use now to see her again?

JESTER: Well, you've broken your doll yourself and now 2.80
you're crying. You didn't heed my words, and I'm a Brahmin.

KING: What didn't I do?

JESTER: Ah, now you've forgotten that! I told you, "Go to her, without a word," but you, sir, entering at the crucial moment, were so uncouth and full of false learning that you reproved her with sharp words like, "Oh, do not despair," and so forth. So why are you crying now? And even asking me about the means to see her again.

KING: How can the fool call encouragement reproof?

JESTER: It's easy to tell who's the fool in this case. But what's the good of all this? The god of a thousand rays is longing to go home. So come, let us go inside.

KING: *(looking)* Yes, the day has almost bent to its close. Ah 2.85
well. For now:

> The splendour of the day, like my dearest,
> has gone,
> stealing the lustre of the lotus beds.
> There seems to be more *passion : redness*
> in the orb of sun,
> than in this heart of mine.

dhyāyan nalinyās taṭe.
saṃjātā sahasā, mam' êva, bhuvanasy'
âpy andha|kārā diśaḥ. [10]

iti niṣkrāntāḥ sarve.

iti dvitīyo 'ṅkaḥ.

The ruddy goose,* like me, stands on
the bank of the lotus pond,
thinking of his mate.
And the quarters of the sky have suddenly
become dark
for the whole world, as it is for me.

Exit all.

End of Act Two.

ACT III

tataḥ praviśati MANORAMĀ.

MANORAMĀ: ⌜āṇatta mhi devīe Vāsavadattāe: «hañje Maṇorame, jaṃ taṃ Saṃkiccāyaṇīe ajja|uttassa mama a uttantaṃ ṇāḍa'|ôvaṇibaddhaṃ, tassa ṇaccidavva|sesaṃ ajja tumhehiṃ komudī|mah"|ûsave ṇaccidavvan ti.» hio kkhu Āraṇṇiāe pia|sahīe suṇṇa|hiaāe aṇṇahā evva ṇaccidaṃ. ajja uṇa Vāsavadattā|bhūmiāe tāe jaï taha karīadi tado avassaṃ devī kuppadi. tā kahiṃ dāva tāṃ pekkhia uvālambhissaṃ.⌟ *(vilokya)* ⌜esā Āraṇṇiā appaṇā evva kiṃ vi kiṃ vi mantaantī digghiā|tīle kadalī|gharaaṃ pavisadi. tā gumm|antariā bhavia suṇissaṃ dāva se visaddha|jappidāṇiṃ.⌟

tataḥ praviśaty āsana/sthā kām'/âvasthāṃ nāṭayanty ĀRAṆYIKĀ.

3.5 ĀRANYIKĀ: *(niḥśvasya)* ⌜hiaa, dul|laha|jaṇaṃ patthaanto tumaṃ kīsa maṃ dukkhidaṃ karesi?⌟

MANORAMĀ: ⌜taṃ edaṃ edasya suṇṇa|hiaattaṇassa kāraṇaṃ. kiṃ uṇa esā patthedi. avahidā dāva suṇissaṃ.⌟

ĀRAṆYIKĀ: *(s'/âsram)* ⌜kahaṃ taha ṇāma somma|daṃsaṇo bhavia mahā|rāo evvaṃ saṃdāvedi maṃ. accariaṃ, accariaṃ.⌟ *(niḥśvasya)* ⌜aha vā maha evva esā a|bhāaheadā. ṇa uṇa mahā|rāassa doso.⌟

MANORAMĀ: *(sa/bāṣpam)* ⌜kahaṃ, mahā|rāo evva se patthaṇijjo. sāhu, pia|sahī, sāhu. abhijāa|sariso de ahilāso.⌟

[Time: A few days later. Late afternoon.]

Enter MANO·RAMA.

MANO·RAMA: Queen Vásava·datta has commanded me, saying: "Mano·rama, today, at the festival of moonlight,* you must perform the remaining part of the play that Sankrityáyani wrote about what happened to my husband and myself." Now, yesterday, my dear friend Arányika seemed absent minded and played her part all wrong. If she plays the part of Vásava·datta like that again today, the queen is sure to get angry. So, where can I find her to warn her? *(looking)* Here is Aránvika now, saying something to herself as she goes into the banana bower on the bank of the long pond. I'll hide behind this thicket of trees and listen as she murmurs to herself in confidence.

Enter ARÁNYIKA, *seated and miming love-sickness.*

ARÁNYIKA: *(sighing)* My heart, why do you cause me such 3.5
pain, wanting someone out of reach?

MANO·RAMA: So this is the cause of her absentmindedness. But what does she want? I'll listen carefully.

ARÁNYIKA: *(in tears)* How can the great king be so very handsome that he torments me like this? It's amazing, quite amazing. *(sighing)* Or is it just my own bad luck and not the king's fault at all?

MANO·RAMA: *(tearfully)* Why, it's the great king himself that she wants! Bravo, dear friend, bravo! This desire befits your good breeding.

ĀRAṆYIKĀ: ⌜kassa dāva edaṃ uttantaṃ ṇivedia sajjha|veaṇaṃ via dukkhaṃ kāraïssaṃ.⌟ *(vicintya)* ⌜aha vā atthi me hiaa|ṇivvisesā pia|sahī Maṇoramā. tāe vi edaṃ lajjāe ṇa pāremi kahiduṃ. savvahā maraṇaṃ vajjia kudo me hiaassa aṇṇā ṇivvudī?⌟

3.10 MANORAMĀ: *(s'|âsram)* ⌜haddhi! haddhi! adibhūmiṃ gadā se tavassiṇīe aṇurāo. tā kiṃ dāṇiṃ ettha karissaṃ?⌟

ĀRAṆYIKĀ: *(s'|âbhilāṣam)* ⌜aaṃ so uddeso jassiṃ mahu|arehiṃ āāsijjantī olambia mahā|rāeṇa samassāsida mhi, «bhīru, mā bhaāhi tti.»⌟

MANORAMĀ: *(sa|harṣam)* ⌜kahaṃ esā, vi diṭṭhā mahā|rāeṇa! savvahā atthi se jīvidassa uvāo. jāva uvasappia samassāsemi ṇaṃ.⌟ *(sahas" ôpasṛtya)* ⌜juttaṃ ṇāma hiaassa vi lajjiduṃ.⌟

ĀRAṆYIKĀ: *(sa|lajjam, ātma|gatam)* ⌜haddhi! haddhi! savvaṃ sudaṃ edāe. tā ettha juttaṃ evva paāsaïduṃ.⌟ *(prakāśaṃ, haste gṛhītvā)* ⌜pia|sahī, mā kuppa, mā kuppa. lajjā evva ettha avarajjhadi.⌟

MANORAMĀ: *(sa|harṣam)* ⌜sahi, alaṃ saṃkāe. edaṃ me āakkha. saccaṃ evva tumaṃ mahā|rāeṇa diṭṭhā ṇa vetti.⌟

3.15 ĀRAṆYIKĀ: *(sa|lajjam, adho|mukhī)* ⌜sudaṃ evva pia|sahīe savvaṃ.⌟

MANORAMĀ: ⌜jaï diṭṭhā mahā|rāeṇa tumaṃ, tā alaṃ saṃtappideṇa. so evva dāṇiṃ daṃsaṇ'|ôvāa|pajjāulo bhavissadi.⌟

ARÁNYIKA: Whom can I tell about this affair, to make the pain a bit more bearable? *(thinking)* But I do have a dear friend who is no different from my own heart, Mano·rama. Yet I would be too shy to tell even her about this. In the end, where can my heart find rest, but in death?

MANO·RAMA: *(in tears)* Oh no! No! The poor girl's love has 3.10
reached its zenith. What can I do about this now?

ARÁNYIKA: *(with longing)* This is the very spot where, when the bees were bothering me, I clung to the great king and he encouraged me, saying, "Oh, do not despair, timorous woman!"

MANO·RAMA: *(with joy)* Why, the great king has already seen her! Then, in the end, there is indeed a way for her to go on living. I'll go up to her and encourage her. *(suddenly approaching)* Is it right to be shy even toward your own heart?*

ARÁNYIKA: *(shyly, to herself)* Oh no! No! She's heard everything! Well, then it will be all right to reveal it to her. *(aloud, taking her by the hand)* Don't be angry, dear friend, don't be angry. It's all the fault of my shyness.

MANO·RAMA: *(with joy)* My friend, enough of this hesitation. Tell me this. Is it or is it not true that the great king saw you?

ARÁNYIKA: *(shyly, hanging her head)* My dear friend heard it 3.15
all.

MANO·RAMA: If the great king saw you, stop fussing. He himself will now preoccupy himself with devising ways to see you.

ĀRAṆYIKĀ: ˹aaṃ sahī|aṇo pakkha|vādeṇa mantedi. aï sahi|pakkha|vādiṇī, devī|guṇa|ṇiala|ṇibaddhe kkhu tassiṃ jaṇe kudo edaṃ?˼

MANORAMĀ: *(vihasya)* ˹halā a|paṇḍide! kamaliṇī|baddh'|âṇurāo vi mahu|aro māladiṃ pekkhia ahiṇava|vara|ras'|assāda|lampaḍo kudo taṃ aṇ|āsādia ṭṭhidiṃ karedi?˼

ĀRAṆYIKĀ: ˹kiṃ ediṇā a|saṃbhāvideṇa? tā ehi. ahiaṃ kkhu sarad|ādaveṇa saṃtappāiṃ ajja vi ṇa me aṅgāiṃ saṃdāvaṃ muñcandi.˼

3.20 MANORAMĀ: ˹aï lajj"|āule ṇa juttaṃ ed'|āvatthaṃ gadāe vi de appā pacchādiduṃ.˼

ĀRAṆYIKĀ *mukham avanamayati.*

MANORAMĀ: ˹aï, a|visaṃbha|sīle, kiṃ dāṇiṃ pacchādesi? ṇīsāsa|ṇiha|viṇiggao diahaṃ rattiṃ vi tujjha aṇurāo a|virada|paḍanta|kusuma|sara|sara|ṇivaha|paütta|huṃ|kāra|saddo via ṇa bhaṇaï?˼ *(ātma/gatam)* ˹aha vā ṇa hu aaṃ kālo uvālambhassa. tā jāva ṇaliṇī|pattāiṃ se hiae dāissaṃ.˼ *(utthāya, dīrghikāyā nalinī/patrāṇi gṛhītv"* ĀRAṆYIKĀYĀ *hṛdaye dadatī)* ˹samassasadu sahī, samassasadu sahī!˼

tataḥ praviśati VIDŪṢAKAḤ.

VIDŪṢAKAḤ: ˹adimahanto kkhu pia|vaassassa Āraṇṇiāe uvari aṇurāo. jeṇa pariccatta|rāa|kajjo tāe evva daṃsaṇ'|ôvāaṃ cintaanto appāṇaṃ viṇodei.˼ *(vicintya)* ˹kahiṃ dāṇiṃ

ARÁNYIKA: My friend here counsels with partiality. You are partial to your friend, but that person is bound by the chains of the queen's virtues. How can he do this?

MANO·RAMA: *(laughing)* O you innocent child! Even though the bee is bound in love with the lotus plant, when it sees the jasmine, it lusts to taste a juice with a new flavor, and then how can it stay put without having it?

ARÁNYIKA: But what's the good of all this, that cannot be? Come, let's go. The autumn heat has made my limbs even hotter, and the heat won't leave them even now.

MANO·RAMA: You're so shy, but it's not right for you to hide 3.20
your true self even when you're in such a state.

ARÁNYIKA *lowers her face.*

MANO·RAMA: Oh, it's in your very nature to be distrustful. But what can you hide now? Night and day, doesn't your love speak of it? It slips out in the semblance of your sighs, as if it were the humming sound made by the ceaseless cascade of arrows sent by the god of flower arrows. *(to herself)* No, this is not the time to tease her. First, I'll put some lotus leaves on her heart. *(getting up, taking lotus leaves from the long pond and putting them on* ARÁNYIKA*'s heart)* Courage, my friend, courage, my friend.

Enter the JESTER.

JESTER: My dear friend's love for Arányika is really too great. For he has neglected the affairs of the kingdom and spends all his time devising means to see her. *(thinking)* taṃ pekkhe? aha vā tahiṃ evva dāva digghiāe aṇṇesāmi.⌟ *(parikrāmati)*

3.25 MANORAMĀ: *(ākarṇya)* ⌜pada|saddo via suṇīadi. tā kadalī|gumm|antaridā bhavia pekkhamha dāva, ko eso tti.⌟

ubhe tathā kṛtvā paśyataḥ.

ĀRAṆYIKĀ: ⌜kahaṃ, so evva mahā|rāassa passa|parivaṭṭhī bamhaṇo.⌟

MANORAMĀ: ⌜kahaṃ, Vasantao evva.⌟ *(sa|harṣam, ātma|gatam)* ⌜avi ṇāma taha have.⌟

VIDŪṢAKAḤ: *(diśo 'valokya)* ⌜kiṃ dāṇiṃ Āraṇṇiā saccaṃ evva saṃvuttā?⌟

3.30 MANORAMĀ: *(sa|smitam)* ⌜sahi, rāa|vaasso kkhu bamhaṇo tumaṃ uddisia mantedi. tā dāva avahidā suṇamha.⌟

ĀRAṆYIKĀ *sa|spṛhaṃ sa|lajjaṃ ca śṛṇoti.*

VIDŪṢAKAḤ: *(s'|ôdvegam)* ⌜jadā dāva mae guru|maaṇa|saṃdāva|ṇīsaha|sarīrassa pia|vaassassa vaaṇeṇa devīṇaṃ Vāsavadattā|Padumāvadīṇaṃ aṇṇāṇaṃ a devīṇaṃ bhavaṇāiṃ aṇṇesanteṇa ṇa sā diṭṭhā, tadā «jahiṃ digghiāe diṭṭhā, idaṃ vi dāva pekkhissaṃ, ti» āado mhi. tā jāva iha vi ṇ' atthi. kiṃ dāṇiṃ karissaṃ?⌟

MANORAMĀ: ⌜sudaṃ pia|sahīe?⌟

VIDŪṢAKAḤ: *(vicintya)* ⌜aha vā bhaṇido evva ahaṃ vaasseṇa, «jaï taṃ aṇṇesanto ṇa pekkhasi, tā tado vi dāva digghiādo tāe kara|ala|pparisa|diuṇia|suha|ssīalāiṃ ṇaliṇī|pattāiṃ geṇhia āaccha, tti.» tā kahaṃ edāiṃ jāṇidavvāiṃ?⌟

Where can I find her now? I know; I'll look for her right there by the long pond. *(He walks around.)*

MANO·RAMA: *(hearing)* I hear what seem to be footsteps. 3.25
Let's hide behind this banana thicket and see who it is.

The two of them do this, and watch.

ARÁNYIKA: Why, it's that same Brahmin who's the sidekick of the great king.

MANO·RAMA: Why, it's Vasántaka! *(with joy, to herself)* Oh, I hope it will be all right!

JESTER: *(looking in all directions)* Has she actually become a Lady of the Jungle?*

MANO·RAMA: *(smiling)* My friend, this Brahmin, the king's 3.30
friend, is talking about you! So let's listen very carefully!

ARÁNYIKA *listens with longing and shyness.*

JESTER: *(upset)* When my dear friend's body could no longer bear the heat and torment of his heavy passion, he told me to search the palaces of the two queens, Vásava·datta and Padmávati, and of the other queens,* but I didn't find her there. So I came here, thinking, "I'll look for her by the long pond, where I saw her before." But she's not here, either. What shall I do now?

MANO·RAMA: Did my dear friend hear that?

JESTER: *(thinking)* On the other hand, my friend said to me, "If you look for her and still can't find her, then at least take from that long pond some of the lotus leaves that the palms of her hands touched and made twice as

3.35 MANORAMĀ: ⌈aaṃ me avasaro.⌋ *(upasṛtya,* VIDŪṢAKAṂ *haste gṛhītvā)* ⌈Vasantaa, ehi! ahaṃ de jāṇāvemi.⌋

VIDŪṢAKAḤ: *(sa|bhayam)* ⌈kassa tumaṃ jāṇāvesi? kiṃ devīe? ṇa hu mae kiṃ vi mantidaṃ.⌋

MANORAMĀ: ⌈Vasantaa, alaṃ saṃkāe. jādisī Āraṇṇiāe kide attaṇo pia|vaassassa avatthā tue vaṇṇidā, tado diuṇadaro bhaṭṭiṇo vi kide mama pia|sahīe avatthā. tā pekkha, pekkha.⌋

apasṛty' ĀRAṆYIKĀṂ *darśayati.*

VIDŪṢAKAḤ: *(dṛṣṭvā, sa|harṣam)* ⌈sa|phalo me parissamo. sotthi hodīe.⌋

3.40 ĀRAṆYIKĀ *sa|lajjaṃ kamalinī|patrāṇy apanīy' ôttiṣṭhati.*

MANORAMĀ: ⌈ajja|Vasantaa, tuha daṃsaṇeṇa evva avagado pia|sahīe saṃdāvo jeṇa saaṃ evva ṇaliṇī|pattāiṃ avaṇei. tā aṇugaṇhādu ajjo imāiṃ.⌋

ĀRAṆYIKĀ: *(s'|āvegam)* ⌈aï, parihāsa|sīle. kīsa maṃ lajjāvesi?⌋

kiṃ cit parāṅ|mukhī tiṣṭhati.

VIDŪṢAKAḤ: *(sa|viṣādam)* ⌈ciṭṭhandu dāva ṇaliṇī|pattāiṃ. adilajj"|āluā de pia|sahī. tā kahaṃ edāṇaṃ samāamo bhavissadi?⌋

cool and refreshing, and bring them to me." But how will I tell which they are?

MANO·RAMA: This is my golden opportunity. *(approaching* 3.35
the JESTER *and taking him by the hand)* Vasántaka, come. I'll tell you.

JESTER: *(with fear)* You'll tell on me? To whom? To the queen? I didn't really say anything.*

MANO·RAMA: Vasántaka, don't worry. The state that, as you describe it, your dear friend is in because of Arányika—my own dear friend is in twice as bad a state, because of the king. Look at it, look!

She goes toward ARÁNYIKA *and points her out.*

JESTER: *(seeing, with joy)* All my efforts have borne fruit! Bless you, my lady!

ARÁNYIKA *throws off the lotus leaves, with embarrassment, and* 3.40
stands up.

MANO·RAMA: Good Vasántaka, the mere sight of you has dispelled my dear friend's burning anguish so that she herself is throwing off the lotuses leaves. Please take them, sir.

ARÁNYIKA: *(upset)* You're always making jokes. Why do you embarrass me?

She stands with her face turned slightly away.

JESTER: *(despairing)* Never mind the lotus leaves. Your dear friend is too easily embarrassed. So how will the two of them meet?

MANORAMĀ: *(kṣaṇaṃ vicintya, sa|harṣam)* ⌜Vasantaa, evvaṃ via.⌟

karṇe kathayati.

VIDŪṢAKAḤ: ⌜sāhu, pia|sahi, sāhu.⌟ *(apavārya)* ⌜jāva evva tuho ṇevaccha|ggahaṇaṃ karettha dāva evva ahaṃ vi vaassaṃ geṇhia āacchāmi.⌟

iti niṣkrāntaḥ.

MANORAMĀ: ⌜adikovaṇe, uṭṭhehi uṭṭhehi! ṇaccidavvaṃ amhehiṃ tassa evva ṇāḍaassa ṇaccida|sesaṃ. tā ehi. pekkhā|gharaṃ evva gacchamha.⌟ *(parikramy' âvalokya)* ⌜idaṃ pekkh"|āgāraṃ. jāva ehi, pavisamha.⌟ *(praviṣṭaken' âvalokya)* ⌜sāhu, sāhu, savvaṃ sajjī|kidaṃ. devīe āantavvaṃ.⌟

tataḥ praviśati devī, SĀṄKṚTYĀYANĪ, *vibhavataś ca parivāraḥ.*

VĀSAVADATTĀ: ⌜bhaavadi, aho de kavittaṇaṃ! jeṇa edaṃ gūḍh'|uttantaṃ ṇāda'|ôvaṇibaddhaṃ s'|âṇubhavaṃ vi amhāṇaṃ ajjautta|caridaṃ a|diṭṭha|puvvaṃ via disantaṃ ahiaaraṃ kodūhalaṃ vaḍḍaadi.⌟

SĀṄKṚTYĀYANĪ: āyuṣmati, āśraya|guṇa ev' âyam īdṛṣo yad a|sāram api kāvyam avaśyam eva śṛṇvatāṃ śravaṇa|sukham utpādayati. paśya:

prāyo yat kiṃ cid api
  prāpnoty utkarṣam āśrayān mahataḥ.
matt'|êbha|kumbha|taṭa|gatam
  eti hi śṛṅgāratāṃ bhasma. [1]

MANO·RAMA: *(thinking for a moment, then, with joy)* Vasán- 3.45
taka, this is how.

She tells it in his ear.

JESTER: Bravo, dear friend, bravo! *(aside)* While you two are putting on your costumes, I'll go and get my friend.

Exit.

MANO·RAMA: My, you've got a temper. Get up, get up. We have to act the remaining part of that play. So, come. Let's go to the theatre. *(walking around and looking)* Here's the theatre. Come, let's go inside. *(entering the stage and looking around)* Bravo, bravo, everything is ready for the queen to come.

Enter the queen, SANKRITYÁYANI, *and the entourage according* 3.50
to rank.

VÁSAVA·DATTA: My dear lady, what a poet you are! For even though we lived through this adventure of our husband, with its secret incidents, still, now that you have made it into a play, when we see it, it seems like something never seen before, and much more interesting.

SANKRITYÁYANI: This subject matter, your highness, is such that even a poem with no substance will inevitably, through none of its own doing, delight the ears of those who hear it. Look:

> Generally, any trifling thing at all becomes
> important
> through its connection with something great.
> For ashes become decorative on the
> swollen temples

VĀSAVADATTĀ: *(sa|smitam)* ⌜bhaavadi, «savvassa vallaho jāmādo hodi, tti» jāṇiadi evva edaṃ. tā kiṃ ediṇā kah"|âṇubandheṇa? varaṃ taṃ evva ṇaccidavvaṃ daṭṭhuṃ!⌟

3.55 SĀṄKṚTYĀYANĪ: evam. Indīvarike, prekṣā|gṛham ādeśaya.

CEṬĪ: ⌜edu, edu bhaṭṭiṇī.⌟

sarvāḥ parikrāmanti.

SĀṄKṚTYĀYANĪ: *(vilokya)* aho prekṣaṇīyatā prekṣā|gṛhasya.

ābhāti ratna|śata|śobhita|śātakumbha|
stambh"|âvasakta|pṛthu|mauktika|dāma|ramyam
adhyāsitaṃ yuvatibhir vijit'|âpsarobhiḥ
prekṣā|gṛhaṃ sura|vimāna|samānam etat. [2]

3.60 MANORAM"|ĀRAṆYIKE: *(upasṛtya)* ⌜jedu, jedu bhaṭṭiṇī.⌟

VĀSAVADATTĀ: ⌜Maṇorame, adikkandā kkhu saṃjjhā tā gacchamha. lahu gaṇhaha ṇevacchaṃ.⌟

UBHE: ⌜jaṃ devī āṇavedi.⌟

iti prasthite.

VĀSAVADATTĀ: ⌜Āraṇṇie, edehiṃ evva mad|aṅga|piṇaddhehiṃ ābharaṇehiṃ ṇevaccha|bhūmiṃ gadua appāṇaṃ pasāhehi.⌟ *(ābharaṇāny aṅgād avatāry'* ĀRAṆYIKĀYĀḤ *samarpayati.)* ⌜Maṇorame, tumaṃ vi ṇalagiri|ggahaṇa|pari-tuṭṭheṇa tādeṇa ajja|uttassa diṇṇāiṃ ābharaṇāiṃ Indī-

of a rutting bull elephant.

VÁSAVA·DATTA: *(smiling)* My dear lady, it's well-known that, as they say, "Everyone loves his son-in-law best."* So what's the use of going on with this conversation? Better to see the play itself!

SANKRITYÁYANI: Right. Indívarika, show us the theatre. 3.55

INDÍVARIKA: Come, your highness, come.

They all walk around.

SANKRITYÁYANI: *(looking)* How lovely the theatre is.

> Garlands of large pearls draped on golden columns
> studded with hundreds of jewels,
> and the young women in the audience,
> surpassing the courtesan nymphs of heaven,
> make this charming theatre seem
> just like a floating palace of the gods.

MANO·RAMA *and* ARÁNYIKA: *(approaching)* Victory, victory 3.60
to the queen.

VÁSAVA·DATTA: Mano·rama, it is past twilight now. So go, and quickly put on your costume.

BOTH: As your highness commands.

The two of them start to go.

VÁSAVA·DATTA: Arányika, go backstage and put on these pieces of jewelry that I'm wearing now. *(She takes off the jewels from her body and gives them to* ARÁNYIKA.*)* Mano·rama, as for you, take from Indívarika the decorations that my father gave to my husband in gratitude for capturing the Reed-mountain elephant,* and go backstage

variā|saāsādo geṇhia ṇevaccha|bhūmiaṃ gadua appāṇaṃ maṇḍehi jeṇa su|sadisī dīsasi mahā|rāassa.⌟

3.65 MANORAMĀ INDĪVARIKĀ / *sakāśād ābharaṇāni gṛhītvā sah'* ĀRAṆYIKAYĀ *niṣkrāntā.*

INDĪVARIKĀ: ⌜edaṃ āsaṇaṃ. uvavisadu bhaṭṭiṇī.⌟

VĀSAVADATTĀ: *(āsanaṃ nirdiśya)* ⌜uvavisadu bhaavadī.⌟

ubhe upaviśataḥ.

3.70 *tataḥ praviśati gṛhīta/nepathyaḥ* KAÑCUKĪ.

KAÑCUKĪ:

> *antaḥ/purāṇāṃ* vihita|vyavasthaḥ,
>   *pade pade* 'haṃ *skhalitāni* rakṣan,
> jar"|āturaḥ saṃprati *daṇḍa/nītyā*
>   sarvaṃ nṛpasy' ânukaromi vṛttam. [3]

bho, ājñāpito 'smi vimānit'|â|śeṣa|śatru|sainyena yathārtha|nāmnā Mahāsenena: «samādiśyatām antaḥ|pureṣu yathā, ‹śvo vayam Udayan'|ôtsavam anubhavāmaḥ. ato yuṣmābhir utsav'|ânurūpa|veṣ'|ôjjvalena parijanena saha Manmath'|ôdyānaṃ gantavyam› iti».

and put them on, so that you'll closely resemble the great king.

MANO·RAMA *takes the decorations from* INDÍVARIKA *and exits with* ARÁNYIKA. 3.65

INDÍVARIKA: Here is a seat. Please sit down, ma'am.

VÁSAVA·DATTA: *(indicating a seat [to* SANKRITYÁYANI*])* My dear lady, please be seated.

The two of them sit down.

[Scene: PRADYÓTA MAHA·SENA*'s palace]**

Enter the CHAMBERLAIN, *in costume.* * 3.70

CHAMBERLAIN:

Suffering from old age,
I imitate all the actions of a king,
by *leaning on my cane* : *devising government policy*
to guard against *stumbling at every step* : *lapses of duty in every province,*
and to keep order *in the women's inner quarters* : *within the cities.**

Maha·sena, "The king who has a Great Army," aptly named indeed, since he scorns the armies of all his enemies, has commanded me to have this announced in the women's quarters: "Tomorrow we celebrate the Festival of Údayana.* Therefore you must go to the Garden of Passion with your entourage dressed in splendid clothes suitable for the festival."

SĀṄKṚTYĀYANĪ: *(*KAÑCUKINAṂ *nirdiśya)* rāja|putri, pravṛttā prekṣā. dṛśyatām.

3.75 KAÑCUKĪ: tad etad ādeṣṭavyaṃ, «parijanena saha gantavyam iti.» na «gṛhīta|nepathyen' êti.» kutaḥ:

pādair nūpuribhir, nitamba|phalakaiḥ
śiñjāna|kāñcī|guṇair,
hār'|āpādita|kāntibhiḥ stanataṭaiḥ,
keyūribhir bāhubhiḥ,
karṇaiḥ kuṇḍalibhiḥ, karaiḥ sa|valayaiḥ,
sa|svastikair mūrdhajair,
devīnāṃ paricārikā|parijano 'py
eteṣu saṃdṛśyate. [4]

na khalu kiṃ cid atr' âpūrvam anuṣṭheyam. kevalaṃ «svāmy'|ādeśa, iti» matv" âhaṃ samādiṣṭas tad ājñā|śeṣaṃ rāja|putryai nivedayāmi. *(parikramy' âvalokya ca)* iyaṃ sā Vāsavadattā vīṇā|hastayā Kāñcanamālay" ânugamyamānā gandharva|śālāṃ praviṣṭā. yāvad asyāḥ kathayāmi.

parikrāmati.

*tataḥ praviśati gṛhīta|*VĀSAVADATTĀ*|nepathy" āsanasth"* ĀRAṆYIKĀ, *vīṇā|hastā* KĀÑCANAMĀLĀ *ca.*

3.80 ĀRAṆYIKĀ: ⌜halā Kāñcaṇamāle, kīsa uṇa cirāadi ajja vi vīṇ"|āārio?⌟

SANKRITYÁYANI: *(pointing to the* CHAMBERLAIN*)* Princess, the play has begun. Please watch it.

CHAMBERLAIN: So I must tell them to "go . . . with your entourage," but not "in stage costume."* For: 3.75

Among them, even the entourage that belongs to
the queen's maids is showy:
anklets on their feet,
tinkling girdle-bands on their broad hips,
pearl necklaces on their full breasts,
armlets on their arms,
hoop-earrings on their ears,
bracelets on their hands,
and good-luck symbols in their hair.*

So there's no need to do anything about this that hasn't been done already. When I received my orders I thought, "Just my master's instructions," and so I'll announce the rest of the command to the princess. *(walking around and looking around)* Here is Vásava·datta, just entering the music hall, and Kánchana·mala right after her, with a lute in her hand. I'll tell her now.

He walks around.

Enter ARÁNYIKA, *seated, wearing* VÁSAVA·DATTA*'s costume, and* KÁNCHANA·MALA, *with a lute in her hand.*

ARÁNYIKA: Kánchana·mala, why is the lute teacher late again today?* 3.80

KĀÑCANAMĀLĀ: ⌜bhaṭṭi|dārie, diṭṭho deṇa ekko ummatto. tassa vaaṇaṃ suṇia citteṇa bhāvido ohasanto ciṭṭhaï.⌟

ĀRAṆYIKĀ: *(sa|hasta|tālaṃ vihasya)* ⌜hañje, suṭṭhu edaṃ pucchadi. «sarisā sarise rañjanti, tti» duve ettha ummattā.⌟

SĀṄKṚTYĀYANĪ: rāja|putryāḥ sadṛśam ākāraṃ paśyāmy asyās. tādṛśen' âkāreṇ' âvaśyaṃ tvadīyāṃ bhūmikāṃ saṃbhāvayiṣyati.

KAÑCUKĪ: *(upasṛtya)* rāja|putri, devas tvām ājñāpayati: «śvo 'vaśyam asmābhir vīṇāṃ vādayantī śrotavyā. tat tvayā nava|tantrī|sajjayā ‹Ghoṣavatyā› stheyam iti.»

3.85 ĀRAṆYIKĀ: ⌜ayya, jaï evvaṃ, lahu vīṇ"|āāriaṃ visajjehi.⌟

KAÑCUKĪ: eṣa Vatsa|rājaṃ preṣayāmi.

iti niṣkrāntaḥ.

ĀRAṆYIKĀ: ⌜Kañcaṇamāle, uvaṇehi me Ghosavadīṃ, jāva se tantīo parikkhemi.⌟

KĀÑCANAMĀLĀ *vīṇām arpayati.* ĀRAṆYIK" *ôtsaṅge vīṇāṃ kṛtvā sārayati.*

3.90 *tataḥ praviśati gṛhīta|*VATSA|RĀJA*|nepathyā* MANORAMĀ.

MANORAMĀ: *(sva|gatam)* ⌜cirāadi kkhu mahā|rāo. kiṃ ṇa kahidaṃ Vasantaeṇa? aha vā devīe bhāadi? jaï dāṇiṃ āacche, tado ramaṇijjaṃ have.⌟

KÁNCHANA·MALA: Princess, he saw a madman, and as he listened to him talk he was struck with wonder, and now he's staying there laughing at him.*

ARÁNYIKA: *(clapping her hands and laughing)* It's good that he's questioning him. "Like likes like," they say, and they're both quite mad.

SANKRITYÁYANI: I see that she looks just like a princess, and with such looks she'll certainly appear to be you when she acts your part.*

CHAMBERLAIN: *(approaching)* Princess, his majesty directs you: "Tomorrow, without fail, we will hear you play the lute. So you must have the lute named 'Sonorous' fitted with new strings."

ARÁNYIKA: If so, sir, then send the lute teacher right away. 3.85

CHAMBERLAIN: I'll go myself and send the king of Vatsa.

Exit.

ARÁNYIKA: Kánchana·mala, bring "Sonorous" to me so that I can test its strings.

KÁNCHANA·MALA *gives her the lute.* ARÁNYIKA *puts it on her lap and tunes it.*

Enter MANO·RAMA *wearing the costume of the* KING OF VATSA. 3.90

MANO·RAMA: *(to herself)* The great king is quite late. Is it possible that Vasántaka didn't tell him? Or is he afraid of the queen? If he comes now it would still be fine.

tataḥ praviśati RĀJ" *âvaguṇṭhita|śarīro,* VIDŪṢAKAŚ *ca.*

RĀJĀ:

saṃtāpaṃ prathamaṃ tathā na kurute
śīt'|âṃśur ady' âiva me.
niśvāsā glapayanty ajasram adhun" âiv'
ôṣṇās tathā n' âdharam.
saṃpraty eva mano na śūnyam, alasāny
aṅgāni no pūrvavad.
duḥkhaṃ yāti mano|ratheṣu tanutāṃ
saṃcintyamāneṣv api. [5]

3.95 vayasya, satyam ev' ôktaṃ Manoramayā, «yath" âiṣā mama priya|sakhī mahā|rājasya devyā darśana|pathād api rakṣyate, tad ayaṃ samāgam'|ôpāyaḥ. adya rātrāv asmābhir ‹Udayana|caritaṃ› nāma nāṭakaṃ devyāḥ purato nartitavyam. tatr' Āraṇyikā Vāsavadattā bhaviṣyati. aham api Vatsa|rājaḥ. tac|cariten' âiva sarvaṃ śikṣitavyam. tad āgatya svayam eva svāṃ bhūmikāṃ kurvāṇaḥ Samāgam'|ôtsavam anubhavatv» iti?

VIDŪṢAKAḤ: ⌜jaï maṃ ṇa pattiāasi, esā Maṇoramā tuha vesaṃ dhāraantī ciṭṭhaï. tā uvasappia saaṃ eva puccha.⌟

RĀJĀ: (MANORAMĀM *upasṛtya)* Manorame, satyam idaṃ yad Vasantako 'bhidhatte?

MANORAMĀ: ⌜bhaṭṭā, saccaṃ evva. maṇḍaa edehiṃ ābharaṇehiṃ appāṇaṃ.⌟

Enter the KING, *with his body veiled, and the* JESTER.

KING:

> The cool rays of the moon do not burn me
> today as they did at first.
> Nor do hot sighs constantly scorch my lower lip
> now as they did then.
> I am not so absent-minded now,
> nor are my limbs so languid as before.
> Misery grows thin when desires are
> about to be realized.

My friend, did Mano·rama really say this? "Since the queen keeps my dear friend even out of the king's range of vision, this is the way for them to meet. Today, at night, we are to perform for the queen the play called 'The Adventures of Údayana.' In it, Ványika will play the queen, and I will play the king of Vatsa. I must learn to do everything just as he did it. So let him come and act his own part himself and in that way enjoy the Festival of the Rendezvous."* 3.95

JESTER: If you don't believe me, here is Mano·rama wearing your costume. Go up to her and ask her yourself.

KING: *(approaching* MANO·RAMA*)* Mano·rama, is what Vasántaka says true?

MANO·RAMA: Sire, it's really true. Put on these decorations.

ity ābharaṇāny aṅgād avatārya RĀJÑE *samarpayati.*

3.100 RĀJĀ *paridadhāti.*

VIDŪṢAKAḤ: ⌜ede kkhu rāṇāo dāsīe vi evvaṃ ṇaccāvianti. aho kajjassa garuadā.⌟

RĀJĀ: *(vihasya)* mūrkha, n' âiṣa kālaḥ parihāsaya. nibhṛtena citra|śālāṃ praviśya Manoramayā sah' âsman|nṛttaṃ paśyatā sthīyatām.

ubhau tathā kurutaḥ.

ĀRAṆYIKĀ: ⌜Kañcaṇamāle, ciṭṭhadu vīṇā. pucchissaṃ dāva kiṃ vi.⌟

3.105 RĀJĀ: śṛṇomi tāvat katamo 'yam uddeśo vartate.

ity avahitaḥ śṛṇoti.

KĀÑCANAMĀLĀ: ⌜pucchadu bhaṭṭi|dāriā.⌟

ĀRAṆYIKĀ: ⌜saccaṃ eva tādo mantedi evvaṃ, jaha «jaï vīṇaṃ vādaanto avaharedi maṃ Vaccha|rāo, avassaṃ bandhaṇādo muñcemi, tti»?⌟

RĀJĀ: *(praviśya paṭā|kṣepeṇa sa|harṣaṃ, vastr'|ânte grathitaṃ badhnāti.)* evam etat. kaḥ saṃdehaḥ?

3.110 sa|parijanaṃ Pradyotaṃ
vismayam upanīya vādayan vīṇām
Vāsavadattām apaharāmi
na cirād ev', êti paśyāmi. [6]

She takes the decorations from her own body and gives them to the KING.

The KING *puts them on.* 3.100

JESTER: So even a slave girl can make these kings play their parts like that. This is getting serious.

KING: *(laughing)* You idiot, this is no time for joking. Go quickly into the picture gallery with Mano·rama and stay there, watching us act.

They both do this.

ARÁNYIKA: Kánchana·mala, never mind the lute. I want to ask you something.

KING: I'll listen to find out what place in the play they've 3.105
reached.

He listens carefully.

KÁNCHANA·MALA: Ask, please, princess.

ARÁNYIKA: Is it true that my father is saying this? "If the king of Vatsa carries me away with his lute playing, I'll certainly release him from prison."

KING: *(entering* [the play within the play] *with a toss of the curtain, joyously, knotting the hem of his garment)** Yes! No doubt about it!

I've amazed Pradyóta and his entourage 3.110
by my lute-playing
and I see that before long
I'll carry away Vásava·datta.

yataḥ su|saṃvihitaṃ sarvaṃ Yaugandharāyaṇena.

VĀSAVADATTĀ: *(sahas" ôtthāya)* ⌜jedu, jedu ajja|utto.⌟

RĀJĀ: *(sva|gatam)* kathaṃ, pratyabhijñāto 'smi devyā?

SĀṄKṚTYĀYANĪ: *(sa|smitam)* rāja|putri, alam alaṃ saṃbhrameṇa. prekṣaṇīyakam etat.

3.115 RĀJĀ: *(ātma|gataṃ, sa|harṣam)* idānīm ucchvāsito 'smi.

VĀSAVADDATĀ: *(sa | vilakṣa | smitam upaviśya)* ⌜kahaṃ Maṇoramā esā. mae uṇa jāṇidaṃ, ajja | utto eso tti. sāhu Maṇorame, sāhu. sohaṇaṃ ṇaccidaṃ.⌟

SĀṄKṚTYĀYANĪ: rāja|putri, sthāna eva kṛtā bhrāntis te Manoramayā. paśya:

rūpaṃ tan nayan'|ôtsav'|āspadam idaṃ,
  veṣaḥ sa ev' ôjjvalaḥ;
sā matta|dvirad'|ôcitā gatir iyaṃ,
  tat sattvam atyūrjitam.
līlā s" âiva, sa eva sāndra|jalada|
  hrād'|anukārī svaraḥ.
sākṣād darśita eṣa naḥ kuśalayā
  Vats'|êśa ev' ânayā. [7]

VĀSAVADATTĀ: ⌜hañje Indīvarie. baddheṇa ajja | utteṇa ahaṃ vīṇaṃ sikkhāvidā. tā se karehi ṇīl'|uppala|dāmaeṇa ṇialaṇaṃ.⌟

3.120 *śiraso 'panīya nīl'|ôtpala|dām' ârpayati.* INDĪVARIKĀ *tathā kṛtvā punas tatr' âiv' ôpaviśati.*

For Yaugándharáyana has set everything up very well.

VÁSAVA·DATTA: *(suddenly standing up)* Victory, victory to my husband!

KING: *(to himself)* What? Has the queen recognized me?

SANKRITYÁYANI: *(smiling)* Princess, none of this confusion! This is just a performance.

KING: *(to himself, with joy)* Now I can breathe again. 3.115

VÁSAVA·DATTA: *(sitting down with a smile of embarrassment)* Why, that's Mano·rama! I could have sworn it was my husband. Bravo, Mano·rama, bravo! Superb acting!

SANKRITYÁYANI: Princess, it was quite natural that Mano·rama confused you. Look:

> There's his handsome form, a pleasure to look at;
> and that's his very own gorgeous costume;
> that's his walk, like an elephant in rut,
> and his own powerful majesty.
> That's precisely his grace, and that voice of his
> like the thunder of dense clouds.
> It really is the Lord of Vatsa
> that that talented girl has shown us in the flesh.

VÁSAVA·DATTA: Indívarika, my husband taught me to play the lute when he was in chains. So now chain him up with this garland of blue lotuses.

She takes a garland of blue lotuses from her own head and gives 3.120
it to her. INDÍVARIKA *does as directed and sits down again in the same place.*

ĀRAṆYIKĀ: ⌜Kañcaṇamāle, kahehi, kahehi. ṇaṃ saccaṃ evva mantedi tādo «jaï vīṇaṃ vādaanto avaharedi maṃ Vaccha|rāo tado avassaṃ bandhaṇādo muñcemi tti.»⌟

KĀÑCANAMĀLĀ: ⌜bhaṭṭi|dārie, saccaṃ. taha karehi jaha Vaccha|rāassa avassaṃ bahu|madā hosi.⌟

RĀJĀ: niṣpāditam eva Kāñcanamālayā yat tad" âsmābhir abhilaṣitam.

ĀRAṆYIKĀ: ⌜jaï evvaṃ tā ādareṇa vādaïssaṃ.⌟

3.125 *gāyantī vādayati.*

⌜*ghaṇa/bandhaṇa/saṃruddhaṃ*
gaaṇaṃ daṭṭhūṇa *Māṇasaṃ* eduṃ
ahilasaï *rāa/haṃso*
daïaṃ gheūṇa appaṇo vasaïṃ.⌟ [8]

VIDŪṢAKO *nidrāṃ nāṭayati.*

MANORAMĀ: *(hastena cālayantī)* ⌜Vasantaa, pekkha, pekkha. pia|sahī me ṇaccaï.⌟

VIDŪṢAKAḤ: *(sa/roṣam)* ⌜dāsīe sude, tumaṃ vi ṇa desi suviduṃ. jada ppahudi pia|vaasseṇa Āraṇṇiā diṭṭhā, tada ppahudi teṇa saha mae rattaṃ|divaṃ ṇiddā ṇa diṭṭhā. tā aṇṇado ṇikkamia suvissaṃ.⌟

3.130 *niṣkramya śete.*

ARÁNYIKA: Kánchana·mala, tell me, tell me. Is it true that my father is saying this? : "If the king of Vatsa carries me away with his lute playing, I'll certainly release him from prison."

KÁNCHANA·MALA: Princess, it's true. So act so that the king of Vatsa will have to think highly of you.

KING: [*(to himself)*] Kánchana·mala has actually achieved what I wanted.

ARÁNYIKA: If so, I'll take special care to play well.

She plays the lute and sings: 3.125

When the *swan of kings* : *royal swan* sees the sky
shut out by thick prison walls :
obscured by bands of clouds,
he longs to go to *the land of his heart's desire* :
Lake Mánasa,
his own home, taking his beloved with him.*

The JESTER *mimes sleeping.*

MANO·RAMA: *(shaking him with her hand)* Look, Vasántaka, look! My dear friend is playing her part.

JESTER: *(in fury)* You daughter of a slave girl, even you don't let me sleep. From the moment when my dear friend saw Arányika, he and I haven't even caught a glimpse of sleep, night or day. I'm going some place else, to sleep.

He goes away and lies down. 3.130

ĀRAṆYIKĀ *punar gāyati.*

⌜ahiṇava|rāa|kkhittā mahu|ariā vāmaeṇa kāmeṇa
uttammaï, patthantī daṭṭhuṃ pia|daṃsaṇaṃ daïaṃ.⌟ [9]

RĀJĀ: *(tat|kṣaṇaṃ śrutvā, sahas" ôpasṛtya)* sādhu, rāja|putri, sādhu! aho gītam, aho vāditram. tathā hi:

vyaktir Vyañjana|dhātunā daśa|vidhen'
âpy atra labdh" âdhunā.
vispaṣṭo druta|madhya|lambita|pari-
cchinnas tridh" âyaṃ layaḥ.
Gopuccha|pramukhāḥ krameṇa yatayas-
tisro 'pi saṃpāditās.
tattv'|augh'|ânugatāś ca vādya|vidhayaḥ
samyak trayo darśitāḥ. [10]

3.135 ĀRAṆYIKĀ: *(vīṇāṃ pariṣvajy' āsanād utthāya,* RĀJĀNAṂ *s'| âbhilāṣaṃ paśyantī)* ⌜uvajjhāo, paṇamāmi.⌟

RĀJĀ: *(sa|smitam)* yad aham icchāmi, tat te bhūyāt.

KĀÑCANAMĀLĀ: *(*ĀRAṆYIKĀYĀ *āsanaṃ nirdiśya)* ⌜iha evva uvavisadu uvajjhāo.⌟

RĀJĀ: *(upaviśya)* rāja|putrī kv' êdānīm upaviśatu?

KĀÑCANAMĀLĀ: *(sa|smitam)* ⌜dāṇiṃ evva bhaṭṭi|dāriā vijjā|māṇena paritosidā tumhehiṃ. tā aruhadi evva esā uvajjhāa|pīṭhiāe.⌟

ARÁNYIKA *sings again:*

> Perverse Desire hurls the female honey-bee into
> a new passion, and she pines away,
> longing to see her lover, who shows his love.*

KING: *(hearing the song at that moment and immediately approaching)* Bravo, princess, bravo. What singing, what playing! For:

> All ten forms of the "Distinguishing" mode
> of playing
> are now clearly distinct.
> The tempo is clearly marked off in three cadences:
> allegro, moderato, and adagio.
> The three pauses, beginning with the "Cow's Tail,"
> have been used in the right order.
> And all three of the modes of playing
> —"true," "animated," and "following"—
> have been well demonstrated.*

ARÁNYIKA: *(clasping the lute, rising from her seat, and looking at the* KING *with longing)* I bow to you, my teacher. 3.135

KING: *(smiling)* May my wish for you come true.*

KÁNCHANA·MALA: *(pointing to* ARÁNYIKA*'s seat)* Will the teacher please sit here?

KING: *(sitting)* Where should the princess sit now?

KÁNCHANA·MALA: *(smiling)* You have just rewarded the princess with your high opinion of her skill. So she really deserves to sit on the teacher's seat.

3.140 RĀJĀ: upaviśastv; arh" êyam ardh'|āsanasya. rāja|putri, sthīyatām.

ĀRĀNYIKĀ KĀÑCANAMĀLĀṂ *paśyati.*

KĀÑCANAMĀLĀ: *(sa|smitam)* ⌜bhaṭṭi|dārie, uvavisa. ko ettha doso? sissa|viseso kkhu tumaṃ.⌟

ĀRAṆYIKĀ *sa|lajjam upaviśati.*

VĀSAVADATTĀ: *(sa|lajjam)* ⌜bhaavadīe ahiaṃ kappidaṃ kajjaṃ. ṇa hu ahaṃ tassiṃ kāle ek'|āsaṇe ajja|utteṇa saha uvaviṭṭhā.⌟

3.145 RĀJĀ: rāja|putri, punaḥ śrotum icchāmi. vādaya vīṇām.

ĀRAṆYIKĀ: *(sa|smitam)* ⌜Kāñcaṇamāle, ciraṃ khu mama vādaantīe parissamo jādo. dāṇiṃ ṇissahāiṃ aṅgāiṃ. tā ṇa sakkuṇomi vādaïduṃ.⌟

KĀÑCANAMĀLĀ: ⌜uvajjhāa, suṭṭhu parissantā bhaṭṭi|dāriā. kavola|tala|baddha|sea|lavāe, pekkha, se vevanti agga|hatthā. tā samassattā hodu muhuttaaṃ.⌟

RĀJĀ: Kāñcanamāle, yuktam abhihitam.

hastena grahītum icchati. ĀRAṆYIKĀ *hastam apasārayati.*

3.150 VĀSAVADATTĀ: *(s'|âsūyam)* ⌜bhaavadi, ahiaṃ edaṃ vi tue kidaṃ. ṇa hu aaṃ Kañcaṇamālā|kavveṇa vañcaïdavvā.⌟

SĀṄKṚTYĀYANĪ: *(vihasya)* āyuṣmati, īdṛśam eva kāvyaṃ bhaviṣyati.

KING: Let her sit here; she deserves half of the seat. Princess, 3.140
do please stay.

ARÁNYIKA *looks at* KÁNCHANA·MALA.

KÁNCHANA·MALA: *(smiling)* Princess, sit down. What fault is there in that? You're a very special pupil.

ARÁNYIKA *sits down, shyly.*

VÁSAVA·DATTA: *(with embarrassment)* My dear lady, you've added to the poem. I certainly did not sit with my husband on a single seat at that time.

KING: Princess, I want to hear more. Play the lute. 3.145

ARÁNYIKA: *(smiling)* Kánchana·mala, I've played for such a long time that I'm exhausted, and now my limbs are so weak that I can't play.*

KÁNCHANA·MALA: The princess is entirely exhausted, professor. See how drops of sweat cling to her cheek, and her fingers are trembling. So let her catch her breath for a moment.

KING: You're right, Kánchana·mala.

He tries to take ARÁNYIKA *by the hand, but she pulls away her hand.*

VÁSAVA·DATTA: *(with indignation)* My dear lady, you've 3.150
added this, too. I certainly won't let Kánchana·mala's poetry betray me.*

SANKRITYÁYANI: *(laughing)* Your highness, this is just the art of poetry.

ĀRAṆYIKĀ: *(sa|roṣam iva)* ⌜avehi, Kañcaṇamāle, avehi. ṇa me bahu|madā si.⌟

KĀÑCANAMĀLĀ: *(sa|smitam)* ⌜jaï ahaṃ ciṭṭhantī ṇa bahu madā tā esā gacchamhi.⌟

iti niṣkrāntā.

3.155 ĀRAṆYIKĀ: *(sa|saṃbhramam)* ⌜Kañcaṇamāle, ciṭṭha, ciṭṭha. ahaṃ se agga|hattho samappido.⌟

RĀJĀ: *(ĀRAṆYIKĀYĀ hastaṃ gṛhītvā)*

sadyo 'vaśyāya|bindu|vyatikara|śiśiraḥ
kiṃ bhavet padma|kośo?
hrāditvaṃ n' âsya manye sadṛśam idam uṣasy
eva vīt'|ātapasya.
muñcanty ete him'|aughaṃ nakha|rajanikarāḥ-
pañca? kiṃ so 'pi dāhī?
jñātaṃ: sved'|âpadeśād a|viratam amṛtaṃ
syandate, vyaktam etat. [11]

api ca:

etena bāla|vidruma|pallava|śobh"|âpahāra|dakṣeṇa
hṛdaye mama tvay" âyaṃ nyasto *rāgaḥ* sva|hastena. [12]

3.160 *iti* garbha|nāṭakam.

ĀRAṆYIKĀ: *(sparśa|viśeṣaṃ nāṭayantī)* ⌜haddhi! haddhi! edaṃ Maṇoramaṃ parisantīe aṇ|atthaṃ evva me aṅgāiṃ karenti.⌟

ARÁNYIKA: *(pretending to be angry)* Go away, Kánchana·mala, go away. I don't think much of you.*

KÁNCHANA·MALA: *(smiling)* If you don't think much of me when I stay here, I'll go.

Exit.

ARÁNYIKA: *(in agitation)* Stay, Kánchana·mala, stay! His fingertips are touching me! 3.155

KING: *(taking* ARÁNYIKA *by the hand)*

> Can this be a lotus bud, suddenly cooled
>   by a spray of dewdrops?
> No, I don't think a bud is so delightful
> even at dawn when the sun doesn't touch it.
> Could these be five moons in the form of nails,
> sending out a shower of snow?
>   But can that also burn?
> I know: clearly this is ceaselessly flowing ambrosia,
> pretending to be sweat.

And:

> Your hand, that so skillfully steals the beauty
> of the sprays of young coral trees,
> has planted this *redness : passion* in my heart.

End of the Play within a Play.* 3.160

ARÁNYIKA: *(miming a special sensation of touch)* Oh no! No! When I touch Mano·rama my limbs do something that makes no sense to me.*

VĀSAVADATTĀ: *(sahas" ôtthāya)* ⌜bhaavadi, pekkha tumaṃ. ahaṃ uṇa aliaṃ ṇa pāremi pekkhiduṃ.⌟

SĀṄKṚTYĀYANĪ: rāja|putri, dharma|śāstra|vihita eṣa gāndharvo vivāhaḥ. kim atra lajjā|sthānam? prekṣaṇīyakam idam. tan na yuktam a|sthāne rasa|bhaṅgaṃ kṛtvā gantum.

VĀSAVADATTĀ *parikrāmati.*

3.165 INDĪVARIKĀ: *(vilokya)* ⌜bhaṭṭiṇi, Vasantao citta|sālā|duvāre pasutto ciṭṭhaï.⌟

VĀSAVADATTĀ: *(nirūpya)* ⌜Vasantao evva eso.⌟ *(vicintya)* ⌜raṇṇā vi ettha hodavvaṃ. tā bodhia pucchissaṃ dāva ṇaṃ.⌟

prabodhayati.

VIDŪṢAKAḤ: *(nidrā|jaḍam utthāya, sahasā vilokya)* ⌜Maṇorame, kiṃ ṇaccia āado via|vaasso? ādu ṇaccadi evva?⌟

VĀSAVADATTĀ: *(sa|viṣādam)* ⌜kahaṃ, ajja|utto ṇaccadi? Maṇoramā dāṇiṃ kahiṃ?⌟

3.170 VIDŪṢAKAḤ: ⌜esā citta|sālāe ciṭṭhaï.⌟

MANORAMĀ: *(sa|bhayam, ātma|gatam)* ⌜kahaṃ, aṇṇahā evva hiae karia devīe mantidaṃ, edeṇa vi mukkha|baḍueṇa aṇṇahā evva buddhia savvaṃ āulī|kidaṃ.⌟

VĀSAVADATTĀ: *(sa|roṣaṃ hasantī)* ⌜sāhu, Maṇorame, sāhu! sohaṇaṃ tue ṇaccidaṃ.⌟

VÁSAVA·DATTA: *(suddenly standing up)* My dear lady, see it, yourself. But as for me, I can't watch this lie.

SANKRITYÁYANI: Princess, even the dharma texts condone this marriage by mutual desire.* What occasion for shame is there in this? This is a performance. It's not right to leave at the wrong place, breaking the mood.

VÁSAVA·DATTA *walks around.*

INDÍVARIKA: *(looking on)* Ma'am, Vasántaka is lying fast asleep at the door of the picture gallery. 3.165

VÁSAVA·DATTA: *(looking sharply)* Yes, it's Vasántaka. *(thinking)* Then the king must be here too. I'll just wake him and ask him.

She wakes him.

JESTER: *(standing up, still dazed from sleep, suddenly looking around)* Mano·rama, has my dear friend finished acting and come back, or is he still acting?

VÁSAVA·DATTA: *(in dismay)* What! My husband is acting? Then where is Mano·rama now?

JESTER: She's standing right here in the picture gallery. 3.170

MANO·RAMA: *(in terror, to herself)* What! The queen spoke, meaning it in one sense, and this Brahminical idiot thought she meant it in another sense, and ruined everything.*

VÁSAVA·DATTA: *(laughing in fury)* Bravo, Mano·rama, bravo! Superb acting, on your part.

MANORAMĀ: *(sa|bhayaṃ kampamānā, pādayor nipatya)* ⌜bhaṭṭiṇi, ṇa hu ahaṃ ettha avarajjhāmi. edeṇa khu had'|āseṇa balādo alaṃkaraṇāiṃ geṇhia duvāra|ṭṭhideṇa iha ṇiruddhā. ṇa uṇa maha akkandantīe saddo muraaṇi|gghos|antario keṇa vi sudo.⌟

VĀSAVADATTĀ: ⌜hañje, uṭṭhehi. jāṇidaṃ savvaṃ. Vasantao kkhu Āraṇṇiā|uttanta|ṇāḍae sutta|dhāro.⌟

3.175 VIDŪṢAKAḤ: ⌜saaṃ evva cintehi: kahiṃ Āraṇṇiā, kahiṃ Vasantao tti?⌟

VĀSAVADATTĀ: ⌜Maṇorame, su|ggahīdaṃ karia ṇaṃ āaccha dāva. pekkhaṇīaṃ se pekkhamhi.⌟

MANORAMĀ: *(sva|gatam)* ⌜dāṇiṃ samassasida mhi.⌟ *(*VIDŪṢAKAṂ *kare badhnāti. prakāśam)* ⌜had'|āsa, dāṇiṃ aṇubhava attaṇo duṇ|ṇaassa phalaṃ.⌟

VĀSAVADATTĀ: *(sa|saṃbhramam upasṛtya)* ⌜ajja|utta paḍihadaṃ edaṃ a|maṅgalaṃ.⌟ *(iti pādayor nil'|ôtpala|dām' âpanayantī, s"|ôtprāsam)* ⌜marisadu ajja|utto jaṃ Maṇoram" êtti karia ṇīl'|uppala|dāmaeṇa bandhāvido si.⌟

ĀRAṆYIKĀ *sa|bhayam apasṛtya tiṣṭhati.*

3.180 RĀJĀ: *(sahas" ôtthāya,* VIDŪṢAKAṂ MANORAMĀṂ *ca dṛṣṭv", ātma|gatam)* kathaṃ, vijñāto 'smi devyā?

MANO·RAMA: *(trembling in terror and falling at her feet)* Your highness, this was not my fault! This damn fool took the decorations from me by force and stood at the door to keep me shut in here. And no one heard the sound of my cries, since the noise of the drums drowned them out.*

VÁSAVA·DATTA: Get up. I know it all. Vasántaka was indeed the stage director of the play, 'The Adventures of Arányika.'

JESTER: Think about it yourself: What has Vasántaka to do 3.175
with Arányika?

VÁSAVA·DATTA: Mano·rama, bind him securely and come along. I'm going to see the performance he directed.

MANO·RAMA: *(to herself)* Now I can breathe again. *(She binds the* JESTER*'s hands. Aloud:)* You damn fool, now reap the fruit of your own scheming.

VÁSAVA·DATTA: *(approaching in haste)* My husband, this evil omen has been averted. *(removing the garland of blue lotuses from his feet as she speaks and remarking, with sarcasm)* Forgive me, my husband, for chaining you with a garland of blue lotuses when I thought you were Mano·rama.

ARÁNYIKA *moves away in fear and remains there.*

KING: *(standing up suddenly, seeing the* JESTER *and* MANO· 3.180
RAMA, *to himself)* What? Has the queen recognized me?

vailakṣyaṃ nāṭayati.

SĀṄKṚTYĀYANĪ: *(sarvān avalokya, sa|smitam)* katham, anyad ev' êdaṃ prekṣaṇīyakaṃ saṃvṛttam? a|bhūmir iyam asmad|vidhānām.

iti niṣkrāntā.

RĀJĀ: *(sva|gatam)* a|pūrvo 'yaṃ kopa|prakāraḥ. dur|labham atr' ânunayaṃ paśyāmi. *(vicintya)* evaṃ tāvat kariṣye. *(prakāśam)* devi, tyajyatāṃ kopaḥ.

3.185 VĀSAVADATTĀ: ⌜ajja|utta, ko ettha kuvido?⌟

RĀJĀ: kathaṃ na kupit" âsi?

snigdhaṃ yady api vīkṣitaṃ nayanayos,
tāmrā tath"|âpi dyutir.
mādhurye 'pi sati skhalaty anupadaṃ
te gadgadā vāg iyam.
niśvāsā niyatā api stana|bhar'|ôt-
kampena saṃlakṣitāḥ.
kopas te prakaṭa|prayatna|vidhṛto 'py
eṣa sphuṭaṃ lakṣyate. [13]

(pādayor nipatya) prasīda, priye, prasīda.

VĀSAVADATTĀ: ⌜Āraṇṇie, tumaṃ kuvida, tti saṃbhāvaanto ajja|utto «pie, pasīda, tti» pasādaadi. tā uvasappa.⌟

3.190 *iti hasten' ākarṣati.*

He mimes embarrassment.

SANKRITYÁYANI: *(looking at everyone, smiling)* Why, this little performance has turned into something quite different. This is no place for people like us.

Exit.

KING: *(to himself)* She's never been angry like this before. I can see that it will be hard to win her over this time. *(thinking)* This is how I'll do it. *(aloud)* My queen, let go of your anger.

VÁSAVA·DATTA: My husband, who's angry here? 3.185

KING: Aren't you angry?

> Though your glance is affectionate,
> there's a red glow in your eyes.
> Though there is honey in it,
> your stammering speech
> stumbles with every foot.
> Your deep sighs, though restrained, are revealed
> by the heaving of your heavy breasts.
> This anger of yours is clearly visible
> even in your obvious efforts to contain it.*

(falling at her feet) Relent, my dear, relent.

VÁSAVA·DATTA: Aránуika, my husband thinks you're angry and so is trying to appease you, saying, "Relent, my dear, relent." Go to him.

She drags her by the hand. 3.190

ĀRAṆYIKĀ: *(sa|bhayam)* ⌜bhaṭṭiṇi, ṇa hu ahaṃ kiṃ vi jāṇāmi.⌟

VĀSAVADATTĀ: ⌜Āraṇṇie, tumaṃ kahaṃ ṇa āṇāsi? dāṇiṃ de sikkhāvemi. Indīvarie, geṇha edaṃ.⌟

VIDŪṢAKAḤ: ⌜hodi, ajja komudī|mah'|ūsave tuha cittaṃ avaharidumṃ vaasseṇa pekkhaṇīaṃ aṇuciṭṭhidaṃ.⌟

VĀSAVADATTĀ: ⌜edaṃ tumhāṇaṃ duṇ|ṇaaṃ pekkhia hāso me jāadi.⌟

3.195 RĀJĀ: devi, alam anyathā vikalpitena. paśya:

bhrū|bhaṅgaiḥ kriyate lalāṭa|śaśinaḥ
kasmāt kalaṅko mudhā?
vāt'|âkampita|bandhujīva|samatāṃ
nīto 'dharaḥ kiṃ sphuran?
madhyaś c' âdhika|kampita|stana|bhareṇ'
âyaṃ punaḥ khidyate?
kopaṃ muñca. tav' âiva citta|haraṇāy'
âitan mayā krīḍitam. [14]

devi, prasīda, prasīda.

iti pādayoḥ patati.

VĀSAVADATTĀ: ⌜hañje, ṇivuttaṃ pekkhaṇaaṃ. tā ehi. abbhantaraṃ evva pavisamha.⌟

3.200 *iti niṣkrāntā.*

ARÁNYIKA: *(in terror)* Your highness, I don't know anything at all about this.

VÁSAVA·DATTA: Aránjika, how could you not know? Well, I'll teach you now. Indívarika, seize her.

JESTER: My lady, my friend acted in this performance to divert your thoughts today during the Festival of Moonlight.

VÁSAVA·DATTA: When I see all your scheming, it does make me laugh.

KING: Stop imagining things to be other than they are. Look: 3.195

Why do your frowning brows make a mark
on the moon of your forehead
for no reason?
Why is your lower lip trembling like a
bandhu·jiva flower
shaken by a wind?
Why do your heavy breasts oppress your waist
even more, with their increased throbbing?
Let go of your anger. I played this game
only to divert your mind.*

Relent, my queen, relent.

He falls at her feet.

VÁSAVA·DATTA: La comedia e finita. So come, let's go into the women's quarters.

Exit. 3.200

RĀJĀ: *(vilokya)* katham a|kṛtv" âiva prasādaṃ gatā devī?

sved'|âmbhaḥ|kaṇa|bhinna|bhīṣaṇatara|
bhrū|bhaṅgam ekaṃ ruṣā,
trāsen' âparam utplut'|ôtpluta|mṛga|
vyālola|netr'|ôtpalam,
utpaśyann aham agrato mukham idaṃ
devyāḥ, priyāyās tathā,
bhītaś c' ôtsuka|mānasaś ca, mahati
kṣipto 'smy ahaṃ saṃkaṭe. [15]

tad yāvad idānīṃ śayanīyaṃ gatvā devyāḥ prasādan'|ôpāyaṃ cintayāmi.

iti niṣkrāntāḥ sarve.

3.205 *iti tṛtīyo 'ṅkaḥ.*

KING: *(looking)* How could the queen have left without relenting?

When I see before me the face of the queen and
the face of my beloved,
the one, in anger, marked by frowns and,
more frightening still,
streaked with drops of sweat,
the other, in terror, eyes lolling about
like those of a gazelle
leaping and leaping,
I'm thrown into a great dilemma,
between fear and the longing of my heart.

So I'll go to bed and think of some way to appease the queen.

Exit all.

End of Act Three.

PRELUDE TO ACT IV

tataḥ praviśati MANORAMĀ.

MANORAMĀ: *(s'|ôdvegam)* ⌜aho diggha|rosadā devīe. ettiaṃ kālaṃ baddhāe pia|sahīe Āraṇṇiāe uvari aṇukampaṃ ṇa geṇhaï. sā tavassiṇī attaṇo bandhaṇassa kileseṇa taha ṇa saṃtappadi, jaha bhaṭṭiṇo daṃsaṇa|ṇirāsadāe. īrisaṃ ca se dukkhaṃ jeṇa ajja evva attāṇaṃ vāvādaantī mae kahaṃ vi ṇivāridā. «edaṃ uttantaṃ bhaṭṭiṇo ṇivedehi, tti» Vasantaaṃ bhaṇia āada mhi.⌟

tataḥ praviśati KĀÑCANAMĀLĀ.

4.5 KĀÑCANAMĀLĀ: ⌜kahaṃ, aṇṇesantīe vi mae bhaavaī Saṅkiccāaṇī ṇa diṭṭhā.⌟ *(vilokya)* ⌜tā edaṃ vi dāva Maṇoramaṃ pucchissaṃ.⌟ *(upasṛtya)* ⌜Maṇorame, avi jāṇāsi, kahiṃ bhaavaī Saṅkiccāaṇi, tti?⌟

MANORAMĀ: *(viloky' âśrūṇi pramṛjya)* ⌜halā Kañcaṇamāle, diṭṭhā. kiṃ uṇa tāe paoaṇaṃ?⌟

KĀÑCANAMĀLĀ: ⌜Maṇorame, ajja devīe Aṅgāravadīe leho pesido. tassiṃ vācide bappha|puṇṇa|ṇaaṇā diḍhaṃ saṃtappiduṃ āraddhā devī. tā viṇodaṇa|ṇimittaṃ tāe bhaavadiṃ aṇṇesāmi.⌟

MANORAMĀ: ⌜halā, kiṃ uṇa tassiṃ lehe ālihidaṃ?⌟

KĀÑCANAMĀLĀ: ⌜«jā maha bhaïṇī sā tava jaṇaṇī evva. tāe bhattā Diḍhavammā tādo te. tā tava kiṃ edaṃ āakkhidavvaṃ? tassa samahiaṃ saṃvaccharaṃ Kaliṅga|hadaeṇa baddhassa. tā ṇa juttaṃ edaṃ uttantaṃ aṇiṭṭhaṃ

[Time: A few days later.]

Enter MANO·RAMA.

MANO·RAMA: *(upset)* The queen stays angry for so long! She hasn't taken pity on my dear friend Aránvika all this time, even though Aránvika's been in prison. The poor girl suffers not so much from the hardship of her own imprisonment as from the hopelessness of seeing the king. She is so unhappy that just today I barely managed to keep her from doing away with herself. I've just come from telling Vasántaka to report this episode to the king.

Enter KÁNCHANA·MALA.

KÁNCHANA·MALA: How can this be? Though I've searched 4.5
for the good lady Sankrityáyani, I haven't seen her. *(looking)* Here's Mano·rama; I'll ask her. *(approaching)* Mano·rama, do you know where the good lady Sankrityáyani is?

MANO·RAMA: *(looking at her and wiping her tears)* I've seen her, Kánchana·mala, but why do you need her?

KÁNCHANA·MALA: Mano·rama, today Queen Angáravati sent a letter.* When the queen read it, her eyes filled with tears and she began to be terribly upset. So I'm looking for the good lady to cheer her up.

MANO·RAMA: But what was written in the letter?

KÁNCHANA·MALA: This: "My sister is like a mother to you, and her husband Dridha·varman is like your father. But why should this story have to be told to you? For more than a year the vile king of Kalínga has held him captive. It's not right for your husband, who borders his kingdom

suṇia samīva|ṭṭhidassa samatthassa bhaṭṭuṇo de evvaṃ udāsīṇattaṇaṃ olambiduṃ tti.»⌟

4.10 MANORAMĀ: ⌜halā Kañcaṇamāle, jadā dāva «aaṃ uttanto bhaṭṭiṇīe ṇa keṇa vi viṇṇaviidavvo, tti» bhaṭṭiṇā āṇattaṃ tā keṇa uṇa dāṇiṃ so leho suṇāvido?⌟

KĀÑCANAMĀLĀ: ⌜aṇuvāia tuṇhī|bhūdāe maha hatthādo geṇhia saaṃ evva bhaṭṭiṇīe vāido.⌟

MANORAMĀ: ⌜teṇa gaccha tumaṃ. esā kkhu devī tāe evva saha danta|valahīe ciṭṭhaï.⌟

KĀÑCANAMĀLĀ: ⌜teṇa hi bhaṭṭiṇī|saāsaṃ gamissaṃ.⌟

iti niṣkrāntā.

4.15 MANORAMĀ: ⌜ciraṃ khu me Āraṇṇiā|saāsādo āadāe. diḍhaṃ ca ṇivviṇṇā sā tavassiṇī attaṇo jīvideṇa. kadā i accāhidaṃ bhave. tā tahiṃ evva gacchamhi.⌟

iti niṣkrāntā.

iti praveśakaḥ.

and is a great military power, to procrastinate with such indifference after he has heard of this unwelcome event."

MANO·RAMA: But, Kánchana·mala, the king commanded: 4.10
"No one must inform the queen of this event."* Then who in the world let her hear the letter now?*

KÁNCHANA·MAḶA: As I read it in silence, the queen snatched it from my hand and read it herself.

MANO·RAMA: Then go. There's the queen now, with that very lady, in the ivory tower.

KÁNCHANA·MALA: I'll go to the queen.

Exit.

MANO·RAMA: It's been quite a long time since I left Arányi- 4.15
ka and came here. And the poor girl is terribly weary of her own life. Something very bad might happen at any moment. I'll go right there.

Exit.

End of the Prelude.

ACT IV

tataḥ praviśati s'|ôdveg", āsana|sthā VĀSAVADATTĀ, SĀṄKṚTYĀYANĪ, *vibhavataś ca parivāraḥ.*

SĀṄKṚTYĀYANĪ: rāja|putri, alam udvegena. n' êdṛśo Vatsa|rājaḥ. katham ittham|gatam api bhavatyā mātṛ|ṣvasṛ|patiṃ vijñāya Vatsa|rājo niścintaṃ sthāsyati?

4.20 VĀSAVADATTĀ: *(s'|âsram)* ⌜bhaavadi, adiujjuā dāṇiṃ tumaṃ. jassa mae ṇa kajjaṃ, tassa mamakeraeṇa kiṃ kajjaṃ? ajjuāe juttaṃ mama edaṃ ālihiduṃ. sā uṇa ṇa āṇādi, ajja vi tārisī ṇa Vāsavadatt" êtti. tuha uṇa edaṃ Āraṇṇiāe uttantaṃ paccakkhaṃ. tā kahaṃ edaṃ bhaṇāsi?⌟

SĀṄKṚTYĀYANĪ: yata eva me pratyakṣaṃ, tata eva bravīmi. tena nanu Kaumudī|mahotsave tvāṃ hāsayituṃ tathā krīḍitam.

VĀSAVADATTĀ: ⌜bhaavadi, edaṃ ettha saccaṃ. taha hāsida mhi jeṇa bhaavadīe purado lajjāe kahaṃ vi ciṭṭhāmi. tā kiṃ takkerakāe kahāe? ṇaṃ edeṇa evva pakkha|vādeṇa ettiaṃ bhūmiṃ ṇīda mhi.⌟

iti roditi.

SĀṄKṚTYĀYANĪ: alaṃ, rāja|putri, ruditena. n' êdṛśo Vatsa|rājaḥ. *(vilokya)* atha vā prāpta ev' âyaṃ, yas te manyu|pramārjanaṃ karoti.

Enter VÁSAVA·DATTA, *seated, upset, with* SANKRITYÁYANI *and her entourage, in order of rank.*

SANKRITYÁYANI: Princess, don't go on distressing yourself. The king of Vatsa isn't like that. How could the king of Vatsa rest unconcerned, knowing that your highness's mother's sister's husband is in such trouble?

VÁSAVA·DATTA: *(in tears)* My good lady, how straight and simple you are now. Since he won't have anything to do with me, why should he have anything to do with mine? It was right for my mother to write to me about this. But she doesn't know that Vásava·datta today is not what she used to be. You, on the other hand, saw this business with Aranyika with your own eyes. So how can you say this? 4.20

SANKRITYÁYANI: It's precisely because I saw it with my own eyes that I can speak like this. He really did play that game at the Festival of Moonlight just to make you laugh.

VÁSAVA·DATTA: My good lady, that's certainly the truth of the matter: he made me laughed at so much that I can hardly stand before a good woman like you, for sheer embarrassment. So why talk about that story? My partiality toward him is what has brought me where I am now.

She weeps.

SANKRITYÁYANI: No more weeping, princess. The king of Vatsa isn't like that. *(looking)* But, here he comes now, the very man who will wipe away your anger.

4.25 VĀSAVADATTĀ: ⌜maṇo|rahā dāṇiṃ ede bhaavadīe.⌟

tataḥ praviśati RĀJĀ VIDŪṢAKAŚ *ca.*

RĀJĀ: vayasya, ka idānīm abhyupāyaḥ priyāṃ mocayitum?

VIDŪṢAKAḤ: ⌜bho vaassa, muñca visādaṃ. ahaṃ de uvāaṃ kahaïssaṃ.⌟

RĀJĀ: *(sa|harṣam)* vayasya, tvaritataram abhidhīyatām.

4.30 VIDŪṢAKAḤ: ⌜bho, tumaṃ dāva aṇea|samara|saṃghaṭṭa|ppa-hāva|bāhu|sālī. puṇo vi aṇea|gaa|turaa|paāi|duv|visa-ha|bala|samudido. tā savva|bala|saṃdoheṇa ante|uraṃ su|pīḍiaṃ karia dāṇiṃ evva Āraṇṇiaṃ muñcāvehi.⌟

RĀJĀ: vayasya, a|śakyam upadiṣṭam.

VIDŪṢAKAḤ: ⌜kiṃ ettha a|sakkaṃ? jado dāva kujja|vāmaṇa| vuḍḍha|kañcui|vajjido maṇusso avaro ṇatthi tahiṃ.⌟

RĀJĀ: *(s'|âvajñam)* mūrkha, kim asaṃbaddhaṃ pralapasi! devyāḥ prasādaṃ muktvā n' ânyas tasyā mokṣaṇ'|âbhyu-pāyaḥ. tat kathaya, kathaṃ devīṃ prasādayāmi?

VIDŪṢAKAḤ: ⌜bho, mās'|ôvavāsaṃ karia jīvidaṃ dhārehi. ev-vaṃ *devī Caṇḍī* pasīdissadi.⌟

4.35 RĀJĀ: *(vihasya)* alaṃ parihāsena. kathaya, kathaṃ devīṃ prasādayāmi.

VÁSAVA·DATTA: These are just your own hopes now, good lady. 4.25

Enter the KING *and the* JESTER.

KING: My friend, what's the way to set my beloved free now?

JESTER: My friend, set yourself free from despair. I'll tell you the way.

KING: *(with joy)* Hurry, my friend, tell it!

JESTER: Well, you have two arms that have proved their power in many a close combat. And an irresistible army of elephants, horses, and foot soldiers enhances your power. So just lay siege to the women's quarters with your entire massed forces, and set Aranyika free right now. 4.30

KING: My friend, it's impossible to do what you advise.

JESTER: What's impossible about it? There's not a single man there except for the hunchbacks and dwarfs and the old chamberlain.

KING: *(with contempt)* You idiot, why do you babble such nonsense? There's no way to set her free but appeasing the queen. So tell me, how shall I appease the queen?

JESTER: Stay alive by fasting for a month. That's how to appease a *Fierce Goddess : an angry queen.**

KING: *(laughing)* Stop joking. Tell me: How can I appease the queen? 4.35

dhṛṣṭaḥ kiṃ purato 'varudhya vihasan
gṛhṇāmi kaṇṭhe priyāṃ?
kiṃ vā cāṭu|śata|prapañca|racanā|
prītāṃ kariṣyāmi tām?
kiṃ tiṣṭhāmi kṛt'|âñjalir, nipatito
devyāḥ puraḥ pādayoḥ?
satyaṃ, satyam aho na vedmy anunayo
devyāḥ kathaṃ syād, iti. [1]

tad ehi. devī|sakāśam eva gacchāvaḥ.

VIDŪṢAKAḤ: ⌜bho, gaccha tumaṃ. ahaṃ dāṇiṃ evva bandhaṇādo kahaṃ vi paribbhaṃsia āado mhi. tā ṇa gamissaṃ.⌟

RĀJĀ: *(vihasya, kaṇṭhe gṛhītvā balān nivartayati.)* mūrkha, āgamyatām, āgamyatām. *(parikramy' âvalokya ca)* iyaṃ devī danta|balabhī|madhyam adhyāste. yāvad upasarpāmi.

4.40 *sa/lajjam upasarpati.*

VĀSAVADATTĀ *sa/khedam āsanād uttiṣṭhati.*

RĀJĀ:

kiṃ muktam āsanam? alaṃ mayi saṃbhrameṇa.
n' ôtthātum ittham ucitam mama, tānta|madhye.
dṛṣṭi|prasāda|vidhi|mātra|hṛto jano 'yam
atyādareṇa kim iti kriyate vilakṣaḥ? [2]

Shall I brazenly bar her way, smile, and clasp my
beloved around the neck?
Or shall I delight her with a masterpiece of false
praise, with a hundred flatteries?
Or should I fall at the queen's feet and stay there
before her, palms folded together?
In truth, in sad truth,
I don't know how to win over the queen.

Come, then. Let's go to the queen.

JESTER: Go yourself. I, on the other hand, have just now barely escaped from prison. So I'm not going.

KING: *(laughing, clasping him around the neck, and turning him around by force)* Come on, you idiot, come on. *(walking around and looking around)* Here's the queen, sitting in the middle of the ivory tower. I'll go to her.

He approaches, shyly. 4.40

VÁSAVA·DATTA *gets up from her seat, wearily.*

KING:

Why did you leave your seat?
Don't disturb yourself on my account.
It's not right for you, with so slender a waist,
to stand up for me.
Why does such excessive respect make this person,
whom you can transport by the mere favor
of the casting of a glance,
feel so ashamed?

VĀSAVADATTĀ: *(mukhaṃ nirūpya)* ⌜ajja|utta, vilakkho dāṇiṃ tumaṃ hosi.⌟

4.45 RĀJĀ: priye, satyam ahaṃ vilakṣaḥ. yat pratyakṣa|dṛṣṭ'|âparādho 'pi bhavatīṃ prasādayituṃ vyavasito 'smi.

SĀṄKṚTYĀYANĪ: *(āsanaṃ nirdiśya)* mahā|rāja, kriyatām āsana|parigrahaḥ.

RĀJĀ: *(āsanaṃ nirdiśya)* ita, ito devy upaviśatu.

VĀSAVADATTĀ *bhūmāv upaviśati.*

RĀJĀ: āḥ kathaṃ, bhūmāv upaviṣṭā devī. aham apy atr' âiv' ôpaviśāmi. *(iti bhūmāv upaviśya, kṛt'|âñjaliḥ)* priye, prasīda, prasīda. kim evaṃ praṇate 'pi mayi gambhīrataraṃ kopam udvahasi?

4.50 bhrū|bhaṅgaṃ na karoṣi, rodiṣi muhur,
mugdh'|êkṣaṇe, kevalaṃ.
n' âtiprasphurit'|âdhar" ânavarataṃ
niḥśvāsam ev' ôjjhasi.
vācaṃ n' âpi dadāsi, tiṣṭhasi paraṃ
pradhyāna|namr'|ānanā.
kopas te stimito nipīḍayati māṃ
gūḍha|prahār'|ôpamaḥ. [3]

priye, prasīda, prasīda.

iti pādayoḥ patati.

VĀSAVADATTĀ: ⌜adisuhido ṇaṃ si. kiṃ dāṇiṃ dukkhidaṃ jaṇaṃ viāresi? uṭṭhehi. ko ettha kuvido?⌟

VÁSAVA·DATTA: *(looking closely at his face)* So now, my husband, you feel ashamed.

KING: My dear, I am, truly, ashamed. For even though my guilt was exposed before your eyes, still I'm trying to appease you. 4.45

SANKRITYÁYANI: *(pointing to a seat)* Great king, please take a seat.

KING: *(pointing to a seat)* Let the queen sit here.

VÁSAVA·DATTA *sits on the ground.*

KING: Oh, the queen has sat on the ground. Then I too will sit right here. *(sitting on the ground and folding his palms together)* Relent, dear, relent. Why do you bear still deeper anger toward me, even when I have bowed to you like this?

> You don't frown, but just weep again and again, 4.50
> with your innocent eyes.
> Your lower lip doesn't quiver too much,
> but you sigh ceaselessly.
> You don't speak, but your face remains bowed in deep thought.
> Your suppressed anger torments me
> like a concealed stab.

Relent, my dear, relent.

He falls at her feet.

VÁSAVA·DATTA: You're certainly excessively happy. Why then are you making an unhappy person feel even worse now? Get up. Who's angry here?

SĀṄKṚTYĀYANĪ: uttiṣṭha mahā|rāja. kim anena? anyad eva tāvad udvega|kāraṇam asyāḥ.

4.55 RĀJĀ: *(sa|saṃbhramam)* bhagavati, kim anyat?

SĀṄKṚTYĀYANĪ *karṇe kathayati.*

RĀJĀ: *(vihasya)* yady evam, alam udvegena. may" âpi jñātam. «siddha ev' âsmin prayojane devīṃ tu diṣṭyā vardhayiṣyām', îti» n' ôktam. anyathā katham ahaṃ Dṛḍhavarma|vṛttānte visrabdhas tiṣṭhāmi? tat katipayāny ahāni tad|vārtāyā āgatāyāḥ. idaṃ ca tatra vartate.

asmad|balair Vijayasena|puraḥsarais tair
ākrānta|bāhya|viṣayo, vihata|pratāpaḥ,
durgaṃ Kaliṅga|hatakaḥ sahasā praviśya
prākāra|mātra|śaraṇo 'śaraṇaḥ kṛto 'sau. [4]

tad|avasthaṃ ca taṃ

4.60 nirdiṣṭ'|ākrānta|mandaṃ, pratidina|viramad|
vīra|dāsera|vṛttaṃ,
śaśvat|saṃśīryamāṇa|dvipa|turaga|nara|
kṣīṇa|niḥśeṣa|sainyam,
adya śvo vā vibhagne jhaṭiti mama balaiḥ
sarvatas tatra durge,
baddhaṃ, yuddhe hataṃ vā, bhagavati, na cirāc
chroṣyasi tvaṃ Kaliṅgam. [5]

SANKRITYÁYANI: Get up, great king. This is no use. Indeed, her distress has quite another cause.

KING: *(confused)* Good lady, what is that other cause? 4.55

SANKRITYÁYANI *tells him in his ear.*

KING: *(laughing)* If that's it, then there'll be no more distress! I knew this, too, but I said nothing, thinking, "I'll tell the queen, 'Good fortune smiles on you,' when this undertaking has been successful." Otherwise, how could I remain so calm about this Dridha·varman affair? Well, it's been several days since we had news of it. This is what is happening there:

> Our forces, led by Víjaya·sena, overran the
> outlying territory
> and smashed his power.
> The vile Kalínga quickly went into his fortress,
> with nothing but the rampart for his defense,
> for he had no defense.

And when he was in these straits,

> Our attack, as described, had made him weak, 4.60
> and his soldiers and slaves did less every day.
> His army wasted away to nothing,
> as his elephants, horses, and men
> were constantly cut down.
> Today or tomorrow my forces will shatter
> his fortress on all sides,
> suddenly, just like that, my good lady,
> and soon you will hear that Kalínga
> has been captured or killed in battle.

SĀṄKṚTYĀYANĪ: rāja|putri, prathamataram eva bhavatyāḥ kathitaṃ mayā,«katham a|pratividhāya Vatsa|rājaḥ sthāsyat'? îti.»

VĀSAVADATTĀ: ⌜jaï evvaṃ, piaṃ me.⌟

praviśya

PRATĪHĀRĪ: ⌜jedu, jedu bhaṭṭā. eso kkhu Viaaseṇo Diḍhavamma|kañcuī|sahido harisa|samuppula|loaṇo piaṃ ṇivedidu|kāmo duvāre ciṭṭhaï.⌟

4.65 VĀSAVADATTĀ: *(sa/smitam)* ⌜bhaavadi, jaha takkemi, paridosida mhi ajja|utteṇ' êtti.⌟

SĀṄKṚTYĀYANĪ: Vatsa|rāja|pakṣa|pātinī khalv ahaṃ na kiṃ cid api bravīmi!

RĀJĀ: śīghraṃ praveśaya tau.

PRATĪHĀRĪ: ⌜taha.⌟

iti niṣkrāntā.

4.70 *tataḥ praviśati* VIJAYASENAḤ KAÑCUKĪ *ca.*

VIJAYASENAḤ: bhoḥ kañcukin, adya svāmi|pādā draṣṭavyā, iti yat satyam, an|upamaṃ kam api sukh'|âtiśayam anubhavāmi.

KAÑCUKĪ: Vijayasena, a|vitatham etat. paśya:

SANKRITYÁYANI: Princess, at the very start I told your highness, “How can the king of Vatsa stay without making a counter attack?”

VÁSAVA·DATTA: If this is so, it pleases me.

Enter the GATE-KEEPER.

GATE-KEEPER: Victory, victory to the king. Here is Víjaya·sena with Dridha·varman’s chamberlain, standing at the door. His lotus eyes are blooming with joy and he wishes to tell you some good news.

VÁSAVA·DATTA: *(smiling)* My good lady, I suspect that my husband has fully satisfied me. 4.65

SANKRITYÁYANI: Being rather partial to the king of Vatsa, I won’t say anything at all.

KING: Let them both come in right away.

GATE-KEEPER: Yes.

Exit.

Enter VÍJAYA·SENA *and the Chamberlain [*VÍNAYA·VASU*].* 4.70

VÍJAYA·SENA: Good chamberlain, the realization that I will see my master’s feet today makes me experience something that truly exceeds all happiness, beyond compare.

CHAMBERLAIN: Víjaya·sena, that’s indisputable. See:

sukha|nirbharo 'nyath" âpi
svāminam avalokya bhavati bhṛtya|janaḥ,
kiṃ punar ari|bala|vighaṭana|
nirvyūḍha|prabhu|niyoga|bharaḥ? [6]

UBHAU: *(upasṛtya)* jayatu, jayatu svāmī!

RĀJĀ *ubhāv api pariṣvajate.*

KAÑCUKĪ: deva, diṣṭyā vardhase.

hatvā Kaliṅga|hatakaṃ hy asmat|svāmī niveśito rājye.
devasya samādeśo nirvyūḍho Vijayasenena. [7]

VĀSAVADATTĀ: ⌜aï bhaavaï, ahijāṇāsi edaṃ kañcuiṃ?⌟

SĀṄKṚTYĀYANĪ: kathaṃ n' âbhijānāmi? nanu sa eṣa yasya haste mātṛ|ṣvasā te patrikām anupreṣitavatī.

RĀJĀ: sādhu! Vijaysenena mahā|vyāpāro 'nuṣṭhitaḥ.

VIJAYASENAḤ *pādayoḥ patati.*

RĀJĀ: devi, diṣṭyā vardhase. pratiṣṭhito rājye Dṛḍhavarmā.

VĀSAVADATTĀ: *(sa|harṣam)* ⌜aṇuggahida mhi.⌟

VIDŪṢAKAḤ: ⌜īrise abbhudae assiṃ rāaule edaṃ karaṇijjaṃ.⌟ (RĀJĀNAṂ *nirdiśya, vīṇā|vādanaṃ nāṭayan)* ⌜guru|pūā.⌟

Even under other circumstances,
a servant is overwhelmed with happiness
when he sees his master.
But how much more,
when he has carried out his lord's command
by routing the armies of his enemies?

BOTH: *(approaching)* Victory, victory to our master.

The KING *embraces both of them.* 4.75

CHAMBERLAIN: Your majesty, good fortune smiles on you!

Víjaya·sena has slain the vile Kalínga,
restored my master to his kingdom,
and fulfilled your majesty's command.

VÁSAVA·DATTA: My good lady, do you recognize this chamberlain?

SANKRITYÁYANI: How could I not recognize him? Of course, he's the one by whose hand your mother's sister sent the letter.

KING: Bravo! Víjaya·sena has accomplished a great undertaking. 4.80

VÍJAYA·SENA *falls at his feet.*

KING: My queen, good fortune smiles on you! Dridha·varman's kingdom has been restored to him.

VÁSAVA·DATTA: *(with joy)* I am deeply grateful.

JESTER: At a time of rejoicing such as this, the following must be done in the royal palace: *(pointing to the* KING *and miming playing the lute)* worshipping a teacher;

(ātmano yajñ'|ôpavītaṃ darśayan) ⌜bamhaṇassa sak|kāro.⌟ *(*ĀRAṆYIKĀṂ *sūcayan)* ⌜savva|bandhaṇa|mokkho tti.⌟

4.85 RĀJĀ: *(*VĀSAVADATTĀM *apavārya choṭikāṃ dadat)* sādhu, vayasya, sādhu!

VIDŪṢAKAḤ: ⌜hodi, kahaṃ tumaṃ ṇa kiṃ vi ettha samādisasi?⌟

VĀSAVADATTĀ: *(*SĀṄKṚTYĀYANĪM *avalokya, sa/smitam)* ⌜moido kkhu had'|āseṇa Āraṇṇiā.⌟

SĀṄKṚTYĀYANĪ: kiṃ vā tapasviny" ânayā baddhayā?

VĀSAVADATTĀ: ⌜jaha bhaavadīe roadi.⌟

4.90 SĀṄKṚTYĀYANĪ: yady evam, aham eva gatvā tāṃ mocayiṣyāmi.

iti niṣkrāntā.

KAÑCUKĪ: idam aparaṃ saṃdiṣṭaṃ mahā|rājena Dṛḍhavarmaṇā: «tvat|prasādāt sarvam eva yath"|âbhilaṣitaṃ saṃpannam. tad ete prāṇās tvadīyāḥ. yath"|êṣṭam imān viniyoktuṃ tvam eva pramāṇam iti.»

RĀJĀ *sa/lajjam adho/mukhas tiṣṭhati.*

VIJAYASENAḤ: deva, na śakyam eva devaṃ prati prativiśeṣaṃ Dṛḍhavarmaṇaḥ kathayitum.

4.95 KAÑCUKĪ: «yady api tubhyaṃ pratipāditāyāḥ Priyadarśikāyā asmad|duhituḥ paribhraṃśān na me saṃbandho jāta, iti duḥkham āsīt, tath" âpi Vāsavadattāyāḥ pariṇetr" âpi tvayā tad apanītam eva.»

(showing his own Brahmin's initiatory thread) rewarding a Brahmin; *(indicating* ARÁNYIKA*)* and releasing all prisoners.

KING: *(out of* VÁSAVA·DATTA*'s hearing, snapping his fingers)* Bravo, my friend, bravo! 4.85

JESTER: My lady, why don't you give some order about this?

VÁSAVA·DATTA: *(looking at* SANKRITYÁYANI, *with a smile)* This damn fool has virtually set Arányika free.

SANKRITYÁYANI: What's the good of keeping the poor girl in prison?

VÁSAVA·DATTA: As it please you, my good lady.

SANKRITYÁYANI: If so, I myself will go and set her free. 4.90

Exit.

CHAMBERLAIN: The great king Dridha·varman has sent this other message: "By your favor, everything I wanted has been achieved. My very life's breaths belong to you. Make use of them as you wish; you have the authority over them."

The KING *stands with his head lowered in embarrassment.*

VÍJAYA·SENA: Your majesty, it is not possible to express Dridha·varman's special affection for your majesty.

CHAMBERLAIN: [*(continuing the message)*] "I was very sorry that, although my daughter Priya·dárshika was betrothed to you, she was lost, and so no alliance between us was made. But your marriage to Vásava·datta erased this regret." 4.95

VĀSAVADATTĀ: *(s'|âsram)* ⌜ajja kañcui, kahaṃ me bhaïṇī paribbhaṭṭā?⌟

KAÑCUKĪ: rāja|putri, tasmin Kaliṅga|hatak'|âvaskande, vidruteṣv itas tato 'ntaḥ|pura|janeṣu, diṣṭyā dṛṣṭām «idānīṃ na yuktam atra sthātum, iti» tām ahaṃ gṛhītvā Vatsa|rāj'|ântikaṃ prasthitaḥ. tataḥ saṃcintya tāṃ Vindhyaketor haste nikṣipya nirgato 'smi. yāvat pratīpam āgacchāmi, tāvat kair api tat sthānaṃ saha Vindhyaketunā smartavyatāṃ nītam.

RĀJĀ: *(sa|smitam)* Vijayasena, kiṃ kathayasi?

KAÑCUKĪ: tatra c' ânviṣyatā mayā na prāptā. tadā prabhṛti n' âdy' âpi vijñāyate, kva vartata iti.

4.100 *praviśya* MANORAMĀ

MANORAMĀ: ⌜bhaṭṭiṇī, pāṇa|saṃsae vaṭṭhaï sā tavassiṇī.⌟

VĀSAVADATTĀ: *(s'|âsram)* ⌜kiṃ uṇa tumaṃ Piadaṃsaṇā|uttantaṃ jāṇāsi?⌟

MANORAMĀ: ⌜ṇa hu ahaṃ Piadaṃsaṇā|uttantaṃ jāṇāmi. esā kkhu Āraṇṇiā kalla|vvavadeseṇa āṇīdaṃ visaṃ pāia pāṇa|saṃsae vaṭṭhadi, tti evvaṃ mae ṇivedidaṃ. tā parittāadu bhaṭṭiṇī.⌟

rudatī pādayoḥ patati.

VÁSAVA·DATTA: *(in tears)* Good chamberlain, how was my sister lost?

CHAMBERLAIN: Princess, in the attack by the vile Kalínga, the inhabitants of the women's quarters ran this way and that. By good luck I happened to see her, and thinking, "It's not wise to stay here now," I took her and set out to come to the king of Vatsa. But after reconsidering, I put her in the hands of Vindhya·ketu and went away. And by the time I returned, some people had made that place, and Vindhya·ketu, nothing but a memory.

KING: *(smiling)* Víjaya·sena, what do you say?*

CHAMBERLAIN: I looked for her there, but didn't find her. And from that time even to today, her whereabouts have remained unknown.

Enter MANO·RAMA. 4.100

MANO·RAMA: Your highness, the poor girl's life is in grave danger.

VÁSAVA·DATTA: *(in tears)* How do *you* know what's happened to Priya·dárshana?*

MANO·RAMA: I don't know anything at all about what's happened to Priya·dárshana. But Arányika here had poison brought to her in the guise of wine, and drank it, and her life is, as I said, in grave dange. Save her, please, your highness!

She falls at her feet, weeping.

4.105 VĀSAVADATTĀ: *(sva/gatam)* ⌜haddhi, haddhi. Piadaṃsaṇā|dukkhaṃ vi me antaridaṃ Āraṇṇiā|uttanteṇa. adidujjaṇo kkhu loo. kadā i maṃ aṇṇahā saṃbhāvaïssadi? tā edaṃ ettha juttaṃ.⌟ *(prakāśaṃ, sa/saṃbhramam)* ⌜Maṇorame, lahu iha evva āṇehi taṃ. ṇāa|loādo gahida|visa|vijjo ajja|utto ethha kusalo.⌟

niṣkrāntā MANORAMĀ.

tataḥ praviśati MANORAMAYĀ *dhṛtā, sa/viṣa/vegam ātmānaṃ nāṭayanty* ĀRAṆYIKĀ.

ĀRAṆYIKĀ: ⌜halā Maṇorame, kīsa dāṇiṃ maṃ andha|āraṃ pavesesi?⌟

MANORAMĀ: *(sa/viṣādam)* ⌜haddhi! haddhi! diṭṭhi vi se saṃkantā viseṇ' êvva.⌟ (VĀSAVADATTĀṂ *dṛṣṭvā)* ⌜bhaṭṭiṇi, lahu parittāehi, lahu parittāehi. guruī|bhūdaṃ se visaṃ.⌟

4.110 VĀSAVADATTĀ: *(sa/saṃbhramaṃ,* RĀJĀNAṂ *haste gṛhītvā)* ⌜ajja|utta, uṭṭhehi, uṭṭhehi. lahu vivajajjaï kkhu esā tavassiṇī.⌟ *(sarve paśyanti.)*

KAÑCUKĪ: *(vilokya)* su|sadṛśī khalv iyaṃ mama rāja|putryāḥ Priyadarśanāyāḥ. (VĀSAVADATTĀṂ *nirdiśya)* rāja|putri, kuta iyaṃ kanyakā?

VĀSAVADATTĀ: ⌜ajja, Viñjhakeuṇo duhidā. taṃ vāvādia Vijayaseṇeṇa āṇīdā.⌟

VÁSAVA·DATTA: *(to herself)* Oh no! No! What's happened to Arányika has eclipsed even my sorrow about Priya·dárshana. The world is certainly full of very bad people. Perhaps they will imagine that I am other than I am. So this is what I'll do about this. *(aloud, in agitation)* Mano·rama, bring her right here, right away. My husband is an expert in this matter; he learned the magic of poisons from the *naga* world.* 4.105

Exit MANO·RAMA.

Enter ARÁNYIKA, *supported by* MANO·RAMA, *miming the symptoms of poisoning.*

ARÁNYIKA: O Mano·rama, why are you leading me now into darkness?

MANO·RAMA: *(in despair)* Oh No! No! The poison has affected her vision, too! *(looking at* VÁSAVA·DATTA*)* Your highness, save her, quickly, save her, quickly. The poison has had serious effects on her.

VÁSAVA·DATTA: *(in haste, taking the* KING *by the hand)* Get up, my husband, get up. This poor girl is sinking fast. *(All look.)* 4.110

CHAMBERLAIN: *(looking)* She certainly resembles, very closely indeed, my princess, Priya·dárshana. *(addressing* VÁSAVA·DATTA*)* Princess, where did this young girl come from?

VÁSAVA·DATTA: Sir, she is Vindhya·ketu's daughter. Víjaya·sena killed him and brought her here.

KAÑCUKĪ: kutas tasya duhitā? s" âiv' êyaṃ mama rāja|putrī. hā, hato 'smi mandabhāgyaḥ! *(iti nipatya bhūmāv, utthāya)* rāja|putri, iyaṃ sā Priyadarśikā bhaginī te.

VĀSAVADATTĀ: ⌜ajja | utta, parittāehi, parittāehi. mama bhaïṇī vivajjaï.⌟

4.115 RĀJĀ: samāśvasihi, samāśvasihi! paśyāmas tāvat. kaṣṭaṃ, bhoḥ kaṣṭam!

saṃjāta|sāndra|makaranda|rasāṃ krameṇa
  pātuṃ gataś ca kalikāṃ kamalasya bhṛṅgaḥ.
dagdhā nipatya sahas" âiva himena c' âsau.
  vāme vidhau na hi phalanty abhivāñchitāni. [8]

Manorame, pṛcchyatāṃ tāvat, «kiṃ te bodha? iti.»

MANORAMĀ: ⌜sahi, kiṃ te bodhaḥ?⌟ *(s'|âsraṃ, punaś cālayantī)* ⌜sahi, ṇaṃ bhaṇāmi, kiṃ de bodho tti?⌟

PRIYADARŚIKĀ: *(a|vispaṣṭam)* ⌜jaṃ edaṃ avasthānaṃ gadāe vi mae ṇa mahā|rāo diṭṭho.⌟

4.120 *ity ardh'|ôkte bhūmau patati.*

RĀJĀ: *(s'|âsram)*

eṣā mīlayat' îdam īkṣaṇa|yugaṃ,
    jātā mam' ândhā diṣaḥ.
  kaṇṭho 'syāḥ pratirudhyate, mama giro
    niryānti kṛcchrād imāḥ.
etasyāḥ śvasitaṃ hṛtaṃ, mama tanur

CHAMBERLAIN: How could she be his daughter? She *is* my princess. This is the ruin of me, unlucky man that I am! *(falling to the ground as he says this, and then getting up again)* Princess, this girl is that sister of yours, Priya·dárshika.

VÁSAVA·DATTA: Save her, my husband, save her! My sister is dying!

KING: Courage, courage! First let's see. [*(aside)*] Oh no! No! 4.115

> The bee went to drink from the unopened bud
> of the lotus,
> which had just filled up with thick honey nectar.
> But suddenly a frost struck the bud and
> scorched it.
> When fate is perverse, wishes never bear fruit.

Mano·rama, ask her now, "Are you conscious?"

MANO·RAMA: My friend, are you conscious? *(in tears, shaking her again)* My friend, I'm talking to you! Are you conscious?

PRIYA·DÁRSHIKA: *(murmuring)* Even in this sorry condition, I didn't see the great king.

She falls to the ground in mid-sentence. 4.120

KING: *(in tears)*

> She is closing her eyes,
> and the quarters of the sky grow dark for me.
> Her throat is choked,
> and these words of mine can scarcely come out.
> Her breathing has stopped,
> and my body is paralyzed.

niśceṣṭatām āgatā.
manye 'syā viṣa|vega eva hi paraṃ,
sarvaṃ tu duḥkhaṃ mama. [9]

VĀSAVADATTĀ: *(s'|âsram)* ⌜Piadaṃsaṇe, uṭṭhehi, uṭṭhehi! pekkha, eso mahā|rāo ciṭṭhaï. kahaṃ, veaṇā vi se ṇaṭṭhā? kiṃ dāṇiṃ mae avarajjhaṃ aāṇantīe, jeṇa kuvidā ṇ' ālavasi? tā pasīda, pasīda. uṭṭhehi, uṭṭhehi! ṇa hu puṇo avarajjhissaṃ.⌟ *(ūrdhvam avalokya)* ⌜hā devva|hadaa. kiṃ dāṇiṃ mae avakidaṃ jeṇa edāvatthaṃ gadā me bhaïṇī ādaṃsidā.⌟

PRIYADARŚIKĀYĀ *upari patati.*

4.125 VIDŪṢAKAḤ: ⌜bho, vaassa. kahaṃ tumaṃ mūḍho via ciṭṭhasi? ṇa eso visādassa kālo. visamā kkhu gaī visassa. tā daṃsehi appaṇo vijjā|pahāvaṃ.⌟

RĀJĀ: satyam ev' âitat. (PRIYADARŚIKĀM *ālokya)* mūḍha ev' âham etāvatīṃ velām. tad aham enāṃ jīvayāmi. salilaṃ, salilam!

VIDŪṢAKAḤ: *(niṣkramya, punaḥ praviśya)* ⌜bho, edaṃ salilam.⌟

RĀJ" *ôpasṛtya* PRIYADARŚANĀYĀ *upari hastaṃ nidhāya mantra|smaraṇaṃ nāṭayati.* PRIYADARŚIKĀ *śanair uttiṣṭhati.*

VĀSAVADATTĀ: ⌜ajja|utta, diṭṭhiā paccujjīvidā me bhaïṇī.⌟

4.130 VIJAYASENAḤ: aho devasya vidyā|prabhāvaḥ!

The poison is racing through her,
but I think all the great suffering is mine.

VÁSAVA·DATTA: *(in tears)* Get up, Priya·dárshana, get up! See, the great king is standing here. What! Has she lost consciousness too? Have I unknowingly offended you now in some way, so that you are angry and will not speak to me? Relent, then, relent! Get up, get up! I won't ever offend you again. *(looking up)* Oh, vile fate! What did I do wrong now that I should see my sister in such a sorry state?

She falls over PRIYA·DÁRSHIKA.

JESTER: My friend, why are you standing there like someone 4.125
in a daze? This is no time for despair. The poison is having rough effects. So demonstrate the power of your magic.

KING: That's absolutely true. *(looking at* PRIYA·DÁRSHIKA*)* I have indeed been in a daze all this time. But I will bring her back to life. Water, water!

JESTER: *(going out and coming back)* Here's water.

The KING *approaches, puts his hand on* PRIYA·DÁRSHANA *and mimes the silent incantation of a mantra.* PRIYA·DÁRSHIKA *gradually gets up.*

VÁSAVA·DATTA: My husband, thank goodness, you have revived my sister.

VÍJAYA·SENA: How great is the power of the king's magic! 4.130

KAÑCUKĪ: aho sarvatr' â|pratihatā *nar'|êndratā* devasya!

PRIYADARŚIKĀ: *(śanair utthāy' ôpaviśya ca, jṛmbhikāṃ nāṭayantī, sa|viṣādam, a|vispaṣṭam)* ⌜Maṇorame, ciraṃ khu sutta mhi.⌟

VIDŪṢAKAḤ: ⌜bho vaassa! ṇivyūḍhaṃ de vedittaṇaṃ.⌟

PRIYADARŚIKĀ *s'|âbhilāṣaṃ* RĀJĀNAṂ *nirūpya, sa|lajjaṃ kiṃ cid adho|mukhī tiṣṭhati.*

4.135 VĀSAVADATTĀ: *(sa|harṣam)* ⌜ajja|utta, kiṃ dāṇiṃ vi esā aṇṇah" êvva karedi?⌟

RĀJĀ: *(sa|smitam)*

svabhāva|sthā dṛṣṭir
 na bhavati, giro n' âtiviśadās.
 tanuḥ sīdaty eṣā,
 prakaṭa|pulaka|sveda|kaṇikā.
yathā c' âyaṃ kampaḥ
 stana|bhara|parikleśa|jananas,
 tathā n' âdy' âpy asyā
 niyataṃ akhilaṃ śāmyati viṣam. [10]

KAÑCUKĪ: (PRIYADARŚIKĀṂ *nirdiśya)* rāja|putri, eṣa te pitur ājñā|karaḥ.

iti pādayoḥ patati.

4.140 PRIYADARŚIKĀ: *(vilokya)* ⌜kahaṃ, kañcuī ajja|Viṇaavasū.⌟ *(s'|âsram)* ⌜hā tāda. hā ajjūe.⌟

KAÑCUKĪ: rāja|putri, alaṃ ruditena. kuśalinau te pitarau. Vatsa|rāja|prabhāvāt punas tad|avastham eva rājyam.

CHAMBERLAIN: Ah, the king's *power over men : power over poisons* goes everywhere unobstructed.

PRIYA·DÁRSHIKA: *(gradually getting up, sitting, miming yawning, despairing, murmuring indistinctly)* Mano·rama, I slept for a long, long time.

JESTER: My friend, you certainly proved your skill as a physician.

PRIYA·DÁRSHIKA, *watching the* KING *with longing, stands shyly, her face slightly lowered.*

VÁSAVA·DATTA: *(with joy)* My husband, why does she act so 4.135
oddly even now?

KING: *(smiling)*

> Her vision is not quite restored to its natural state,
> and her speech is not very clear.
> Her body tends to collapse, and her skin,
> covered with beads of sweat, thrills.
> Her trembling troubles her heavy breasts.
> All of this shows that even now
> not all of the poison in her is fully extinguished.*

CHAMBERLAIN: *(addressing* PRIYA·DÁRSHIKA*)* Princess, I am your father's servant.

He falls at her feet.

PRIYA·DÁRSHIKA: *(looking at him)* Why, it's the good Vína- 4.140
ya·vasu, our chamberlain! *(in tears)* Father! Mother!

CHAMBERLAIN: Princess, no more crying! Your parents are alive and well. The power of the king of Vatsa has restored the kingdom as it was before.

VĀSAVADATTĀ: *(s'|âsram)* ⌜ehi, alia|sīle. dāṇiṃ vi de bhaïṇiā|siṇehaṃ daṃsehi.⌟ *(kaṇṭhe gṛhītvā)* ⌜dāṇiṃ samassattha mhi.⌟

VIDŪṢAKAḤ: ⌜hodi, tumaṃ bhaïṇiṃ geṇhia kaṇṭhe evvaṃ parituṭṭhā si. vodiassa pāridosiaṃ visumaridaṃ.⌟

VĀSAVADATTĀ: ⌜Vasantaa, ṇa visumaridaṃ.⌟

4.145 VIDŪṢAKAḤ: *(*RĀJĀNAṂ *nirdiśya, sa|smitam)* ⌜vodia, pasārehi hatthaṃ. bhaïṇīe agga|hatthaṃ de pāridosiaṃ dāvissaṃ.⌟

RĀJĀ *hastaṃ prasārayati.*

VĀSAVADATTĀ PRIYADARŚIKĀ*|hastam arpayati.*

RĀJĀ: *(hastam upasaṃhṛtya)* kim anayā? saṃpraty eva katham api prasādit" âsi.

VĀSAVADATTĀ: ⌜ko tumaṃ a|gaṇhiduṃ? puḍhamaṃ evva tādeṇa iaṃ diṇṇā.⌟

4.150 VIDŪṢAKAḤ: ⌜bho, māṇaṇīā kkhu devī. mā se paḍiūlaṃ karehi.⌟

VĀSAVADATTĀ RĀJÑO *hastaṃ balād ākṛṣya,* PRIYADARŚIKĀM *arpayati.*

RĀJĀ: *(sa|smitam)* devī prabhavati. kuto 'smākam anyathā kartuṃ vibhavaḥ?

VĀSAVADATTĀ: ⌜ajja|utta, ado vi paraṃ kiṃ de piaṃ karīadu?⌟

VÁSAVA·DATTA: *(in tears)* Come, you little liar. Now, at least, show some sisterly affection. *(embracing her by the neck)* Now I am encouraged.

JESTER: Ma'am, embracing your sister by the neck is your reward. But you have forgotten to reward the physician.

VÁSAVA·DATTA: Vasántaka, I have not forgotten.

JESTER: *(addressing the* KING, *and smiling)* Physician, 4.145
stretch out your hand. I will have the hand of your sister given to you as your reward.

The KING *stretches out his hand.*

VÁSAVA·DATTA *offers him* PRIYA·DÁRSHIKA*'s hand.*

KING: *(withdrawing his hand)* What have I to do with her? You've only been appeased just now, and with considerable difficulty.

VÁSAVA·DATTA: Who are you to refuse? Her father gave her in the first place.

JESTER: The queen's wishes certainly ought to be respected. 4.150
Don't oppose her.

VÁSAVA·DATTA *pulls the* KING*'s hand by force and offers* PRIYA·DÁRSHIKA.

KING: *(smiling)* The queen rules supreme. Where could we find the power to do otherwise?

VÁSAVA·DATTA: My husband, what more do you want me to do?

RĀJĀ: kim ataḥ paraṃ priyam? paśya:

4.155 niḥ|śeṣaṃ Dṛḍhavarmaṇā punar api
svaṃ rājyam adhyāsitaṃ.
tvaṃ kopena su|dūram apy apahṛtā
sadyaḥ prasannā mama.
jīvantī Priyadarśanā ca bhaginī
bhūyas tvayā saṅgatā.
kiṃ tat syād aparaṃ priyaṃ, priyatame,
yat sāṃprataṃ prārthyate? [11]

tath" âp' îdam astu.

bharata|vākyam

urvīm uddāma|sasyāṃ janayatu visṛjan
Vāsavo vṛṣṭim iṣṭām.
iṣṭais traiviṣṭapānāṃ vidadhatu vidhivat
prīṇanaṃ vipra|mukhyāḥ.
ā|kalp'|ântaṃ ca bhūyāt sthira|samupacitā
saṃgatiḥ saj|janānāṃ,
niḥśeṣaṃ yāntu śāntiṃ piśuna|jana|giro
duḥ|sahā vajra|lepāḥ. [12]

iti niṣkrāntāḥ sarve.

4.160 *iti caturtho 'ṅkaḥ*

samāpt" êyaṃ Priyadarśikā nāma nāṭikā.

KING: What more could anyone want? Look:

Dridha·varman has his own kingdom back again, 4.155
entire.
Though you were carried far away by anger,
all at once I have appeased you.
And your sister Priya·dárshana is not only alive
but united with you.
What other dear thing, my dearest,
could anyone want now?*

And in addition, this:

The actors' epilogue

May Indra, sending down the desired rain,
make the earth bring forth abundant crops.
May the leading Brahmins please the gods
with sacrifices properly done.
May good people live together 'til
the end of the eon,
heaping up happiness.
And may the words of slanderers,
so hard to overcome because
their stain is as permanent as diamonds,
rest in peace.

Exit all.

End of Act Four. 4.160

End of the play called 'The Lady who Shows her Love.'

CHĀYĀ

The following is a Sanskrit paraphrase (chāyā) *of the Prakrit passages (marked with* ⌜corner brackets⌟*) in the play. References are to chapter and paragraph.*

The Lady of the Jewel Necklace

1.17 ārya|putra, iyam asmi. ājñāpayatv āryaḥ ko niyogo 'nuṣṭhīyatām iti.

1.19 ārya|putra niś|cinta idānīm asi tvaṃ, tat kasmān na nṛtyasi? mama punar manda|bhāgyāyā ek" âiva duhitā. s" âpi tvayā kasminn api deś'|ântare dattā. katham evaṃ dūra|deśa|sthitena bhartrā sah' âsyāḥ pāṇi|grahaṇaṃ bhaviṣyat' îty anayā cintay" ātm" âpi me na pratibhāti. kiṃ punar nartitavyam!

1.37 ājñāpayatu bhavān!

1.40 bho vayasya! evaṃ nv idam. ahaṃ punar jānāmi: na bhavato, na Kāma|devasya, mam' âiv' âikasya brāhmaṇasy' âyaṃ Madana|mah"|ôtsavaḥ, yasya priya|vayasyen' âivaṃ mantryate.

1.40 tat kim anena? prekṣasva tāvad asya madhu|matta|kāminī|jana|svayaṃ|grāha|gṛhīta|śṛṅgaka|jala|prahāra|nṛtyan|nāgara|jana|jānita|kautūhalasya samantataḥ śabdāyamāna|mardal'|ôddāma|carcarī|śabda|mukhara|rathyā|mukha|śobhino prakīrṇa|paṭa|vāsa|puñja|piñjarita|daśa|diśā|mukhasya sa|śrīkatāṃ Madana|mah"|ôtsavasya.

1.45 idam api tāvat su|vidagdha|jana|bharita|śṛṅgaka|jala|prahāra|mukta|sīt|kāra|mano|haraṃ vāra|vilāsinī|jana|vilasitam avalokayatu priya|vayasyaḥ!

1.48 bho, eṣā khalu Madanikā madana|vaśa|visaṃṣṭhulaṃ Vasant'|âbhinayaṃ nṛtyantī Cūtalatikayā sah' êta ev' āgacchati. tad avalokayatv etāṃ priya|vayasyaḥ!

1.51 Kusum'|āyudha|priya|dūtako mukulāyita|bahu|cūtakaḥ / śithilita|māna|grahaṇako vāti dakṣiṇa|pavanakaḥ.

1.52 vikasita|bakul'|âśokakaḥ kāṅkṣita|priya|jana|melakaḥ / pratipālan'|â|samarthakas tāmyati yuvati|sārthakaḥ.

1.53 iha prathamaṃ Madhu|māso janasya hṛdayāni karoti mṛdulāni, / paścād vidhyati Kāmo labdha|prasaraiḥ kusuma|bāṇaiḥ.

1.56 bho vayasya! aham apy etayor madhye gatvā nṛtyan gāyan Madana|mah"|ôtsavaṃ mānayiṣyāmi.

1.58 bhavati Madanike, bhavati Cūtalatike! mām apy etāṃ Carcarīṃ śikṣayatam!

1.59 hat'|āśa! na khalv eṣā Carcarī.

1.60 tat kiṃ khalv etat?

1.61 Dvi|padī|khaṇḍaṃ khalv etat.

1.62 kim etena khaṇḍena modakāḥ kriyante?

1.63 na hi, na hi! paṭhyate khalv idam.

1.64 yadi paṭhyate, tad alaṃ mam' âitena! vayasyasya sakāśam eva gamiṣyāmi.

1.65 ehi, krīḍāmaḥ. Vasantaka, kutra gacchasi?

1.66 vayasya, nartito 'smi. na hi, na hi. krīḍitvā palāyito 'smi.

1.68 hañje Madanike! ciraṃ khalv āvābhyāṃ krīḍitam. tad ehi. nivedayāvas tāvad bhartryāḥ saṃdeśaṃ mahā|rājāya.

1.69 sakhi, evaṃ kurvaḥ.

1.70 jayatu, jayatu bhartā! bhartaḥ, devy ājñāpayati—

1.70 na hi, na hi! vijñāpayati.

1.72 āḥ, dāsyāḥ putri. kiṃ devy ājñāpayati?

1.73 evaṃ devī vijñāpayati: «adya khalu mayā Makarand'|ôdyānaṃ gatvā rakt'|âśoka|pāda|pa|tale saṃsthāpitasya bhagavataḥ kusum'|āyudhasya pūjā nirvartayitavyā. tatr' ārya|putreṇa saṃnihitena bhavitavyam.»

1.75 bho vayasya, tad uttiṣṭha. tatr' âiva gacchāmo, yena tatra gatasya mam' âpi brāhmaṇasya svasti|vācanaṃ kim api bhaviṣyati.

1.77 yad bhart" ājñāpayati.

1.79 yad bhavān ājñāpayati. etv, etu bhavān.

1.81 bho, etat tan Makarand'|ôdyānam. tad ehi. praviśāvaḥ.

1.82 bho, vayasya! prekṣasva, prekṣasva! etat khalu tan Malaya|mārut'|āndolana|praphullat|sahakāra|mañjarī|reṇu|paṭala|pratibaddha|paṭa|vitānaṃ matta|madhu|kara|mukta|jhaṅ|kāra|milita|madhura|kokil'|ārāva|saṃgīta|śruti|sukhaṃ tav' āgamana|darśit'|ādaram iva Makarand'|ôdyānaṃ lakṣyate. tat prekṣyatāṃ bhavān.

1.87 bho vayasya! n' âitena madhu|karā nūpura|śabdam anuharanti. nūpura|śabda eva âiṣa devyāḥ parijanasya.

1.90 hañje Kāñcanamāle! ādesaya me Makarand'|ôdyānasya mārgam.

1.91 etu, etu bhartrī.

1.92 hañje Kāñcanamāle! atha kiyad dūre sa rakt'|âśoka|pāda|po yatra mayā bhagavataḥ kusum'|āyudhasya pūjā nirvartayitavyā?

1.93 bhartri, āsanna eva. kiṃ na prekṣate bhartrī? iyaṃ khalu sā nirantar'|ôdbhinna|kusuma|śobhinī bhartryā parigṛhītā mādhavī|latā. eṣ" âpy aparā navamālikā latā, yasyā a|kāla|kusuma|samudgama|śraddhālunā bhartrā anu|dinam āyāsyata ātmā. tad etām atikramya dṛśyata eva sa rakt'|âśoka|pāda|po, yatra devī pūjāṃ nirvartayiṣyati.

1.94 tad ehi, tatr' âiva laghu gacchāmaḥ.

1.95 etu, etu bhartrī.

1.97 bhartri, ayaṃ khalu sa rakt'|âśoka|pāda|po yatra devī pūjāṃ nirvartayiṣyati.

1.98 tena hi me pūjā|nimittāny upakaraṇāny upanaya.

1.99 bhartri, etat sarvaṃ sajjam.

1.100 aho, pramādaḥ parijanasya! yasy' âiva darśana|pathāt prayatnena rakṣyate, tasy' âiva dṛṣṭi|gocare patitā bhavet. bhavatu, evaṃ tāvad bhaṇiṣyāmi:

1.100 hañje Sāgarike! kasmāt tvam adya Madana|mah"|ôtsava|parādhīne parijane sārikām ujjhitv" êh' āgatā? tat tatr' âiva laghu gaccha. etad api sarvaṃ pūj"|ôpakaraṇaṃ Kāñcanamālāyā haste samarpaya.

1.101 yad bhartry ājñāpayati.

1.101 sārikā mayā punaḥ Susaṃgatāyā haste samarpitā. etad apy asti me prekṣituṃ kautūhalaṃ: kiṃ yathā tātasy' ântaḥ|pure bhagavān Anaṅgo 'rcyate ih' âpi tath" âiva, kim anyath" êti. tad a|lakṣitā bhūtvā prekṣiṣye. yāvad iha pūjā|samayo bhavati, tāvad aham api bhagavantam Anaṅgam eva pūjayituṃ kusumāny avaceṣyāmi.

1.102 Kāñcanamāle, pratiṣṭhāpay' âśoka|mūle bhagavantaṃ Pradyumnam.

1.103 yad bhartry ājñāpayati.

1.104 bho, vayasya! yathā viśrānto nūpura|śabdas, tathā tarkayāmi: āgatā devy aśoka|mūlam iti.

1.108 katham ārya|putraḥ! Jayatu jayatv ārya|putraḥ! etad āsanam. atr' ôpaviśatv ārya|putraḥ.

I.110 bhartri, sva|hasta|datta|kuṅkuma|carcikā|śobhitaṃ kṛtvā rakt'|âśoka|pāda|pam arcyatām bhagavān Pradyumnaḥ.

I.111 upanaya me pūj"|ôpakaraṇāni.

I.119 bhartri, arcito bhagavān Pradyumnaḥ. tat kuru bhartur ucitaṃ pūjā|sat|kāram.

I.120 tena hy upanaya me kusumāni vilepanaṃ ca.

I.121 bhartri, etat sarvaṃ sajjam.

I.123 hā dhik! hā dhik! kathaṃ, kusuma|lobh'|ôtkṣipta|hṛdayay" âti|ciram eva mayā kṛtam! tad yāvad anena sindhuvāra|viṭapen' âpavārita|śarīrā bhūtvā prekṣe.

I.123 kathaṃ, pratyakṣa eva bhagavān Kusum'|āyudha iha pūjāṃ pratīcchati. asmākaṃ tātasy' ântaḥ|pure punaś citra|gato 'rcyate. tad aham ap' îha sthit" âiv' âibhiḥ kusumair bhagavantaṃ Kusum'|āyudhaṃ pūjayiṣye.

I.123 namas te bhagavan Kusum'|āyudha! a|mogha|darśano ma idānīṃ tvaṃ bhaviṣyasi!

I.123 dṛṣṭaṃ yad draṣṭavyam. tad, yāvan na ko 'pi māṃ prekṣate, tāvad eva gamiṣyāmi.

I.124 ārya|Vasantaka, ehi! sāṃprataṃ tvam api svasti|vācanaṃ pratīccha.

I.125 ārya, svasti|vācanaṃ pratīccha.

I.126 svasti bhavatyai.

I.129 katham, ayaṃ sa rājā Udayano, yasy' âhaṃ tātena dattā.

I.129 tat para|preṣaṇa|dūṣitam api me jīvitam etasya darśanen' êdānīṃ bahu|mataṃ saṃvṛttam.

1.133 kathaṃ, prasthitā devī. bhavatu. tad aham api tvaritaṃ gamiṣyāmi.

1.133 hā dhik! hā dhik! manda|bhāginyā mayā prekṣitum api ciraṃ na pārito 'yaṃ janaḥ.

2.3 hā dhik! hā dhik! kutr' êdānīṃ mama haste sārikā|pañjaraṃ nikṣipya gatā me priya|sakhī Sāgarikā? tat kva punar enāṃ prekṣiṣye?

2.3 katham, eṣā khalu Nipuṇik" êta ev' āgacchati. tad yāvad enāṃ prakṣyāmi.

2.5 āścaryam, āścaryam! an|anya|sa|dṛśaḥ prabhāvo manye devatāyāḥ. upalabdaḥ khalu mayā bhartur vṛtt'|ântaḥ. tad gatvā bhaṭṭinyai nivedayiṣyāmi.

2.6 sakhi Nipuṇike! kv' êdānīṃ tvaṃ vismay'|ôtkṣipta|hṛday" êv' êha sthitāṃ māṃ avadhīry' êto 'tikrāmasi?

2.7 kathaṃ, Susaṃgatā! halā Susaṃgate! su|ṣṭhu tvayā jñātam. etat khalu mama vismayasya kāraṇam: adya kila bhartā Śrī|parvatād āgatasya Śrīkhaṇḍadāsa|nāma|dheyasya dhārmikasya sakāśād a|kāla|kusuma|saṃjanana|dohadaṃ śikṣitv" ātmanaḥ parigṛhītāṃ navamālikaṃ kusuma|samṛddhi|śobhitāṃ kariṣyat' îti. tatr' âitaṃ vṛtt'|ântaṃ jñātuṃ devyā preṣit" âsmi. tvaṃ punaḥ kutra prasthitā?

2.8 priya|sakhīṃ Sāgarikām anveṣṭum.

2.9 sakhi, dṛṣṭā mayā te priya|sakhī Sāgarikā gṛhīta|citra|phalaka|vartikā|samudgakā samudvign" êva kadalī|gṛhaṃ praviśantī. tad gaccha tvam. aham api devyāḥ sakāśaṃ gamiṣyāmi.

2.13 hṛdaya, prasīda prasīda! kim anen' āyāsa|mātra|phalena dur|labha|jana|prārthan'|ânubandhena? anyac ca: yen' âiva dṛṣṭena ta īdṛśaḥ saṃtāpo nanu vardhate, tam eva punar api prekṣitum abhilaṣas' îty, aho te mūḍhatā! kathaṃ c' âti|nṛśaṃsa janmataḥ prabhṛti saha|saṃvardhitaṃ imaṃ janaṃ parityajya, kṣaṇa|mātra|darśana|paricitaṃ janam anugacchan na lajjase? atha vā kas tava doṣaḥ! Anaṅga|śara|patana|bhītena tvay" âivam adya vyavasitam.

2.13 bhavatu. Anaṅgaṃ tāvad upālapsye.

2.13 bhagavan Kusum'|āyudha! nirjita|sakala|sur'|âsura bhūtvā strī|janaṃ praharan kathaṃ na lajjase?

2.13 atha vā an|aṅgo 'si.

2.13 sarvathā mama manda|bhāginyā maraṇam ev' ânena dur|nimitten' ôpasthitam.

2.13 tad yāvan na ko 'p' îh' āgacchati, tāvad ālekhya|samarpitaṃ tam abhimataṃ janaṃ prekṣya yathā|samīhitaṃ kariṣyāmi.

2.13 yady api me 'ti|sādhvasena vepate ayam ati|mātram agra|hastas, tath" âpi n' âsti tasya janasy' ânyo darśan'|ôpāya iti yathā|tath" ālikhy' âinaṃ prekṣiṣye.

2.15 etat tat kadalī|gṛham. tat praviśāmi.

2.15 eṣā me priya|sakhī Sāgarikā. kiṃ punar eṣā guruk'|ânurāg'|ôtkṣipta|hṛday" êva kim apy ālikhantī na māṃ prekṣate? bhavatu. tad yāvad asyā dṛṣṭi|pathaṃ parihṛtya nirūpayiṣyāmi kim eṣ" ālikhat' îti.

2.15 kathaṃ, bhart" ālikhitaḥ! sādhu, Sāgarike, sādhu! atha vā na kamal'|ākaraṃ varjayitvā rāja|haṃsy anyatr' âbhiramate!

2.16 ālikhitaḥ khalu may" êṣaḥ. kiṃ punar an|avarata|nipatad|bāṣpa|salilena na me dṛṣṭiḥ prekṣituṃ prabhavati.

2.16 kathaṃ, priya|sakhī Susaṃgatā! sakhi, ita upaviśa.

2.17 sakhi, ka eṣa tvay" âtr' ālikhitaḥ?

2.18 sakhi, pravṛtta|Madana|mah"|ôtsave bhagavān Anaṅgaḥ.

2.19 aho te nipuṇatvam! kiṃ punaḥ, śūnyam iv' âitac citraṃ pratibhāti. tad aham apy ālikhya Rati|sa|nāthaṃ kariṣyāmi.

2.20 Susaṃgate, kasmāt tvay" âham atr' ālikhitā?

2.21 sakhi, kim a|kāraṇaṃ kupyasi? yādṛśas tvayā Kāma|deva ālikhitas, tādṛśī mayā Ratir ālikhitā. tad anyathā|saṃbhāvini, kiṃ tav" âiten' ālapitena? kathaya tāvat sarvaṃ vṛtt'|ântam.

2.22 nanu jñāt" âsmi priya|sakhyā.

2.22 priya|sakhi, mahatī khalu me lajjā. tat tathā kuru, yathā na ko 'py apara etaṃ vṛtt'|ântaṃ jānāti.

2.23 sakhi, mā lajjasva. īdṛśasya kanyā|ratnasy' âvaśyam ev' ēdṛśe vare abhilāṣeṇa bhavitavyam. tath" âpi, yathā na ko 'py apara etaṃ vṛtt'|ântaṃ jñāsyati, tathā karomi. etayā punar medhāvinyā sārikay" âtra kāraṇena bhavitavyam. kad" âpy eṣ" âsy' ālāpasya gṛhīt'|âkṣarā bhūtvā kasy' âpi purato mantrayiṣyate.

2.24 tat kim idānīm atra kariṣyāmi? ato 'py adhikataraṃ me saṃtāpo vardhate.

2.26 sakhi, samāśvasihi, samāśvasihi. yāvad asyā dīrghikāyā nalinī|patrāṇi mṛṇālikāś ca gṛhītvā laghv āgacchāmi.

2.27 sakhi, apanay' êmāni nalinī|patrāṇi mṛṇāla|valayāni ca. alam etaiḥ. kim|ity a|kāraṇa ātmanam āyāsayasi? nanu bhaṇāmi—

2.28 dur|labha|jan'|ânurāgo, lajjā gurvī, para|vaśa ātmā— / priya|sakhi, vi|ṣamaṃ prema, maraṇaṃ śaraṇaṃ na varam ekam?

2.30 sakhi Sāgarike, samāśvasihi, samāśvasihi.

2.35 sakhi, uttiṣṭh' ôttiṣṭha. eṣa khalu duṣṭa|vānara ita ev' āgacchati. tad a|lakṣitaṃ tamāla|viṭap'|ândha|kāre praviśy' âinam ativāhayāvaḥ.

2.36 Susaṃgate! kathaṃ, tvayā citra|phalaka ujjhitaḥ. kad" âpi ko 'pi taṃ prekṣate.

2.37 ayi, su|sthite, kim ady' âpi citra|phalakena kariṣyasi? eṣa khalu dadhi|bhakta|lampaṭo sārikā|pañjaram udghāṭy' âpakrānto duṣṭa|vānaraḥ. medhāviny apy uḍḍīn" âiṣā gacchati. tad ehi. laghv anusarāvaḥ. asy' ālāpasya gṛhīt'|âkṣarā kasy' âpi purato mantrayiṣyate.

2.38 sakhi, evaṃ kurvaḥ.

2.39 hī hī, bhoḥ! āścaryam āścaryam!

2.40 Susaṃgate, jñāyate punar api sa duṣṭa|vānara āgacchat' îti.

2.41 ayi kātare, mā bibhīhi. bhartuḥ pārśva|vartī ārya|Vasantakaḥ khalv eṣaḥ.

2.42 sakhi Susaṃgate, darśanīyaḥ khalv ayaṃ janaḥ.

2.43 ayi su|sthite, kim anena dṛṣṭena? dūre bhavati khalu sārikā. tad ehi. anusarāvaḥ.

2.46 hī hī, bhoḥ! āścaryam, āścaryam! sādhu re, Śrīkhaṇḍadāsa dhārmika, sādhu! yena datta|mātreṇ' âiva tena dohaden' ēdṛśī navamālikā saṃvṛttā yena nir|antar'|ôdbhinna|kusuma|guccha|śobhita|viṭapā upahasant" îva lakṣyate devī|parigṛhītāṃ mādhavī|latām. tad yāvad gatvā priya|vayasyaṃ vardhayiṣyāmi.

2.46 eṣa khalu priya|vayasyas tasya dohadasya labdha|pratyayatayā parokṣam api tāṃ navamālikāṃ pratyakṣāṃ iva kusumitāṃ prekṣamāṇaḥ harṣ'|ôtphulla|locana ita ev' āgacchati. tad yāvad enam upasarpāmi.

2.51 jayatu jayatu priya|vayasya! bho vayasya, diṣṭyā vardhase.

2.55 etv, etu bhavān.

2.58 bho vayasya, ehi, palāyāvahe.

2.60 etasmin bakula|pāda|pe ko 'pi bhūtaḥ prativasati.

2.62 bho, eṣa khalu sphuṭ'|âkṣaram eva mantrayate. tad yadi mama vacanaṃ na pratyeṣi, tad agrato bhūtvā svayam eva tāvad ākarṇaya.

2.66 āḥ, kathaṃ, satyam eva sārikā!

2.66 āḥ, dāsyāḥ putri, kiṃ tvayā jñātaṃ satyam eva Vasantako bibhet' îti? tat tiṣṭha muhūrtam, yāvad anena piśuna|jana|hṛdaya|kuṭilena daṇḍa|kāṣṭhena paripakvam iva kapittha|phalam asmād bakula|pāda|pād āhatya bhūmau tvāṃ pātayiṣyāmi.

2.69 bho vayasya, śrutaṃ tvayā yad etayā mantritam? eṣā bhaṇati: «sakhi, ka eṣa tvy" âtr' ālikhitaḥ?»«sakhi, pravṛtta|Madana|mah"|ôtsave bhagavān Anaṅga iti.» punar apy eṣā bhaṇati: «sakhi, kasmāt tvay" âham atr' ālikhitā?»«sakhi, kim a|kāraṇaṃ kupyasi? yādṛśas tvayā Kāma|deva ālikhitas, tādṛśī mayā Ratir ālikhit" êti. tad anyathā|saṃbhāvini, kiṃ tav' âiten' ālapitena? kathaya sarvaṃ vṛtt'|ântam!» bho vayasya, kiṃ nv idam?

2.71 bho vayasya, yujyate. evaṃ khalv etat.

2.73 bho, eṣā bhaṇati: «sakhi, mā lajjasva. īdṛśasya kanyā|ratnasy' âvaśyam ev' ēdṛśe vare 'bhilāṣeṇa bhavitavyam.» bho vayasya, y" âiṣā ālikhitā, sā khalu darśanīyā.

2.75 bho vayasya, śrutaṃ tvayā yad etayā mantritam? «sakhi apanay' êmāni nalinī|patrāṇi mṛṇāla|valayāni ca. alam etena. katham a|kāraṇa ātmānam āyāsayasi?»

2.77 bho, mā tvaṃ pāṇḍitya|garvam udvaha. ahaṃ ta etasyā mukhāc chrutvā sarvaṃ vyākhyāsyāmi. tac chṛṇuvaḥ. ady' âpi kurukurāyate eva eṣā sārikā dāsyāḥ putrī.

2.79 bho vayasya, eṣā khalu sārikā dāsyā duhitā catur|vedī brāhmaṇa iva ṛcaḥ paṭhituṃ pravṛttā.

2.81 bho, etad etayā paṭhitam.

2.82 dur|labha|jan'|ânurāgo, lajjā gurvī, para|vaśa ātmā— / priya|sakhi, vi|ṣamaṃ prema, maraṇaṃ śaraṇaṃ na varam ekam?

2.84 tataḥ kiṃ nu khalv idam?

2.86 kiṃ gāthā?

2.88 bhoḥ, kim etair vakra|bhaṇitaiḥ? ṛjv eva kiṃ na bhaṇasi yathā: «mām an|āsādayanty" êti.» anyathā ko 'nyaḥ Kusuma|cāpa|vyapadeśen' âivaṃ nihnūyate?

2.91 bho, eṣā khalu kadalī|gṛham eva gatā. tad ehi, laghv anusarāvaḥ.

2.94 etv, etu bhavān.

2.94 bho, etat khalu kadalī|gṛham. yāvat praviśāvaḥ.

2.96 bho, gatā dāsyāḥ putrī. atra tāvan manda|mārut'|ôdvellad|bāla|kadalī|dala|śītale śilātala upaviśya muhūrtaṃ viśrāmyāvaḥ.

2.100 bhoḥ! etena khal' ûdghāṭita|dvāreṇa tasyāḥ sārikāyāḥ pañjareṇa bhavitavyam. eṣo 'pi sa citra|phalakaḥ. yāvad enaṃ gṛhṇāmi.

2.100 bho vayasya, diṣṭyā vardhase!

2.102 bho, etat khalu tad, yan mayā bhaṇitam: «tvam ev' âtr' ālikhitaḥ. ko 'nyaḥ kusuma|cāpa|vyapadeśena nihnūyata iti?»

2.104 na te darśayiṣyāmi. s" âpi kanyak" âtr' âiv' ālikhitā tiṣṭhati. tat kiṃ pāritoṣikeṇa vin" ēdṛśaṃ kanyā|ratnaṃ darśyate?

2.110 sakhi, na samāsādit" āvābhyāṃ sārikā. tac citra|phalakam api tāvad asmāt kadalī|gṛhād gṛhītvā laghv āgacchāvaḥ.

2.111 sakhi, evaṃ kurvaḥ.

2.113 bho vayasya, kasmāt punar eṣ" avanata|mukhy" ālikhitā?

2.114 sakhi, yathā Vasantako mantrayate, tathā tarkayāmi bhartr" âpi atr' âiva bhavitavyam. tat kadalī|gulm'|ântarite bhūtvā prekṣāvahe tāvat.

2.117 sakhi, diṣṭyā vardhase! eṣa te hṛdaya|vallabhas tvām eva nirvarṇayaṃs tiṣṭhati.

2.118 kasmāt parihāsa|śīlatay" êmaṃ janaṃ laghuṃ karoṣi?

2.119 nanu bhaṇāmi: kasmād eṣ" âvanata|mukhy" ālikhit" êti?

2.121 sakhi, darśitaṃ khalu Medhāviny ātmano medhāvitvam.

2.122 bho vayasya, api sukhayati te locanam?

2.123 kim eṣa bhaṇiṣyat' îti yat satyaṃ jīvita|maraṇayor antare varte.

2.126 sakhi, śrutaṃ tvayā.

2.127 tvam eva śṛṇu, yasyā ālekhya|vijñānam evaṃ varṇyate.

2.128 bho vayasya, yasya punar īdṛśyo 'py evaṃ samāgamaṃ bahu manyante, tasy" âpy ātmana upari kaḥ parābhavaḥ, yen' âtr' âiva tay" ālikhitam ātmānaṃ na prekṣase?

2.131 hṛdaya, samāśvasihi samāśvasihi. mano|ratho 'pi ta etāvatīṃ bhūmiṃ na gataḥ.

2.132 sakhi, tvam ev' âikā ślāghanīyā, yayā bhart" âpi evaṃ mantryate.

2.133 bho vayasya, etat sa|rasa|kamalinī|dala|mṛṇāla|viracitaṃ tasyā eva madan'|âvasthā|sūcakam śayanīyaṃ lakṣyate.

2.138 bho vayasya, ayam aparas tasyā eva pīna|stan'|ôṣmā|kliśyamāna|komala|mṛṇāla|hāraḥ. tat prekṣatāṃ bhvān.

2.141 hā dhik! hā dhik! gurv|ânurāg'|ôtkṣipta|hṛdayo bhart" â|saṃbaddham api mantrayituṃ pravṛttaḥ. tan na yuktam ataḥ param upekṣitum. bhavatu. evaṃ tāvat.

2.141 sakhi, yasya kṛte tvam āgatā, so 'yaṃ te puratas tiṣṭhati.

2.142 Susaṃgate, kasya kṛte 'ham atr' āgatā?

2.143 ayi anya|śaṅkite, nanu citra|phalakasya. tad gṛhāṇ' âitam.

2.144 a|kuśal" âsmi tav' ēdṛśānām ālāpānām. tad anyato gamiṣyāmi.

2.145 ayi a|sahane, iha tiṣṭha tāvan muhūrtaṃ, yāvad asmāt kadalī|gṛhāc citra|phalakaṃ gṛhītv" āgacchāmi.

2.146 sakhi, evaṃ kuru.

2.148 bho vayasya, pracchāday' âitaṃ citra|phalakam. eṣā khalu devyāḥ paricārikā Susaṃgat" āgatā.

2.150 jayatu, jayatu bhartā!

2.154 bhartaḥ, na kevalaṃ tvam, ayam api citra|phalakena saha sarvo vṛtt'|ânto mayā vijñātaḥ. tad gatvā devyai nivedayiṣyāmi.

2.155 bho vayasya, sarvaṃ saṃbhāvyate. mukharā khalv eṣā garbha|dāsī. pāritoṣikeṇa saṃprīṇay' âinām.

2.157 bhartaḥ, alaṃ śaṅkayā. may" âpi bhartuḥ prasādena krīḍitam eva. tat kiṃ karṇ'|ābharaṇena? eṣa eva me guruḥ prasādo yat «kasmāt tvay" âham atra citra|phalaka ālikhit" êti?» kupitā me priya|sakhī Sāgarikā. tad gatvā prasādayatv enāṃ bhartā.

2.159 ita, ito bhartā.

2.160 bho, gṛhṇāmi etaṃ citra|phalakam. kad" âpi punar apy etena kāryaṃ bhaviṣyati.

2.161 bhartaḥ! iyaṃ sā.

2.163 hā dhik! hā dhik! etaṃ prekṣy' âti|sādhvasena na śaknomi padāt padam api gantum. tat kim idānīm atra kariṣyāmi?

2.164 hī hī, bhoḥ! āścaryam, āścaryam! īdṛśaṃ rūpaṃ manuṣya|loke na punar dṛśyate. tat tarkayāmi Prajāpater apy etan nirmāyya vismayaḥ samutpanna iti.

2.167 sakhi, īdṛśaḥ citra|phalakas tvayā ānītaḥ.

2.170 bhartaḥ, ati|kopanā khalv eṣā. tadd haste gṛhītvā prasāday' âinām.

2.172 bho, eṣā khalu tvayā '|pūrvā Śrī samāsāditā.

2.175 sakhi, ati|niṣṭhur" êdānīm asi tvaṃ, y" âivaṃ bhartrā haste gṛhīt" âpi kopaṃ na muñcasi.

2.176 ayi Susaṃgate, ady' âpi na viramasi?

2.178 eṣā khalv aparā devī Vāsavadattā.

2.180 Susaṃgate, kim idānīm atra kariṣye?

2.181 sakhi, etāṃ tamāla|vīthikām antarayitvā niṣkrāmāvaḥ.

2.184 bhoḥ! na jānāmi kva sā. may" «âiṣā khalv aparā devī Vāsavadatt" âti|dīrgha|roṣatay" êti» bhaṇitam.

2.188 hañje Kāñcanamāle, atha kiyad dūra idānīṃ s" ārya|putreṇa parigṛhītā navamālikā?

2.189 bhartri, etat kadalī|gṛham atikramya dṛśyata eva.

2.190 tad ādeśaya mārgam.

2.191 etu, etu bhartri.

2.193 bhartri, yathā samīpe bhartā mantrayate, tathā tarkayāmi bhartrīm eva pratipālayaṃs tiṣṭhat' îti. tad upasarpatu bhartrī.

2.194 jayatu, jayatv ārya|putraḥ!

2.197 ārya|putra, atha kusumitā navamālikā?

2.199 ārya|putra, mukha|rāgād eva mayā jñātaṃ yathā kusumitā navamālik" êti. tan na gamiṣyāmi.

2.200 hī hī bhoḥ! jitaṃ, jitam asmābhiḥ!

2.202 bho, mā kupya. tūṣṇīkas tiṣṭha. aham ev' âtra jñāsyāmi.

2.203 bhartri, prekṣasva tāvat kim atra citra|phalake ālikhitam.

2.204 Kāñcanamāle, ayaṃ ārya|putraḥ. iyaṃ punaḥ Sāgarikā. kiṃ nv etat?

2.205 bhartri, aham apy etad eva cintayāmi.

2.206 ārya|putra, ken' êdam ālikhitam?

2.208 bho, mā cintaya. aham uttaraṃ dāsyāmi.

2.208 bhavati, m" ânyathā saṃbhāvaya. «ātmā kila duḥkhen' ālikhyata iti» mama vacanaṃ śrutvā priya|vayasyen' âitad ālekhya| vijñānaṃ darśitam.

2.210 ārya|putra, eṣ" âpi y" âparā tava samīpa ālikhitā, tat kim ārya| Vasantakasya vijñānam?

2.212 bhavati, satyaṃ satyam. śape brahma|sūtreṇa yad īdṛśī kad" âpy asmābhir dṛṣṭa|pūrvā.

2.213 bhartri, ghuṇ'|âkṣaram api kad" âpi saṃbhavaty eva.

2.214 ayi ṛjuke, Vasantakaḥ khalv eṣaḥ. na jānāsi tvam etasya vakra| bhaṇitāni.

2.214 ārya|putra, mama punar etac citra|phalakaṃ prekṣamāṇāyāḥ śīrṣa|vedanā samutpannā. tad gamiṣyāmy aham.

2.217 ārya|putra, m" ânyathā saṃbhāvaya. satyam eva māṃ śīrṣa|vedanā bādhate. tad gamiṣyāmi.

2.219 bho, diṣṭyā vardhase! kṣemeṇ' âsmākam atikrāntā 'kāla|vāt'| āvalī.

3.3 Kauśāmbike! Kauśāmbike! api dṛṣṭā tvayā bhartuḥ sakāśe Kāñcanamālā na vā?

3.3 kiṃ bhaṇasi? «ko 'pi kālas tasyā āgatya gatāyā iti?» tat kutr' êdānīṃ prekṣiṣye?

3.3 katham, eṣā khalu Kāñcanamāl" êta ev' āgacchati. tad yāvad enām upasarpāmi.

3.5 sādhu, re amātya|Vasantaka sādhu! atiśayitas tvay" âmātya Yaugandharāyaṇo 'nayā saṃdhi|vigraha|cintayā.

3.6 halā Kāñcanamāle, kim ārya|Vasantakena kṛtaṃ, yena sa evaṃ ślāghyate?

3.7 halā Madanike, kiṃ tav' âitena jñātena? tvam idaṃ rahasyaṃ rakṣituṃ na pārayasi.

3.8 śape devyāś caraṇābhyāṃ, yadi kasy' âpi purataḥ prakāśayāmi.

3.9 yad evaṃ, tac chṛṇu. adya khalu mayā rāja|kulāt pratinivartamānayā citra|śālikā|dvāre Vasantakasya Susaṃgatayā samam ālāpaḥ śrutaḥ.

3.10 sakhi, kīdṛśaḥ?

3.11 yathā: «Susaṃgate, na khalu Sāgarikāṃ varjayitvā anyat kim api priya|vayasyasy" â|svasthatāyā kāraṇam. tac cintay' âtra pratīkāram iti.»

3.12 tataḥ Susaṃgatayā kiṃ bhaṇitam?

3.13 evaṃ tayā bhaṇitam: «adya khalu devyā citra|phalaka|vṛttānta|śaṅkitayā Sāgarikāṃ rakṣituṃ mama haste samarpayantyā yan nepathyaṃ me prasādī|kṛtaṃ ten' âiva viracita|bhaṭṭinī|veṣāṃ Sāgarikāṃ gṛhītv" âham api Kāñcanamālā|veṣa|dhāriṇī bhūtvā pradoṣa ih' āgamiṣyāmi. tvam ap' îh' âiva citra|śālikā|dvāre māṃ pratipālayiṣyasi. tato mādhavī|latā|maṇḍape tayā saha bhartuḥ samāgamo bhaviṣyat' îti.»

3.14 Susaṃgate, hat" âsi khalu tvaṃ, y" âivaṃ parijana|vatsalāṃ devīṃ vañcayase.

3.15 halā, tvam idānīṃ kutra prasthitā?

3.16 ahaṃ khalv a|svastha|śarīrasya bhartuḥ kuśala|vṛttāntaṃ jñātuṃ gatā tvaṃ cirayas' îty uttāmyantyā devyā tava sakāśaṃ preṣit" âsmi.

3.17 ati|ṛjuk" êdānīṃ sā devī, y" âiva pratyeti! eṣa khalu bhartā '|svasthatā|miṣeṇ' ātmano madan'|âvasthāṃ pracchādayan danta|toraṇa|valabhyāṃ tiṣṭhati. tad ehi. etaṃ vṛtt'|āntaṃ bhartryai nivedayāvaḥ.

3.31 hī hī, bhoḥ! Kauśambī|rājya|lābhen' âpi na tādṛṣaḥ priya|vayasyasya paritoṣa āsīd, yādṛṣo 'dya mama sakāśāt priya|vacanaṃ śrutvā bhaviṣyat' îti tarkayāmi. tad yāvad gatvā priya|vayasyasya nivedayiṣyāmi.

3.31 katham, eṣa priya|vayasya imām eva diśam avalokayaṃs tiṣṭhati, tathā tarkayāmi mām eva pratipālayat' îti. tad upasarpāmy enam.

3.31 jayatu, jayatu priya|vayasyaḥ! bho vayasya, diṣṭyā vardhase samīhit'|âbhyadhikayā kārya|siddhyā.

3.33 bho, a|cireṇa svayam eva prekṣya jñāsyasi.

3.35 bhoḥ, kasmān na bhaviṣyati yasya te upahasita|Bṛhaspati|buddhi|vibhavo 'ham amātyaḥ!

3.37 evam evam.

3.39 bho, imaṃ tāvac chuddha|suvarṇa|kaṭaka|maṇḍita|hastam ātmano brāhmaṇyai gatvā darśayiṣyāmi.

3.41 bhoḥ, prekṣasva prekṣasva! eṣa khalu gurv|anurāg'|ôtkṣipta|hṛdayaḥ saṃdhyā|vadhū|datta|saṃketa iv' âsta|giri|śikhara|kānanam anusarati bhagavān sahasra|raśmiḥ.

3.47 bhoḥ, śobhanaṃ bhaṇitam.

3.48 bho vayasya, prekṣasva prekṣasva. eṣa khalu bahalī|kṛta|vira-la|vana|rāji|saṃniveśo gṛhīta|ghana|paṅka|pīvara|vana|varā-ha|māhiṣa|kṛṣṇa|cchaviḥ prasarati pūrva|diśaṃ pracchādayaṃs timira|saṃghaḥ.

3.52 etv, etu priya|vayasya.

3.54 bho vayasya, etat khalu samāsannaṃ saṃsakta|bahala|patra|pā-da|pa|latābhiḥ piṇḍī|kṛt'|ândha|kāram iva Makarand'|ôdyā-nam. tat katham atra mārgo lakṣyate?

3.58 bho, etaṃ khalu nipatan|matta|madhu|karaṃ kusum'|āmoda|vāsita|daśa|diśaṃ masṛṇa|marakata|maṇi|śilā|kuṭṭima|sukhā-yamāna|caraṇa|saṃcāra|sūcitaṃ tam eva mādhavī|latā|maṇḍa-paṃ saṃprāptau svaḥ. tad ih' âiva tiṣṭhatu bhavān, yāvad ahaṃ devī|veṣa|dhāriṇīṃ Sāgarikāṃ gṛhītvā laghv āgacchāmi.

3.60 bho, mā uttāmya. eṣa āgato 'smi.

3.65 hañje Kāñcanamāle, satyam eva mama veṣaṃ kṛtvā Sāgarik" ārya|putram abhisariṣyati?

3.66 katham anyathā bhaṭṭinyai nivedyate? atha vā citra|śālikā|dvāre sthito Vasantaka eva te pratyayam utpādayiṣyati.

3.67 tena hi tatr' âiva gacchāvaḥ.

3.68 etv, etu bhaṭṭinī.

3.70 yathā citra|śālikā|dvāre pada|śabdaḥ śrūyate, tathā tarkayāmy āgatā Sāgarik" êti.

3.71 bhaṭṭini, iyaṃ sā citra|śālikā. tad yāvad Vasantakasya saṃjñāṃ karomi.

3.72 Susaṃgate, su|ṣṭhu khalu kṛtas tvayā eṣa Kāñcanamālāyā veṣaḥ. atha Sāgarik" êdānīṃ kutra?

3.73 nanv eṣā.

3.74 eṣā sphuṭam eva devī Vāsavadattā!

3.75 katham, jñāt" âsmi!

3.76 bhavati Sāgarike, ita āgaccha.

3.77 hat'|āśa, smariṣyasy' êtad ātmano vacanam.

3.78 tvaratāṃ, tvaratāṃ Sāgarikā. eṣa khalu pūrva|diśa udgacchati bhagavān mṛga|lāñchanaḥ.

3.81 bhavati Sāgarike, eṣa khalu priya|vayasyas tvām ev' ôddiśy' ôtkaṇṭhā|nirbharaṃ mantryate. tan nivedayāmy asmai tav' āgamanam.

3.83 bho vayasya, diṣṭyā vardhase! eṣā khalu may" ānītā Sāgarikā.

3.85 nanv eṣā.

3.88 Kāñcanamāle, evam api mantrayitv" ārya|putraḥ punar api mām ālapiṣyat' îty, aho, āścaryam!

3.89 bhartri, evaṃ nv idam. kiṃ punaḥ sāhasikānāṃ puruṣānāṃ na sambhāvyate?

3.90 bhavati Sāgarike, viśrabdhā bhūtvā priya|vayasyam ālapa. ady' âpi tāvad asya nitya|ruṣṭāyā devyā Vāsavadattāyā duṣṭa|vacanaiḥ kaṭukite śrotre sāmprataṃ sukhayatu tava madhura|vacan'|ôpanyāsaḥ.

3.91 Kāñcanamāle, aham īdṛśī kuṭu|bhāṣiṇī. ārya|Vasantakaḥ punaḥ priyaṃ|vadaḥ.

3.92 hat'|āśa, smariṣyasy etad vacanam.

3.93 bho vayasya, prekṣasva prekṣasva. eṣa khalu kupita|kāminī|kapola|saṃnibhaḥ pūrva|diśaṃ prakāśayann udito bhagavān mṛga|lāñchanaḥ.

3.98 ārya|putra, satyam ev' âhaṃ Sāgarikā. tvaṃ punaḥ Sāgarik"|ôt-
kṣipta|hṛdayaḥ sarvam eva Sāgarikā|mayaṃ prekṣase.

3.100 bho vayasya, kim aparam? asmākaṃ jīvita|saṃśayo jāta eṣaḥ.

3.102 ārya|putra, m" âivaṃ bhaṇa. anya|gatān' îmāny akṣarāṇi.

3.103 kim idānīm atra kariṣyāmi? bhavatv evaṃ tāvat.

3.103 bhavati, mah"|ânubhāvā khalu tvam. tat kṣamyatāṃ tāvad eko
'parādhaḥ priya|vayasyasya.

3.104 ārya|Vasantaka, nanu prathama|saṃgame vighnaṃ kurvatyā
may" âiv' âitasy' âparāddham.

3.107 ārya|putra, uttiṣṭh' ôttiṣṭha. nir|lajjaḥ khalu sa jano ya ārya|pu-
trasy' ēdṛśaṃ hṛdayaṃ jñātvā punar api kupyati. tat sukhaṃ
tiṣṭhatv ārya|putraḥ. gamiṣyāmy aham.

3.108 bhartri, kuru prasādam. evaṃ caraṇa|patitaṃ mahā|rājam uj-
jhitvā gatāyā devyā avaśyaṃ paścāt|tāpena bhavitavyam.

3.109 apehy a|paṇḍite! kim atra prasādasya paścāt|tāpasya vā kāra-
ṇam? tad ehi, gacchāvaḥ.

3.112 bho, uttiṣṭha! gatā devī. tat kim atr' âraṇya|ruditaṃ karoṣi?

3.114 kathaṃ na kṛtaḥ prasādo, yad ady' âpy a|kṣata|śarīrau tiṣṭhāvaḥ?

3.117 bho, ruṣṭā devi kiṃ kariṣyat' îti na jānāmi. Sāgarikā punar
duṣ|karaṃ jīviṣyat' îti tarkayāmi.

3.120 diṣṭyā n' âham anena viracita|devī|veṣeṇ' âsyās citra|śālikāyā
niṣkrāmantī ken' âpi lakṣit" âsmi. tad idānīṃ kiṃ kariṣyāmi?

3.121 bhoḥ! kiṃ mūḍha iva tiṣṭhasi? cintay' âtra pratīkāram!

3.124 varam idānīṃ svayam ev' ātmānam udbadhy' ôparatā, na pu-
nar jñāta|saṃketa|vṛtt'|ântayā devyā paribhūt" âsmi. tad yāvad
aham aśoka|pāda|paṃ gatvā yathā|samīhitaṃ kariṣyāmi.

3.125 tiṣṭha tāvat, tiṣṭha bhoḥ! pada|śabdaḥ śrūyate. jānāmi kad" âpi gṛhīta|paścāt|tāpā punar api devy āgatā bhavet.

3.127 yad bhavān ājñāpayati.

3.128 tad yāvad etāyā mādhavī|latāyāḥ pāśaṃ viracayy' âśoka|pāda|pa ātmānam udbadhya vyāpādayāmi.

3.128 hā tāta, hā amba, eṣ" êdānīm aham a|nāth" â|śaraṇā vipadye manda|bhāginī.

3.129 kā punar eṣā? katham, devī Vāsavadattā!

3.129 bho vayasya, paritrāyasva paritrāyasva! eṣā khalu devī Vāsavadatt" ôdbadhy' ātmānaṃ vyāpādayati.

3.131 nanv eṣā!

3.134 ammo, katham, eṣa bhartā!

3.134 yat satyam: enaṃ prekṣya punar api me jīvit'|âbhilāṣaḥ saṃvṛttaḥ. atha v" âinaṃ prekṣya kṛt'|ârthā bhūtvā sukhen' âiva jīvitaṃ parityakṣyāmi.

3.134 muñcatu, muñcatu māṃ bhartā! parādhīnaḥ khalv ayaṃ janaḥ, na punar īdṛśam avasaraṃ martuṃ prāpnoti.

3.138 bho, evaṃ nv idaṃ, yady a|kāla|vāt'|āvalī bhūtvā n' āyāti devī Vāsavadattā.

3.140 hañje Kāñcanamāle, taṃ tathā caraṇa|nipatitam ārya|putram avadhīry' āgacchantyā may" âti|niṣṭhuraṃ kṛtam. tad idānīṃ svayam eva gatv" ārya|putram anuneṣyāmi.

3.141 ko 'nyo devīṃ varjayitv" âinaṃ bhaṇituṃ jānāti? varaṃ sa eva devo dur|jano, na punar devī. tad etv, etu bhaṭṭinī.

3.144 bhaṭṭini, eṣa khalu yathā samīpe bhartā mantrayate, tathā tarkayāmi tvām ev' ânunetum ita ev' āgacchati.

3.145 tena hy a|lakṣit" âiva pṛṣṭhato gatvā kaṇṭhe gṛhītvā prasādayiṣyāmi.

3.146 bhavati Sāgarike, viśvastā bhūtvā priya|vayasyam ālapa.

3.147 Kāñcanamāle! katham, Sāgarik" êta ev' āgatā? tac chroṣyāmi tāvat paścād upasarpsyāmi.

3.148 bhartaḥ, kim eten' âlīka|dākṣinyena jīvitād api vallabhatarāyā devyā ātmānam aparādhinaṃ karoṣi?

3.151 ārya|putra, yuktam etat, sa|dṛśam etat!

3.153 ārya|putra, uttiṣṭha uttiṣṭha. kim ady' âpi saha|j'|âbhijātāyāḥ sevayā duḥkham anubhūyate?

3.155 bhavati, tvaṃ kim udbadhy' ātmānaṃ vyāpādayas' îti veṣa|sādṛśya|mohitena mayā priya|vayasyo 'tr' ānītaḥ. yadi mama vacanaṃ na pratyeṣi, tat prekṣasv' âitaṃ latā|pāśam.

3.157 Kāñcanamāle, eten' âiva latā|pāśena baddhvā gṛhāṇ' âinaṃ brāhmaṇam. etāṃ ca dur|vinītāṃ kanyakām agrataḥ kuru.

3.158 yad devy ājñāpayati.

3.158 hat'|āśa, anubhav' êdānīm ātmano dur|nayasya phalam. Sāgarike, tvam apy agrato bhava.

3.159 hā dhik! katham a|kṛta|puṇyayā mayā martum apy ātmana icchayā na pāritam.

3.160 bho vayasya, smara mām a|nāthaṃ devyā bandhanād vipadyamānam.

4.3 hā priya|sakhi Sāgarike, hā lajjāvati, hā udāra|śīle, hā sakhī|jana|vatsale, hā saumya|darśane! kutr' êdānīṃ tvaṃ mayā prekṣitavyā?

4.3 ayi, daiva|hataka a|karuṇa! a|sāmānya|rūpa|śobhā tādṛśī tvayā yadi nirmitā, tat kasmāt punar īdṛśam avasth"|ântaraṃ prāpitā?

iyaṃ ca ratna|mālā jīvita|nir|āśayā tayā «kasy' âpi brāhmaṇasya haste pratipāday' êti» bhaṇitvā mama haste samarpitā. tad yāvat kam api brāhmaṇam anviṣyāmi.

4.3 aye, eṣa khalv ārya|Vasantaka ita ev' āgacchati. tad yāvad etasmā ev' âitāṃ pratipādayiṣyāmi.

4.5 hī hī, bhoḥ! adya khalu priya|vayasyena prasāditayā tatra|bhavatyā Vāsavadattayā bandhanān mocayitvā sva|hasta|dattair modakaiś cirasya tāvat kālasy' ôdaram me su|pūritaṃ kṛtam. anyac c' âitac paṭṭ'|âṃśuka|yugalaṃ karṇ'|ābharaṇaṃ ca dattam. tad yāvad idānīṃ gatvā priya|vayasyaṃ prekṣe.

4.6 ārya|Vasantaka, tiṣṭha tāvan muhūrtam.

4.7 kathaṃ, Susaṃgatā! Susaṃgate, kiṃ|nimittaṃ rudyate? na khalu Sāgarikāyā aty|āhitaṃ kim api saṃvṛttam?

4.8 ārya|Vasantaka, etad eva nivedayiṣyāmi. sā khalu tapasvinī devyā Ujjayinīṃ nīyata iti pravādaṃ kṛtv" ôpasthite 'rdha|rātre na jñāyate kutra nīt" êti.

4.9 ati|nirghṛṇaṃ khalu kṛtaṃ devyā.

4.10 iyaṃ ca ratna|mālā tayā jīvita|nir|āśayā «ārya|Vasantakasya haste pratipāday' êti» bhaṇitvā mama haste samarpitā. tad gṛhṇātv etām āryaḥ.

4.11 bhavati, na ma īdṛśe prastāve hastau grahītuṃ prasarataḥ.

4.13 tasyā ev' ânugrahaṃ kurvann aṅgī|karotv etām āryaḥ.

4.14 atha v" ôpanaya, yen' ânay" âiva Sāgarikā|viraha|duḥkhitaṃ priya|vayasyaṃ vinodayiṣyāmi.

4.16 Susaṃgate, kutaḥ punas tasyā īdṛśasy' âlaṃ|kārasya samāgamaḥ?

4.17 ārya, may" âpi sā kautūhalena pṛṣṭ" âiv' āsīt.

4.18 tatas tayā kiṃ bhaṇitam?

4.19 tataḥ s" ōrdhvaṃ prekṣya, dīrghaṃ niḥśvasya: «Susaṃgate, kim idānīṃ tav' âitayā kathay" êti» bhaṇitvā rodituṃ pravṛttā.

4.20 nanu kathitam eva sāmānya|jana|dur|labhen' ânena paricchadena: sarvathā mahā|kula|prasūtayā tayā bhavitavyam iti. Susaṃgate, priya|vayasya idānīṃ kutra?

4.21 ārya, eṣa khalu bhartā devī|bhavanān niṣkramya sphaṭika|śilā|maṇḍapaṃ gataḥ. tad gacchatv āryaḥ. aham api devyāḥ pārśva|vartinī bhaviṣyāmi.

4.22 evam.

4.32 eṣa khalu nirbhar"|ôtkaṇṭh"|parikṣāmām api ślāghanīya|lāvaṇyāṃ tanuṃ samudvahann udita iva dvitīyā|candro 'dhikataraṃ śobhate priya|vayasyaḥ. tad yāvad enam upasarpāmi.

4.32 svasti bhavate! diṣṭyā dṛṣṭo 'si devī|hasta|gaten' âpi mayā punar apy etābhyām akṣibhyām.

4.38 a|priyaṃ te nivedayituṃ na pārayāmi.

4.40 samāśvasitu, samāśvasitu priya|vayasyaḥ!

4.43 bho vayasya, m" ânyathā saṃbhāvaya. sā khalu tapasvinī devy" Ôjjayinīṃ preṣit" êti śrūyate. ato mayā «'|priyam» iti bhaṇitam.

4.45 bhoḥ! Susaṃgatayā. anyac ca, mama haste tayā kim api nimittam iyaṃ ratna|mālā preṣitā.

4.51 yad bhavān ājñāpayati.

4.53 bho vayasya, m" âivam uccair mantrayasva. kad" âpi ko 'pi devy" êha saṃcarati.

4.55 jayatu, jayatu bhartā! bhartaḥ, eṣa khalu Rumaṇvato bhāgineyo Vijayavarmā priyaṃ kim api nivedayitu|kāmo dvāre tiṣṭhati.

4.57 yad deva ājñāpayati.

4.57 Vijayavarman, eṣa khalu bhartā. tad upasarpatv āryaḥ.

4.67 bho, laghv ācakṣva. vepata iva me hṛdayam.

4.73 jayatu, jayatu bhavān! jitam asmābhiḥ!

4.77 yad deva ājñāpayati.

4.79 ājñāpt" âsmi devyā yathā: «hañje, Kāñcanamāle, gaccha. etam aindra|jālikam ārya|putrāya darśaya.»

4.79 eṣa khalu bhartā. tad yāvad usarpāmi.

4.79 jayatu, jayatu bhartā! devī vijñāpayati: «eṣa khal' Ûjjayinītaḥ Sarvasiddhir nām' āindra|jālika āgataḥ. tat prekṣatām enam ārya|putra iti.»

4.81 yad deva ājñāpayati.

4.84 praṇamata caraṇāv Indrasy' êndra|jālaka|pinaddha|nāmnaḥ, / tath" âiva Śambarasya, māyā|su|pratiṣṭhita|yaśasaḥ.

4.85 bhartaḥ, eṣa khalv āindra|jālikaḥ.

4.86 jayatu, jayatu devaḥ! deva,

4.87 kiṃ dharaṇyāṃ mṛg'|âṅka, ākāśe mahī|dharo, jale jvalanaḥ, / madhy'|âhne pradoṣo darśyatāṃ? dehy ājñaptim!

4.88 atha vā kiṃ bahunā jalpitena?

4.89 mama pratijñ" âiṣā: yad yad hṛdayen' ēhase saṃdraṣṭum, / tat tad darśayāmy ahaṃ guror mantra|prabhāveṇa.

4.90 bho vayasya, avahito bhava. īdṛśo 'sy' âvaṣṭambho, yena sarvaṃ saṃbhāvyate.

4.92 yad bhart" ājñāpayati.

4.94 Kāñcanamāle, Ujjayinīta āgata ity asti me tasminn aindra|jālike pakṣa|pātaḥ.

4.95 jñāti|kula|bahu|mānaḥ khalv eṣa bhartryāḥ. tad etv, etu bhartrī.

4.96 jayatu, jayatv ārya|putraḥ.

4.100 yad deva ājñāpayati.

4.101 Hari|Hara|Brahma|pramukhān devān darśayāmi deva|rājaṃ ca / gagane Siddha|Cāraṇa|sura|vadhū|sārthāṃ ca nṛtyantam.

4.102 tat prekṣatāṃ devaḥ.

4.105 āścaryam, āścaryam!

4.106 āḥ, dāsyāḥ putra aindra|jālika! kim etair devair apsarobhiś ca darśitaiḥ? yadi te 'nena parituṣṭena kāryaṃ, tat Sāgarikāṃ darśaya.

4.108 jayatu, jayatu bhartā! amātyo Yaugandharāyaṇo vijñāpayati: «eṣa khalu Vikramabāhoḥ pradhān'|âmātyo Vasubhūtir Bābhravyena kañcukinā sah' āgataḥ. tad arhati devo 'sminn eva sundara|muhūrte prekṣitum. aham api kārya|śeṣaṃ samāpy' āgata ev' êti.»

4.109 ārya|putra, tiṣṭhatu tāvad indra|jālam. mātula|gṛhāt pradhān'|âmātyo Vasubhūtir āgataḥ. taṃ tāvat prekṣatām ārya|putraḥ.

4.111 yad deva ājñāpayati.

4.111 ekaḥ punar mama khelo 'vaśyaṃ devena prekṣitavyaḥ.

4.113 Kāñcanamāle, gaccha tvaṃ, dehy asya pāritoṣikam.

4.114 yad devy ājñāpayati.

4.116 yad deva ājñāpayati.

4.122 etv, etv amātyaḥ.

4.126 bho, eṣa khalu mahā|rājaḥ. tad upasarpatv amātyaḥ.

4.131 etad āsanam. upaviśatv amātyaḥ.

4.135 amātya, eṣā devī Vāsavadattā praṇamati.

4.136 ārya, praṇamāmi.

4.142 hā dhik! hā dhik! kim idānīṃ Vasubhūtiḥ kathayiṣyati?

4.147 ārya|putra, na jñāyate ko 'līkaṃ mantrayata iti.

4.148 tatas tasyāḥ kiṃ vṛttam?

4.150 hā, hat" âsmi manda|bhāginī! hā, bhagini Ratnāvali, kutr' êdānīm asi? dehi me prativacanam.

4.152 ārya|putra, yujyata etat. paraṃ kuto mam' âitāvad bhāga|dheyam?

4.159 ārya|putra, paritrāyasya paritrāyasya!

4.161 ārya|putra, may" ātmanaḥ kṛte na bhaṇitam. eṣā khalu mayā nirghṛṇy" êha nigaḍena saṃyamitā Sāgarikā vipadyate. tat tāṃ paritrāyatām ārya|putraḥ.

4.165 vayasya, mā khalv evaṃ sāhasaṃ kuru!

4.168 kathaṃ, mama duḥkha|bhaginyā vacanād evam adhyavasitam ārya|putreṇa! tad aham apy ārya|putram ev' ânugamiṣyāmi.

4.169 bhavati, aham api te pathy|upadeśako bhavāmi.

4.174 hā dhik! samantataḥ prajvalito huta|vahaḥ.

4.174 adya hutavaho diṣṭyā kariṣyati mama duḥkh'|âvasānam.

4.176 katham, ārya|putraḥ! tad etaṃ prekṣya punar api me jīvit'|âbhilāṣaḥ saṃvṛttaḥ.

4.176 paritrāyatāṃ, paritrāyatāṃ bhartā!

4.183 diṣṭyā ’|kṣata|śarīra ārya|putraḥ.

4.192 jayatu, jayatu bhavān!

4.195 bho, mā saṃdehaṃ kuru. indra|jālam ev’ êdam. bhaṇitaṃ tena dāsyāḥ putreṇ’ āindra|jālikena yath” «âiko mama punaḥ khelo ’vaśyaṃ devena prekṣitavya iti.» tat tad ev’ âitat.

4.197 ārya|putra, jñātaṃ mayā.

4.203 amātya, «eṣā khalu sāgarāt prāpt” êti» bhaṇitv” âmātya|Yaugandharāyaṇena mama haste nikṣiptā. ata eva Sāgarik” êti śabdyate.

4.206 katham, amātyo Vasubhūtiḥ!

4.209 hā tāta, hā amba! kutr’ âsi? dehi me prativacanam.

4.211 ārya|kañcukin, iyaṃ sā mama bhaginī Rātnāvalī?

4.213 bhagini, samāśvasihi samāśvasihi.

4.215 prathamam eva mayā jñātaṃ: na khalu sāmānya|janasy’ ēdṛśaḥ paricchado bhavat’ îti.

4.217 kṛt’|âparādhā khalv ahaṃ devyā na śaknomi mukhaṃ darśayitum.

4.219 ehy, ehy ati|niṣṭhure! idānīm api tāvat snehaṃ darśaya.

4.219 ārya|putra, lajje khalv anen’ ātmano nṛśaṃsatvena. tad apanay’ âsyā bandhanam.

4.221 ārya|putra, amātya|Yaugandharāyaṇen’ âitāvantaṃ khalu kālaṃ dur|janī|kṛt” âsmi, yena jānat” âpi na niveditam.

4.233 bho, an|ākhyātam apy etaj jñāyata eva, yathā: antaḥ|pura|gatā sukhena te nayana|pathaṃ gamiṣyat’ îti.

4.238 ārya, sphuṭam eva kiṃ na bhaṇasi, yathā: pratipāday' âsmai Rātnāvalīm iti.

4.239 bhavati, su|ṣṭhu tvayā jñāto 'mātyasy' âbhiprāyaḥ.

4.240 ehi Ratnāvali, ehi. etāvad api tāvan me bhaginik"|ânurūpaṃ bhavatu.

4.240 ārya|putra, pratīcch' âinām.

4.242 ārya|putra, dūre khalv etasyāḥ pitṛ|kulam. tat tathā kuru, yathā na bandhu|janaṃ smarati.

4.244 hī hī bhoḥ! pṛthvī khalv idānīṃ hasta|gatā priya|vayasyasya.

The Lady who Shows her Love

1.25 bho vayasya. kathaṃ tam eva dāsyāḥ putraṃ bandhana|hatakaṃ praśaṃsasi? tad idānīṃ vismṛtam? yat tathā nava|graha iva gaja|patiḥ khalakhalāyamāna|loha|śṛṅkhalā|bandha|pratiskhalac|caraṇaḥ, śūnya|mukha|puṣkara|piśunita|hṛdaya|saṃtāpo, roṣa|vaś'|ôttambhita|dṛṣṭir, guruka|kara|sphoṭita|dharaṇi|mārgo, rajanīṣv apy a|nidrā|sukham anubhūto 'si.

1.28 bhoḥ! yadi tāvad bandhanaṃ sukha|nibandhanaṃ bhavati, tat kasmāt tvaṃ, Dṛḍhavarmā baddha, iti Kaliṅga|rājasy' ôpari roṣaṃ badhnāsi?

1.31 jayatu jayatu devaḥ! eṣa khalu Vijayaseno 'mātyo, Rumaṇvān api pratīhāra|bhūmim upasthitau.

1.33 yad deva ājñāpayati.

1.63 yad deva ājñāpayati.

2.3 nanu bhaṇito 'sm' Îndīvarikayā yathā, «ārya, upavāsa|niyama|sthitā devī Vāsavadattā svasti|vācana|nimittaṃ śabdāyet' êti.» tad yāvad dhārā|gṛh'|ôdyāna|dīrghikāyāṃ snātvā devī|pārśvaṃ gatvā kukkuṭa|vādaṃ kariṣyāmi. anyathā katham asmābhiḥ sadṛśā brāhmaṇā rāja|kule pratigrahaṃ kurvanti?

2.3 katham, eṣa priya|vayasyo 'dya devyā virah'|ôtkaṇṭhā|vinodana|nimittaṃ dhārā|gṛh'|ôdyānam eva prasthitaḥ. tad yāvad vayasyena sah' âiva gatvā yath"|ôditam anuṣṭhāsyāmi.

2.7 svasti bhavate! vardhatāṃ bhagavān!

2.9 arcati khalu devī brāhmaṇam.

2.11 bhoḥ! īdṛśaḥ khalu brāhmaṇaḥ, yaś catur|veda|pañca|veda|ṣaḍ|veda|brāhmaṇa|sahasra|paryākule rāja|kule prathamam aham eva devī|sakāśāt svasti|vāyanaṃ labhe.

2.13 yad deva ājñāpayati.

2.15 bho ehi, gacchāvaḥ.

2.15 bho vayasya, paśya, paśya a|virata|pata|dvividha|kusuma|sukumāra|śilā|tal'|ôtsaṅgasya, parimala|nilīna|madhukara|bhara|bhagna|bakula|mālatī|latā|jālakasya, kamala|gandha|grahaṇ'|ôddāma|māruta|paryavabuddha|bandhūka|bandhanasya, a|virala|tamāla|taru|pihit'|ātapa|prakāśasy' âsya dhārā|gṛh'|ôdyānasaya saśrīkatām.

2.18 bho vayasya! etad api tāvat paśya, paśya. ya eṣo '|virala|patat|kusuma|nikaro 'dy' âpi patr'|ântara|galad|varṣ'|âvasāna|salila|bindur iva lakṣyate sapta|parṇa|pādapaḥ.

2.22 ājñapt" âsmi devyā Vāsavadattayā: «hañje Indīvarike, adya may" Âgastya|maharṣaye 'rgho dātavyaḥ. tad gaccha tvam. śephalikā|kusuma|mālāṃ laghu gṛhītv" āgacch'! êti. eṣ" âpy Āraṇyikā dhārā|gṛh'|ôdyāna|dīrghikāyā yāvad eva vikasitāni kamalāni n' âst'|âbhilāṣiṇā sūryeṇa mukulāyyante, tāvad eva laghv avacity' āgacchatv iti.» eṣā tapasvinī tāṃ dīrghikāṃ na jānāti. tad gṛhītvā tāṃ gamiṣyāmi.

2.22 ita ita, Āraṇyike, ehi.

2.24 tathā nāma tādṛśe vaṃśa utpannay", ânya|janam ājñāpya sthitayā, sāṃpratam parasya may" ājñaptiḥ kartavy", êti n' âsti khalu duṣ|karaṃ daivasya. atha vā mam' âiv' âiṣa doṣo, yena jānaty" âpi na vyāpādita ātmā. tat kiṃ sāṃpratam kariṣyāmi? atha vā duṣkaram idānīṃ mayā cintitam. varam ev' âitad api. na punar ātmano mah"|ârghaṃ prakāśayantyā mayā laghū|kṛta ātmā. tat kā gatiḥ? yathā|bhaṇitam anuṣṭhāsyāmi.

2.25 ita ehy, Āraṇyike.

2.26 iyam āgacchāmi.

2.26 hañje dūre kim ady' âpi dīrghikā?

2.27 eṣā śephālikā|gulm'|ântaritā. tad ehi avatarāvaḥ.

2.30 bhoḥ, tvaṃ tāvad etad anyac ca paśyann utkaṇṭhā|nirbharaṃ vinodayasy' ātmānam. mama punar|brāhmaṇasya svasti|vācana|vel" âtikrāmati. tad yāvad ahaṃ tvaritaṃ dīrghikāyāṃ snātvā devyāḥ sakāśaṃ gamiṣyāmi.

2.35 bho vayasya, paśya, paśya! k" âiṣā kusuma|parimala|sugandha|veṇi|madhukar'|āvalir, vidruma|lat'|âruṇa|hasta|pallavā, ujjvalat|tanu|komala|bāhu|latā satyaṃ pratyakṣa|car" îv' ôdyāna|devatā strī dṛśyate?

2.38 eṣā khalu devyāḥ paricārik" Êndīvarikā. tad gulm'|ântaritau bhūtvā paśyāvaḥ.

2.40 Āraṇyike, avacinu tvaṃ padmāni. aham apy etasmin nalinī|patre śephālikā|kusumāny avacitya devī|sakāśaṃ gamiṣyāmi.

2.43 halā Indīvarike! na śaknomi tvayā vinā muhūrtam apy atr' āsitum.

2.44 yādṛśam adya mayā devyā mantritaṃ śrutaṃ, tādṛśena ciram eva mayā vinā tvay" āsitavyam.

2.45 kiṃ devyā mantritam?

2.46 etat. «tad" âiṣ" âhaṃ mahā|rājena bhaṇitā yathā: ‹yad" âisā Vindhyaketu|duhitā vara|yogyā bhaviṣyati tad" âhaṃ smārayitavya iti.› tat sāṃprataṃ mahā|rājaṃ samārayāmi, yen' âsyā vara|cintā|paryākulo bhaviṣyati.»

2.48 tad gaccha tvam. na mama tvay" â|saṃbaddha|pralāpinyā prayojanam.

2.52 bho vayasya, paśya, paśya. āścaryam āścaryam! eṣā salila|calat|kara|pallava|prabhā|vistṛten' âpahasita|śobhaṃ karoti kamala|vanam avacinvatī.

2.55 hā dhik! hā dhik! ete khalv apare parityajya kamalinīṃ nīl'|ôt-pala|vanāni samāpatanto nipuṇataraṃ bādhamānā āyāsayanti māṃ duṣṭa|madhukarāḥ.

2.55 halā Indīvarike, paritrāyasva māṃ, paritrāyasva mām. ete khalu duṣṭa|madhukarāḥ paribhaviṣyanti.

2.56 bho vayasya, pūrṇās te manorathāḥ. yāvad eva garbha|dāsyāḥ sutā n' āgacchati, tāvad eva tvam api tūṣṇīko bhūtv" ôpasar-pa. eṣ" âpi salila|śabda|sūcitena pada|saṃcāreṇ', Êndīvarik" āgacchat' îti jñātvā tvām ev' âvalambiṣyate.

2.59 Indivarike, lagh'|ûpasarpa, lagh'|ûpasarpa. ākulī|kṛt" âsmi duṣ-ṭa|madhukaraiḥ.

2.63 kathaṃ, n' âiṣ" Êndīvarikā!

2.63 Indīvarikā, laghv āgaccha, laghv āgaccha! paritrāyasva mām.

2.64 bhavati, sakala|pṛthvī|paritrāṇa|samarthena Vatsa|rājena pari-trāyamāṇā ceṭīm Indīvarikām ākrandasi!

2.66 ayaṃ khalu sa mahā|rājo yasy' âhaṃ tātena dattā. sthāne khalu tātasaya pakṣa|pātaḥ.

2.68 āyāsitā khalv Āraṇyikā duṣṭa|madhukaraiḥ. tad yāvad upasar-pya samāśvāsayāmi. Āraṇyike mā bibhihi. eṣ" ôpagat" âsmi.

2.69 bho, apasar', âpasara. eṣā khalv Indīvarik" āgatā. etaṃ vṛttān-taṃ prekṣya devyai nivedayiṣyati.

2.69 tad idam eva kadalī|gṛhaṃ praviśya muhūrtaṃ tiṣṭhāvaḥ.

2.71 hañje Āraṇyike, kamala|sadṛśasya tava vadanasy' âyaṃ doṣo, yan madhukarā evam aparādhyanti.

2.71 tad" êhi, gacchāvaḥ. pariṇato divasaḥ.

2.73 hañje Indīvarike, atiśiśiratayā salilasy' ôru|stambha iva samut-pannaḥ. tac chanaiḥ śanair gacchāvaḥ.

2.74 tathā.

2.76 bho, ehi, niṣkrāmāvaḥ. tāṃ gṛhītv" âiṣā dāsyāḥ sut" Êndīvarikā gatā.

2.80 bhoḥ, tvam eva puttalikāṃ bhaṅktv" êdānīṃ rodiṣi. na mama khalu brāhmaṇasya vacanaṃ karoṣi.

2.82 tad idānīṃ vismṛtam. yathā «tūṣṇīko bhūtv" ôpasarp', êti» mayā bhaṇitam. atisaṃkaṭe bhavān praviśy'|âlīka|pāṇḍitya|durvidagdhatayā, «ayi visṛja viṣādam, ity» etair anyaiś ca kaṭu|vacanair nirbhartsya sāṃprataṃ kiṃ rodiṣi? punar apy upāyaṃ pṛcchasi.

2.84 jñātam eva, ko 'tra mūrkha iti. tat kim etena. astam|ay'|âbhilāṣī bhagavān sahasra|raśmiḥ. tad ehy, abhyantaram eva praviśāvaḥ.

3.3 ājñapt" âsmi devyā Vāsavadattayā: «hañje Manorame, yaḥ sa Sāṅkṛtyāyany" ārya|putrasya mama ca vṛttānto nāṭak'|ôpanibaddhas, tasya nartitavya|śeṣam adya yuṣmābhiḥ kaumudī|mah"|ôtsave nartitavyam iti.» hyaḥ khalv Āraṇyikayā priya|sakhyā śūnya|hṛdayay" ânyath" âiva nartitam. adya punar Vāsavadattā|bhūmikayā tayā yadi tathā kriyate tato 'vaśyaṃ devī kupyati. tat kutra tāvat tāṃ prekṣy' ôpālapsye?

3.3 es" Āraṇyik" ātman" âiva kim api kim api mantrayamāṇā dīrghikā|tīre kadalī|gṛhaṃ praviśati. tad gulm'|ântaritā bhūtvā śroṣyāmi tāvad asyā viśrabdha|jalpitāni.

3.5 hṛdaya durlabha|janaṃ prārthayamānaṃ tvaṃ kasmān māṃ duḥkhitāṃ karoṣi.

3.6 tad etad asyāḥ śūnya|hṛdayatvasya kāraṇam. kiṃ punar eṣā prārthayate? avahitā tāvac chroṣyāmi.

3.7 kathaṃ tathā nāma saumya|darśano bhūtvā mahā|rāja evaṃ saṃtāpayati mām! āścaryam, āścaryam!

3.7 atha vā mam' âiv' âiṣ" â|bhāgadheyatā. na punar mahā|rājasya doṣaḥ.

3.8 kathaṃ, mahā|rāja ev' âsyāḥ prārthanīyaḥ. sādhu, priya|sakhi, sādhu. ābhijātya|sadṛśas te 'bhilāṣaḥ.

3.9 kasmai tāvad etaṃ vṛttāntaṃ nivedya sahya|vedanam iva duḥkaṃ kariṣyāmi.

3.9 atha vā asti me hṛdaya|nirviśeṣā priya|sakhī Manoramā. tasyā apy etal lajjayā na pārayāmi kathayitum. sarvathā maraṇaṃ varjayitvā kuto me hṛdayasy' ânyā nirvṛtiḥ?

3.10 hā dhik! hā dhik! atibhūmiṃ gato 'syās tapasvinyā anurāgaḥ. tat kim idānīm atra kariṣyāmi?

3.11 ayaṃ sa uddeśo yasmin madhukarair āyāsyamān" âvalambya mahā|rājena samāśvāsit" âsmi, «bhīru, mā bibhīh'! îti.»

3.12 katham, eṣ" âpi dṛṣṭā mahā|rājena! sarvath" âsty asyā jīvitasy' ôpāyaḥ. yāvad upasṛtya samāśvāsayāmy enām.

3.12 yuktaṃ nāma hṛdayasy' âpi lajjitum.

3.13 hā dhik! hā dhik! sarvaṃ śrutam etayā. tad atra yuktam eva prakāśayitum.

3.13 priya|sakhi, mā kupya, mā kupya. lajj" âiv' âtr' âparādhyati.

3.14 sakhi, alaṃ saṅkayā. etan ma ācakṣva. satyam eva tvaṃ mahā|rājena dṛṣṭā, na v' êti?

3.15 śrutam eva priya|sakhyā sarvam.

3.16 yadi dṛṣṭā mahā|rājena tvaṃ, tad alaṃ saṃtāpitena. sa ev' êdānīṃ darśan'|ôpāya|paryākulo bhaviṣyati.

3.17 ayaṃ sakhī|janaḥ pakṣa|pātena mantrayate. ayi sakhi|pakṣa|pātini, devī|guṇa|nigaḍa|nibaddhe khalu tasmiñ jane kuta etat?

3.18 halā a|paṇḍite! kamalinī|baddh'|ânurāgo 'pi madhu|karo mālatīṃ prekṣy' âbhinava|ras'|āsvāda|lampaṭaḥ kutas tām an|āsādya sthitiṃ karoti?

3.19 kim eten' â|saṃbhāvitena? tad ehi. adhikaṃ khalu śarad|ātapena saṃtaptāny ady'|âpi na me 'ṅgāni saṃtāpaṃ muñcanti.

3.20 ayi lajj"|ākule na yuktam etad avasthāṃ gatay" âpi ta ātmā pracchādayitum.

3.22 ayi, aviśrambha|śīle, kim idānīṃ pracchādayasi? niśvāsa|nibha|vinirgato divasaṃ rātrim api tav' ânurāgo 'virata|patat|kusuma|śara|śara|nivaha|pravṛtta|huṅ|kāra|śabda iva na bhaṇati?

3.22 atha vā na khalv ayaṃ kāla upālambhasya. tad yāvan nalinī|patrāṇy asyā hṛdaye dāsyāmi.

3.22 samāśvasitu sakhī, samāśvasitu sakhī.

3.24 atimahān khalu priya|vayasyasy' Āraṇyikāyā upary anurāgaḥ. yena parityakta|rāja|kāryas tasyā eva darśan'|ôpāyaṃ cintayann ātmānaṃ vinodayati.

3.24 kutr' êdānīṃ tāṃ prekṣe? atha vā tatr' âiva tāvad dīrghikāyām anviṣyāmi.

3.25 pada|śabda iva śrūyate. tat kadalī|gulm'|ântarite bhūtvā prekṣāvahe tāvat, ka eṣa iti.

3.27 kathaṃ, sa eva mahā|rājasya pārśva|parivartī brāhmaṇaḥ.

3.28 kathaṃ, Vasantaka eva!

3.28 api nāma tathā bhavet.

3.29 kim idānīm Āraṇyikā satyam eva saṃvṛttā?

3.30 sakhi, rāja|vayasyaḥ khalu brāhmaṇas tvām uddiśya mantrayate. tat tāvad avahite śṛṇuvaḥ.

3.32 yadā tāvan mayā guru|madana|saṃtāpa|nissaha|śarīrasya priya|vayasyasya vacanena devyor Vāsavadattā|Padmāvatyor anyāsāṃ ca devīnāṃ bhavanāny anviṣyatā na sā dṛṣṭā, tadā «yatra dīrghikāyāṃ dṛṣṭ", edam api tāvat prekṣiṣya, ity» āgato 'smi. tad yāvad ih' âpi n' âsti. kim idānīṃ kariṣye?

3.33 śrutaṃ priya|sakhyā?

3.34 atha vā bhaṇita ev' âhaṃ vayasyena, «yadi tām anviṣyan na prekṣase, tat tato 'pi tāvad dīrghikātas tasyāḥ kara|tala|sparśa|dviguṇita|sukha|śītalāni nalinī|patrāṇi gṛhītv" āgacch', êti.» tat katham etāni jñātavyāni?

3.35 ayaṃ mam' âvasaraḥ.

3.35 Vasantaka, ehi. ahaṃ te jñāpayāmi.

3.36 kasya tvaṃ jñāpayasi? kiṃ devyāḥ? na khalu mayā kim api mantritam.

3.37 Vasantaka, alaṃ śaṅkayā. yādṛśy Āraṇyikāyāḥ kṛta ātmanaḥ priya|vayasyasy' âvasthā tvayā varṇitā, tato dviguṇatarā bhartur api kṛte mama priya|sakhyā avasthā. tat paśya, paśya.

3.39 saphalo me pariśramaḥ. svasti bhavatai!

3.41 ārya|Vasantaka, tava darśanen' âiv' âpagataḥ priya|sakhyāḥ saṃtāpo, yena svayam eva nalinī|patrāṇy apanayati. tad anugṛhṇātv ārya imāni.

3.42 ayi parihāsa|śīle. kasmān māṃ lajjayasi?

3.44 tiṣṭhantu tāvan nalinī|patrāṇi. atilajjālukā te priya|sakhī. tat katham etayoḥ samāgamo bhaviṣyati?

3.45 Vasantaka, evam iva.

3.47 sādhu, priya|sakhi, sādhu!

3.47 yāvad eva yuvāṃ nepathya|grahaṇaṃ kuruthas, tāvad ev' âham api vayasyaṃ gṛhītv" âgacchāmi.

3.49 atikopane, uttiṣṭh', ôttiṣṭha. nartitavyam asmābhis tasy' âiva nāṭakasya nartita|śeṣam. tad ehi. prekṣā|gṛham eva gacchāvaḥ.

3.49 idaṃ prekṣ"|āgāram. yāvad ehi, praviśāvaḥ.

3.49 sādhu, sādhu, sarvaṃ sajjī|kṛtam. devy" āgantavyam.

3.51 bhagavati, aho te kavitvam! yen' âitad gūḍha|vṛttāntaṃ nāṭak'|ôpanibaddhaṃ s'|ânubhavam apy asmākam āryaputra|caritam a|dṛṣṭa|pūrvam iva dṛśyamānam adhikataraṃ kautūhalaṃ vardhayati.

3.54 bhagavati, «sarvasya vallabo jāmātā bhavat', îti» jñāyata ev' âitat. tat kim etena kath"|ânubandhena? varaṃ tad eva nartitavyaṃ draṣṭum!

3.56 etu, etu bhaṭṭinī.

3.60 jayatu, jayatu bhaṭṭinī!

3.61 Manorame, atikrāntā khalu saṃdhyā. tad gacchatam. laghu gṛhṇītaṃ nepathyam.

3.62 yad devy ājñāpayati.

3.64 Āraṇyike, etair eva mad|aṅga|pinaddhair ābharaṇair nepathya|bhūmiṃ gatv" ātmānaṃ prasādhaya.

3.64 Manorame, tvam api Nalagiri|grahaṇa|parituṣṭena tāten' ārya|putrasya dattāny ābharaṇān' Îndīvarikā|sakāśād gṛhītvā nepathya|bhūmiṃ gatv" ātmānaṃ maṇḍaya, yena su|sadṛśī dṛśyase mahā|rājasya.

3.66 idam āsanam. upaviśatu bhaṭṭinī.

3.67 upaviśatu bhagavatī.

3.79 halā Kāñcanamāle, kasmāt punaś cirayaty ady' âpi vīṇ"|ācāryaḥ?

3.80 bhartṛdārike, dṛṣṭas ten' âika unmattaḥ. tasya vacanaṃ śrutvā citreṇa bhāvito 'pahasaṃs tiṣṭhati.

3.81 hañje, suṣṭhv etaṃ pṛcchati. «sadṛśāḥ sadṛśe rajanta, iti» dvāv atr' ônmattau.

3.84 ārya, yady evaṃ, laghu vīṇ"|ācāryaṃ visarjaya.

3.87 Kāñcanamāle, upanaya me Ghoṣavatīṃ, yāvad asyās tantrīḥ parīkṣe.

3.90 cirayati khalu mahā|rājaḥ. kiṃ na kathitaṃ Vasantakena? atha vā devyā bibheti? yad' îdānīm āgacchet tato ramaṇīyaṃ bhavet.

3.95 yadi māṃ na pratyāyayasy, eṣā Manoramā tava veṣaṃ dhārayantī tiṣṭhati. tad upasṛtya svayam eva pṛccha.

3.97 bhartaḥ, satyam eva. maṇḍay' âitair ābharaṇair ātmānam.

3.100 ete khalu rājāno dāsy" âpy evaṃ nartyante. aho kāryasya gurutā!

3.103 Kāncanamāle, tiṣṭhatu vīṇā. prakṣyāmi tāvat kim api.

3.106 pṛcchatu bhartṛ|dārikā.

3.107 satyam eva tāto mantrayate evaṃ, yathā «yadi vīṇāṃ vādayann apaharati māṃ Vatsa|rājo, 'vaśyaṃ bandhanān muñcām', îti»?

3.111 jayatu jayatv ārya|putraḥ!

3.115 kathaṃ! Manoram" âiṣā! mayā punar jñātam, ārya|putra eṣa iti. sādhu Manorame sādhu. śobhanaṃ nartitam.

3.118 hañje Indīvarike, baddhen' ārya|putreṇ' âhaṃ vīṇāṃ śikṣitā. tad asya kuru nīl'|ôtpala|dāmakena nigaḍanam.

3.120 Kāñcanamāle kathaya kathaya. nanu satyam eva mantrayate tāto «yadi vīṇāṃ vādayann apaharati māṃ Vatsa|rājas tato 'vaśyaṃ bandhanām muñcāmi iti.»

3.121 bhartṛdārike satyam. tathā kuru yathā Vatsa|rājasya' âvaśyam bahumatā bhavasi.

3.123 yady evaṃ, tad ādareṇa vādayiṣyāmi.

3.125 ghana|bandhana|saṃruddhaṃ gaganaṃ dṛṣṭvā Mānasam etum / abhilaṣati rāja|haṃso dayitāṃ gṛhītv" ātmano vasatim.

3.127 Vasantaka, paśya, paśya. priya|sakhī me nṛtyati.

3.128 dāsyāḥ sute, tvam api na dadāsi svaptum! yadā prabhṛti priya|vayasyen' Āraṇyikā dṛṣṭā, tadā prabhṛti tena saha mayā rātraṃ|divaṃ nidrā na dṛṣṭā. tad anyato niṣkramya svapsyāmi.

3.131 abhinava|rāga|kṣiptā madhu|karikā vāmakena kāmena / uttāmyati, prārthayamānā draṣṭuṃ priya|darśanaṃ dayitam.

3.134 upādhyāya, praṇamāmi.

3.136 ih' âiv' ôpaviśat' ûpādhyāyaḥ.

3.138 idānīm eva bhartṛ|dārikā vidyā|mānena paritoṣitā yuṣmābhiḥ. tad arhati ev' âiṣ" ôpādhyāya|pīṭhikāyāḥ.

3.141 bhartṛdārike, upaviśa. ko 'tra doṣaḥ? śiṣya|viśeṣā khalu tvam.

3.143 bhagavaty" âdhikaṃ kalpitaṃ kāvyam. na khalv ahaṃ tasmin kāla ek' āsane ārya|putreṇa sah' ôpaviṣṭā.

3.145 Kāñcanamāle, ciraṃ khalu mama vādayantyāḥ pariśramo jātaḥ. idānīṃ niḥsahāny aṅgāni. tan na śaknomi vādayitum.

3.146 upādhyāya, suṣṭhu pariśrāntā bhartṛ|dārikā. kapola|tala|baddha|sveda|lavāyāḥ, pasy', âsyā vepete agra|hastau. tat samāśvastā bhavatu muhūrtam.

3.149 bhagavati, adhikam etad api tvayā kṛtam. na khalv ahaṃ Kāñcanamālā|kāvyena vañcayitavyā.

3.151 apehi, Kāñcanamāle, apehi. na me bahumat" âsi.

3.152 yady ahaṃ tiṣṭhantī na bahu matā tad eṣā gacchāmi.

3.154 Kāñcanamāle, tiṣṭha, tiṣṭha. ayam asy' âgra|hastaḥ samarpitaḥ.

3.160 hā dhik! hā dhik! etāṃ Manoramāṃ sparśantyā an|artham eva me 'ṅgāni kurvanti.

3.161 bhagavati, paśya tvam. ahaṃ punar alīkaṃ na pārayāmi prekṣitum.

3.164 bhaṭṭini, Vasantakaś citra|śālā|dvāre prasuptas tiṣṭhati.

3.165 Vasantaka ev' âiṣaḥ.

3.165 rājñ" âpy atra bhavitavyam. tad bhodayitvā prakṣyāmi tāvad enam.

3.167 Manorame kiṃ nartitv"|āgataḥ priya|vayasyaḥ? atha vā nṛtyaty eva?

3.168 katham, ārya|putro nṛtyati? Manoram" êdānīṃ kutra?

3.169 eṣā citra|śālāyāṃ tiṣṭhati.

3.170 katham, anyath" âiva hṛdaye kṛtvā devyā mantritam, eten' âpi mūrkha|baṭuken' ânyath" âiva buddhvā sarvam ākulī|kṛtam.

3.171 sādhu, Manorame, sādhu! śobhanaṃ tvayā nartitam!

3.172 bhaṭṭini, na khalv aham atr' âparādhyāmi. etena khalu hat'|āśena balād alaṃkaraṇāni gṛhītvā dvāra|sthiten' êha niruddhā. na punar man' ākrandantyāḥ śabdo muraja|nirghoṣ'|ântaritaḥ ken' âpi śrutaḥ.

3.173 hañje, uttiṣṭha. jñātaṃ sarvam. Vasantakaḥ khalv Āraṇyikā|vṛttānta|nāṭake sūtra|dhāraḥ.

3.174 svayam eva cintaya: kutr' Āraṇyikā, kutra Vasantaka iti?

3.175 Manorame su|gṛhītaṃ kṛtv" âinam āgaccha tāvat. prekṣaṇīyam asya paśyāmi.

3.176 idānīṃ samāśvasit" âsmi.

3.176 hat'|āśa, idānīm anubhav' ātmano dur|nayasya phalam.

3.177 ārya|putra, pratihatam etad a|maṅgalam!

3.177 marṣatv ārya|putro yan Manoram" êti kṛtvā nīl'|ôtpala|dāmakena bandhito 'si.

3.184 ārya|putra, ko 'tra kupitaḥ?

3.188 Āraṇyike, tvaṃ kupit", êti saṃbhāvayann ārya|putraḥ «priye, prasīd', êti» prasādayati. tad upasarpa.

3.190 bhaṭṭini, na khalv ahaṃ kim api jānāmi.

3.191 Āraṇyike, tvaṃ kathaṃ na jānāsi? idānīṃ te śikṣayāmi. Indīvarike, gṛhāṇ' âinām.

3.192 bhavati, adya Kaumudī|mahotsave tava cittam apahartuṃ vayasyena prekṣaṇīyam anuṣṭhitham.

3.193 etaṃ yuṣmākaṃ dur|nayaṃ prekṣya hāso me jāyate.

3.198 hañje, nivṛttaṃ prekṣaṇakam. tad ehi. abhyantaram eva praviśāvaḥ.

4.3 aho dīrgha|roṣatā devyāḥ! etāvantaṃ kālaṃ baddhāyā api priya|sakhyā Āraṇyikāyā upary anukampāṃ na gṛhṇāti. sā tapasviny ātmano bandhanasya kleśena tathā na saṃtapyate, yathā bhartur darśana|nirāśatayā. īdṛśaṃ c' âsyā duḥkhaṃ yen' âdy' âiv' ātmānaṃ vyāpādayantī mayā katham api nivāritā. «etaṃ vṛttāntaṃ bhartre niveday', êti» Vasantakaṃ bhaṇitv" āgat" âsmi.

4.5 katham, anviṣyanty" âpi mayā bhagavatī Sāṅkṛtyāyanī na dṛṣṭā.

4.5 tad etām api tāvan Manoramāṃ prakṣyāmi.

4.5 Manorame, api jānāsi, kutra bhagavatī Sāṅkṛtyāyan", îti?

4.6 halā Kāñcanamāle, dṛṣṭā. kiṃ punas tayā prayojanam?

4.7 Manorame, adya devy" Âṅgāravatyā lekhaḥ preṣitaḥ. tasmin vācite bāṣpa|pūrṇa|nayanā dṛḍhaṃ saṃtaptum ārabdhā devī. tad vinodana|nimittaṃ tasyā bhagavatīm anviṣyāmi.

4.8 halā, kiṃ punas tasmiĩ lekha ālikhitam?

4.9 «yā mama bhaginī sā tava janany eva. tasyā bhartā Dṛḍhavarmā tātas te. tat tava kim etad ākhyātavyam? tasya samadhikaṃ saṃvatsaraṃ Kaliṅga|hatakena baddhasya. tan na yuktam etaṃ vṛttāntam aniṣṭaṃ śrutvā samīpa|sthitasya samarthasya bhartus ta evam udāsīnatvam avalambitum iti.»

4.10 halā Kāñcanamāle. yadā tāvad «ayaṃ vṛttānto bhaṭṭinyai na ken' âpi vijñāpitavya, iti» bhartr" ājñaptaṃ, tat kena punar idānīṃ sa lekhaḥ śrāvitaḥ?

4.11 anuvācya tūṣṇīṃ bhūtāyā mama hastād gṛhītvā svayam eva bhaṭṭinyā vācitaḥ.

4.12 tena gaccha tvam. eṣā khalu devī tay" âiva saha danta|valabhyāṃ tiṣṭhati.

4.13 tena hi bhaṭṭinī|sakāśaṃ gamiṣyāmi.

4.15 ciraṃ khalu ma Āraṇyikā|sakāśād āgatāyāḥ. dṛḍhaṃ ca nirviṇṇā sā tapasviny ātmano jīvitena. kadā cid atyāhitaṃ bhavet. tat tatr' âiva gacchāmi.

4.20 bhagavati, atyṛjuk" êdānīṃ tvam. yasya mayā na kāryaṃ, tasya madīyena kiṃ kāryaṃ? mātur yuktaṃ mam' âitad ālikhitum. sā punar na jānāty, ady' âpi tādṛśī na Vāsavadatt" êti. tava punar eṣa Āraṇyikā|vṛttāntaḥ pratyakṣaḥ. tat katham etad bhaṇasi?

4.22 bhagavati, etad atra satyam. tathā hāsit" âsmi yena bhagavatyāḥ purato lajjayā katham api tiṣṭhāmi. tat kiṃ tadīyayā kathayā? nanv eten' âiva pakṣa|pāten' âitāvatīṃ bhūmiṃ nīt" âsmi.

4.25 manorathā idānīm ete bhagavatyāḥ.

4.28 bho vayasya muñca viṣādam. ahaṃ ta upāyaṃ kathayiṣyāmi.

4.30 bhoḥ, tvaṃ tāvad aneka|samara|saṃghaṭṭa|prabhāva|bāhu|śālī. punar apy aneka|gaja|turaga|padāti|durviṣaha|bala|samuditaḥ. tat sarva|bala|saṃdohen' ântaḥ|puraṃ su|pīḍitaṃ kṛtv" êdānīm ev' Āraṇyikāṃ mocaya.

4.32 kim atr' â|śakyam? yatas tāvat kubja|vāmana|vṛddha|kañcuki| varjito manuṣyo 'paro n' âsti tatra.

4.34 bho, mās'|ôpavāsaṃ kṛtvā jīvitaṃ dhāraya. evaṃ devī Caṇḍī prasatsyati.

4.38 bho, gaccha tvam. ahaṃ punar idānīm eva bandhanāt katham api paribhraśy' āgato 'smi. tan na gamiṣyāmi.

4.44 ārya|putra, vilakṣa idānīṃ tvaṃ bhavasi!

4.53 atisukhito nanv asi. kim idānīṃ duḥkhitaṃ janaṃ vikārayasi? uttiṣṭha. ko 'tra kupitaḥ?

4.62 yady evaṃ, priyaṃ me.

4.64 jayatu jayatu bhartā! eṣa khalu Vijayaseno Dṛḍhavarma|kañcuki|sahito harṣa|samutphulla|locanaḥ priyaṃ nivedayitu|kāmo dvāre tiṣṭhati.

4.65 bhagavati, yathā tarkayāmi, paritoṣit" âsmy ārya|putreṇ' êti.

4.68 tathā.

4.78 ayi bhagavati, abhijānāsy etaṃ Kañcukinam?

4.83 anugṛhīt" âsmi.

4.84 īdṛśe 'bhyudaye 'smin rāja|kula etat karaṇīyam.

4.84 guru|pūjā.

4.84 brāhmaṇasya sat|kāraḥ.

4.84 sarva|bandhana|mokṣa iti.

4.86 bhavati, kathaṃ tvaṃ na kim apy atra samādiśasi?

4.87 mocitā khalu hat'|āśen' Āraṇyikā.

4.89 yathā bhagavatyai rocate.

4.96 ārya Kañcukin, kathaṃ me bhaginī paribhraṣṭā?

4.101 bhaṭṭini, prāṇa|saṃśaye vartate sā tapasvinī.

4.102 kiṃ punas tvaṃ Priyadarśanā|vṛttāntaṃ jānāsi?

4.103 na khalv ahaṃ Priyadarśanā|vṛttāntaṃ jānāmi. eṣā khalv Āraṇyikā kalya|vyapadeśen' ānītaṃ viṣaṃ pītvā prāṇa|saṃśaye vartata, ity evaṃ mayā niveditam. tat paritrāyatāṃ bhaṭṭinī.

4.105 hā dhik, hā dhik! Priyadarśanā|duḥkham api me 'ntaritam Āraṇyikā|vṛttāntena. atidurjanaḥ khalu lokaḥ. kadā cin mām anyathā saṃbhāvāyiṣyati. tad etad atra yuktam.

4.105 Manorame, laghv ih' âiv' ānaya tām. Nāga|lokād gṛhīta|viṣa|vidya ārya|putro 'tra kuśalaḥ.

4.108 halā Manorame, kasmād idānīṃ māṃ andhakāraṃ praveśayasi?

4.109 hā dhik! hā dhik! dṛṣṭir apy asyāḥ saṃkrāntā viṣeṇ' âiva.

4.109 bhaṭṭini, laghu paritrāyasva, laghu paritrāyasva. gurū|bhūtam asyā viṣam.

4.110 ārya|putra, uttiṣṭh', ôttiṣṭha. laghu vipadyate khalv eṣā tapasvinī.

4.112 ārya, Vindhyaketor duhitā. taṃ vyāpādya Vijayasenen' ānītā.

4.114 ārya|putra, praitrāyasva, paritrāyasva. mama bhaginī vipadyate.

4.118 sakhi, kiṃ te bodhaḥ?

4.118 sakhi, nanu bhaṇāmi, kiṃ te bodha iti?

4.119 yad etad avasthāy" âpi mayā na mahā|rājo dṛṣṭaḥ.

4.123 Priyadarśane, uttiṣṭh', ôttiṣṭha! paśy', âiṣa mahā|rājas tiṣṭhati. katham, vedan" âpy asyā naṣṭā? kim idānīṃ may" âparāddham a|jānatyā, yena kupitā n' âlapasi? tat prasīda, prasīda! uttiṣṭh', ôttiṣṭha! na khalu punar aparātsyāmi.

4.123 hā daiva|hataka! kim idānīṃ may" âpakṛtaṃ yen' âitad avasthāṃ gatā me bhaginy ādarśitā?

4.125 bho vayasya, kathaṃ tvaṃ mūḍha iva tiṣṭhasi? n' âiṣa viṣādasya kālaḥ! viṣamā khalu gatir viṣasya. tad darśay' ātmano vidyā|prabhāvam.

4.127 bho, etat salilam.

4.129 ārya|putra, diṣṭyā pratyujjīvitā me bhaginī.

4.132 Manorame, ciraṃ khalu supt" âsmi.

4.133 bho vayasya nirvyūḍhaṃ te vaidyatvam.

4.135 ārya|putra, kim idānīm apy eṣ" ânyath" âiva karoti?

4.140 kathaṃ Kañcuky ārya|Vinayavasuḥ!

4.140 hā tāta! hā mātaḥ!

4.142 ehy, alīka|śīle. idānīm api tāvad bhaginī|snehaṃ darśaya.

4.142 idānīṃ samāśvasit" âsmi.

4.143 bhavati, tvaṃ bhaginīṃ gṛhītvā kaṇṭha evaṃorituṣṭ" âsi. vaidyasya pāritoṣikaṃ vismṛtam.

4.144 Vasantaka, na vismṛtam.

4.145 vaidya, prasāraya hastam. bhaginyā agra|hastaṃ te pāritoṣikaṃ dāpayiṣyāmi.

4.149 kas tvam a|grahītum? pratham eva tāten' êyaṃ dattā.

4.150 bho, mānanīyā khalu devī. m" âsyāḥ pratikūlaṃ kuru.

4.153 ārya|putra, ato 'pi paraṃ kiṃ te priyaṃ kriyatām?

NOTES

Bold *references are to the English text;* ***bold italic*** *references are to the Sanskrit text. An asterisk (*) in the body of the text marks the word or passage being annotated.*

The Lady of the Jewel Necklace

1.3 **Benediction**: Sanskrit plays generally begin with verses of benediction, which foreshadow the action of the play that follows. Traditionally, they are spoken by the stage director (literally, the "string-holder" or "curtain-puller"), who, being a Brahmin, is qualified to speak a blessing. Since there is no stage direction for the stage director to enter before he speaks in the prelude, I am assuming that he enters before the benediction, and have inserted that direction. I have also put in the time and the scene.

1.4 The verses of benediction in this play are dedicated to the three-eyed god Shiva (here called **Shambhu**, "The one who brings contentment"). In this verse Shiva is with Párvati, the **Daughter of the Mountain**, his wife. She is bringing him **flowers** to propitiate him in his divine aspect, perhaps on the occasion, before their marriage, when she hoped to persuade him to marry her. She experiences three of the eight traditional signs of erotic excitement: goose-flesh, trembling, and sweating. The conceit of this verse is that in her nervousness, and prevented by her breasts' weight from standing up high enough to raise her hands over Shiva's head, Párvati spills the flowers meant for Shiva, and those flowers fall between them and, as it were, on the audience. The erotic ambivalence of Párvati foreshadows that of Ságarika in Act One, and the flowers will be Ságarika's flowers.

1.6 Here Shiva's wife is named **Gauri**, "the Golden One," and the encounter takes place on their wedding night. Again she is ambivalent, and Shiva laughs at her ambivalence. The god's laughter is auspicious and forms the blessing "good for you," literally "for your auspiciousness" (***śivāya***), which also means "for Shiva." This verse foreshadows the moment when Ságarika will be aroused in Údayana's presence and by his touch, in Act Two.

1.8 The verses [1], [2], and [3] of the benediction are generally believed to be by Harsha and a part of this play; verse [4] is accepted by many, though not all, editors. This verse, [2a], is rejected by most, including KALE, but it is about jealousy, a central theme of the play, and the figure of speech it employs, called *śleṣa*, or paronomasia, is well suited to express the play as a whole, a story of mistaken identities. Read in one way, the central lines are spoken by Párvati, the Daughter of the Mountain (Himálaya), to Shiva, and refer to the myth in which Shiva burnt to ashes Kama, the god of love, sex, and pleasure, when Kama was attempting to force Shiva to marry Párvati. Kama's banner is emblazoned with the image of a sea-monster that he had killed (while the ocean has sea serpents that function like banners). Shiva now holds in his hair the river Ganges, who goes on three paths (the Milky Way in the sky, the Ganges on earth, and the Sarásvati under the earth); his relationship with the Ganges excites Párvati's jealousy. Shiva's neck became blue-black when he swallowed the poison that came out of the ocean when the gods churned it to obtain the elixir of immortality. Read in a second way, the central verses are spoken by Lakshmi, goddess of good fortune, Vishnu's consort (who is also sometimes called the Daughter of the Ocean), to Vishnu, and refer to another aspect of that same myth of churning, for Vishnu became a tortoise who supported the mountain used as the churn; the churning produced many things, including Lakshmi. Now, as Krishna, an incarnation of Vishnu, Vishnu excites Lakshmi's jealousy by his attentions to the crooked hunchback Kubja, whom Krishna made both whole and beautiful, and who then fell in love with him. (*Bhāgavata Purāṇa* 10.1.47.1–10).

1.10 Shiva is here telling his wife the story of his destruction of the sacrifice of **Daksha**, who was the father of Sati, Shiva's previous wife, now reincarnate as Párvati. Daksha disapproved of Shiva as a son-in-law and failed to invite him to his sacrifice; this insult to her husband inspired Sati to commit suicide in a fire that she generated from within herself, and to avenge her death Shiva simultaneously destroyed Daksha's sacrifice and carried it out, using Daksha himself as the sacrificial beast whom he beheaded. The **mischievous mob** consists of the crowd of Shiva's ***gaṇa***s, goblins and other impish demigods in his train. The **three fires** are those that every Hindu householder ideally maintains: the householder's fire, received from his father; the fire for oblations; and the ceremonial fire. The three eyes are Shiva's, as in verse I.I. This laugh is louder and rougher than the one in the previous verse. (I prefer the reading of ***aṭṭa*** to that of *āṭṭa*.) This verse foreshadows the fire in Act Four.

I.12 Harsha, as is common with kings (cf. Rama·chandra), is here given an epithet that likens him to the **moon**. Both he and king Údayana are, moreover, said to be in the lunar dynasty, ultimately descended from the moon. M. R. KALE suggests that the line about the **bulls of the twice-born** (that is, the preeminent Brahmins) implies that they had been harassed in the past, perhaps even by Harsha himself during his pro-Buddhist period, but would no longer be so, and that the triumph of the moon is Harsha's triumph over his own Buddhist tendencies, while the **reverence to the gods** is his return to the Hindu fold. As a result of this, the Hindu gods, pleased, will send rain, the moon (also called the lord of herbs) will encourage growth, and there will be **abundant harvests**. This verse foreshadows the final victory of Údayana and his kingdom in Act IV.

I.14 Plays in ancient India were often presented on the occasion of festivals, in this case the **Spring festival** in honor of Kama, celebrated to this day as the Holi festival. The stage director acknowledges that this play borrows a well-known plot but boasts that it has made new variations on the old theme.

I.14 The play in question is a *nāṭikā*.

I.15 Harsha is the king of Vatsa; for Vatsa, and all geographical references, see the map on p. 59.

1.21 Like the benediction, this verse hints at events in the play to follow. Yaugándharáyana is about to reveal the second meaning: Ratnávali will be rescued from the sea, brought from a distant land, and so forth.

1.22 "**Son of an actor**," more precisely "son of Bharata," Bharata being the author of the textbook on acting.

1.31 He uses the word ***Madana***, passion, another name for Kama.

1.32 Another paronomastic verse, referring simultaneously to the king, who has silenced **talk of war** (since he has no more enemies), has the people's **love**, has a jester named **Vasántaka** ("little Spring"), and can call the spring **festival** his own (because he is its patron); and to the god Kama, the god whose **bow** is made of **flowers** (as are his arrows), who cannot talk of his body (because Shiva burnt it to ashes), whose wife is **Rati** ("Love," or "Sexual Pleasure"), whose season is **Spring**, and who can call the Spring festival his because it is in his honor.

1.35 That the king (followed, later, by other people) is said to enter, seated, tells us that "enter" may mean "is revealed to the audience," perhaps by the removal of a curtain.

1.37 The jester, even though he is a Brahmin, and the women (even the queen) speak a dialect, Prakrit, rather than the Sanskrit spoken by the (other) upper-class men.

1.39 Queen Vásava·datta is the daughter of **Pradyóta**.

1.40 ⌜***paḍa/vāsa***⌟ (*paṭa/vāsa*) usually and literally designates cloth garments, but here it seems to mean a perfumed powder or, as glossed by the dictionary called the *Amarakoṣa*, a red-yellow powder, such as people squirt on one another during Holi celebrations to this day.

1.42 The **god of wealth** is Kubéra. **Kaushámbi** is the capital city of the kingdom of Vatsa; see Introduction and map (p. 59). The **ashóka** (or *Jonesia Asoka Saraca*) is a small, leguminous tree with magnificent red-yellow flowers.

1.47 "**Lounge-lizards**" translates ***bhujaṅ/ga***, which means serpents ("who move on their bellies") but also designates (i) a class of voluptuaries, paramours of prostitutes and parasites of princes, and (ii) the demigods called *nāgas*, who live in the underworld, are serpents below the waist and anthropomorphic above, and have jewels embedded in their hoods, in contrast with the human snakes who wear a lot of jewels.

1.49 What I have somewhat literally translated as the **Two-feet Suite** (***dvi/padī/khaṇḍa***) is a song in a meter that is actually divided into four quarters or feet (with 13 metrical units in each).

1.51 The **wind from the south** is cool and perfumed, hence welcomed by lovers.

1.52 The **bákula** (*Mimusops Elengi*), also called the Spanish cherry, is a large, tall tree with dark green leaves, said to blossom when a beautiful woman sprays it with water from her mouth. The sweet fruit of this species is eaten, and the small, round white flowers have a lovely perfume. The **ashóka** is said to blossom when a beautiful woman kicks it.

1.55 I follow KALE here in taking ***pīḍay" êva*** ("**as if in pain**") with each line; the **hair**, personified, is loathe to give up its **garland**; the **anklets** cry out in pain; the **necklace** in its pain strikes her breast as if to try, in vain, to stop her from dancing; and she stoops in pain under the weight of her **breasts**.

1.62 ⌜***khaṇḍa***⌟ means a "**piece**" of music, or of molasses candy. Brahmins in general, and jesters in particular, are said to be too fond of food.

1.70 The words for "command" and "report" are very much alike (⌜***ā-ṇavedi***⌟/*ā-jñāpayati* and ⌜***vi-ṇṇavedi***⌟/*vi-jñāpayati*), both based on the causative of the verb "to know" (*jñā*), and the women accidentally use the wrong one, before they quickly correct themselves.

1.75 The "**auspicious present**" is the ⌜***sotthi/vāaṇa***⌟ (*svasti/vācana*), literally "saying, 'It is good,'" that a person performing a vow gives to a Brahmin, who speaks a blessing in return. It usually consists of sweets, but sometimes also rice, cloth, and so forth.

1.82 The **Málayas** are a range of mountains forming an eastern spur to the southern Ghats, south of Mysore. The sandal trees and cardamom that grow there perfume the winds that blow from there through north India in the spring.

1.86 Several conventions are embedded in this verse, including those noted for 1.52 [verse 14] (women spraying/kicking trees to make them bloom in spring) and another, the custom of perfuming wine with flowers. The **chámpaka** (*Michelia Campaka*) is a large tree with fragrant yellow blossoms, related to jasmine; the chámpakas are said to shine at last because they enjoy the mouthfuls of wine the women have sprayed on them and they blossom when the women smile on them.

1.93 The **mádhavi vine** (*Gaertnera Racemosa* or *Laguncularia*, white buttonwood) has fragrant white flowers. Women in Sanskrit dramas, and occasionally men, adopt certain plants and animals from time to time. The verb also means "to take prisoner" or "to marry."

1.93 The **new jasmine** is a kind of double jasmine, with large and fragrant white flowers. The king's efforts to make it bloom out of season will be realized in Act Two.

1.98 The things needed for the ritual would be flowers, perfumes, fragrant powders, and so forth.

1.100 The **carelessness of the servants** consists, as we are about to learn, in their failure to keep Ságarika behind, with the mynah bird, where she would have been safely out of the king's sight.

1.101 Kama is **bodiless** because Shiva destroyed his body; invisible now, he pervades the erotic world.

1.101 At this point, Ságarika is watching the queen, unseen; and now the king is about to watch the queen, also unseen; but the king and Ságarika do not yet see one another.

1.102 When Shiva burnt Kama to ashes, Kama was reborn as **Pradyúmna**, the son of Krishna and Rúkmini.

1.106 The **bow** as well as the arrows of Kama are made of flowers, and the staff of the bow is smaller in the middle, like her **waist**, made smaller by her **vow**, probably a fast, perhaps to keep her straying husband's love.

1.114 **Kusúmbha** flowers (*Carthamus Tinctorius*), safflower, are bright yellowish-red.

1.116 ***Smara*, Memory**, is another name of the god of love.

1.118 Kama, having no body, cannot feel what is felt by the image that represents him. The word for "**festival**" (***utsava***) also means "joy": her touch is both a joy and an expression of the festival.

1.123 The **sinduvára tree** (*Vitex Negundo*, known in China as the "Five-Leaved Chaste Tree") has tiny pink and white blossoms.

1.123 The word ⌜***daṃsaṇa***⌟ (*darśana*, "sight") has a built-in pun, for it designates both the auspicious sight that a person has of a god or king or other special person and the auspicious gaze that that special person casts on the onlooker.

1.128 Údayana's name means "rising." His **feet** rob the lotuses of their lustre because they are more beautiful than lotuses, while the **rays of the moon** rob them because they make the day-lotuses close up at night.

1.131 The moon, lord of the night, makes the eastern face of the sky pale, just as the thought of her lover makes the woman pale.

1.135 The bees' humming is put to shame by the sweeter singing of the courtesans.

2.7 ⌜***Siri/pavvata***⌟ (*Śrī/parvata*, also called *Śrī/śaila*) is a holy mountain, still visited by pilgrims, and believed to be the site of miracles.

2.7 "**What plants want**" is a ⌜***dohalaa***⌟ (*dohada*, literally, "heartsickness"), a term that usually means what pregnant women long to eat (hence a kind of morning-sickness-preventative). Here, however, it means what a plant, pregnant with its blossoms, wants to eat, a kind of organic fertilizer.

2.7 This verb, which occurs in Act One in the sense of "adopt" (when Vásava·datta "adopted" a certain flower), here, I think, is better translated with the male equivalent, "marry."

2.13 She decides she cannot blame Kama for his lack of chivalry toward a woman (the lawbooks have a rule against striking women) because he has no body and therefore no heart, no opportunity for compassion.

2.13 "**This bad omen**" is her falling in love with a person beyond her reach; unrequited love often ends in death, in Sanskrit literature.

2.13 "**What I want**" probably means looking at the king. SYLVAIN LÉVI translates it, "satisfy the desires of my eyes."

2.15 Though there are no stage directions here, Susángata says her entire speech to herself, as does Ságarika.

2.15 KALE says that the reference to a **swan in a lotus pond** means that king Údayana is a suitable person for her to be in love with.

2.19 "**How clever**" may mean both "How well you paint" and "How cunning you are to conceal your desire for the king."

2.23 "**Ace Reporter**" is my translation of ⌜***medhāviṇī***⌟ (*medhāvinī*), which means, more literally (and according to the *Amarakoṣa*), "one who has the faculty of retaining memory," which KALE takes to signify that she will reveal secrets.

2.28 Ságarika is in the power of someone else, namely, Vásava·datta, who also happens to be the wife of the man out of her reach.

2.34 The **people of the third sex** are ***varṣa/vara***s (literally, "semen-withholders"), who guard the harem. Some commentaries call them eunuchs and say that they are castrated in order to serve in the harem; but others say that they have merely taken a vow of chastity or continence, or are simply "neither men nor women" through their inherently liminal sexuality. SYLVAIN LÉVI says that the *varṣa/dhara* (*sic*) is an effeminate servant, castrated, employed in love affairs. The **Scattered Wanderers** (an ingenious etymology that Harsha plays upon) are Kirátas, hill tribesmen who guard the women's quarters. All of these characters people the women's quarters of the palace, or the harem, where the women and children live.

2.35 **Tamála trees** (*Xanthochymus pictorius*) have dark bark and thick, dark green leaves, and therefore provide a dark place to hide.

2.49 The ***madana*** ("Passion") tree may be the thorn-apple (*Vanguiera Spinosa*). She is beginning to yawn because she is sleepless from making love all night.

2.53 The magic Káustubha jewel hangs around the **throat of the best of men** (Vishnu). Magic spells keep the serpents and serpent-people (*nāgas*) trapped under the earth. The *Rāmāyaṇa* tells us that Megha·nada (also called Índrajit), the son of Rávana, killed Rama's brother Lákshmana and their monkey allies, but the monkey Hánuman brought a magic herb from a distant mountain and revived them.

2.106 **Lake Mánasa** ("The Lake of the Mind"), on Mount Kailása, is where geese and swans are said to migrate each year to mate.

2.108 The moon that is her face is unprecedented because it is always full and always present, unlike the real moon. The god Brahma sits on a lotus, and lotuses close at night.

2.118 "**This person**" is probably the king, whom Ságarika accuses Susángata of insulting by attributing to him an infatuation with a person like herself. But "this person" can also refer to the speaker, in this case Ságarika herself.

2.125 It is a conventional sign of beauty in a woman's body that it has three folds of skin in the midriff.

2.166 Brahma, the Creator, has four heads.

2.174 Shri, the **Goddess of Fortune**, also called Lakshmi, was churned from the ocean along with the *pārijāta* tree, the tree of paradise, and the ambrosia. That Ságarika combines the properties of both the goddess and the tree makes her unprecedented. Perspiration is one of the signs of erotic excitement (as in 2.130 [verse 12]).

2.178 I have used the phrase "**Queen Vásava·datta all over again,**" with its ambiguous meaning (i) "Ságarika is just like Vásava·datta" (which is what the jester means) and (ii) "Here comes the queen again" (which is what the king mistakenly thinks the jester means), to translate ⌜***avarā Vāsavadattā***⌟ (*aparā Vāsavadattā*), "another Vásava·datta," which the jester intends as "a second Vásava·datta" and the king hears as "another woman, Vásava·datta."

2.186 The king does not yet know that Ságarika is Ratnávali, but the verse contains a double entendre on "jewel necklace" which is a kind of Freudian slip, a truth that he does not consciously know to be true.

2.211 When the queen has caught the king red-handed with his portrait of Ságarika, the king struggles to justify his far-fetched and hastily improvised claim that he has painted, out of sheer imagination, a woman he claims he has never seen.

2.212 Every Brahmin is given a **sacred thread** at his initiation, and he never takes it off. When the jester says, "**We never saw such a girl before,**" he is both lying and telling the truth, for the adjective "never seen before" can describe Ságarika's unprecedented beauty, but of course they have indeed seen her earlier on this day and at that time already remarked that she was like none before.

2.213 The word she uses here for **coincidence** (⌜***ghuṇ'/akkharaṃ***⌟, *ghuṇ'/âkṣaram*) literally designates an alphabet letter eaten into a page by a bookworm, somewhat like our quantum metaphor of the odds against a monkey randomly typing out the works of Shakespeare.

3.26 To be reduced to the **five elements** is to die. The five arrows cause five progressive stages of love-sickness, from early infatuation to death.

3.28 The king clearly intends this to apply to Ságarika, to whom he has just referred. But he has also mentioned the queen, and it seems to me that this verse could just as easily apply to her. This the king does not see; but does Harsha?

3.35 **Brihas·pati** is the counselor of Indra, king of the gods, and said to be the original author of the *Arthaśāstra*, the ancient Indian textbook of political science.

3.43 The idea is that the sun, worried about the strength of a one-wheeled chariot, steals a second wheel from the sky, the wheel formed by the rays that radiate out into the sky at sunset.

3.45 The **sun** (*sūrya*) is also (according to the commentator) a specific term for a type of *nāyaka* or hero in a drama. The double entendre applies to the lotus plant and to a woman, whom the hero consoles as he leaves either because, for the sun, it is the time for sunset or because the lover has a rendezvous with another woman. The day-lotus closes at sunset and opens at sunrise. The epithet Lotus-eyes has a double application, meaning one whose lotuses are its eyes (the plant) or one whose eyes are like lotuses (the woman). The sun puts his rays on the mountain as he speaks to the plant, and the lover puts his hands on the woman's bowed head as he speaks to her.

3.48 The **darkness** makes the sparse forests seem dense as it fills in the spaces between them.

3.50 **Shiva's neck** became dark when he swallowed the poison that emerged from the churned ocean.

3.77 This line seems to me to be out of place here; it is far more appropriate when it appears again, verbatim, later in this Act (3.92).

3.78 Indians see a **hare** in the moon where Europeans see a man's face.

3.80 This can mean both that on a particular day during the monsoon, the heat becomes intense right before the downpour, or that in the days before the onset of the monsoon season, the heat is most intense. Both are true.

3.87 This verse is so laden with every cliché in the Sanskrit thesaurus for beautiful women that it may be meant to show how totally out of his mind Údayana is at this moment. Vásava·datta's scorn for the way the king is talking may be literary as well as sexual.

3.97 There are textual problems with the text of this verse, such as the absence of a subject, which KALE fudges by taking "face-moon" both as a locative, which is how it appears in the verse (***vaktr'|êndau***), and as a nominative (*vaktr'|ênduḥ*), which does not appear. But the meaning is fairly straightforward: the primary paronomastic pun is on her face as the moon, while the secondary paronomastic pun is on Kama as the ocean (with a large fish (*jhaṣa*) on or as its banner). The **bimba** fruit (*Momordica Monadelpha*) is bright red; *bimba* also means a disk, particularly the lunar disk. Her **moon face** eclipses the beauty of lotuses both in the sense of destroying it, because lotuses close at night, and surpassing it, because she is more beautiful than they are. The ocean swells when the moon rises and Kama increases when she is near. And Hindu mythology tells us both that the gods store their ambrosia in the moon and that the gods churned the ocean to obtain the ambrosia when they lost it; her face, the poet says, also has that ambrosia.

3.106 Women in ancient India would paint the palms of their hands, soles of their feet, and lips with a red dye, called **lac**, made from an insect similar to the one that supplies cochineal. ***Uparāga*** means both "redness" and "an eclipse," which makes the moon red; anger is like that eclipse, reddening her face.

3.111 There is no stage direction here, but Vásava·datta and Kánchana·mala are said to enter a few pages later, and clearly they are not present during the intervening scene.

3.116 The "**slip**," like a Freudian slip, is more precisely a stumbling, usually (in Sanskrit poetry) a stumbling on the name (*nāma|skhalitam*), calling one woman by the name of another (particularly in the throes of passion), which is precisely what Údayana has done here, spectacularly. Once again the king's words might refer to Vásava·datta or to Ságarika, or to both. The Jester refers to both women in his response to this poem. "**Day by day**" suggests that the queen is meant here, since the king has just met Ságarika; but several days have passed since Act One, and it is Ságarika for whom he first voices concern after the verse. He has offended both women and fears that he has driven them to the brink of suicide; though Ságarika has not yet learned about all this, she is the one who will in fact attempt suicide, though even then his assumption is that Vásava·datta is the suicidal one.

3.137 "**A bolt out of the blue**" translates the Sanskrit phrase "rain without clouds" (***an/abhrā vṛṣṭiḥ***), which is used in the same way, to denote unexpected good fortune. The jester has already replied to this phrase with the metaphor of the hurricane to describe Vásava·datta's unexpected and unwelcome intrusion, in Act Two.

4.27 The commentary explains that the oaths were deceptive because he had to say words that would, on the one hand, make the queen trust him and, on the other hand, not actually lie (presumably about his intentions toward Ságarika). The king is, as we have seen, a past master of paronomasia.

4.29 The idea is that Ságarika became liquefied when he touched her, but was still able to enter his heart through the five paths made by the five arrows of Kama, the Intoxicator.

4.42 A difficult verse. The first part seems to mean that although the king did not oblige Ságarika by following her into death, his breath should oblige him by leaving him and thus accomplishing what he failed to accomplish. The second part seems to mean that if the breaths do not leave of their own accord he will kill himself and thus steal them, to catch up with Ságarika who has had such a head start. Female elephants, contrary to European assumptions about elephants, walk very gracefully, and women in Sanskrit poems are often said to walk like them, though not to look like them.

4.79 "**All-powerful**" translates ⌜*Savvasiddhi*⌟ (*Sarvasiddhi*), literally, possessing all of the eight magical powers or siddhis—making yourself invisible, very small, flying, and so forth.

4.84 **Indra** is the king of the gods, and master of illusion and magic. **Shámbara** is the name of a demon who is the patron of magic; he abducted Pradyúmna, who killed him. Magicians carry peacock fans that they wave in the course of their tricks, like magic wands.

4.94 Vásava·datta also comes from **Ujjain**, the capital of Avánti, where her father was the ruler.

4.101 **Siddhas** are demigods with magical powers, the eight siddhis. (The seer who made the prediction that Yaugándharáyana refers to at the very start of the play was a Siddha.) Cháranas are heavenly bards who travel about in heaven. The **women of the gods** are the heavenly courtesans or nymphs, called ápsarases.

4.104 The **Demon-killer** is Vishnu, identified by the icons on each of his four arms. The **king of the gods** is Indra.

4.109 Víkrama·bahu is Vásava·datta's mother's brother.

4.125 The word he uses for "**correspondence**" is ***saṃvāda***, literally a conversation, a meeting. The commentary glosses it as "resemblance" (*sādṛśyam*) and says that Vasu·bhuti means that it might be another, resembling jewel. Vasu·bhuti seemed at first quite certain about the unique identity of the necklace, and here is perhaps prevaricating, preventing Babhrávya from making a direct assault on the intimate friend of the great king until he finds out more about the circumstances attending the transmission of the necklace.

4.150 Vásava·datta calls Ratnávali her sister in the way that South Asians in general apply "sister" and "brother" to close relatives (and African Americans to even more distant members of their ethnicity). Ratnávali is her sister in that she is of noble birth and hence may be a distant relative, perhaps a cousin. In *Priyadarśikā*, Priya·dárshika's father is married to Vásava·datta's mother's sister, making them actually cousins, and Vásava·datta calls Priya·dárshika her sister.

4.156 **Lavánaka** is a village in Vatsa, near Mágadha.

4.171 Literally, why should the [survival of] the race descended from Bharata climb into the balance-scale of uncertainty for no good reason? **Bharata** was the ancestor of the great lunar line of kings that included Údayana.

4.221 The queen tries to throw the blame onto Yaugándharáyana for not telling her that Ságarika was in fact Ratnávali, in the vain hope that this will justify her cruel and jealous treatment of Ságarika.

4.224 KALE's Sanskrit commentary, summarizing the *Kathāsaritsāgara*, spells it out: In the past, Yaugándharáyana enlightened her by saying, "Let the king of Vatsa obtain the earth." The queen, having as her only concern the welfare of her own husband, agreed to be separated from her husband for a certain time and agreed to his taking another wife.

4.251 "**Stain . . . permanent as diamonds**" translates ***vajra/lepa***, which means, literally, "adamantine-stain" or a kind of glue that sticks on forever. This verse puns on the name of Vásava·datta by calling Indra by his epithet of "Vásava." The word I have translated "**rest in peace**" more literally means "be brought to *śānti*," a word which literally means the extinguishing of a fire but has religious overtones of the final liberation of the soul.

The Lady who Shows her Love

1.2 The verses of benediction in this play are dedicated to the three-eyed god Shiva (here called **Hara**, the Remover). Shiva's wife is named Gauri, "the Golden One," and the encounter takes place at their wedding. The smoke is from the fire used in the wedding ceremony; and Shiva wears the crescent moon in his hair. She is shy of showing her face in front of Brahma, perhaps because of the tradition, preserved in many myths, that Brahma desired her himself at the wedding, and was punished by Shiva. She is jealous of the goddess Ganges, whom Shiva bears in his hair but whom she regards as a rival. She experiences the first of the eight traditional signs of erotic excitement, horripilation, when he takes her hand as the defining act of the wedding ceremony. The blessing "good for you," literally "for your auspiciousness" (*śivāya*), also means "for Shiva." The benediction also refers, paronomastically, to the plot of the play to follow. Gauri's tears and delight suggest Priya·dárshika's sorrow at her father's defeat and her delight at his restoration; Gauri/Priya·dárshika gazes at Shiva/Údayana; Gauri/Priya·dárshika is shy in front of Brahma/Vásava·datta.

1.4 This time the ambivalence is Shiva's. According to the myth, the ten-headed demon Rávana raised up **mount Kailása** and terrified Párvati (who is here called **Uma**) until Shiva pressed it down with his foot, imprisoning Rávana under it. This verse imagines that Rávana caused an earthquake that triggered a series of events, as earthquakes tend to do: the shaking aroused the curiosity of Shiva's **gang of goblins** (*gaṇa*s), who rushed out of the caves where they live. When Shiva's little son **Kumára** saw them, he hid, abandoning his mount, the peacock, who is the enemy of snakes. The **snake** that Shiva wears as his belt recoiled from the peacock, since birds, especially large birds like peacocks, are the enemies of snakes. This made Shiva mad (and, according to some poems on this theme, embarrassed), but his **anger** was easily overpowered by his pleasure in the final event in the chain reaction, Uma's frightened **embrace** (triggered both by the initial earthquake and by the snake). The secondary overtones of the plot may be seen as referring to Uma/king Dridha·varman being overthrown (when Rávana/the king of Kalínga rebels) and restored (when Shiva/Údayana suppresses him), and of Shiva/Vásava·datta being first angry and then reconciled with Párvati/Údayana.

1.6 The stage director acknowledges that this play borrows a well-known plot but boasts that it has made new variations on the old theme, what we would call *bricolage*. Indeed, this whole speech (together with the following paragraph, 1.7, verse 3) is taken straight out of *Ratnāvalī*, in which it is more appropriate, since that play takes place at the Spring festival, while *Priyadarśikā* begins in autumn. Kósala is a kingdom on the Ganges, east of Kanauj.

1.7 Údayana is the **king of Vatsa**.

1.8 This seems to imply that the stage director will play the part of the king.

1.12 The **chamberlain**, a stock character, is an old man wearing a long robe, who complains a lot. Always a Brahmin, he was in charge of the women's quarters of the palace.

1.15 The king's **powers** were traditionally said to be the power of the army and treasury, of the advice of wise ministers, and of the personal energy of the king. **Raghu** and **Dilípa** are famous kings in the line of Rama, and **Nala** a great hero of the *Mahābhārata* (though also a king famous for first suffering and then emerging from serious misfortunes, and therefore a subtly apt person to compare now with a king in trouble).

1.15 In one of a number of instances of intertextuality in this play, the **king of Kalínga** echoes the name of one of Údayana's earlier wives, Kalínga·sena ("Army of Kalínga") in the 'Ocean of the Rivers of Story.'

1.16 From this it is evident that the king who had imprisoned Údayana was Pradyóta, the king of Avánti, and that, in escaping from him, Údayana stole his daughter, Vásava·datta.

1.16 From this it appears that this is still the same day of the attack that killed Vindhya·ketu.

1.17 The paronomasia is so complete and parallel that it seemed best to put the entire double entendre into the second half of the translation.

1.29 We have already encountered **Vindhya·ketu** as the ally of king Dridha·varman and protector of Vásava·datta, and we know that he was killed; now we learn that Údayana's army was the one that attacked "like demons" and killed him. Vindhya·ketu thus appears in this play in the role that the king of Kósala played in *Ratnāvalī*: a worthy enemy, king of the "jungle" (*araṇya*), more precisely ruler of the Vindhya mountains that formed the gateway to the south, significantly, I think, precisely the part of India that Harsha himself tried in vain to conquer. Harsha never gives any reason for Údayana's attack on either of these kings (Kósala or Vindhya·ketu), but he does not have to: it was the duty of a king to attack the countries on his border, to expand his kingdom. It is, however, a bit surprising that he should attack the ally of the king whose daughter he was trying to marry. In fact, there are several interconnected martial clashes in this play: the king of Kalínga attacks and captures Dridha·varman (Priya·dárshika's father); Údayana's general, Víjaya·sena, attacks and kills Dridha·varman's ally Vindhya·ketu (who had adopted Priya·dárshika); and, finally, Údayana sends Víjaya·sena to attack the king of Kalínga, and free Priya·dárshika's father.

1.57 The three parts of the **army** are infantry, cavalry, and armor (tanks, or, in this case, elephants).

1.68 "**Minnow**" translates ***śaphara***, the smallest of fishes. The **bee** hovers near the elephant's cheek because he is attracted by the sweet ichor that drips down from the forehead of an elephant in rut, and by the shade it affords.

2.3 This seems to be the jester's blasphemous way of referring to the chanting of Vedic prayers at dawn. The 'Rig Veda' likens chanting Brahmins to frogs croaking in a pond (*Ṛg Veda* 7.103). The **fountain-house** is a kind of summer house fitted with cooling fountains.

2.11 Some Brahmins are named *tri/vedin* ("Knowing Three Vedas") because they know the *Ṛc*, *Sāman*, and *Yajur Veda*s, the main three; and some *catur/vedin* ("Knowing Four Vedas") because they also know the *Atharvaveda*, a supplementary text often regarded as the fourth Veda. And although certain texts (such as the *Mahābhārata*) claim, metaphorically, to be the "Fifth Veda," there are no *pañca/vedin* ("Five-Veda") Brahmins, and no one speaks of a "Six-Veda" Brahmin.

2.15 **Bandhúka** flowers are bright red and are said to bloom at noon and fall the next morning.

2.17 The **Sad Tree** (***śephālika***, *Nyctanthes Arbor Tristis*) is a small tree with fragrant flowers. The **Seven-leaved tree** (***sapta/cchada***, *Alstonia Scholaris*) is a large tree that, allegedly, smells like rutting elephants. The **wine of the flowers** is honey.

2.20 The **shirísha** (*Acacia Sirissa*) is a tall tree with delicate blossoms.

2.34 The oval **pond** is likened to an eye, and the eye of a goddess gives you darshan, blessing you both by your sight of her and by her sight of you.

2.37 A **serpent princess** is a *nāginī*, cobra from the waist down, beautiful woman from the waist up; they inhabit a water world beneath the earth. Údayana's adventures in the world of the *nāga*s are part of Hindu mythology, documented in the *Bṛhatkathāmañjarī* [2.56–60]. The **goddess Shri**, goddess of good fortune, usually holds a lotus.

2.73 **Numb thighs** is one of the signs of extreme erotic excitement.

2.78 The lotus thorns remain up, as if in horripilation, one of the early signs of erotic excitement.

2.86 The **ruddy goose** is the *cakravāka*, a bird that loses its mate every evening and cries for her all night.

3.3 The autumn **festival of the moon** is celebrated on the full-moon day of Áshvina (late September to late October), when the moon is particularly bright after the rains.

3.12 Mano·rama is referring to Aránylka's remark that Mano·rama was no different from her own heart.

3.29 That is, has Aránylka become true to her name, "**Lady of the Jungle**," either by reverting to the jungle or behaving like a naïve country girl instead of cooperating with the king, as a lady of the court would have done. The jester speculates like this because he cannot find her.

3.32 Another moment of intertextuality: Údayana marries Padmávati in a story told in the 'Ocean of the Rivers of Story' and in Bhasa's play, 'Vásava·datta in a Dream.' The **other queens** the jester refers to may be Kalínga·sena and perhaps even Ratnávali.

3.36 The jester has, as usual, misunderstood the meaning of a word. "Tell" in English has some of the multiple meanings that the verb *jñā* has in Sanskrit, first (in the indicative) to recognize (i. e., to distinguish which leaves are the right ones), then (in the causative) to cause someone to recognize or to report to someone. The jester fears that Mano·rama will tell Vásava·datta that the king is in love with Aránylka.

3.54 I take this rather cryptic saying to mean that people are always prejudiced in favor of their own family, and so Vásava·datta will naturally be inclined to like a play about her own life.

3.64 There are several stories about this **elephant**. In Buddhist texts, this is the elephant that a wicked king sent to kill the Buddha, who, however, tamed the elephant. In Hindu traditions, it was said to belong to Maha·sena Pradyóta, Vásava·datta's father. There is also a legend that when Údayana ran away with Vásava·datta, riding a female elephant, he was pursued by one of Pradyóta's sons riding Nala·giri. And finally, most relevant, in Kali·dasa's *Meghadūta* 27: "The king of Vatsa brought the daughter of Pradyóta here, and the Nala·giri elephant roamed here, when he had uprooted, in fury, the post to which he had been tied." Apparently Údayana captured the elephant and stopped him from wreaking havoc in Pradyóta's city, which he did by playing his magic lute that had, like Orpheus's lyre and Mozart's magic flute, the power to tame wild animals. According to the 'Ocean of the Rivers of Story' (II.3), when Údayana was just a boy he rescued a powerful *nāga* (semi-serpent) from a snake-charmer; in return, the *nāga* gave him a lute, "Sonorous," which he used to tame wild elephants. (According to the *Bṛhatkathāmañjarī* of Ksheméndra, Údayana also married the *nāga*'s daughter.) When Pradyóta captured Údayana, he ordered Údayana to teach music to Vásava·datta, an opportunity that he used to win her over and elope with her. This is about to be alluded to in the play within the play.

3.69 This marks the beginning of the "Play within a Play" (*garbha/nāṭaka*). Speech in it is printed in a different font for clarity.

3.70 The **Chamberlain** is playing the Chamberlain, and Kánchana·mala is playing Kánchana·mala. It is therefore not clear what his costume would be, other than what he has been wearing in the play all along.

3.72 The basic pun is on ***daṇḍa***, which basically means a rod, and then comes to mean punishment ("spare the rod . . . "), or government, particularly the army ("carry a big stick"), and still designates a stick that someone old and/or lame, like the chamberlain, might use.

3.73 Presumably a festival to celebrate Údayana's marriage to Vásava·datta. KALE suggests that it might celebrate the capture of Údayana, but surely this would be rather tactless, even for Pradyóta.

3.75 The implication is that there is to be a performance at the festival, which would be a play within the play by Sankrityáyani within the play by Harsha announced by the stage director within the play by Harsha. And since everyone is already so gorgeously dressed, there is no need to put on an extra costumes for the performance.

3.75 The **good-luck symbols** are swastikas, a Sanskrit word literally meaning "Something that says 'it-is-good,'" designating an auspicious diagram that took various forms, including the one appropriated by the Nazis.

3.79 The **lute teacher** turns out to be Údayana, the king of Vatsa. See note to 3.64.

3.80 The madman is Yaugándharáyana in the disguise that he used, according to the old story, to get into Pradyóta's prison and set Údayana free.

3.82 Though there is no stage direction here, Sankrityáyani is clearly speaking outside the play within the play, and to Vásava·datta.

3.94 Since the play will closely follow Údayana's adventures and the actress is to imitate his mannerisms closely, Údayana will be able to say his lines correctly without any rehearsal. **The Festival of the Rendezvous** is a lighthearted twist on The Festival of Údayana: Údayana is going to celebrate his own festival by meeting his new love.

3.108 **Knotting the hem** seems to have the same meaning as "girding his loins:" tightening up the lower garments in preparation for some vigorous action.

3.125 The **royal swan** (*rāa/haṃsa*, Sanskrit *rāja/haṃsa*) is said to return to his home, Lake Mánasa, every year to mate, at the time of the monsoon.

3.131 "**Who shows his love**," or, "good to look at," (***pia/daṃsaṇa***, Sanskrit *priya/darśana*) may be a subtle, even subconscious, signal from Aranyika to Údayana, telling him that she is, in fact, Priya·dárshika.

3.133 Indian musical theory is extremely complex, and there seems little point in trying to explain it briefly here. The verse makes it clear that both Údayana and Priya·dárshika-as-Aranyika-as-Vásava·datta are expert in it.

3.135 "**For you**" (*te*) is a pun: ostensibly, I wish that you may get your/my wish, but really, I wish to have you. Therefore while he seems to be saying, may you be a fine musician, he is really saying, may you be my queen.

3.145 Her **limbs** are actually weak with passion for the king and, perhaps, increasingly so because of her growing subconscious suspicion that it is the king, and not Mano·rama, who is playing the part of the king.

3.149 What she means is that she won't allow Kánchana·mala to describe her in a state of erotic excitement (for the queen clearly gets the double entendre of Aranyika's signs of "exhaustion"). But what she says without knowing it is also true, that she does not want Kánchana·mala to say the words that allow the king to betray her with Aranyika.

3.151 Aranyika, playing the queen, expresses the queen's **anger**, but perhaps she is also expressing her own, on the subconscious level. The king is making a move on both of them simultaneously.

3.159 According to KALE's judgment, the performance of the play within the play ends at 3.200, but the actual lines said in the play ends here.

3.160 Her **limbs make no sense** because she cannot explain her arousal by a woman, as she thinks that the king is Mano·rama. KALE's Sanskrit commentary glosses this line to mean, "Some distortion of my mind, difficult to bear, enflames my limbs."

3.162 The **marriage by mutual desire** is the ***gāndharva*** marriage, in which the only witnesses are the gandhárvas, demigods who encourage music and fertility.

3.170 That is, the queen meant, "If the king is acting in place of Mano·rama, what part is Mano·rama playing?" But the jester thought she meant, literally, "Where is Mano·rama physically now?" and his answer simultaneously revealed her whereabouts and showed that she was colluding with the king.

3.172 Mano·rama is wildly improvising, counting on the jester to back her up, as he does.

3.186 A pun on "**foot**," referring both to syllables of speech and to feet that might stumble.

3.195 The **moon** has the mark of a hare on it. The **bandhu·jiva flower** ("living in groups," *Pentapetes Phoenicea*) is a plant with a red flower, which opens at noon and withers the next morning.

4.7 **Queen Angáravati** was Vásava·datta's mother, the wife of Pradyóta Maha·sena. Angáravati's sister, Priya·dárshika's mother, is unnamed.

4.10 Apparently Vásava·datta did not know until now that her uncle, Dridha·varman, had been deposed.

4.10 Though Kánchana·mala read the letter silently, letters were sometimes read aloud, hence heard rather than seen.

4.34 The word ***devī*** means both **goddess** and **queen**; and Chandi ("**Fierce**") is the name of a particular goddess. People fast to appease a goddess, though not usually a queen, but in a more informal way women often fast in order to get their way with men; Gandhi copied this habit in fasting against the British.

4.98 The king smiles and calls on Víjaya·sena because he knows that Víjaya·sena found the girl alive and brought her to his court, where she lives as Aránvika, and he invites him now to give this welcome piece of information to the chamberlain. (They are interrupted before he can do so.) At this moment only Yaugándharáyana, Priya·dárshika, and the king know that Aránvika is Priya·dárshika, and the king has only just found it out.

4.102 **Priya·dárshana** is an alternative form of Priya·dárshika. (See 3.132 [verse 9].) The queen assumes that Mano·rama is talking about the present subject, Priya·dárshika, which, though neither of them knows it, she is, though Mano·rama thinks she is just talking about Aránvika.

4.105 Údayana's adventures in the **naga world** are part of the folklore, as we have noted. Though his knowledge of **poisons** is not well known, his interest in magic is clear from his skill with the magic of plants in *Ratnāvalī* as well as his expressed interest in the magician's craft. The word that I have translated as "**magic**" (***vidyā***) can also be translated as "science," a lesson for us all.

4.137 In this final masquerade, the king presents the symptoms of love-sickness in the guise of symptoms of poisoning (with poison that masqueraded as wine in the first place), a final wedding of political and erotic intrigue.

4.155 This verse puns on the name of **Priya·dárshana** by the repeated use of "**dear**" (***priya***).

INDEX

Sanskrit words are given in the English alphabetical order, according to the accented CSL pronunciation aid. They are followed by the conventional diacritics in brackets.

Permitted finals:

k	ṭ	t	p	ṅ	n	m	*(Except āḥ/aḥ)* ḥ/r	āḥ	aḥ	*Initial letters:*
k	ṭ	t	p	ṅ	n	ṃ	ḥ	āḥ	aḥ	k/kh
g	ḍ	d	b	ṅ	n	ṃ	r	ā	o	g/gh
k	ṭ	c	p	ṅ	ṃś	ṃ	ś	āś	aś	c/ch
g	ḍ	j	b	ṅ	ñ	ṃ	r	ā	o	j/jh
k	ṭ	ṭ	p	ṅ	ṃṣ	ṃ	ṣ	āṣ	aṣ	ṭ/ṭh
g	ḍ	ḍ	b	ṅ	ṇ	ṃ	r	ā	o	ḍ/ḍh
k	ṭ	t	p	ṅ	ṃs	ṃ	s	ās	as	t/th
g	ḍ	d	b	ṅ	n	ṃ	r	ā	o	d/dh
k	ṭ	t	p	ṅ	n	ṃ	ḥ	ā	aḥ	p/ph
g	ḍ	d	b	ṅ	n	ṃ	r	ā	o	b/bh
ṅ	ṇ	n	m	ṅ	n	ṃ	r	ā	o	*nasals* (n/m)
g	ḍ	d	b	ṅ	n	ṃ	r	ā	o	y/v
g	ḍ	d	b	ṅ	n	ṃ	*zero*[1]	ā	o	r
g	ḍ	l	b	ṅ	l̃[2]	ṃ	r	ā	o	l
k	ṭ	c ch	p	ṅ	ñ ś/ch	ṃ	ḥ	āḥ	aḥ	ś
k	ṭ	t	p	ṅ	n	ṃ	ḥ	āḥ	aḥ	ṣ/s
gg h	ḍḍ h	dd h	bb h	ṅ	n	ṃ	r	ā	o	h
g	ḍ	d	b	ṅ/ṅṅ[3]	n/nn[3]	m	r	ā	a[4]	*vowels*
k	ṭ	t	p	ṅ	n	m	ḥ	āḥ	aḥ	*zero*

[1]ḥ or r disappears, and if a/i/u precedes, this lengthens to ā/ī/ū. [2]e.g. tān+lokān=tāl̃ lokān.
[3]The doubling occurs if the preceding vowel is short. [4]Except: aḥ+a=o '.

Final vowels:

a	ā	i	ī	u	ū	ṛ	e	ai	o	au	*Initial vowels:*
' â	" â	y a	y a	v a	v a	r a	e '	ā a	o '	āv a	a
' ā	" ā	y ā	y ā	v ā	v ā	r ā	a ā	ā ā	a ā	āv ā	ā
' ê	" ê	' î	" î	v i	v i	r i	a i	ā i	a i	āv i	i
' ē	" ē	' ī	" ī	v ī	v ī	r ī	a ī	ā ī	a ī	āv ī	ī
' ô	" ô	y u	y u	' û	" û	r u	a u	ā u	a u	āv u	u
' ō	" ō	y ū	y ū	' ū	" ū	r ū	a ū	ā ū	a ū	āv ū	ū
a' r	a" r	y ṛ	y ṛ	v ṛ	v ṛ	' ṛ̂	a ṛ	ā ṛ	a ṛ	āv ṛ	ṛ
' âi	" âi	y e	y e	v e	v e	r e	a e	ā e	a e	āv e	e
' āi	" āi	y ai	y ai	v ai	v ai	r ai	a ai	ā ai	a ai	āv ai	ai
' âu	" âu	y o	y o	v o	v o	r o	a o	ā o	a o	āv o	o
' āu	" āu	y au	y au	v au	v au	r au	a au	ā au	a au	āv au	au

THE CLAY SANSKRIT LIBRARY

Current Volumes

For more details please consult the CSL website.

1. The Emperor of the Sorcerers (*Bṛhatkathāślokasaṃgraha*) (vol. 1) by *Budhasvāmin*. SIR JAMES MALLINSON
2. The Heavenly Exploits (*Divyāvadāna*) JOEL TATELMAN
3. Maha·bhárata III: The Forest (*Vanaparvan*) (vol. 4) WILLIAM J. JOHNSON
4. Much Ado about Religion (*Āgamaḍambara*) by *Bhaṭṭa Jayanta*. CSABA DEZSŐ
5. The Birth of Kumára (*Kumārasaṃbhava*) by *Kālidāsa*. DAVID SMITH
6. Ramáyana I: Boyhood (*Bālakāṇḍa*) by *Vālmīki*. ROBERT P. GOLDMAN
7. The Epitome of Queen Lilávati (*Līlāvatīsāra*) (vol. 1) by *Jinaratna*. R.C.C. FEYNES
8. Ramáyana II: Ayódhya (*Ayodhyākāṇḍa*) by *Vālmīki*. SHELDON I. POLLOCK
9. Love Lyrics (*Amaruśataka, Śatakatraya & Caurapañcāśikā*) by *Amaru, Bhartṛhari & Bilhaṇa*. GREG BAILEY & RICHARD GOMBRICH
10. What Ten Young Men Did (*Daśakumāracarita*) by *Daṇḍin*. ISABELLE ONIANS
11. Three Satires (*Kaliviḍambana, Kalāvilāsa & Bhallaṭaśataka*) by *Nīlakaṇṭha, Kṣemendra & Bhallaṭa* SOMADEVA VASUDEVA
12. Ramáyana IV: Kishkíndha (*Kiṣkindhākāṇḍa*) by *Vālmīki*. ROSALIND LEFEBER

13. The Emperor of the Sorcerers (*Bṛhatkathāślokasaṃgraha*) (vol. 2)
 by *Budhasvāmin*. Sir James Mallinson
14. Maha·bhárata IX: Shalya (*Śalyaparvan*) (vol. 1)
 Justin Meiland
15. The Rákshasa's Ring (*Mudrārākṣasa*)
 by *Kālidāsa*. Michael Coulson
16. Messenger Poems (*Meghadūta, Pavanadūta & Haṃsadūta*)
 by *Kālidāsa, Dhoyī & Rūpa Gosvāmin*. Sir James Mallinson
17. Ramáyana III: The Forest (*Araṇyakāṇḍa*) (vol. 4)
 by *Vālmīki*. Sheldon I. Pollock
18. The Epitome of Queen Lilávati (*Līlāvatīsāra*) (vol. 2)
 by *Jinaratna*. R.C.C. Feynes
19. Five Discourses of Worldly Wisdom (*Pañcatantra*)
 by *Viṣṇuśarman*. Patrick Olivelle
20. Ramáyana V: Súndara (*Sundarakāṇḍa*)
 by *Vālmīki*. Robert P. Goldman & Sally J. Sutherland Goldman
21. Maha·bhárata II: The Great Hall (*Sabhāparvan*)
 Paul Wilmot
22. The Recognition of Shakúntala (*Abhijñānaśākuntala*) (Kashmir Recension) by *Kālidāsa*. Somadeva Vasudeva
23. Maha·bhárata VII: Drona (*Droṇaparvan*) (vol. 1)
 Vaughan Pilikian
24. Rama Beyond Price (*Anargharāghava*)
 by *Murāri*. Judit Törzsök
25. Maha·bhárata IV: Viráta (*Virāṭaparvan*)
 Kathleen Garbutt
26. Maha·bhárata VIII: Karna (*Karṇaparvan*) (vol. 1)
 Adam Bowles
27. The Ocean of the Rivers of Story (*Kathāsaritsāgara*) (vol. 1)
 by *Somadeva Bhaṭṭa*. Sir James Mallinson

THE CLAY SANSKRIT LIBRARY

To Appear in 2007

28. "Friendly Advice" (*Hitopadeśa*) by *Nārāyaṇa* &
    "King Vikrama's Adventures" (*Vikramacarita*). JUDIT TÖRZSÖK
29. Handsome Nanda (*Saundarananda*)
    by *Aśvaghoṣa*. LINDA COVILL
30. "How the Nagas were Pleased" (*Nāgānanda*) by *Harṣa* &
    "The Shattered Thighs" (*Ūrubhaṅga*) by *Bhāsa*
    ANDREW SKILTON
31. Maha·bhárata V: Preparation for War (*Udyogaparvan*) (vol. 1)
    KATHLEEN GARBUTT
32. Maha·bhárata VI: Bhishma (*Bhīṣmaparvan*) (vol. 1)
    ALEX CHERNIAK
33. Maha·bhárata IX: Shalya (*Śalyaparvan*) (vol. 2)
    JUSTIN MEILAND
34. The Ocean of the Rivers of Story (*Kathāsaritsāgara*) (vol. 2)
    by *Somadeva Bhaṭṭa*. SIR JAMES MALLINSON
35. Rama's Last Act (*Uttararāmacarita*)
    by *Bhavabhūti*. SHELDON I. POLLOCK